The Secrets of Eliminating Stress Forever

**Your Journey
From slavery
To freedom**

The Secrets of Eliminating Stress Forever

Your Journey From slavery To freedom

Copyright © 2004 by Marcel Limbasan

Printed in United States of America

All rights reserved. No part of this book may be reproduced or transmitted in any form, or by any means, electronic or mechanical, including photocopying, recording, or any information storage and retrieval system, without permission in writing from the Publisher.

Although based on scientific discoveries, the information from this book are not intended as medical advice, or prescribe the use of any technique either directly or indirectly as a form of treatment for physical or medical problems without the advice of a physician.

The author and the publisher, assume no responsibility for your actions, in the event that you use any of the information from this book, although you have the constitutional right to do so.

Library of Congress Cataloging-in-Publication Data.

ISBN 0-9719500-0-8.

Published in U.S.A. by Future Horizons International. 2004.

About the Book

New Breakthrough in Stress Research. The New Theory of Stress. The new book:
"The Secrets of Eliminating Stress forever, your journey from slavery to freedom"
takes you into an unbelievable journey from slavery to freedom, by showing you what stress really is, where it comes from, and how you could eliminate it from your life.

PREFACE.

- "Necessity is the mother of invention" -

This expression is universally accepted as truth, and like many others, I also had the chance to experience it to be true.
Born in Eastern Europe, since my childhood I have had to deal with many challenges from which I had many important lessons to learn. Though I came from a modest family, with limited financial possibilities, I always remember myself as a person interested in acquiring knowledge and wisdom. For some reason, I had this inner thirst to know more and more, and to appreciate the value of knowledge.

In 1984, I left Europe, and came to America, with the same hope that was burning in the hearts of millions of eastern Europeans, to find a better life. Leaving one kind of problems, and challenges behind, I had to face different ones here. And, because they were new for me, I also had to learn how to deal with them. The most painful challenge to deal with was *stress*. I had no idea that the notion of stress is used in the medical domain. I knew about *stress* since I was in school, but only as a technical word, I was not aware of the fact that here in America, stress is seen as the root of most medical problems that people have to deal with. Being used to facing challenges and overcoming them, I became preoccupied with this subject, knowing that the most suitable person to deal with my high level of stress was myself. I was familiar with an old saying: "Give a command, and then do it yourself, if you want it to be done properly."
So, I started to gather information in this area from most prestigious and well-known specialists in this field, knowing that the best way to accomplish something fast is to learn from the professionals. This is what I have done. Soon I realized that I am facing a new challenge: the top professionals in stress believe there is no cure for stress, an idea that I just could not accept. I always knew that, for everything I do, I am responsible. Stress is the result of a certain kind of behavior, and behaviors could be changed. I honestly could not accept the theory of stress as being realistic. I challenged myself to find the answer to this problem. I recalled the saying of Doug Larson: "Some of the world's greatest feats were accomplished by people not smart enough to know they were impossible"
And after countless hours of personal studies, little by little I started to realize that stress is not an invincible enemy that was to control and affect people's life forever in a negative way.
And, pretty soon I started to understand what stress really is, how it works, and also how it could be eliminated. Once I understood that, I tested on myself, to see if it was going to work. And it did very well. Realizing the importance of a discovery like this, I felt its my duty to write this book and make it known to everybody who might be interested in a permanent solution for stress.

The major problem in dealing with stress today, is that since the present theory has been accepted as truth many decades ago, most professionals in this field, are not looking to challenge it, but to find a way to manage it, or get the best out of it. And of course that, if they believe that there is no cure for stress, they won't look for a solution for eliminating it.

But, if somebody will start to challenge this theory, he might be surprised to find out that it will not stand anymore to the latest tests. By reading the information contained in this book, you have the chance to prove to yourself that whatever I am writing is true, and by understanding and applying this simple information, the life that you improve is yours, and that of those whom you do love.

The author.

Table of contents

Part 1. Who really are we?..page 1.

Introduction...page 3.

Secret # 1. "The one who knows the rules of the game…"
Chapter 1. The game of life has its own rules..page 11.

Secret # 2. "Knowing the rules of our game…"
Chapter 2. Which are the rules of our game?..page 19.

Secret # 3. "The *vehicle* that takes you…"
Chapter 3. Human body..page 35.
    Human spirit...page 50.

Secret # 4. "The *designer* of your own heaven or hell"
Chapter 4. Human mind...page 53.
    The anatomy of human mind..page 54.
    The anatomy of a blueprint..page 61.
    The three major abilities..page 66.
    Reasoning..page 68.
    Imagination...page 70.
    Emotion..page 72.

Secret # 5. "What we become through what we do."
Chapter 5. Human behavior..page 79.
    Awareness..page 79.
    Desire...page 96.
    Decision...page 107.

Secret # 6. "The hidden reasons behind our actions"
Chapter 6. Motivation..page 113.
    Discipline...page 118.

Secret # 7. "Who's behind our inner drive for happiness?"
Chapter 7. The propulsion mechanism...page 133.

Secret # 8. "Your invisible protective *guardian*."
Chapter 8. The self-defense mechanism...page 147.

Part 2. What are we dealing with?..page 155.

Secret # 9. "The *monsters* that play mind games on you."
Chapter 9. Who really are the stressors?..page 157.
    New dictionary...page 160.
    Unchangeable versus changeable..page 167.

Solvable versus unsolvable..page 169.
Dreams versus reality..page 171.
Inner needs and fears..page 173.
Is the past really gone?...page 180.

Part 3. When the impossible becomes possible..............................page 183.

Secret # 10. "Free yourself from the past..."
Chapter 10. Solving the mystery of stress...page 185.
    Stop producing new stress...page 187.

Secret # 11. "Eliminating stress from negative past experiences..."
Chapter 11. Healing the past...page 199.
    The reasoning method..page 200.
    Make peace with yourself...page 201.
    Make peace with your neighbor..page 206.
        Attitude...page 208.
        Communication..page 211.
    Make peace with the environment..page 216.
    Make peace with your Maker..page 219.
    The substitution method...page 222.
    When bad things happen..page 226.

Secret # 12. "Wisdom the practical application..."
Chapter 12. Make up your mind..page 231.
    Let's remember...page.234.

The Touch of the Masters Hand.

" Twas battered and scarred, and the auctioneer thought it scarcely worth his while
To waste much time on the old violin, but held it up with a smile;
"What am I bidden, good folks," he cried,
"Who'll start the bidding for me? A dollar, a dollar, then two! Only two?
Two dollars, and who'll make it three? Three dollars, once; three dollars twice; going for three…"
But no, from the room, far back, a gray-haired man came forward and picked up the bow;
Then, wiping the dust from the old violin, and tightening the loose strings,
He played a melody pure and sweet as caroling angel sings.

The music ceased, and the auctioneer, with a voice that was quiet and low, said;
"What am I bid for the old violin?" And he held it up with the bow.
"A thousand dollars, and who'll make it two? Two thousand! And who'll make it three?
Three thousand, once, three thousand, twice, and going and gone," said he.
The people cheered, but some of them cried,
"We do not quite understand what changed its worth." Swift came the reply:
"The touch of the Master's hand."
…………………………………….."

By Myra Brooks Welch.

How many of us are feeling just like this old violin, battered and scarred by ravaging bondage of the cruel stress that is stopping us from enjoying a happy life without any relief in sight?
I don't know about you, but many times in my life I felt like this old violin loosing touch of my real worth. Somehow I rekindle the inner fire that was still burning inside me, motivating me to do something about my situation which gave me the strength to get up and take the responsibility of my life.

Even though millions today have lost the zest for life and barely struggle to survive, you yourself can take courage. The end of this struggle is near because a beautiful rainbow starts to appear on the horizon. A rainbow to brighten your days and bring relief to your stressful life.

Before you start reading this book, you were probably not aware that you are a wonderful human being equipped with amazing abilities and deserving to live a stress free life. Much like the old violin, the continuous negative effects of stress discounted your worth to *a few dollars*.
The message of this book will help you regain your real worth and value that you were born with.
Read it, understand it, and master it and enjoy the journey to a stress free life.

Part 1.

Who Really Are We?

Part 1.

Who Really Are We?

Introduction.

- The journey to the highest mountain starts with the first step. -

Imagine how life would be without stress; would that be possible? Or, maybe that's impossible, you might say. Nobody until now came up with such a statement.

This damaging negative state of mind, the "psychological stress" has been with us for so long and we got so much used to it. People's main concern is to learn how to better manage it. To eliminate it might sound impossible but today you have the chance to see how this could come true.
Do you know why nobody until now has found a way to eliminate it?
One reason is because everybody believes that it is impossible to eliminate it, so believing that, nobody has tried to find a way to do so.
As far as I am concern, the first time I heard that it's impossible to eliminate stress, it didn't sound right to me. I didn't believe it's as realistic as it should be and couldn't agree with the idea. I always knew that there must be a way and a few years ago I started to look for the possibility of eliminating stress. And like the saying:
"Watch out for what you are looking for, you may just find it!" After searching for the truth in this matter I eventually found it. Once I understood it, I felt that is my duty to make it known to others. That's why I decided to write this book.

Imagine that you have a car and you learned to drive from some friends or some of your relatives. Now, also you got some driving habits by following what you saw them doing.
One of the habits is that anytime you go through a kind of negative or difficult situation, you pull like the emergency brake. In the beginning, nothing happens with the car. But after a while, because little by little you keep pulling the emergency brake, you start realizing that the engine doesn't have as much power as before. The transmission seems like it might be slipping and hardly shifting. The brakes are getting hotter than normal. The grease on the wheel bearings starts melting down because of excessive heat. In other words the *health* of the car starts to deteriorate little by little. Becoming aware of this, you start to do what you saw others doing. You learn how to manage your car better. You start using oil treatment for the engine, special transmission oil for better friction. Then you keep replacing the brake pads that are getting worn out faster than normal. Also you pay more attention to greasing the wheel bearing because the grease keep melting and the bearings are in danger of breaking down. Even though you do your best on managing your car, its *health* is still your concern. There should be a better solution to deal with this kind of problem. But where is a better solution found? Everybody does the same thing. Now, what's the real problem here? Is the special oil treatment not efficient enough? Or you don't change the brake pads often enough? Or maybe you should use higher-grade grease for the wheel bearings? Well, you could improve all these, but the problem still remains. Why? Because looking to manage the situation, the best you can do is to improve the management of it. Then, what's the solution? Well, the best and lasting way to deal with this is to find out what's the source of it. Eliminate the source and all the *symptoms* will disappear by themselves. But to do that, we need to focus our attention into a totally different area. From the area of many and sophisticated products used for stress management; to the area of personal behavior. We need to learn and understand the difference between good driving habits and not so good or even bad driving habits and the side effects *some* driving behaviors have on the *health* of the car. By doing that, we realize that we become responsible for its *health*. It's not the quality

Introduction.

of the oil, or the brake pads or the grease; it's the quality of our driving habits that really could solve the *health* problems of our car. I think that this example could bring a little light to our problem with stress. We can focus all our attention on how to better manage stress but still we would still live a stressful life. We need to change our focus into a different area: that of personal behavior. Why? We are going to find out from this book, through our *unhealthy habits,* we are the creators of our stressful environment. That being the case, we are also the ones capable of solving this *impossible* task. You may have heard the definition of insanity: "Doing the same old thing and expecting different results."

Well if it didn't work in other areas of life, it won't work when it comes to solving the problem of stress either. Therefore, in order to get different results, we are going to do something different than stress management. We are going to learn how to eliminate this problem, not just manage it; hoping that it will eventually go away. Let me tell you a little *story* about this.

There were three people in hell from three different religions *paying* for their *sins*. The first one was asked: Why are you here?
"Well, I think that I didn't pray enough, plus some other things;" the first one said.
How about you? the second one was asked.
"Well, I think I didn't have enough faith, plus some other things," was the reply.
What about you? What did you do to be punished in this tormenting place the third one was asked.
"Who, me? It's not hot, and I am not here," was the reply.
We might not want to behave like the third one. We need to deal with the reality, no matter how good or bad it might be. The information from this book will help us to get a better understanding of reality and how to properly deal with it. And each of us can learn how to do that and dream like this is very possible.
Impossible? No. Did you ever hear these sayings?
"For the one who wants to believe, I have a thousand proves, but for the one who doesn't want, I have none"
"Everything is possible to the one that wants to believe it."

Many of us might be familiar with the word paradigm. The word defines a set of rules or fundamental understandings that people accept and follow even though they might have been proven as truths. Today there is a universal paradigm about stress. This paradigm says that as long as we live, we are *blessed* with *the plague of our generation* and the best we can do is to manage it. If we are familiar with the word paradigm, we also might be familiar with the notion *paradigm shifting* which basically means that even though the paradigms are fundamental beliefs or rules; many times new understandings produce a powerful and decisive shift in some of them and the need for major changes arrives. So, this book basically is going to produce a powerful shift from the old paradigm of stress to a new one.

The old paradigm has been reigning for many decades but now the time has arrived for a new and better one. Of course, as in the case with any other paradigm shifting, this one might go through the same stages. First, some might accept it right the way, but some might ridicule and laugh at it. Then some might even attack it. But after a while it will be accepted and embraced as better than the old one.

We know that in order to get a full benefit of our goals, we need to ask ourselves the right questions that will produce the results we want. The old paradigm required questions like: How can we manage stress better? How can we avoid stress? What's the best we can do under stress and other similar ones?
By asking ourselves these kinds of questions, we get answers accordingly. The best we can do is to become better and better managers over something we all hate –stress. We will never get an answer on how to eliminate stress; unless we ask the questions:
How do we eliminate stress? Why do we experience stress in our life? What is stopping millions of people today from living a stress free life? There are two major reasons:
1. Unconsciously we produce new stress by giving a negative meaning to new information that enters our mind.
2. Unconsciously we *recycle or relieve* old stress that was already *stored* in our memory banks.

In order to be able to live a stress free life, we need to learn how to stop producing new stress and learn how to remove the stress already *stored* in our memory from the past. To stop producing new stress, we

Introduction.

need to understand the laws and principles that govern the functions of our mind and body. Once we become aware that it is our responsibility to make sure we obey them. When we start removing the old stress, we need to start with the beginning, in other words, with the early years of our life coming down to our present day. We know that our brain is like a vast data storing mechanism that stores all the bits of information we come in contact daily. It not only stores, but also classifies them in *files*. We have a file for each subject of our life. Like: Family file, working file, health file, entertainment file, education file, stress file, etc. Now, what do we have in the *stress file*? Do we have information on how to live a stress free life? If not, where can we find this information? Nobody is talking about this subject; all we have is how to manage a stressful life. Beside the files we have in our memory banks, each file has a blueprint used by our subconscious mind in accomplishing the tasks required for each particular file. Again, how many of us have the file *living a stress free life* and a blueprint for it? Probably none. But how many has the file *living a stressful life* and the blueprint for it?

For our mind to accomplish this dream of living a stress free life, it needs to create a new file and a blueprint for it. And it needs to have enough information in the file so the mind is able to bring it into reality anytime we want. Not only that, but we need to clear or delete the old file of all the information that is producing negative emotions. We do this by learning how to *talk* to our subconscious mind.

This is not something new; we all talk to our subconscious mind every day. But we are just not aware of it. If somebody asks you: How old are you? Or, what is your height or weight? You don't need to look in your wallet to find out. As a command to your subconscious mind, it brings to your conscious awareness the requested information previously stored and classified in your memory banks about your age, height or weight. By asking ourselves serious questions, we actually send a command to our subconscious mind on how to accomplish that task. The subconscious mind takes the command and based on the information stored in the memory banks about that particular subject, brings it into realization. Then the reticular activating system in our brain will start to direct our attention toward the things that will help us accomplish this task. This reticular system is like a laser guided missile, once locked on a target, will keep follow it until it reaches it. The so-called *impossible* becomes possible. Unless we start to look at the possibility of eliminating stress, we will never be able to accomplish it. You might have heard the saying:

"A blind man cannot understand what darkness is, because he never saw the light."

I will not start to fill up your mind with all the negative effect of stress, because I know that since you started to read this book, you already know what stress is and how badly you might be you are searching for a permanent solution. Probably, you are tired of so many people who want to teach you how to manage something they themselves cannot. See, any manager in order to manage well, has to have among other things, something to manage. For you to learn to manage stress, you need to get stressed and then learn to manage it if you can. Now, who in the world would want to manage something that he/she hates? Does anybody like stress? I don't think so. Then why would we want to manage it and not to eliminate it?

If you think like me, you would like a permanent solution, a way to eliminate it, not only to manage it.

By paying close attention, understanding and following the information from this book, you will not become a manager but a stress free person. This is what this information is providing you. A way to understand what we really are; what are we dealing with when it comes to stress, how it is formed, and how to eliminate it forever. Not only to manage it, but to eliminate it. In case you still want to be a stress manager, this information is not for you. But, if you really desire to fix this problem for good, here is the solution. This information is very easy to understand. There aren't any scientific terms, so you might not need the dictionary to learn word meanings. Everything in this book is simple but also contains powerful statements for anybody to understand and apply.

Imagine you have to take a test. Once done, the proctor takes and analyses it. Then you get the results. As you expected, they are not too good, some are ok, but many are pretty bad. Would you be appreciative if the proctor of your test comes to you, gives your test back, and let you have another chance to review and redo it as you like? Would you be glad to be given a second chance?

Introduction.

I think you would. Well, we are not going to have the chance to actually *relieve* again our life: the past, present and its future. Through this information, we have the chance to go back in the past and *redo, or repair* it. By doing that, we are changing our present and future into a better and more positive one. Being freed by our negative and stressful past, we stop being conditioned negative by it, and become able to live our life the way we want it. Much of the stress that we have to deal with daily is caused by our past. By *repairing or healing the past,* we are redesigning our present and our future.

If we go back in history and remember a few centuries ago, most scientists believed that the earth was flat. Those who came up with different opinions were ridiculed, but after a while what they claim to be true, it was indeed proven to be so. See, as the saying goes: "Beauty is in the eyes of the beholder," what we call reality proves to be our own interpretation of it. Many times we just do not have enough information to get a full understanding of some complicated things in life.

We know that many years ago everybody was watching a black and white TV. Then suddenly somebody came with a new idea. A color TV! Wow! That's amazing, some have said. But some others were skeptics. It's not possible; nobody until now came with this kind of TV. Must be impossible, it's just a joke. Now, how many people would like to watch a black and white TV? None, but first they had to see it to believe it. Remember not long ago we didn't have a TV remote control either. Any time we wanted to switch the channel, we had to get up from our comfortable chair, go to the TV, switch the channel and then sat down again. Then suddenly somebody came up with a new invention. You don't need to get up anytime you want to switch the channel. You just push a little button and…miracle! The TV switches the channel by itself.
Wow! Many have said. It's impossible, others argued. Nobody came up with this kind of product before. Today, how many people buy a TV without a remote control? None.

Something similar happens with our subject of eliminating stress. There are a few interpretations of what stress is. Many decades ago, Hans Selye, the father of stress theory, defined stress as: "Our body's response to any demand upon it." Eastern philosophies view stress as an inner imbalance or an absence of inner peace. Some others believe the one's inability to cope with a perceived or real threat results in a series of physiological responses and adaptations. Each of these interpretations has a piece of truth in them. It's true that stress is the result of a response. Also it's true that one's inability to cope with a real or perceived threat creates a series a series of physiological responses that in turn disturbs the inner balance thus reducing or even eliminating the inner peace.

By making a careful observation of all these interpretations, I realized that there is an important factor that needs to be addressed in order to get a clear and complete picture of what stress really is and how to properly deal with it. We need to address not only the dynamics and mechanics of stress, but even more, who controls their sources. The environment? or the individual? If it's the environment, we know that we cannot control it entirely; therefore we are doomed to live with stress all our lives. But, if it's the individual, what does it take for one to learn and master the control of the dynamics and mechanics in such a way that eliminate the negative effects of stress? That led me into the study of human behavior and mind-body communication. Getting deeply in these subjects I realized that our brain continuously absorbs information from our environment. Once absorbed it is processed by it and the results of this process through our nervous system is sent throughout our body to be felt as what we commonly call emotions.

One of the main reasons that I decide to challenge the theory of stress is that I could not believe that stress is our response to any demand. Didn't make any sense to me. If any demand produces stress it means that we are designed to be continuously negatively affected by our interaction with the environment. I could not accept this kind of idea. The confusion I think is made between the word: *Stress* and the words: *Awareness or emotion*. The idea that stress is the response to any demand might be true when it is applied to things. An example, if you keep stressing a piece of material, it becomes weaker and weaker and eventually will break down. When we talk about humans, with the ability to consciously understand the environment, when we go through a process of change, the level of awareness changes because we perceive and understand the change. If the change is toward something that produces pleasure, we accept the change and

Introduction.

feel good about. On the other hand, when the change produces pain, we tend to reject it due to the fact that we are built with a protective mechanism that keeps us away from anything that might cause harm. Also, we are equipped with the ability to choose what meaning we give to our environment or situations we might go through. When we do it properly, our life develops normal. But when unconsciously we give a wrong meaning to the environment or to the situations we go through, we have to pay the consequences of our mistakes. In other words, our response to any stimuli can be an unconscious reaction to it, or could be a response based on a conscious decision we make on each particular stimulus.

Let's take an example:

We all are familiar with cars and know that we use them every day for our needs. In other words, we can say that the car is like a friend that is helping us fulfilling some of our daily needs. Let's say that you are driving on the freeway and thinking about something exciting; you are not aware that the speedometer goes up to 80 miles / hour. Suddenly, you look in the rear view mirror and see red flashing lights of a highway patrol car.

"O boy, I wasn't looking for this!" - you might think but you pull over and probably get a ticket for speeding. Now, can you say that it's the car's fault because you were traveling at this speed? You would recognize that it's your fault and nobody else. That's the normal reaction. The same thing happens when we get stressed but what's our reaction? We blame it on the environment. This is exactly the same thing if we would blame the car for the speeding ticket.

If we take a closer look around us, we can see that in our environment we are surrounded by a large variety of forms of life, objects and things. We can safely say that we perceive their existence in different forms such as simple energy, gases, liquids and finally solids. When it comes to life forms, the basic unit is the cell. Aggregates of many different cells are held together by intercellular supporting structures called molecules. Aggregates of molecules form an organ. Aggregates of organs form a body. All the life forms are made of a combination of different energy forms, gases, liquids and solids. Each form has its unique characteristics that differ from one form to another. For example, we take a plant, an animal and a human being. What do you think is going to happen, if over a period of 3 months, we continuously "stress" each of them? In other words, we continuously create a "stressful environment" by subjecting them to, high winds, rain and lower temperatures. What are we going to find out at the end of this experiment? Well, it depends on their abilities to cope with these stressful environments. The plant for example, stays in one place and will resist the stressful environment based on its strength. Once overstressed, they probably will die by not being able to provide protection or to get away from harm. The animal on the other hand, being a life form that is able to move from one place to another, will look to find safety, by instinctively seeking a safer environment. Still, its protective reactions are limited by the abilities that the animal posses. Now, when it comes to the human beings, the same environment will present much less difficulties because we are equipped with superior abilities. Humans can understand the reason for stressful environments and also can find a way to protect themselves by being creative in finding a safe environment. By using wrong reasoning and focusing on the negativity of the situation, humans could make their situation worst than it actually is.

As human beings, we are designed to be able to understand and define our environment, give them a specific meaning; positive or negative. In other words, we have basic knowledge when it comes to evaluating our environment. What we are not aware of is that we have the ability to change the meaning we give to our environment, how we feel about it, based on our own *interpretations*, not on reality. When we perceive it as negative, our body is going to feel the results of our interpretation as negative emotions. On the other hand, when we perceive it as positive, our body is going to feel results of our interpretations as positive emotions.

Becoming aware of these important facts, we cannot afford any longer to accept the idea that stress is our body reaction to any demand upon it. This is still true when it comes to unconscious things or objects, inferior life forms. It does not include human beings equipped with free will to identify, accept / reject and define negative or positive any demand upon us.

If we take a closer look at the way our body functions, we would recognize a simple truth that humans are designed to continually absorb information from their environments. As long as we are alive our

Introduction.

level of awareness changes all the time. When the level of awareness changes, by itself it does not have any stressful effect over us. But, this happens up to a point. As long as we give right meanings to new information that we continuously absorb, there is no danger of stress.

When we start to improper diagnose the meaning of outside information, things start to change. Because we are *experts* in miss diagnosing, we are the ones that are the creators of our stressful environments. This might sound like powerful statement but try to reason a little bit and you will find out the truth. Let me ask you a simple question: Is there anywhere in the world, any intelligent people will build a product with the intention to work in a safe way and at the same time build it in such a way that the more you use it the more it damages itself? I don't think so. We all know that in all areas of life we are looking to design products that are better and last longer. The competition requires the achieving of more quality rather than inferiority.

Let's ask the car manufactures if they are looking for improving the quality of their products or they are looking for poor quality materials to use in their products.

If we as humans, with our limitations, always want to improve for better; what makes you think that an intelligent designer would build a marvelous human body in such a way that any time when a demand or a change happens to it, will be affected negative and eventually to be destroyed by stress? Does this make any sense to you? Makes no sense to me. This was one of the reasons I decided to do research in this field to find out the truth. It didn't take much to realize that people today are confusing the stress with the level of emotional awareness that changes any time when there is a demand upon our body.

Our body constantly responds to the information that we receive from the outside. Any time this happens the level of emotional awareness changes. Now, some of the information we interpret as positive resulting in a positive state of mind, and other information we interpret as negative resulting in a negative state of mind.

Those that we are interpreting as negative they eventually become what we call *stressors*.

According to the specialists in stress management, we are advised to manage our stressors and find ways to reduce their effect upon us. What makes my program superior than the rest is that it goes to the root of the problem; eliminating the stressors. As a result we are able to live a stress free life. The secret is how can we eliminate the stressors? Can we do that? Here is the good news. Yes. We just need to learn how.

Now, somebody might ask the question:

What qualifies me to write this book and come up with so many things that are useful for people? Well, I have been doing extensive research for more than seven years on how to *eliminate* stress. How many others can say that? Yes, they might have experience in how to manage stress, but what's their experience in eliminating it? Let's take an example to illustrate my point:

What makes a heart surgeon, a good heart surgeon? Or a mechanic, a good mechanic?

They have to combine the knowledge acquired from others, the ability and courage to do the job, and have the necessary tools and equipment needed for the job. All of these have to be properly combined. Just the knowledge, courage/ ability, having right tools/ equipment will not help if one doesn't has the courage to perform the surgery. Or if he doesn't have the right equipment to perform. But, is he the one who built the tools? Or the one that discovered all the knowledge he got from others?

No, he acquired the knowledge/ tools and he trusts and uses them for the job. The same thing happens in our case. Much of the knowledge in this book is known to people today. Of course there are new things in it that nobody has ever heard about. My merit is that I wasn't afraid to take this knowledge, the old and the new and put them into a new light, so each of us gets a better understanding of the reality we are living in daily.

Let me tell you a little story to reflect our point:

One day three friends who all happen to be mechanics were driving to work. One of them was an engine specialist, the second a transmission specialist, and the third one a brake specialist. Suddenly their car broke down on the road. The driver pulls over and opens the hood. The others come out and try to figure out what's wrong with the car. They spend a few hours trying to fix it but they just cannot figure out what's wrong. Then after a while somebody else pulls over and tells them that he can help. The others look at him, thinking; what can he do? He is just another driver on the road. The new driver looks closer under the hood

Introduction.

and asks for a screwdriver. He hits the carburetor's body a few times. After that, he tells the driver to crank the engine. To the amusement of all present the car starts.

"How much do you charge me for this?" The driver asks.

"$100" he says.

"One hundred dollars? Just for hitting the carburetor few times with a screwdriver? You must be kidding."

"No, I am not. One dollar for hitting the carburetor, and $99 for knowing where to hit."

Now, the three mechanics were good mechanics, no doubt about that. They fixed many problems before. It just happened that this one they were not able to figure it out. What about the driver who stopped and solved their problem? The fact that he was driving a car at that particular time means that he was just lucky guessing what to do? Maybe yes, but also he could have been somebody with much more knowledge and experience in this field then the three mechanics.

The whole point is that it's very good to have the right tools but it's more important to know how to use them properly in each particular case. This is what the book is all about. Getting the right knowledge and understanding of how the tools work and how to properly apply them in any particular case.

The difference between me and other professionals in stress management is that I focus all of my attention in finding a way to eliminate stress. On the other hand, other professionals believe that stress cannot be eliminated; they focus all their attention on how to manage it better.

Even though we all are aware of the damaging effects that stress has over our lives, still an interesting question arises; why are we really interested in solving the problem of stress?

Well, actually we don't have too much against stress. It has a lot against us, such as our overall health, happiness and joy of life. All of us want a happy and healthy life. Stress is the element that blocks us from achieving a healthy lifestyle. The happiness, joy and health of our life, depends in the way we handle stress. We can say that stress is part of a bigger picture, involving ourselves in our environment, people events and situations that we are dealing with daily. Understanding the role we play in this big picture will help us to solve our stress problem by eliminating the underlying causes of stress.

Now, let's go back to our example with the car and our driving habits. We all are familiar with cars. Each car has an engine that makes the car run, but also among other things, the car is equipped with a *brake system*. We all agree that the brake system is very necessary so we can safely stop the car. Because many years ago, somebody mistakenly got a *wrong habit* of pulling the emergency brake every time they encountered a difficult or negative situation. As a result, everybody is complaining about the car's performance. The engine overheats, the transmission is barely shifting, the brakes are making a lot of noise, etc. In other words the car seems to fall apart bit by bit. What's the solution? Should we eliminate the braking system because it is the one that is the root of all these problems? No, we cannot do that. But what we can do is to properly understand its role and to get rid of our habit to activate the emergency brake at the wrong time. Once we do that all the problems will disappear. Once we get the right kind of knowledge, then it's just a matter of applying it. Let me ask you a simple question: Why do you stop your car and wait when you see a red signal in front of you? Because you don't like the red color, and want to wait until it gets green? I don't think so. The first time you learned to drive, you also learn that the law requires you to stop on red lights and go on green lights. Once you believed that, your brain paid attention to form a habit of reminding you to stop any time you get to a red light. Still, even though your mind reminds you about the right thing to do, you consciously could decide to obey or not. The same thing happens when we become aware of what is required from us to live a stress-free life. Having the right knowledge and accepting it as truth, our subconscious mind will bring to our conscious awareness the proper way to deal with *stress*. Then we are not slaves to stress and will be able to live a stress free life. As somebody nicely put it: "If it is to be, it's up to me."

Now, once we realized that the root of our stress is not coming from our *environment*, but from our misunderstanding of the role and functions of our *brake system*, we need to learn and understand how it was designed to function. Also, we also need to have an accurate understanding on how we came to have these

Introduction.

driving habits, their source and what does it takes to replace them with better ones. To do that, let's take another example: Let's look at a tree and examine it a little bit closely.

A tree is deeply rooted in the ground through solid roots. Also it has a trunk, branches leaves and fruits. Now what determines the quality of the fruits and the health of the tree? Well, the major factor in is the quality of the soil where the tree is planted. Even though all trees are planted in the ground, the minerals and other ingredients that make up the soil plays the most important factor in its health and quality of its fruits. If we want to improve the quality of its fruits, would it be a good idea to start applying some better color over the unhealthy fruits so they will look better? Or should we do some other work on it? We could do that but this will change only the appearance not the health of the tree. What we should do is to check the quality of the soil and make sure that there are no chemicals or other ingredients that might have a harmful effect on it. A good gardener knows that there is a huge difference between the sweet taste of a good fruit and the taste of ingredients needed by the tree's roots to properly grow and bear good fruits. By treating the soil with the right ingredients, the gardener would get quality fruits from the tree. Now what does this have to do with eliminating stress? Well, like a tree, the quality of our *fruits* is determined by the quality of ingredients we assimilate daily. As we are going to see in next chapters of this book, we need clean air, healthy foods, and maybe the most important; proper information. I say maybe most important because when it comes to stress, air and food has little or no nothing to do with it. The information that we feed our minds plays a major part in the creation and elimination of our stress.

The book is divided in three major parts. Part one: "Who really are we?" helps us to get a better understanding of who really are we. It reminds us that no matter where we come from, or what our background is, each and every one was born a wonderful human being. We all had such a wonderful beginning, but somewhere down the line, we started to allow stress to enter our lives. We forgot so easily that it's our birthright to live a wonderful and stress free life. Overwhelmed with daily problems and difficult situations, we let ourselves be *conditioned* by our environment. As a result, the quality of our life depends on its quality. Of course that by of living in the so-called stressful environment our life identifies with it. As result we are conditioned to live a stressful life. Part one of this book is going to help us remember that we too are wonderful humans beings, deserving to live a stress free life. Part two: "What are we dealing with?" is going to help us get a better understanding of what stress really is, where it comes from and the role we play in its creation. Part three: "When the impossible become possible" is going to help us by providing the necessary tools that we can use in creation of our stress free environment.

We are going to learn about the twelve secrets that if we properly understand and apply them, we are going to be able to eliminate stress forever. I have called them secrets not necessary because you never heard about them but because nobody until now have connected them together so they make sense in this practical, understandable order. So we are going to embark on our unbelievable journey, learn step by step what is required to be able to live a stress free life. We are going to start with the first secret and see how we can better ourselves when we know the rules of the game.

Review Question: In the light of the example used in the beginning about the car whose *health* starts to deteriorate, what it might be useful to consider?

Answer:
- A *paradigm shift* from its management to the real source of the problems; our driving habits.

"By changing our paradigm of stress from stress management to eliminating stress, we learn to use our body according the laws and principle they were designed to and then the impossible becomes possible."

Secret # 1.

"The one who knows the rules of the game can play the game the way he wants to."

Chapter 1. The Game Of Life Has Its Own Rules.

- Warning! By reading this book, you get a lot of knowledge –
- By applying what you learn, you may become a stress free person -

Life, what is life? Is life a game we all have to play no matter what? Does it consist of continuous series of uncertainties, challenges, problems and surprises?
Well, even though life is made up of many surprises, problems, challenges and continuous series of

uncertainties, it's a kind of game. Why? Because if we take a closer look, we can see that they all have some laws and regulation hidden behind them. Nothing happens without reason. We might not be aware of the reasons but they are still there. This is one of the most important principles in life that we should pay attention to. Being aware of it, then we realize that in order to have a successful and joyful life, we should be smart enough to learn and get familiar with these rules. You may have heard the saying:

"The one who knows the rules of the game can play the game the way they want to."

On the other hand, not knowing the rules, we are at the mercy of our *environment* and of those who know them. They are the primary beneficiaries, not us. Let's take an example to illustrate this point:

Suppose there are two people on a boat in stormy weather in the middle of the sea. Both of them are handcuffed to a pole in the middle of the boat. Not only that but they are also blind folded. They can't see anything and one of them has no idea what happened, where they are going, if they will ever survive this ordeal. The other, even though in the same situation, knows that this is just a temporary situation, pretty soon the storm will pass away and they will get back safely to the shore.
Now, what's going to be their state of mind? How will each one get through this difficult situation? We all get the point now. The one that has accurate knowledge is able to apply it. As a result, this person's mental state is different than the one that doesn't have the right knowledge to apply so they could better their situation. Knowing the rules of *the game* by having the right knowledge enables them to play the game the way they wants to. All of us live our lives but how do we live it? The way we want or are we at the discretion of whatever might happen to us? Let's take another example:

Suppose you are not feeling well and you might need to see a doctor. Not being an expert in medicine, you depend on the doctor for treatment. But, if you were a doctor, would you know how to take care of yourself? Of course, you would. Let's elaborate more on this example:

When somebody starts getting sick, what happens most of the time?

They panic and we know now that by doing this many times, it does more damage than the sickness itself. Also, they might start thinking about all the negative consequences that could happen and finally call the doctor. Once there, they find out that it is not such a big deal:

"Just take this medicine and everything will be all right" - the doctor says.

Now, how do you think a doctor reacts when he / she feel sick?

Do you think they will panic and stress themselves? No. Why is that?

Being a doctor, he / she know the *rules of this game* and play the way they want to. Let's take another example:

You are driving your car on the freeway minding your own business, when suddenly you start hearing some noises coming from your car. What is going to be your reaction?

"Something is happening to my car" - you may say, that is a normal response. But, in most cases, if you are not a mechanic, the tendency is to panic. From this point on, you start imagining all the bad results from this situation: Late to work, the extra money you have saved, now you might have to spend to repair the car, and so on. If you were a mechanic the thoughts would be different.

First, you wouldn't have to worry because you would pull over right away and try to find out what the problem is. Most of the time it's minor and by being a mechanic you might have some tools in your car that would take care of the problem. At least you could reduce the risk and expenses necessary to fix the car. You are still a driver on the road, like any other drivers, but the fact that beside the knowledge how to drive the car, you also have some extra knowledge; how to deal with situations when it breaks down, that puts you at advantage over the others. In other words, being a mechanic, you know the *rules of this game*, and that helps to play the way you want to, for your own advantage.

Now, what does it take to become a doctor, mechanic, engineer, or a teacher? I could wish to be a doctor, so I could take care of all my health problems. I could wish to be a mechanic, so I could fix the problems with my car. I could wish to be a teacher, so I could teach others how to do their jobs. I could wish to be a stress free person, so I'll enjoy my life.

All of these wishes are very good but just wishing is not enough. It might be a positive step in the right direction but we need much more. We need to be willing to take the necessary steps to accomplish these kinds of wishes. Let's see some of these necessary steps.

The very first step for us is to become *aware* of the possibility of achieving such goals.

Awareness comes from new information that we come in contact with. It could come from other people's desire to let us know about the new information, or could come from our own desire to research a new area.

This is what this book is basically all about, to make you aware of new information that contains the secrets on how to eliminate your stress. Knowing that each of us like to listen to the *radio station* W.I.I.F.M. (What's In It For Me), and realize that there is much benefit for us; we develop a desire to do the necessary steps to assimilate this information and solve our stress problems.

Now, from the previous examples we can see the difference in outcomes between having the right knowledge and benefiting from it in time of crises, and being uninformed in the specific area and having to pay a high price for it. Understanding the differences in outcomes, we can realize the necessity of having the right kind of knowledge for each specific crisis. The same principal works in eliminating stress.

We need to learn the secrets of what stress really is, how it's formed, and what role do we play in its creation; so we can get rid of it.

We have mentioned before that stress, according to the father of the stress theory, is our body response to any demand upon it. Now, like some other theories, from time to time they might need to be updated. We all know that science progresses continually and based on new information we get new understandings. We could update this theory by saying, when we are talking about humans:

"Stress is the negative response of our body, to *a specific* demand upon our body that we perceive as a stressor."

What is the difference you may ask?

Well, it's a big difference because not all changes produces stress. Each change produces different level of emotional awareness. Out of all the changes, only those we perceive as stressors, result in stress. Later on, we will discuss how the mind processes information, and we'll discover that if only the stressors are having a stressing effect on us, we have a choice in calling a "stressor", a stressor. Or we may call it a regular demand upon our body without the effect of a stressor.

Let's take an example to illustrate this:

One day, on the way to work, you get on the bus, when suddenly at the next stop a bunch of kids get in with their father.

Soon as they get in, they start making a lot of noise, running from one end of the bus to the other, disturbing everyone. You keep looking at them, thinking that the kids really need some discipline from their father. Nothing happens; the father doesn't say anything. After ten minutes of this kind of behavior, you feel the urge to do something about it. You turn to the father, and as polite as possibly ask him to do something about the kids because their behavior is irritating everybody. Then, he turns to you and in a low tone of voice tells you:

"I think you are right but we just came from the hospital, where their mother just died few hours ago and that's why the kids are so irritating."

Now, what happened to you in this moment? You instantly changed your attitude toward the kids. Why? The situation is the same; the only thing that changed was the meaning you give to the same situation; based on the new information received. But changing the meaning of the situation, you also changed the mental state of your mind. Something that, a few minutes ago was defined as a stressor, changed suddenly into an opposite feeling of sorrow and kindness. You probably would apologize and ask the father if you could do anything to help. What can we learn from this example?

We have the choice to choose how we interpret the events and information from around us. Giving them a positive meaning will result in a positive state of mind. If we give them a negative meaning it will result into a negative state of mind. Now you may ask:

"How does a person, in their right mind, could call something that is bad; good?"

Doesn't make any sense. See, the secret is not what the event itself is; negative or positive. That's not so important. What's important is the meaning we give to it, because it triggers our brain to have a positive reaction or a negative one based on our own interpretation; not on the reality of the event. Let me tell you a little story:

Many years ago a friend and I were invited to visit another friend. After we got there, we started talking about different subjects, and then his wife asked us if we would like a cup of tea or a coffee.

"A cup of tea please," I said.

She brought each of us a cup of tea.

Now, I have to tell you that I was born in Europe, and in the area I came from every body that I know of drinks sweet tea. I thought that this was the custom in America also. The people we were visiting though, were from Cambodia, and in that part of the world people drink tea from herbs that doesn't taste anything like sweet! As soon as I tasted it, I almost had to spit it out of my mouth but not wanting to make them feel bad, I just asked my friend how does he likes the tea? He told me that he was satisfied; it tastes good.

"Yours may be good but they surely forgot to add sugar to mine" I said.

"I don't think so, he said, this is the way they drink it."

We had the same drink but because of my past experiences, a "good tea is a sweet tea" and from their past experiences an "unsweetened tea is also a good tea." For them it might have been a pleasure to drink it, but for me it was unpleasant. I did drink a little but I felt like I will never drink that kind of tea again.

We come again to the same conclusion; it is not the event itself. It is the meaning we give to it that makes us happy or unhappy. Somebody very appropriately said:
"It is not what is happening to you but what you do with what happens to you"

Now, before we move on, we need to properly understand the basics functions of our mind, body and what triggers our behavior. Remember that:
"The one who knows the rules of the game, could play the game the way they wants to."
It may sound like we are going into a unknown area but as we will see, the mind and body, like any other sophisticated machinery, works on certain laws and principles. If we learn them, we are able to control our future, destiny and eventually eliminate stress forever.

Now, usually when we hear about laws, we have the tendency to reject the idea because none of us would like to be controlled or cornered. We tend to look for some substitutions for laws. That's why we will try to see this from a better and more acceptable angle.

Let's see what is the real purpose of laws.
To better understand this, we'll start with a broader view.
We know that there exists a gigantic and complex universe around us. There are millions, maybe billions of stars, and countless galaxies in space. For some reasons, there is a perfect balance in the interactions between them.
In other words, there are certain laws and regulations that these outer space components are obeying; never forgetting to respect them.

Imagine what might happen if the sun will just *forget* to follow its route? If that would happen, the functions of our life on earth will be affected or even terminated. We have laws such as: natures, physics, chemistry, and mathematics, biologic and so on. These laws are fixed and we can trust them. When we act in harmony with these laws, we benefit from them also.

Looking at the things around us, we see that all of them are subjected to some rules or laws for one very important reason: balance, and harmony. When they are respected, the harmony and balance exist; when they are broken there is a big price to be paid. Imagine what will happen if you are driving your car and suddenly the systems on the car start going crazy. When you want to stop, the car instead starts to accelerate? That will be something nobody wants to happen to them.
So, anytime that nature laws are broken, what is the result?

You could visualize yourself; it will be disastrous.
This does not happens because the car manufacturer know and understand that the materials used in these components work based on fixed laws that do not change.
A piece of metal will never become plastic or something else; it will always be a piece of metal. Every kind of material has its own properties and car manufacturers know and put their trust in these laws.

As long as they go along with these laws and not against them, everything is fine.
Every time you go home at night, you turn the light on, right?
Yes, you expect that the electric circuit will work properly because it follows its own laws that do not change, unless somebody starts messing them up.
See, the whole universe is like gigantic machinery that works perfect, following its own pre-established rules and regulations. Life on earth could exist likewise.
It's very important to recognize that humans are a part of this complex machinery and we need to do our part in contributing to the balance and harmony. For us to be able to do this we need to understand what are the laws and regulations that govern the functions of our own minds and bodies.
By learning this, we will stop sabotaging our own future, and start directing it to the destination we really want. See, this should be a collective effort because we are all in this together.
The problem is that many of today's scientists are spending their time, energy,

millions of dollars, to try to reach the distant parts of the universe. Instead of trying harder to explore our inner universe, the infinite complexity and capability of our mind and body, it's much closer and the benefits are much more rewarding, because the easiest laws to break are the ones you don't know about.

Most people today know so little about this infinite unexplored continent - the powerful human mind!
As a result, we suffer so much because of this.
When we buy a product, like a TV, VCR, car or a computer, we also get a manual from which we learn how to properly operate the product. The more we understand the instructions, the better we are able to use the product. If we do not follow the manual, we can misuse it or damage the item.

The same principle applies to our mind. It works according to specific laws and regulations. We need to find out what they are and learn how to properly apply them. Otherwise, we are doing guesswork.
Would you hire somebody to do some important computer work for you, if you know that they aren't even familiar with computers?
Unfortunately, most people today have no idea how their minds and bodies work or what controls their behavior. They are living their lives by trial and error. Most die without understanding this, and some by the end of their life, are able to realize this; wishing they found out sooner.

We could do the same, wasting our life by trail and error. Or, we could decide to appreciate the value of knowing to consciously control our life and learn as soon as possible these secrets.
We don't need to know everything about these things but it's important to learn the most important things.

What would you rather have: 2 one hundred dollar bills, or 180 one-dollar bills?
Even though 180 dollar bills sound much more then 2 one hundred dollar bills, their values are established by how much each bill is worth.
So, we do not necessarily need 180-dollar bills; we can do better with only two bills. We have to make sure their value is greater than all 180 one-dollar bills.
The same thing happens in our case. We can have a lot of knowledge (many one dollar bills, which is not bad), but more important is to have the right knowledge so we can apply it to our situation.

Coming back to our main point, we are part of a huge *machinery* we call earth, or nature. Like it or not, we are controlled by its destiny and future. More than any other components, we are much more responsible to what happens to it because we are the only ones designed with superior abilities.
These abilities we are equipped with they have a specific role to play in our developing a joyful or an unpleasant life on this earth.

We have two eyes, right? What for? Just for our selfish desires? Or for even a greater purpose?
We have two ears. What for? Just for listening to what we think is the best for us? Or for a greater purpose? Like learning how to create a better environment for others too? We have two hands. What for? Just to accomplish our egoistic goals? Or for a greater purpose? Once we take a closer look at this, we realize that no man is an island. We are all in this together. Sooner or later our collective behavior will dictate the direction where we are heading, as individuals and as a human race. We don't live any longer in *dark ages,*
We live in a time where through increasing awareness we cannot afford any more to neglect the realities that surround us all. Like somebody once said: "We cannot sink half the ship."

If we take a closer look at the nature, we can safely say that it works as a unit, for the good, peace and harmony of all the elements involved in its complex and continuous existence. For this to happen, all the elements involved, unconsciously keep following some laws, rules or regulations. Humans are a major part of nature and we cannot survive without it. Then it makes perfect sense to believe and understand that we too, are under obligation to follow and live in harmony with the nature's laws, rules and regulations. Actually, our welfare, peace, health and happiness depends how to we integrate ourselves as part of the nature. How much we understand and respect these laws, rules and regulations that govern the functions of our whole earth determines also our overall health. In other words, the whole Nature is equipped with amazing abilities, laws and regulations. And it never forgets to use these for our benefits. Humans as part of this wonderful Nature, we too have the responsibility to learn how to use our abilities to complement the other works of the Nature, not just for our own personal or even selfish desires.

By understanding these realities, we can consciously decide to do our share in creating a better environment for others and for ourselves.

In order to come up with new theory that would be recognized in scientific community, like anyone else, the author is also required to use the scientific method. What is the scientific method you might ask? Well, the scientific method is a series of steps that are used to solve a problem through the use of intelligent questions. Here are the basic steps that need to be addressed in using the scientific method.
1. Observe what happens in the particular subject you are working on.
2. Ask one or more important questions related to the subject.
3. Based on observations, form a hypothesis.
4. Test the hypothesis.
5. Analyze the results.
6. Draw conclusions.
7. Communicate results.

1. Observe what happens.

The first step requires a careful objective observation of a particular subject or event that is to be addressed. It could be done through a series of laboratory tests, or through observations of the behaviors and the results of such. In some instances through laboratory tests one could get enough observation to form a theory. In others due to the psychological or other factors that are involved, more than laboratory tests are required to form a theory. Since the nature of the subject of stress has an important psychological and behavioral aspect related to it, using only physical science or laboratory testing would prove to be insufficient to draw a correct conclusion, even if they are done on humans. Even though the majority of people perceive stress as being caused by stressful situation, the reality is that its creation has largely to do with human behavior. We know that each individual is unique and responds different to stressful situations. One particular situation could be a stressful one for an individual, but non stressful for another.

So in order to observe how stress takes place, we need to look for people that get stressed easily. Observe their view of the environment; do they see it as a pleasant environment, or a stressful on? Observe their view of themselves, do they see themselves as happy optimistic people? Or do they seem to perceive themselves as unhappy or even pessimistic people? Also observe their willingness to explore new ways of dealing with stress.

Due to the progress of our modern society, a great number of rapid changes take place. With the same amount of time at one's disposition, these rapid changes, decreases the leisure time that one needs to function properly, at the same time increasing the number of so-called stressors. Not being able to properly cope with all of these most people stress themselves out that aggravate even more their coping with the situations.

2. Ask questions.

The second step requires the asking of a series of questions related to the subject of stress, such as:
Where does stress come from?
Is it the result of one's reaction to any stimuli, or does it occur only in specific situation? Is it caused by the so-called stressful situations?
If so, what can we do about to solve this major problem that all of us is facing today?
What if stress occurs only when one is unable to deal with a specific situation?
Even more, what if stress is created only when one gives a negative meaning to particular stimuli?
If stress occurs due to ones interpretation of situations and not based on their polarity, could there be a solution, formula, or specific behavior that could reduce or even eliminate the stressful effect that a situation might have on a person?

Does stress occurs only because of present circumstances?
Or there are others factors that have nothing to do with the present?
It is possible that some stress has little to do with the present, but is the result of relieving some memories that contain negative feelings attached to them in the past?
Is there any possibility to get rid and eliminate stress?
Are there any secrets that most people don't know that could bring light into this subject?
What field of science should we focus on to solve these problems?

3. Form a hypothesis.

The third step requires forming one or more hypotheses. In our case, we are going to form two hypotheses.

Hypothesis A. Since we human beings are creatures designed to function in a specific way, and are surrounded by a wonderful and delightful natural environment, it's safe to say that we were also designed as wonderful human beings with an inborn right to live a happy and stress free life.

Hypothesis B. Since stress doesn't occur in any situation, there are two possible sources for it:
    1. When one perceives any stimuli as negative, they consciously or not give a negative meaning to them. The subconscious part of the brain takes the stimuli as negative and therefore harmful to our well-being, triggering the protecting self-defense mechanism. Being understood as negative it is processed and transformed into an electro-chemical reaction (negative emotion) that is sent through our nervous system throughout our body.
    2. When without being aware of, one relieves a memory that has in the past a negative meaning attached to it.

4. Test the hypothesis.

Let's take a simple example. Suppose you own a house for many years and have quite a bit of equity on it. One day you come from work and find a message on your answering machine from your lender. It says that it's important that you contact them as soon as possible because it relates to your mortgage. You call back right a way, but couldn't reach anybody to talk to, just the mailbox.
Now you have a few choices.
One, (because you know first hand some cases when people lost their homes) right the way to display a negative attitude, thinking that something is going wrong with your mortgage and might jeopardize your ownership of the house.
Two, you could start thinking a little bit about the history of your mortgage payments, and knowing that you made them all in time, it couldn't be that the message implies that something is wrong so could jeopardize the ownership of your house. It just could be for reasons related to the house, but not necessarily negative.
Three, you could carefully listen to the tone of voice and entire message and realize that maybe they wants you to refinance your mortgage to a lower rate, so that's why they called.
Now, in each particular choice you make the state of mind differs one from the other. The first choice, by giving a negative meaning to the new information coming in, the mental state becomes negative. If you persist in it, eventually becomes a stressful situation.
The second choice, once you start reasoning and eliminate the factors that could create a negative meaning, you get in a balanced state of mind. In other words, the situation is not critical, and you are waiting for more feed back to make the right judgment.
The third choice, by reasoning this way, your state of mind becomes positive, your mortgage payments could be lowered; and that's good news.

Now, we can use endless number of examples to prove this point. The truth is that we are equipped with enough abilities to make this possible. In other words, to take each situation we go through one at a time and reason it in a positive light, and by doing so the results will become positive. It only requires that we become aware of it; start desiring to make the change, making a decision, finding enough motivation to be able to discipline ourselves in such a way that this become a way of life.

5. Analyze the results.

Hypothesis A. Any individual, who realizes that they are wonderful human beings, should come to the conclusion that they have an inborn right to live a happy and stress free life. As a wonderful human being, each also being equipped with free will, have the ability to choose his / hers own interpretation of the situations we go through or the environment we live in. A characteristic of a wonderful human being is that has a positive outlook in life, he /she has the tendency to see the good out of life and any situation no matter how difficult or negative it might appear to be.

Hypothesis B. Understanding the importance of these any time when life would bring them "lemons", instead of complaining how sour they are, they could go into "lemonade business" and get the best out of it. Learning the rules of the "lemonade business," one could successfully make a profit from any of the so-called "lemons" that many times life has to offer. By learning the secrets of turning lemons into lemonade, one could discipline himself /herself and could make this a way of life, and could truly say that life is a pleasant journey and enjoy its ride.

6. Draw a conclusion.

Based on the previous steps we have taken, we can safely say that as wonderful human beings, and by learning the secrets of eliminating stress, we too can live a stress free life.

7. Communicate the results.

The purpose of this book is doing just that. It offers a simple but powerful way of eliminating stress from our life. In the second step "Ask questions," we asked many questions that are related to this subject. Throughout the book, one by one these questions will be answered.

Now, let's talk about one of the biggest secrets in our lives, the one that has to do with our game of stress and see how by properly understand and apply it, we can enjoy a happier, healthier journey on this earth.

Review Question: In order to play the game of life in such a way that we win it, what is required from us?

Answer:
- Like any other games it also has its own rules that we need to understand and obey in order to win this game of life.

"Acquiring knowledge will make us knowledgeable people. Acquiring accurate knowledge and continuously applying it will help us to win the game of life."

Secret # 2.

"Knowing the rules of our game enables us to play it the way we want to and win."

Chapter 2. Which Are The Rules Of Our Game?

- Wisdom settles in the minds of those not afraid to ask themselves intelligent questions -

If our life is the greatest game we all have to play and it consists of a continuous series of uncertainties, challenges, problems and surprises, it's reasonable to find out what are the rules and elements. We saw the difference in outcomes between being properly equipped and being misinformed or ignorant of the rules of this game.

Coming back to our subject of stress, we can say that dealing with stress is another important game of our life. Being properly equipped to play this game we have great chances to win it. On the other hand, as reality shows, most of us are doing a poor job in dealing with it. The major reason is t we are not properly equipped with the necessary knowledge to apply and win the game.

As you may know, stress is destroying happiness and enjoyment from people's lives. Why? As we just mentioned, it's because we are not aware of what is behind this game.

Many of us might know the story of the young boy David and the giant Goliath. What do you think would have been the outcome if David would have ask himself the question:

How can I *manage* living with this giant?

Well, the outcome would have been totally different, right?

Of course it would. By asking this kind of question he would have come up with an idea on how to coexist with the giant. But e asked himself a different kind of question:

How can I get rid of him, destroy him?

The same thing happens in our case. We also face a huge giant; stress.

We can ask ourselves how can we live with it? Or, we can ask ourselves how we can get rid of it?

The first time I faced this giant, I didn't asked myself how to manage it but how to get rid of it. once and for all. That was the main focus of my research. I wasn't interested in finding a way to manage it but a lasting solution, the elimination of it.

Let's look at some of the elements of our game.

First, as human beings, our bodies are built like no other machinery in the universe. This body is composed of a number of sophisticated organs each doing its job for the well being of the body as a whole.

Second, we have the *mind*, which is the one that controls and directs the body.

Third, when we start to interact with the environment, the mind directs the body to act in a specific way as a response to this interaction. This is what we call *behavior*.

Fourth, for the mind to direct the body towards a specific behavior, the body also needs another element; which we are going to call *life spirit*. We can safely say that the life's spirit is the energy that resides inside living creatures. It activates and maintains all the organs and components of a living creature. If the life's spirit is absent, the body becomes lifeless, or dead.

Now, beside these four elements of our game, humans are equipped with some amazing abilities that make us unique.

Many of us have heard about the so-called mind / body communication, which basically means that there is a strong relationship between our mind and our body.

Because of their continuous interaction humans have some amazing abilities such as:

1. The ability to keep itself alive.

2. The ability to grow, multiply and continuously develop its capacities.

3. The ability to consciously identify, explore, absorb, enjoy and acquire ownership of the environment.

4. Create new events and situations, factual or fiction.

5. To store information in our memory banks.

6. Recreate characters, events or situation from memory.

7. Ruin our health by improper using our mind or body.

8. Maintain, rejuvenate or restore the health of our body, by properly communicate with it.

9. To consciously control and direct our life the way we want it.

Let's take one at a time and elaborate more.

1. The ability to keep itself alive.

Many scientists in the past and present are looking to find the perpetual-mobile, in other words, the machinery that once start working, it continuously keep doing that. Wouldn't that be a wonderful achievement? Of course it would!

Well, it might surprise you to find one by looking in the mirror. Yes, we are the kind of live *machinery* that once born, keeps ticking until we die. Still, it takes a while until that happens. As a matter of fact, we don't die because the live *machinery* was not build properly. Somewhere down the line, we screwed up and as a result, our life span has been reduced to what we live today.

The combination of the body, mind and spirit, all put together in a wonderful way, creates what we call a human being.

Last time I checked, in order to function or recharge our *battery*, we didn't have any electric cord to plug in. All the other man-made devices need an electric source to be connected to; otherwise they wouldn't work. The best and most sophisticated computer isn't good for anything unless we have an electric source for it.

Chapter 2.   Which are the rules.

Also, a human being is needed to turn it on and off, because the computer has no ability to connect itself to an electrical source.
But we humans, even though every evening we go to sleep, automatically wake up in the morning and are able to continue our activities left from the previous day.
This amazing ability is due to the fact that we are equipped with two mechanisms.
One, we are going to call: "The propulsion mechanism"
The other, "The self-defense mechanism"

The propulsion mechanism creates in each of us an inner desire to consciously identify, explore, absorb, enjoy and acquire ownership of the *environment*. In other words, it's like a radar guided missile that continuously seeks and follows its targets until it succeeds in finding them. The targets are love, happiness, enjoyment of the environment, good health, peaceful relationships, peace of mind, etc. In accomplishing its role, the propulsion mechanism uses our nervous system to transmit from the brain the positive messages throughout our body. Then the whole body feels good and happy.

The self-defense mechanism was designed to keep us away and warn of anything that might be hurtful, dangerous, or fatal. Like a good guardian, it continuously watches for our own protection and welfare. This mechanism is doing its job in two ways.
In one way, it triggers an inner desire to stay away from some things, situation, events or people that might present a danger for us; through what we commonly call fear.
Example: We might be afraid to jump from a cliff, a high building, or to walk in the night on a street in a bad neighborhood. That inner fear comes from the self-defense mechanism that is warning us by triggering the feelings of fear.
The other way is by triggering a level of pain in a specific part of our body, when something is not functioning properly. This could be due to the fact that part of our body has been hurt or damaged by somebody or something, and needs our conscious attention.
The self-defense mechanism uses the immune and the nervous system in accomplishing its role. The immune system deals primarily with the security inside the body, making sure that no foreign or domestic agent might enter or disturb its proper functions. Its messengers continuously seek and destroy any invaders.
The nervous system is primarily used to process any kind of information that comes from the environment. When the information is perceived as being negative, it triggers a negative response throughout our body. The intensity of this negative response is based on the level of danger perceived. We commonly might call it: bad mood, anger, anxiety, depression, stress, etc. All of these are triggered by the self-defense mechanism as a response to our brain computing information that is perceived as dangerous.
 One mechanism pushes us forward to enjoy our life and the other protects us from anything that might be dangerous.

2. The ability to grow, multiply and continuously develop its capacities.

How would you like to build a copy machine that not only make copies, but also makes copy machines? How about a car that not only takes you any place you want, but also is able to reproduce itself; so you don't have to buy another one later? How about that? We humans, like all the other creatures, have this capacity to multiply. And all of us who are parents could be very appreciative and thankful for this wonderful capacity. This capacity is so amazing, that it continuously puzzles scientists even today.
It's true that only human beings when they are born, they need somebody to take care of them, otherwise, if left alone they would soon die. There is a special reason for this.
On the other hand, all the other creatures when they are born, shortly after that, they are able to survive on their own.

But, how many of these creatures are able to develop their capacities like humans? None. How many are able to go to school and college, or get a PhD?
None. The reason is that only humans were designed with such capacities.

3. The ability to consciously identify, explore, absorb, enjoy and acquire ownership of the environment.

What do we mean by this? It means that we are not only alive, but also aware of the fact that we are alive, able to understand and direct our live according to our own desires. Even more than that, we also have a deep-rooted inner drive to become the owners of our desired environment or others things that we consider valuable.
Now, in order to accomplish this, we need to keep in mind two important factors:
    1. Our proper behavior towards the environment we live in, result in a joyful life.
On the other hand, an improper behavior will result in a stressful environment, and a stressful life.
    2. Our proper behavior towards others and ourselves results in a joyful and fulfilling life.
By the same token, an improper behavior toward others and ourselves will result in a joyless life.

Let's talk a little bit about consciousness.
We can safely say that as long as we are alive and awake, we are in a state of consciousness. What maintain our consciousness are our senses that continuously absorb information from the environment that are sent to our brain to be perceived or processed. The result is then released to our body and we become conscious of everything that surrounds us.
    We express our continuous interaction with our environment in two different or opposite ways. When we consciously or not are directly involved or actively participate in whatever happens around us, we can say that we are in a state of active consciousness. On the other hand, when we are not directly involved or actively participants, we simply observe whatever happens around us. We can say that we are in a state of passive consciousness. Because of the variety of situations we continuously go through, we often switch from one state to the other, based on our personal interest in whatever happens around us.
    We have mentioned earlier about the four elements: body, mind, spirit and behavior.
When a person is dead, it still has a body but because the spirit of life cease to exist, the mind also cease to function even though the brain or other organs might be in good condition.
When a person is sleeping, they are alive but still unconscious. Why? By sleeping, the senses they are equipped with are turned off. When the senses are turned off, the consciousness is off also. When the person wakes up, their senses become active, and they become conscious.
Consciousness starts when our perceptive senses are activated and in proper working conditions. If we shut off one or more of our senses, our level of consciousness would be reduced also.
When somebody is in a coma, are they conscious of themselves? No. Why? Their conscious perceptive senses are shut off and the brain has a problem receiving or processing the information from them. Being conscious creatures, humans are able to:
    A. Recognize us as distinctive and unique individuals.
    B. Recognize others as distinctive and distinguished individuals.
    C. Become aware of our past, present and future.
    D. Choose what kind of information we absorb from our environment.
    E. Give a particular meaning to any information; no matter of their origin.
    F. Build a relationship with other people, situations or events, by the process of association.
    G. Keep away from other persons, situations or events, by the process of disassociation. .

Let's see how the consciousness process takes place.
There are three steps in the process of consciousness:

> **1. The first step we are going to call reasoning.**
> **2. The second, we are going to call imagination.**
> **3. The third, we are going to call emotions.**

In the first step, a live human being chooses according to his / hers free will the kind of information to absorb from the environment. This is done through the senses such as: sight, hearing, taste, smell, and touch. Beside the fact that he / she has the option to choose what kind of information to accept and absorb, they also have the ability to give a positive or negative meaning to this particular information. If it's given a positive meaning, the information is linked to what we call the propulsion mechanism.
On the other hand, if it's given a negative meaning, the information is linked to the self-defense mechanism. These two mechanisms will be discussed in details later.
In the second step, through what we call imagination, our brain processes bits of information accepted through reasoning, and transforms them into electro-chemical impulses. The brain then sends these impulses as messengers of information to body cells.
In the third step, through what we call emotions, each cell of the body, (or the specific ones to whom were sent), upon receiving the messages, feeds itself with them. As result of this, the body goes through an emotional state. The level of emotion is dictated by the intensity and duration of the messengers.
The result of the processed information, what we call emotion, is the basis of our consciousness.
Let's talk about both states of consciousness starting with the active one.

A. Active consciousness.

By active consciousness, it means we associate ourselves or directly participate in the environment. We become part of the *environment* and we become the *center of attention*. As a result, we feel that we need to control and direct everything in our *environment*. Of course that identifying ourselves with it, our consciousness is affected by the *consciousness* of the *environment*. In other words, we run the risk of molding our consciousness by the polarity of the *environment*. If the *environment* is pleasant and favorable, the overall state of our consciousness is positive. But by the same token, if the *environment* is negative, the overall state of consciousness becomes negative.
When we associate with the *environment*, we relate directly to things, situations, events or the environment itself, others and ourselves. Our body's position is alert to receive every bit of information. The eyes are pretty much wide opened, ears ready to listen, etc. Also, when we associate ourselves to a situation or event, our brain will trigger specific kinds of questions, some like these:
What can I do in this situation?
How can I solve it?
How can I change it?
How can I help?
How can I get rid of it? Etc.
All these questions require our direct involvement. As a result, our brain is directly processing the information. The emotions resulted are felt by our body, as if they are our own, even though they belong to the *environment*.
It's wise to learn to associate only when the situations or events are not stressful ones. Many people get stressed today because they are not aware of this important fact. Not knowing that they have a conscious

choice between associating and disassociating to any situation or event, they stress themselves out by associating to stressful situations or events.
If the situation is stressful, by keeping ourselves emotionally away from it, we keep the stress away from us. By doing this, we are not linking the situation to the self-defense mechanism.
Otherwise, by not doing this, we associate and put ourselves in the position of experiencing its stress by linking it to the self-defense mechanism.
If the situation is a pleasant one, then it's wise to associate with it. By doing this, we create a link between this particular situation and our propulsion mechanism.

B. Passive consciousness.

By passive consciousness, we mean that even though we humans are part of whatever environment we are in, we disassociate ourselves from other people, things, situations, events or the environment. Even though we might be physically active, emotionally we become observers, not being directly involved. Our body's position is not forward, but a little bit backward, and relaxed. Our senses are not at their peak of perceptions, but just idling.
Also, when we disassociate ourselves, our brain will trigger totally different kinds of questions, some like these:
Let's watch what is going on here?
Let's see how these things are going to develop?
What would be a correct response to this?
What could be done to improve this? Etc.
All these questions require an emotionally passive response from us. We play the role of a spectator, not getting directly involved in the situation.
By disassociation from the old stressful situations or events, you remove the previous links to the self-defense mechanism.
Did you happen to see two people going through the same situation, but one getting very anxious and stress about it, and the other seems like doesn't care too much?
Well, the first one unconsciously or not is associating to the situation. As result that person is emotionally involved, feeling the negative charge of the situation. By perceiving the situation as negative and being associated with it, this creates a link in his / her brain between that situation and his /hers self-defense mechanism, which in turn triggers the negative emotion.
On the other hand, the second person, being disassociated from the situation, is not emotionally affected by it. Not being associated with the situation, his / her brain doesn't perceive any danger and there is no linking to the self-defense mechanism to create a negative emotion. Becoming aware of this important fact, we can use this in solving our problems with stress.

4. Create new characters, events or situations, factual or fiction.

Remember when you were just a kid how your imagination used to run wild. How you created in your own mind characters, situations or events? Of course at that time being a naïve child, you imagined many things, but now as an adult they seem so childish and unrealistic. But at that time, they were so real to you. Wasn't it? It was because our subconscious mind cannot make the difference between real or fiction information. Whatever we decide to believe and accept, it processes as true. Any bits of information real or fiction that are collected through our perceptive senses are transformed into electrical impulses and sent to our brain. Inside our brain they create an electro-chemical reaction. The results of these reactions are sent by the brain through its messengers to our body cells to be *fed*. The emotions felt are real even though some of the bits of information were just fiction.

Where do you think our dreams and aspirations come from? Well, all come from this ability we have. On the other hand, where do the worries, anxieties, and much of the stress come from? From the same ability, but in this case, we are using negative information instead of positive.

Imagine the electrical system in a car. We have a battery, and many electrical components that are connected to each other through a complicated *web* of electric wires. The battery has two terminals, one negative and the other positive. When we turn on the engine, the electricity from the battery flows from positive to all the components feeding them with the necessary electric power to function properly.

Now, do you think it's important to make sure that the battery is connected properly? What do you think is going to happen if by mistake we connect the battery terminals the wrong way? Please don't try to do this, you are going to mess up many components of the electrical system, and the car won't start any more. Well, human beings are designed to live a joyful and pleasant life. Which means that we should feed our mind with positive information. Like the way a battery feeds power to the components so it can function properly. Because we are imperfect and live in an imperfect world, consciously or not, with or without our will, we absorb much information that is negative, or give a negative meaning. As a result, we unconsciously *switch the terminals* of *our battery* and of course this result in getting stressed.

5. To acquire and store information in our memory banks.

Memory! What a wonderful ability to possess.

What do you think life would be if our brain wouldn't be able to differentiate between past, present and future? We wouldn't be able to function. The way it was designed to function gives us the ability to differentiate between them, so we can understand when these memories were stored. For example: Do you remember when you were 10 years old? Of course you do. What kind of memory comes to your mind when I asked you this question? Memories from the time you were seven, or eight, or twelve? No, because the brain stores the information in a specific order, so we can remember it the right way. Even though the memory was designed to work so wonderful, and it could be a good friend and joyful companion, it also could be the root of much of our stress.

Well, how could this be? Understanding the purpose of our memory, and the way it was designed to function, we have a great friend and a joyful companion.

On the other hand, not being aware of this, we might have a continuous source of stress that could make our life miserable.

During the day we are going through many kinds of situations and events. All the bits of information from these are stored in our memory banks. During the night when we sleep, the brain selects these bits of information and stores each in the specific file that it belongs to. The bits of information about our work, they go in the *work file*. The bits of information about family go in the *family file*. The bits of information about our health go in the *health file* and so on.

The brain doesn't discriminate the information we feed our mind with. It stores in its memory banks any kind of information, positive or negative. When it stores positive information, it results in positively emotionally charged memories. But, by the same token, when it stores negative information, it results in negative emotionally charged memories.

6. Recreate characters, events or situation from memory.

We have so many great past experiences stored in our memory. Any time we want, we can go back recreate and relive them. Maybe the memory of a good friend who is not here. The pleasant vacations you spent in the mountains with your family. The memorable experience of having your first bundle of joy -your first baby. Other important or memorable events in your life; such as your wedding, birthdays or anniversaries.
By reliving all these memories, you are re-experiencing these wonderful times as many times as you want.
Our memory, with all its amazing abilities, also could be the root of much of our stress.
Understanding its purpose, and the way it was designed to function, we have a great friend and a joyful companion.
On the other hand, not being aware of this might be a continuous source of stress that could make our life miserable.
Well, how could this be?
Specialists tell us that about 75% of all the information that we come in contact with is negative, or perceived to be negative. If that's the case, unconsciously we have a great tendency to remember or recreate negative characters, events or situations from our memory.
When we do this, we are reliving these negative memories that are going to have a negative or even a stressful effect over us.
The implementation of learning, behavior and change are not controlled by our conscious mind, but by our subconscious mind. It's not enough to realize and consciously decide to do something different. In order to accomplish a particular desire or goal, we need to understand the role our subconscious mind plays and work on accomplishing them at the subconscious level first. Acting this way, the results will be more permanent and lasting.
What happens is, we consciously come up with a goal or desire. Once we decided what we want to do, that message goes to the subconscious mind to be brought into reality. The subconscious mind looks in the memory banks for the file and the blueprint that contains information on how to accomplish this. Based on the information found, it takes the necessary steps in bringing into reality our goal or desire. The more clear and concrete information exist about that subject, the easier it will be to accomplish. But if we don't have enough information, or it's just not clear or concrete enough, it will take much longer, if will be accomplish at all.
When we start to worry, we are sending a command to our subconscious mind to accomplish these negative *goals*. The subconscious mind accepts any command and start working on it.
It's wise to learn to control our thoughts, and focus on the ones that are positive, instead of bringing back and relieving the old negative ones and getting stressed because of them.

7. Ruin our health by improperly using our minds or bodies.

Now, ruining our body's health shouldn't be called ability, but this happens because we just don't know, or are not aware of the importance of this.
How do we ruin our own health?
Well, let's see some *methods* we use in doing this.

-Do we know for sure what are the best foods and in what quantity should we use for our body? Of course we do. We eat what we like, and as much as we want. Right? That's why they built supermarkets.

-Do we know what role vegetables and fruits play in our diet?
Of course we do. When asked, what's his favorite vegetable? Someone once said:
"Out of all vegetables, the one I like the most is *meat*." ☺

- Do we know for sure what's the best liquid that our body needs and how much to take in with each meal? Soft drinks, beer, wine, whisky, etc…oh, yeah, and some water.

- Do we know that our brain is in continuous need for food? Do we know what's the right food for it? Of course we do. That's why we invented the radio TV, VCR or the newest in entertainment devices.

- Do we know that there is a direct correlation between the health of our body and our mental state, and vice-versa? Do we know that through our thoughts we can make ourselves sick, and also we can make ourselves well? Of course *we do*. That's why we go to the doctor so often.

- Do we know what' the proper position of our body's bones and muscles, so we could function at the peak of our abilities? Of course we do. We know how to walk, don't we?
Monkeys know how to walk also.

8. Maintain, rejuvenate or restore the health of our body, by properly communicating with it.

Now, even though we might be *lousy owners* of our own body, we can still consider ourselves lucky, because when the blueprint design was made, there was a marvelous provision put there. The bodies own natural ability to restore and rejuvenate itself, if it is given the chance. I said if it is given the chance.
We also can help ourselves very much by learning how to use our body the proper way.
Did you know that the way you position the bones of your body influences the circulatory, the nervous and the immune system? Many of our health problems come from improper posture and maintenance of our body position. Pay attention to others when they walk, the posture of their body. Then ask yourself:
What kind of mental state do they have in this posture? Positive? Or negative? All of us can *read* this. If the mental state is negative, we can read it by the way they walk and their body's posture says this. On the other hand, if the mental state is positive, we can also *read* it on their faces.
Suppose you cut your finger. Even if you leave the cut alone, without treatment, what's going to happen pretty soon? Well, as we all know, pretty soon the process of healing or repairing of the wound starts. In few days the wound closes by itself and the finger is as good as new. How did this come about? If we take any man made object; let's say a radio, and make a hole in it, what's going to happen? Will the radio still be working? Will the hole *heal* or *repair* itself? Well, the radio might still be working (depends where the hole was made in it and how big) but for sure that hole will never repair itself. Why is that?
Because the radio wasn't built with the ability to repair or heal itself.
But we humans were built with this *healing mechanism* that kicks in when damage has been done to our bodies.
 A simple and powerful way to help us live a better life is to learn not to interfere with our healing mechanism. We need to read our body's *language* and use our posture the right and healthier way.

| Chapter 2. | Which are the rules. |

Now, after we gained a little understanding about some of our previous abilities, and what they do to us, let's talk a little bit about the next ability we are equipped with.

9. To consciously control and direct our life the way we want it.

We are what we are because of the way we behave. Somebody who is a doctor displays a doctor's behavior. Somebody who is a mechanic, display a mechanic's behavior. Somebody with a high stress level displays a high stress level behavior, etc.
Our behavior plays an important role in what we are in life.
It's wise to learn to consciously direct our life the way we want it and to stop being at the mercy of others. Actually we all change our behavior from one direction to another; we might just not be aware of that. Let's take a simple example to illustrate this point:
Imagine a small boy playing in the back yard. Then suddenly he falls down and hurt his little knee. Of course, he immediately starts to cry. His mom hears his cry and right the way comes to check on him. Finding him hurt, she picks him up, and gives him a hug and a kiss. Then she brings his favorite toy. Once the kid sees the toy, he suddenly stops crying, takes the toy, and automatically forgets about the pain.
What can we learn from this example?
When he got hurt, his attention was directed toward the incident. In his brain, instantly a link was created between the situation he got in, and his self-defense mechanism.
"That's a wrong thing to do," was the subconscious message from the brain.
"Stay away of such situation, it causes you harm."
Now, when the mother comes with his favorite toy, his focus shifts from the incident to the toy. The link to the self-defense mechanism breaks down or weakens. An instant link is created between his favorite toy and his propulsion mechanism. Having this toy to play with creates so much pleasure for him.
"I'll do anything to get it," is the subconscious message from his brain.
"So, stop focus on the incident," it's not so important now.
Now, understanding this, we can shift our focus from something that causes us pain towards something that causes us pleasure. We are going to apply this principle in eliminating stress. We do this by consciously removing the links between our self-defense mechanism and specific persons, events, or situations. Not only that but we can rearrange them and even link them to the propulsion mechanism. The next time we access them from our memory, we won't feel any negative feelings that used to be attached to them.
Now, let's go further and look at our behavior from a different point of view, by asking a simple question:
The question is how can we influence our behavior or what is triggering our behavior?
There are two important factors that trigger our behavior.
1. Our thoughts are the seat of our behavior.
2. Our willingness to behave in a specific way.
Let's talk a little bit about these two.

1. Who Controls Your Actions?

-If your life is a movie, who's the director? -

One very important principle or rule in our life is this:
"Your actions are controlled by the thoughts you are continuously carrying in your head. The power to control your thought is in your hands."
This sounds like good news and any body could learn how to do this. The thing is that most people are not aware of this ability they have. Not knowing is the easiest way to screw up. Sadly to say but it is true.
Many of our problems are the result of not knowing how to control our actions. If you don't believe me, just go and visit a prison and ask those people why they are there? They will tell you that for some reason they could not control their actions. Most of them, if not all, wish they could turn back the time, so they could think twice before acting.
This is an extreme example with people who committed crimes but what about us? How many times do we regret reacting in a certain way, and later realized that we should have known better?
From time to time, we all are guilty of this.
So, it is very important to learn how we can consciously control our actions. Actually, this is not a difficult thing to do. It is a matter of changing an old thinking habit into a new one that has positive results. This is very important because a bad thinking habit will always trigger a negative state of mind.
When we start getting stressed, two very negative things happens:

1. We loose control of our thinking ability.
2. We loose the ability to concentrate.

That's why, all the bad things people do, are done under a state of stress when they have lost control and concentration. Once these two allies are lost, the results of their actions are most probably negative and eventually they start getting stressed.
It is important to believe and understand this and take the necessary steps to learn how to eliminate stress from its roots.
We should not want to loose control of our thinking ability.
Remember:
"Your thoughts control your actions and you have the power to control your thoughts."
Once you learn to control your thoughts, you will be smart enough to dwell on positive thoughts that will result in a positive state of mind and eventually in a stress less life.
Let's take another example:
Remember the last time you got a speeding ticket? Maybe you never got one, but let's say that you are driving about twenty miles over the speed limit and you are pulled over by a police officer. He / she stops you and asks if you are aware of the speed you are driving. Could you say?
"I am sorry officer, but you know I was not speeding at all. I was just seating comfortably in my car. I just had my foot on the accelerator, the car was speeding; not me."
You may say that but for sure you will be the one to pay for the ticket.
Why? Because you had the control of the accelerator, so that's why the car was speeding. You could say that the accelerator was controlling the speed of the car, that is true, but you had the control of the accelerator.
The same way our thoughts are controlling our actions, but we have the power to control the thoughts.

Now, we can let the events from outside control our thoughts and actions or we could choose to do it consciously; according to our goals and plans that we are setting for ourselves.

Right now, we understand the necessity of taking control of our thoughts. Later on, we are going to learn where our thoughts come from and how can we create a positive environment for the development of our thoughts.

Now, let's discuss who's responsible for our behavior.

2. Who Must Do it For Me?

- If it is to be, it's up to me -

When it comes to taking control of our life and destiny, another very important principle to keep in mind is: "If it is to be it's up to me."
This principle is the basis of our progress, because we and only we should be in charge of our destiny, and cannot pass on this responsibility to somebody else.
We saw that it is very important to understand and get familiar with the *rules of the game*. Then, we saw that we have the ability to control and direct our actions toward our own established goals.
Progressing to the next step that is maybe most important, we need to take the necessary actions in directing and designing our own future.
There is not a substitute for this, we, and only we can do it for ourselves. Nobody should do it for us, I mean, if we really want our life to be controlled by us and not by others. If, like many people today do, we are just reactors to what is happening, of course we do not need to do it ourselves. There are others out there who will do it for us. However, the way they will do it is most probably to benefit themselves at our expenses. That's why there are 1% leaders who are leading the other 99% followers.
The 1% of population is controlling 99% of the wealth. The other 99% are controlling 1% that's left over.
So, we need to learn what the 1% do and follow their example, not of the other 99% who are the followers. The same way that we eat, sleep, and learn for ourselves, is the same way we have to do it for ourselves. This implies action once we learned what to do. In order for us to become people who act instead of react, we need to be aware of the necessity of changing old habits with new ones. For us to do this, we need to analyze and recognize our own habits to see which ones are OK and which ones are not.
The ones that are OK strengthen them, and the ones that are bad, replace them with new ones. It is like starting to learn a new language. Basically, it's the same process.
Let's elaborate a little bit more.
This process takes place in few stages and in a certain order. We need to understand and follow these steps in the order required to be able to learn and master it.
   Step 1: When we don't know the language and are not aware of it. This step is called: *Unconsciously incompetent.*
In other words we don't know that we don't know. We were not exposed yet to the information that might make us aware of it.
   Step 2.: Getting exposed to certain information, we become aware that we do not know. This step is called: *Consciously incompetent.*
In other words, we become aware that we don't know, or we come to realization that we do not know. Becoming aware of this fact, we start developing a desire to know.
   Step 3: Being aware of that we don't know, we start to learn about it. In other words, we take a decision and motivate ourselves to do that.
This step is called: *Consciously competent.* Now, we are aware that we know.
   Step 4: We become so familiar with the subject that it becomes a habit; we do it instantly without conscious thought. In other words, we discipline ourselves enough that it becomes an automatic reaction.
This step is called: *Unconsciously competent.*
These are the four steps we need to go through in order to learn a new language, or to form a new habit.
Remember: In order for us to eliminate stress forever, we need to learn how to replace most of our *bad habits* that are triggering a negative state of mind that results in stress.

I call them *bad habits*, not because they are necessary bad, but because the meaning we give to them is a negative one. In other words, we have an old habit of calling certain situations bad and as a result we experience stress. What we are going to do is learn to call these certain situations different than before.
See, we cannot change the situations themselves but we can change how we look at them.
The way to do this is to learn to give new meanings to the information and events that are taking place around us.

During our life we learned many things and we have a lot of information stored in our memory. What most people are not aware of is that to each bit of information is attached or associated, a certain state of mind. Any time we hear or say certain words or sounds, our brain is going to bring out from our memory anything that it is associated with these words or sounds. This could be positive feelings or negative feelings. We have the choice to let them stay attached and put them back in our memory, or we can remove them, and associate different feelings to these audio and video information. And guess what? Next time when you hear the same words or sounds, the feelings will be different.
Let's take a simple example:

Somebody has the bad habit of talking nasty to you, which most probably irritates and makes you feel bad any time when you see this person. But, if you really want to stop punishing yourself by feeling angry you could learn a little trick. Every time you see this person imagine that a joker or a clown is coming to you and is verbally impaired. This poor person needs some help to learn *a better vocabulary* to communicate properly with you or others.

If you seriously look at him / her this way, what you actually are doing is, replacing this negative association with a different one. Next time when you see him / her, you will not feel irritated by his / her bad language.
Why? He / she is still the same jerk but you are protecting yourself by changing the way you see him /her. See, the way you feel is not determinate by others, but by you. You should be smart enough to recognize this, and be the one who chooses how to feel about it.

As humans, were designed for a special positive purpose. In order to achieve this purpose, our brain was designed to react positive toward anything that causes us pleasure or happiness, and to react negative toward anything that will cause us pain or will put us in danger. In other words, any decision we ever take will be based on these two basic principles:
It will cause us pleasure, and keep us away from pain.
The positive or negative reaction is manifested throughout our body through what we call emotion. When the information, event, or the situation is perceived as positive, the emotion is positive. On the other hand, when the information, event or situation is perceived as negative, the emotion is negative. All bits of information that we feed our mind with during our entire life are stored in our brain through a process of association, between the video and audio information at that particular time.
To each video (image) and audio (sound) information we also associate a feeling that could be positive, negative or just a neutral feeling.
Let's take a simple example:
Let's say that John is your best friend. What comes to your mind when you hear the name John? For sure his picture will come to your mind and also you might smile as a result of a positive feeling toward him. Right?
Why is this? Your mind unconsciously has associated the sound of his name to the picture or his image and because he is your friend, you have associated a positive state of mind. Any time when you hear this name, you start feeling good.
Now, let's say that your good friend John *steals* your dear sweetheart from you. What will you feel when you hear his name again?
I bet you the situation will be totally different. Why?

By causing you pain, your mind subconsciously alongside the sound of his name and picture, have associated a negative feeling. So, any time when you hear this name you start feeling bad. What you have done is, subconsciously removed the positive association to his name and image and substituted a negative state of mind. This is a process that happens every second. During all the time that we are awake, we do associate picture sounds and feelings that happens every second. All of these so-called *neuron- associations* are stored in our brain's memory banks.

We know in America, more than 50% of marriages end up in divorce. Let's see how this is possible. If half the couples that swore to stay together and *love and cherish until death do us part,* ended up in courts fighting like enemies, something must be wrong.

Let's say that our friend John forgets about his former sweetheart and meets another girl we'll call Mary.

Now, in his memory, he has no positive or negative associations about Mary. So, he starts fresh. Being impressed by the way she looks speaks and behaves; he starts to like her.
In other words, his memory starts to fill with positive associations of her picture and the sound of her name. Soon our friend John starts falling in love with Mary and vice- versa. After a few months or years we find out that they are happily married.
Now, there is an important thing we have to mention here. The feeling of stress and the feeling of being in love are triggering the same kind of reaction in our brain. The only difference is that our body rejects feelings of stress, and welcomes feelings of love. So remember what's happening when somebody is stressed?
He or she looses control and concentration.
The same thing happens when we are in love. To some extent, we loose control and concentration.
Our friend John, by being in love, has no idea that before he falls in love with Mary he should do his *homework.* Trying to find out if this beautiful Mary is the right woman for him, the one that will be compatible with him should be top priority He loves her very much and that's enough for him. To be in love with her is enough. After a few years, things start to change. Living together, new kinds of associations start forming in their memories. These new kinds of associations start accumulating because his personality style does not match hers. Unaware of this, instead of meeting each other's inner needs, they are feeding each other's fears. Doing this, they start to associate their negative feelings about each other. After a period of time, these negative associations start to override and replace the positive old associations. Then they start to loose interest, eventually coming to the point of hating each other. Without counseling, they find themselves on the brink of divorce blaming each other for the miserable lives they had together.

This process of overriding old associations with new ones could take place instantly, like in the first example with John's sweetheart, when John's feeling toward his friend changed instantly when he heard that his friend stole his girlfriend.

Or, it could take a period much longer, months or even years. This happens based on the kind of information we put in our minds that might result in a change instantly or gradually.

Our today's actions are the result of our previous thoughts. Our future behavior will be the result of what we are feeding our mind today. That's why it is important to be selective on what kind of thoughts we entertain. Also, what kind of information we feed our mind with, positive or negative.
Because tomorrow we will reap, what we have sown today.
Every day we go through these kinds of changes in our lives. We basically have experience in doing them. Now, we even know how they take place in our mind, so it's up to us to learn to do these kinds of changes purposely, based on our conscious decisions.
Remember*:* "If it is to be it's up to me"
Let's take another example:

Let's say that you live in the United States all your life. For some reason, you have to move for a while to England. What do you think is going to happen with your driving habits? Well, you are going to have a little challenge. Here everybody drives on the right side of the street, and it's normal. In England, the situation is different. If you drive on the right side you are going to get a ticket. Why? Not because they don't know how to drive, but the rules are totally different. Now, should you ask the British to change their laws about driving because you are used to doing the opposite? Are you smart enough to understand the reality and do your best to learn and obey the new rules? In the beginning it's going to feel a little bit weird and you may have the tendency to drive on the other side of the road. Once you understand this necessity, you discipline yourself to obey the new rules.

Basically, the same thing happens in our situation with stress. We got so used to our old way of dealing with stress, that to do something different, it sounds like out of the ordinary. The thing we need to do is, to become aware of the new and better way of dealing with stress, taking a decision to follow it, and learn to discipline ourselves to keep following it daily. As we mentioned earlier: "If it is to be, it's up to me."

After we got a general idea of our human abilities, we need to go on and discuss in more details the four major elements we mentioned at the beginning of this chapter; body, spirit, mind, and behavior.

Let's do this by starting to learn about the third secret: the vehicle that takes us anywhere we go, the most sophisticated living mechanism in universe, our own body.

Review Question: Why it is that no one has yet won the *game* of stress?

Answer:
- It's close to impossible to play and win a game if their rules are not understood and applied properly.

"Acquiring knowledge about the old paradigm of stress will make us managers over something that nobody likes; stress. Acquiring accurate knowledge about the new paradigm and continuously applying it will help us to win the game of stress."

Review Question: What will be a great help in winning the *game* of stress?

Answer:
- Understanding it we start benefiting from our amazing abilities that we all posses. This will help us win this so called *unwinable* game.

"We are not just human beings. We are wonderful human beings designed with amazing abilities."

Secret # 3.

"The vehicle (most sophisticated living mechanism in the universe) that takes you anywhere you go."

Chapter 3. <u>A. Human body.</u>

- Do we get back from life what we want? Or we get what we deserve? -

Is this really true? Could our body be the most sophisticated living mechanism in the universe? Well, lets find out, but before we do this let's discuss a different subject that will help us learn about the human body.

If we want to find a word that defines the characteristic of all the things that surround us, I think that the word will be intelligence. This intelligence is manifested throughout the universe in four major stages.

1. Lifeless, unconscious intelligences.
2. Alive, unconscious intelligences.
3. Alive semi-conscious intelligences.
4. Alive conscious intelligences.

Lets take one at the time and see what are we dealing with.

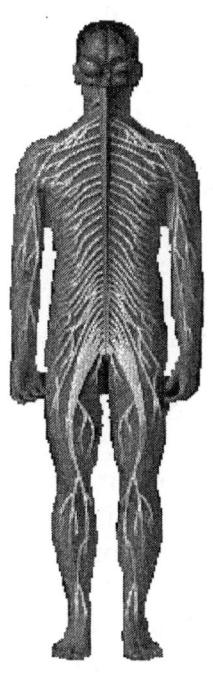

1. Lifeless, unconscious intelligences.

- Obedient though not conscious of themselves. -

Take a look at the universe. Even though the planets are made of lifeless rocks, or certain gases, they manifest an unconscious intelligence, due to the fact that they continually keep following some specific laws. They all strictly follow their own orbit. The sun has the property to radiate a gravitational field that keeps the nine planets of the solar system in perfect balance. Each of them continuously circles the hub of the solar system with the precision of clockwork. For billions of years, the earth keeps moving around the sun with the same speed, on the same orbit, no closer or further from the sun, so the life on earth is continuously maintained. The sun also like the earth, is moving around the center of our galaxy, the Milky Way.

Even though the earth is 109 times smaller than the sun, it was positioned exactly at the right distance from the sun, and its orbit was designed in such away that we have enough heat, day and night, and the benefit of four different seasons. Like a faithful servant, the earth obeys these laws and keeps on moving on the same orbit for billions of years.

If you make a huge investment in something, would you be smart enough to protect your investment? Of course you would. If we take a closer look at our universe, we can see that in order for the earth to be protected and maintain life on it, there are few planets in our solar system that play the role of a watchman. Especially the one we call Mars, which among other things is called: *the garbage can of the universe*. What do I mean by this?

Well, we know that there are millions and maybe billions of meteorites, asteroids and other cosmic debris continuously flying through space. How many of these reach the earth? Compared with how many are continuously falling on the other planets of our solar system, the ones that reach the earth are insignificant in number and size. Mars being the biggest, its powerful gravitational field attracts toward it most of these flying debris; that are getting close to earth. Like Mars, the other planets are all lifeless, so it does not matter how many holes these flying debris makes on them.

The earth also generates a gravitation field that keeps all the things from its surface firmly to the ground. This gravitational field is not too weak, or too strong but perfect to maintain a perfect balance in nature.

As we come closer to earth, on its surface are billions of things, and forms of life that we could call intelligence. Like the others, their *behaviors* are also based on laws and principles.

Did you ever wonder about the complexity of what continuously happens here on earth, even though most of us are not aware of, or do not pay attention?

For example: Do you know that in order for us to be able to drink clean water, each city has built a laborious system of purifying water? If for some reason these would stop working, we would have a huge problem. Did you know that the earth has a global system of purifying and managing the water? It's called the cycle of precipitation. Even though the world's water supply is enormous, (about 325 million cubic miles) less than 1% is available as fresh, usable water. If this supply of fresh water is not properly managed, and continually replenished, all life on earth will soon cease to exist. Because this cycle was firmly established, and the water follows these specific laws, it constantly moves in a complex and never ending cycle. They do an intelligent work, even though it might not be a conscious work from their part.

Lets take another example:

Chapter 3. Human body.

We all are familiar with the telephone, radio, television, computers and other electronic equipment. These are very interesting things because even though they are lifeless and unconscious, they do a very intelligent work. The materials used to build them have specific and interesting properties. Lets take the phone for example:

You pick-up the phone and, and place a call over seas. What the phone does, is, it picks-up your tone of voice, and transforms it into electric impulses, which are sent instantly through the phone line all the way to the desired destination. Once there, these electric impulses are transformed back into sounds, exactly like yours. The person from the other side recognizes your voice, and you can communicate with each other. We are so familiar with these things that we take them for granted, not being aware of the fact that there are specific laws and properties that these materials are constantly obeying. What will happen if out of the blue, these materials stop obeying their own properties? It will be chaos. Imagine driving your car and the metals from which the cars are built, stop being metal and become liquids? Everything will fall apart. Picture your computer, having important information in its files, suddenly looses its property to process and store information. All your work will be gone! You cannot trust it any more.

Visualize that your typewriter stop responding correctly to your commands and instead of typing your message it will type something no one understands? But these things will never happen, you will say, and I agree with you. But why will never happen? Because these materials, even though they are lifeless and unconscious, do intelligent work when they obey specific laws and regulations. The reason; they were *programmed* to do so.

We can go on and on with hundreds of examples, but I think we get the point, so let's go to the second category of intelligences.

2. Alive, unconscious intelligences.

- Obedient to their preset programming. -

In this category, we have the whole world of plants. Starting with the microscopic single celled algae, to the gigantic sequoias, and everything between them.

This world of plants is estimated to have more than 350,000 species. When we take each of them, we see that they grow and live by following specific laws and principles. They constantly obey them, even though plants are not conscious of themselves. Without them, the world of animals might cease to exist. They do their share normal functionality of our earth as a whole.

Isn't that something?

How would you like a product that uses polluted air (carbon dioxide) and release oxygen?
More than that, the plants were designed with multiple uses in mind. One use is to serve as food for animals and humans.
Second, to beautify the earth.
The third use is to purify the air, by absorbing carbon dioxide and eliminating oxygen.

How would you like it if somebody came up with a way of making food, which contains all the nutrients, vitamins, and minerals we need, by using only water, carbon dioxide and sunlight? The whole process would take place in a fraction of a second. How about this?

Well, we may not be able to come up with such an ingenious invention, but the leaves of the plants have been doing it since the beginning of history. For some reasons, they are much smarter than we are, or they were designed to do this.

We can continue to explore the wonderful world of plants, but I think we have enough proof that these plants, even though they are not conscious of themselves, they manifest an intelligent behavior based on specific laws and principles. By doing this, they contribute to the harmony and balance in nature and to the functionality of the earth.

Now, let's go to the next category of intelligences, the animal world.

3. Alive, semi-conscious intelligences.

- Free to move, but still obedient. -

The wonderful world of animals include not only mammals, but also birds, fish, reptiles, frogs, clams, lobsters, jellyfish, worms, and insects. All of these creatures are alive. Semi-conscious because their behavior is controlled by a built in preset program, which they are not able to change or alter.

If we take any species of animals and examine it, we see each has a specific and harmonious way of dealing with the environment. Each grows and develops in its specific, appropriate location, having its own cycle of life well defined. Also, contributing to the harmony of the proper order of nature.

Beside this fact, humans have to learn from many of these animals, because even though we consider ourselves superior to them, they are equipped with some qualities that are almost unbelievable.

Not too many decades ago, scientists discovered jet propulsion and now it's widely used all over the earth. Did you know that for millions of years, the jellyfish and other marine creatures used jet propulsion to move, and they kept moving all the time?

Not long ago, humans discovered the internal combustion engine. The latest models of racecars can run at an unbelievable high rpm (rotations/minute) 7000-8000 rpm. Did you know that the little insects called midges, can vibrate their wings an astonishing 1000 times/ second, not minute? They do not have limited warranties on their locomotion system, but a lifetime. They don't need special lubricants to keep their components in working condition.

During the Second World War, the British were the first ones to discover and use radar to track down enemy planes approaching London. Technology, that saved the country from being devastated by the German war machine. Since then, more sophisticated radar installations are being developed to detect almost anything that moves. Did you know that for millions of years there were animals and birds that use radar technology to guide themselves?

They can migrate from one place of the earth to another, thousands of miles without getting lost. They do not have a central command room with specialists to give them proper directions on when to turn right or left. Many of these species use the sun or the stars at night to navigate. Some of them are *tuned in* to the earth's magnetic field, infrared rays, polarized light or slight changes in barometric pressure. This makes scientists wonder when they might be able to do invent or duplicate these actions.

Did you know that many species of bats use a sonar system, called echolocation, which enables them to navigate, avoid obstacles and find food? Using high-pitched sounds at a rate of 200 per second, their brain analyzes the echoes received from these and determines what would be the proper reaction. Amazingly, a bat can find an insect, chase it and eat it in less than a second!

Chapter 3. Human body.

Most of us know about the story with the ugly frog that with a kiss, turned into a beautiful prince. Some might wish they could experience this transformation. We know that this is just a story that will never happen in reality. Might not happen with humans but there are true story of this kind in nature. Did you know that the beautiful butterfly used to be an ugly caterpillar and transforms itself into a beautiful butterfly we all enjoy seeing? This has been happening for millions of years.

For thousands of years, humans were destined to live in very hot areas of the earth without air conditioning in their houses. Just few decades ago, we were smart enough to invent an air-conditioned house. But did you know that the nature is again ahead of us? For millions of years, even though blind, termites are building their mounds as air-conditioned houses. The rooms inside are built in such a way that it provides an ambient environment inside even in the hot summer days.

More than a century ago we discovered, started using electricity and we benefit from the use of it. But did you know that we again are a little bit behind? Some fish have been generating and using electricity for millions of years. Not just low voltage but even more than 600 volts of electricity! They do it without any sophisticated and expensive installations that require continuously maintenance.

The world is grateful to the Wright brothers, whose courage and perseverance laid the foundation of the airplane industry. Airplanes today are capable of flying from one continent to the other, transporting millions of passengers. Because of the airplane the earth became a much smaller place than before. But, we all know that these sophisticated flying machines are very expensive and require well-trained pilots to operate them. But when a closer look is given at birds, we're amazed at the way they were designed to fly. The bone structure is the perfect structure to help the birds fly. The wings and the feathers are amazingly designed to maximize power and minimize weight. Their lungs and circulatory systems are extremely efficient to cope with the high-energy requirements necessary for long flights. Their muscles are perfect designed to manage the movement of the wings; making the flight of a bird an easy task.

Did you know who used first the gyroscope? Well, again we are millions of years behind. Our sophisticated airplanes are using the gyroscope, in order to maintain right positions in the air. But the fluid filled inner ear of a bird works as a gyroscope, helping the bird maintain level flight.

Now, let's land from the air and dive deep in the ocean to see what interesting things are found. During the Second World War, the German U-boats destroyed hundreds of merchant and war ships, causing tens of thousands in human losses, and millions of dollars in lost cargos. These U-boats were the primitive submarines, having the capability to locate its pray, and destroy it without being seen on the surface of water.

Today, the new and improved submarines are capable of going undetected and delivering even long-range nuclear missiles. But even though we are capable of building such impressive submersible machines, we are still way behind of what some of the marine creature are capable of. Of course these marine creatures are not able to launch intercontinental nuclear missiles, but with ease they are capable to dive deep into the ocean floor even to 20,000 feet, where the water pressure is tremendous. Still, they are capable to live a normal life. Being equipped with their own tiny built-in flashlights, they are able to turn them on and off in order to help find food or protect themselves from predators.

Even though these creatures might have a very advanced and intelligent behavior, it is a behavior based on a preset program encoded in their brains. That's why, within each species, all creatures basically reacts the same way. A cat will always behave like a cat, a fish will always behave like a fish, a bird will always behave like a bird, and so on. They were not equipped with the ability to have a wide range of choices, and consciously decide which one to choose. In other words, they do not have a free will when it comes to choosing their conscious behavior.

We could say that all these intelligences, (lifeless, alive unconscious and semi-conscious) might have a mind of their own, but they do not have a conscious control over it.

Well, we can go forever to study these semi-conscious intelligences, but we have the next category of intelligences that is needed to study.

4. Live conscious intelligences.

- Obedient? We are the only ones to have a choice on this. -

You may guess by now who are these living conscious intelligences? You're right, we are, the human specie. Even though we cannot fly, or swim thousand of feet under water, humans are equipped with something that other species do not posses; the ability to exercise free will. Let's explore other interesting abilities that our bodies are equipped with.

How would you like to own a car that is design in such a way that part of the gasoline is used during driving, and the rest to regenerate itself during the day?

During the day you could drive a few hundreds miles, wearing out the tires, brakes, and other components but over night they regenerate themselves.
Did you know that our own body has these kinds of abilities?
Do you know why we eat and drink?

We are hungry and thirsty you may say. That's a very superficial answer. The real reason we eat and drink is because our body was designed to constantly regenerate itself. To do that, we were equipped with the digestive system, which properly breaks down the food, providing fuel for billions of our body's cells.

How would you like to have another feature? Something like, when somebody makes a dent on the body of your car, the metal used in building the car has the ability to fix itself in short, periods of time.
Most probably you have heard about our immune system. It is a very sophisticated built in defense system that has the role of stalking and eliminating almost any type of foreign substances both alive or inert that are in the body but are not recognized as being part of the body, or might intrude in our body. Imagine having a security system like this in your house or community. Wouldn't that be nice? All of us are equipped with a system like this even though most of us are not aware of it.

How about some more interesting features? How about having a car that the more you use it the better it drives? How about a paint job that the more you use the car the better it looks? Wouldn't this be wonderful?

Many people are overweight today and specialists are encouraging everybody to exercise. They say that the health of our bodies depends on how much we move and exercise. Who do you think is much healthier? An athlete or a *couch potato* who spends most of his time watching TV with a bag of chips and a beer in his hand? We do not necessary have to be an athlete, but the more exercise we do, the more we improve our health and body. Isn't that wonderful?

Contrary to the things humans build (which the more we use them, the faster they wear out and eventually break down); human beings were design exactly the opposite. The more we move the healthier we get.

How would you like to own a copy machine that beside the fact that could make copies also has the property to make copy machines too? How about that?
We are here on earth today for the fact that we were equipped with another wonderful feature: The ability to multiply. How does this process starts? Ask the professionals, and they will tell you how amazing this process is. From almost nothing, that original cell has in its genetic code, all the necessary information and ability to keep multiplying itself until it becomes a little

bundle of joy, your own darling baby. How long do you think it will take until scientist might be able to build such an amazing *thing*?

If we look a little bit closer around us, we can see that all the other living creatures have their own system of multiplying, which also are amazing in their own ways.

How would you like to have a very sophisticated video camera, which is able to continuously take pictures never having to adjust the focus, because it does it automatically?

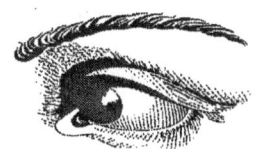
We have two eyes, so we can see and enjoy our surroundings, but do you know how sophisticated our eyes are? When the video information enters the eyes, it's focused by the lens to form an upside-down image on the back of the eye wall. Then each bit of information is transformed into electrical impulses, which are sent to the brain through the optic nerve to be analyzed and interpreted.

How would you like to have a computer so powerful, that it has an infinite memory capacity? How would you like to see a computer built that would keep track of every human being on earth? Not only as a statistic but is able to provide a job for everyone, enough food and clothing, the right environment so each individual could enjoy its job and family. A health care system where none is forgotten, and where everybody is treated equally and with respect. How about that? Wouldn't this be wonderful? Well, we still have to wait for a while until somebody is able to do accomplish this task.

Now, the most sophisticated organ of our body is the brain.

One of the most amazing abilities is its memory capacity. The more that science progresses, the more they recognize its powerful memory capacity. As a matter of fact, the way it is designed to function, our brain has an infinite memory capacity. This might be news for you, but pretty soon all the scientists will come to this conclusion. When it comes to our brain's memory, we shouldn't be misled into thinking that it functions like a computer. A computer needs space to store information. The more information we have, the more space we need. With our brain things are different. It doesn't need any space to store information because its memory works different.

Let's look at another amazing ability of our brain.

Did you know that a human body has about 75 trillion cells, and the brain controls all of them? Each cell receives all it needs to function properly, because the brain controls the circulatory system through which each cell is fed and cared for.

Did you know that the brain is capable of controlling all the body's cells to harmoniously work together to maintain the proper operation of the body? ? There are only about 6 billion people and are divided into many countries. Political, social, and religious ideologies are dividing us. Hate, dishonesty, selfishness and many other *qualities* are keeping us apart. What do you think if suddenly the cells of our body start to behave the way we do?

But they don't. Why? Because, if we look a little closer at the macro and micro universes that surrounds us, they have a common characteristic. They all work in harmony with each other.

Do you know that each signal that enters the brain produces an electrochemical reaction when it passes from the cell's body through the axon with unbelievable speed? After one thousandth of second, it is ready to carry another signal. This process takes place 24 hours a day, 7 days a week, 365 days a year, for a lifetime. What do you think is going to happen if some of those get tired of doing their jobs and stop for a break; arguing that this is too much for them? Like many of us, when we feel that we are working too hard, we stop

From this information we can realize that humans are not just people, but very sophisticated creatures who's functions are based on specific laws and regulations. The more we are aware of this, the easier it will be to master ourselves.

Let's move on to see what our body needs in order to develop and function properly. If we ask people today what they need in order to function properly and have a happy life, the majority will agree that we need clean air to breathe, and healthy foods to feed our bodies. But, we need even more than that.

Imagine, how our life will be if we had the cleanest air and the healthiest foods to feed our bodies but we couldn't see, hear, or feel anything. How would our lives be? Not too pleasant.

So, the third and maybe the most important element is information.

We are equipped with five major senses: Sight, hearing, touching, smelling and taste. All these are special sensors that continuously pick up information from the environment and send them to the brain to be interpreted. Then they are brought to our conscious awareness to be consciously perceived, understood and felt through what we commonly call emotions. By being equipped with these, we are able enjoy a happy life. These sensors make us aware of our beautiful surroundings, people whom we could build relationships with, and also many other wonders that happen around us. By the same token, the same sensors pick up negative information, sends them to the brain to be analyzed. Of course that being negative, or perceived as negative, they will be transformed and felt by our body as a negative emotion.

We can say that there are three major things that we need in order to function properly, and develop a healthy and desirable body.

1. **We need clean air**
2. **We need healthy food.**
3. **We need proper information.**

Let's take one at the time and see what we can learn from them.

1. Clean fresh Air.

- The invisible fuel for our body. -

Even though we do not see it, air still exists and is essential for our existence. Without it all life on earth would disappear in a short period of time. About 78% of air is nitrogen, 21% is oxygen, and the 1% is a mixture of carbon dioxide and other gases.

The human body is made up of trillions of cells, which are connected together, and all of them need oxygen to function properly. As they use oxygen, they give off carbon dioxide as waste, a product that the body must get rid of. The oxygen is carried to the cells through the blood. The cleaner the air the healthier the body becomes. The polluted the air, the unhealthier the body becomes. We cannot expect to live in a very polluted environment and still develop a healthy body.

A simple way to improve our health and well being of our body is to form a habit of doing breathing exercises. This process is very simple to do, and the rewards are great. We begin by breathing three times deeply than normal, and then start to pull air into our lungs counting from one to ten. After our lungs are full of air, hold it for at list until you could count to 15 or even 20. Then release slowly the air by counting from one to ten. Repeat this exercise ten times in a row two or three time a day for ten days. You will be very surprised to see how much you improve your health and energy. You are going to feel energized all day long and full of life. Each of your body's cells will be invigorated with the extra oxygen you feed them during these exercises. The whole body will feel different. You will start to feel that you are really living, full of energy and freshness. That's a lot of gain for such a little investment!

Chapter 3.   Human body.

2. Healthy Foods.

- The visible fuel for our body. -

"Food, food!" cries the hungry. If they are hungry, their cries are justified, because all of us need food; which is the second ingredient that we need to develop a healthy body. If we look around, we observe that we are surrounded with a large variety of foods: natural, artificial, and a combination of both. But, are all these necessary for sustaining our life? Or many are produced because they have a high return of investment for their producers? Well, the reality is that many of today's foods we find on the market, are not the right foods for us, but they bring good profit to those who manufacture them.
Now the question is: How can we be sure, which of these large varieties are the right ones for us? To get a better understanding, we'll see what the body needs to develop healthfully and function properly.
One of our body's major characteristics is the ability to move. And we all know that for anything to move it needs to utilize a specific amount of energy. The same thing happens with our body. It needs a source of continuous energy. Food is a major part of this source. The energy resulted from food is used by the body to feed all its cells.
An important thing that we should know is that for our body to function proper, it has to have a constant temperature. The fat in our body plays an important role in maintaining this temperature. When we become overweight, for some reason our brain gets the impression that it doesn't have enough fat stored in the body. Therefore, it triggers the process of depositing more fat in the body. If we are able to understand what factors determine the triggering of this process and eliminate them, we solve the whole overweight problem.
We know that about 70% of our body is made up of water. To maintain a healthy body, it makes perfect sense to realize that we should eat the kind of foods that contains enough water so we can keep a balance of water in our body. We might consider vegetables and fruits to be part of our daily food.
Another important factor that we should keep in mind is our body is equipped with something that is call metabolism. This is a sophisticated system that regulates the relationship between the amount of food that is burned by the body and the amount of food that is stored in our body as fat or muscle tissue.
A proper understanding of this process, gives us the possibility to have a healthy and desirable body.
Even though we live in the richest country in the world, and benefit from the most advanced and sophisticated discoveries of science, we have a big problem with the way we eat. Many people today are overweight and are jumping from one kind of diet to another, and still cannot find the real answer to their problem.
The main reason is that these diets work on one part of the problem; leaving the most important undone.
To be able to function properly and adapt to various situations, our body was design with the ability to change the relationship between the amount of food used by the body to feed itself, and the amount of food to be stored. It works like a thermostat in your car. It was design to open at a certain temperature. Once the engine reaches that specific temperature, it opens and also the fan starts working to lower the temperature. If somebody changes the set point to a higher temperature, what is going to happen? Will it open to the previous point? Of course it will not. Being set to a higher point, will allow the engine's temperature to get higher, which might cause problems with the proper functions of the car. The same thing happens with our body. If the original set point has been changed, the metabolism's rate has changed also. And more fat is stored in the body than necessary, which will result in being overweight.
Now the big question is what can we do to harmonize our metabolism in such a way that the body will stop storing unwanted fat? There are few factors we have to keep in mind if we want to accomplish this.
First is the quality of the foods we eat. There are foods that help slow the metabolism, and there are foods that help increase it. Having a diet rich in foods that slow the metabolism of course will not help.

Second, the amount of food we eat. Did you know that your stomach is as big as your fist? If that's the case, we can get an idea of the size of our meal should be.

Many times we are under stress and one of its side effects is that it triggers a feeling of hunger. Then we start to eat more than necessarily; adding to our overweight problem.

Third, many times we are under the impression that we are hungry, when actually we are just thirsty. A simple remedy is when we start to feel hungry, drink some water. If we are still hungry, then we can eat, but many times we are just thirsty, and by drinking a cup of water, the *hunger* goes away.

Fourth, we should start to eat food instead of carbohydrates, proteins, cholesterol free, or any other types they call them. Go back in history 50 years, or 100 years or even 1000 years. What do you think people living in those times were eating?

Believe me, they all were eating food.

Our body was designed so sophisticated that it would know to trigger hunger only when it feels that it really needs nourishment, no matter what kind of food we eat.

So, basically food is fuel for our body no matter if it's carbohydrates, or 20% fat, or so much protein, etc. If we consume foods that result in more than necessary energy for the body, the brain will delay the triggering of hunger. On the other hand, if we consume foods that contain less than necessary energy, our brain will trigger the feeling of hunger more often.

Fifth, and maybe the most important, and the most ignored is the information we feed our mind about food. Many of our body's functions were programmed to work according to some specific standards. Some of these we cannot change or reprogram no matter what we do, but some body functions can be reprogrammed. When it comes to metabolism, because during our live we were bombarded with many kinds of information about dieting, unaware of we have wrongly reprogrammed our metabolism. What we have to do is to find a way to bring it back to the original set point. Once it is back to its original specifications, the brain freely will control the metabolism to maintain a perfect balance without any diet.

We can do this by cleaning our mind from all the wrong information we have accepted about the role of food in our lives. In other words, we have to replace the old core beliefs that are governing our thinking regarding foods and dieting, with more realistic ones. To do this, we need to familiarize ourselves with real information about how our body function and metabolism. Then pay less attention to the *get slim quick* programs that make such beautiful promises but get small and temporary results. The reason for this is through our genetic code received at birth, the metabolism's set point was initially set to a perfect balance. During our life, being bombarded with so much information about nutrition, unconsciously we have reprogrammed our metabolism set point getting it out of balance. The original set point of metabolism left alone would have developed a healthy and chemically balanced body. There isn't any need to program it but allow it to go back to the original program. Once back to its original program, it will start working harmoniously to produce a desirable and healthy body.

Now lets go to the third and maybe most important ingredient to maintain a happy and healthy life.

3. *Proper Information.*

- The beauty or the poison of our life. -

Information? Could this be the most important ingredient to maintain a happy and healthy life? How could this be true?

Well, it's very true that without oxygen and food pretty soon we will cease to exist. But, if we have oxygen and food and our life is miserable; is that a good thing? See, we are the kind of beings that want to make the cake and eat it also. We want to be alive, and live a good life; don't just live a life of misery and problems. Now, how can information influence so much our lives? Even though it's ignored by common people professionals know the importance of it. Why do you think that many companies are willing to spend unbelievable sums of money to show you commercials on the TV? They know the power that the information has over the human mind, and they take advantage of this making a huge profit.

We basically need information for two major reasons:
1. For personal development.
2. To be able to communicate with our surroundings, environment, people and everything else.

Let's take the first reason we need information.

1. For our personal development.

For the same reason that we need air and food, we also need individually to feed our minds with information for our personal development. We have this inner desire to grow, to know more, to explore, absorb, and enjoy the environment. None of us wants to be a little baby locked up someplace not knowing what happens around. We all want to progress, to become better, more intelligent and be able to cope with all the daily challenges.

To do this, we are helped by our senses that continuously absorb information from the environment. To this information, we have to react in one way or the other, based on our personal interpretation that is given to it. Based on our interpretation, it will be processed by our brain and transformed into an emotion that will be felt by our body.

We know that we are equipped with five major senses, but we'll focus on the first three, which we are considering more important, seeing, hearing and touching. Through these senses, the brain receives information from the environment, analyzes them, and gives a corresponding command to the body to react in a specific way according to the information received. Our behavior, which is our body reaction to the information received, is influenced by two factors:
1. The quality of information received.
2. The way that we personally interpret the information.

We'll take one at the time and see how they influence our life towards happiness, joy, pain, anxiety and stress.

Quality of information.

Quality, quality, everyone wants quality in life. We want to drive quality cars, wear quality cloths, eat quality foods, and live in quality homes. This is normal but shouldn't it also be normal to look for quality information that we use to feed our mind daily? Yes we should. How many of us are aware of this and really pay close attention what kind of information we let enter our minds? As we just mentioned, our behavior is influenced by the information that enters our mind.

Lets take an example to illustrate this:

Even though we are just one human race, we are divided into many countries, with many different languages and customs.

Now, when a child is born to an American family, is the child's brain programmed to speak English? No, it will learn English because the parents, who speak English, will teach him. But let's say that for some reason the child is taken to a different country where people speak a different language, and stays there for 20 years. Will the child still speak English and behave like an American? I don't think so. Why not? Is he not an American child? Yes he is. But being exposed to different kind of information (language and customs) his mind will accept and process that particular kind. If he comes back to America he has to learn the English language and customs, and then he could practice them, even though he was born in America.

So, as we can see from this example, we humans have all the same brain that works based on the same specific laws and principles.

But, our behavior is influenced by the kind of information we feed our mind with. An American will speak and act like an American.

A Russian will speak and act like a Russian. By the same token a person who feeds his or hers mind with positive information, will speak and behave in a positive manner. A person who feed his or hers mind with much negative or even vulgar information, will speak and behave in a negative manner.

Remember: "Garbage in, garbage out."

Now, what does the information has to do with stress? Well, stress is the result of a certain behavior. And as we mentioned before, the type of information we feed our minds with influences our behavior. We need to learn what kind of information creates a behavior that result is stress. Knowing this, we can choose not to accept this kind of information and of course that stress is eliminated. Does this make any sense to you? It does to me.

If we have a leaky roof, instead of working hard to get the water out of the house, and through the holes more comes in, we better, fix the leak first, and then get the water out. Once the leak is fixed, to have a clean house is just a matter of cleaning the old mess.

To get a better understanding of how information causes us to become stressful persons, look at the next example

Imagine a fruit tree. Even though it is not seen from the outside, it has strong roots underground. Another part, which we can see is the trunk, with many branches, leafs and of course fruits. In many ways we are like a tree. What people see are our bodies, then strong roots, which are our personal strong inner convictions or core beliefs. The trunk and branches are our habits that are growing and developing from the ingredients received from the roots. Here is the key. The information we feed our minds daily, is nothing else but the ingredients that the roots are absorbing from the ground. The ground is our environment. Unlike the tree, which has no choice but to absorb what it finds in the place it grows, we humans have a choice, to accept or reject any information from environment. We are more superior to a tree; we are equipped with free will. We should be smart enough to use it especially when we know that the favor we are doing is for ourselves.

Most people today are working hard trying to change their, or others behavior. They are not being aware that their behaviors are the result of their habits. Their habits are the result of their own core beliefs. And their core beliefs are the result of the kind of information they decide to accept and validate as truth. During our lives we are unaware that we have accepted and validated the kind of information that resulted in wrong core beliefs. Having wrong core beliefs leads to wrong habits resulting in wrong behaviors. As a result, we experience much pain, anxiety and stress. What we need to do is to revise our core believes about stress. Feed our mind with the right kind of information, validate them as truths, and through repetition and discipline, replace the old core beliefs with new ones. Once these are replaced, new behavior changes automatically. After we have done this, we need to remember that being equipped with free will, we have the ability and responsibility, to choose to follow the new core beliefs, or to return to the old ones. It has to become a new way of life, in order for us to continuously enjoy a life free of stress. It's not enough just to know what to do. We need to practice it daily.

The way we personally interpret the information.

Humans are now more than 6 billion people, but are two of us identical? Or, does each of us have our own way of seeing and interpreting things. Even though we are equipped with the same brain, which works based on the same laws and regulations, each of us has his or hers own unique way of interpreting information collected from the environment.

We have common beliefs and views, but when it comes to individual details, each of us has the right to give our own meaning to any information.

Remember the example with the tree? We absorb the information from the environment through the roots, (which are our core believes, or blueprints), and then it grows into a trunk with branches, (which are our habits) and the fruits, which are our behaviors.

Being equipped with free will, we have the choice to give any interpretation to the information, based on our old core believes, or we can give a brand new meaning to it.

Most people, base their decision on their old core believes. For them, the information passes through the path of least resistance. What this mean, is that they tend to do what is familiar to them, rather than change and take new directions in life.

If we want to change our behavior, into a desirable one, we need to change the information we validate for ourselves with the ones that produce desirable core believes, or blueprints. Then these will produce desirable habits that in turn will produce desirable behavior.

When we talk about behavior, we can say that there are two manifestations of our behavior.

One that has to do with our actions, and the other that has to do with the behavior of our body's cells.

In other words, the core beliefs that we build into our subconscious mind could trigger a positive or negative behavior. But, also controls and triggers the behavior of our organs in our body.

Even though we might not be aware, there is a continuously communication between our subconscious mind and all the cells of our body. And based on the quality of these core believes, we maintain a healthy or an unhealthy body.

Later on, we will learn how our subconscious mind creates a blueprint for each core belief that we have. This blueprint is used by the subconscious mind to control and maintain all the functions of our body cells and organs. If these blueprints are based on correct and proper information, they will trigger a positive response, so our body's cells are healthy, and as result, we are healthy. By the same token, if these blueprints are based on incorrect or false information, of course they will trigger a negative response, so our body cells become unhealthy. By maintaining these incorrect or false blueprints, unconsciously we are the ones that keep us in an unhealthy state.

Beside many other side effects of these negative blueprints that are damaging the lives of millions there is another important one: stress.

And of course that by trying to treat stress with medication won't help. We need to go to the root of the problem and take care of it. Then the symptoms will automatically disappear.

2. To be able to properly communicate with our environment.

Now, the second reason we need proper information, is that we are not alone in this earth; a very complex environment surrounds us all. Information is the link between this complex *environment* and us. Through it we understand and perceive, act or react, maintain or change our behavior towards the *environment*. In our case, when we talk about *environment*, we should understand our surroundings, people, places, events and situations.

The end result of our dealing with the environment is the ownership and the proper management of it. So, the information we choose to accept, and the meaning we give to it plays an important role in achieving our purpose. That's why we should become aware of what the proper information is. Because each bit of information is processed by our brain and felt by our body through what we call emotions. Having two kinds of emotions, negative and positive, we realize that they are the result of processing different kind of information. Joy and sorrow, happiness and stress, they all are the result of the kind of information our mind processes in dealing with the *environment*. Beside the fact that our body feels the effects of the information processed through what we call emotion, it also becomes an important factor to our response to the environment. When we process information that we perceive as positive we feel happy, and our response to the *environment* is positive. By the same token, when we process information that we perceive as negative we might stress ourselves, and our reaction to the environment will be negative.

We can have the cleanest air, and the best food available, but if we are not aware of the quality of information we are getting and feeding our mind with, our life will still be unhappy and filled with problems and negative experiences.

Another important thing to remember is that the information we are feeding our mind with, has the ability in time to condition and change our behavior, creating habits that might be helpful or might cause us more trouble then we would like.

Basically, the whole secret of eliminating stress is to understand how to properly use the information we continuously receive from the *environment*.

Now let's learn more about another aspect of our body.

We can say that the body is the vehicle that connects the mind to the environment.

Let's take an example to illustrate this:

Imagine a car. The car has a physical body. Not only that, but the physical body has interesting *abilities*. Nice and comfortable interior. Then it's equipped with a climate control unit that helps the driver to maintain a pleasant temperature inside the car, even though outside the temperature is different. To make the inside environment even more pleasant, it is equipped with a stereo system; radio, cassette or CD. To make the driving experience safer, the car also is equipped with safety devices, such as the break system, signal, horn, etc.

So, we can compare our body with the body of a car. Its entire abilities form the mind. Now, for all these to function, the body is also equipped with an energy source (the battery) and also a system that continuously maintains the energy source to the proper level (Electrical charging system)

We know that the battery is kind of *the life of the car;* it turns on the engine, activates the lights so we can see. Makes the radio and other electrical components from the car work. Being a vital component of the car, if the battery is dead, nothing on the car is going to work.

Our body's battery is called the *spirit,* which enables us to stay alive.

Now for the car to function it needs a driver. A person with experience in driving to take care of it and use it according the rules and regulations specified by manufacturer.

The driver can be compared with our conscious mind. Our conscious mind was designed to use the body according to the specifications of its designer. Like in the case with the car, the body follows orders from the conscious mind, no mater if they are correct or not. If the commands are proper according with the specifications, the results are positive. By the same token, if the conscious mind (the driver) is not aware or careless, the body is going to suffer.

When the spirit activates the body's functions, it turns on the mind. Once the mind starts to work, it directs the body to act in a specific way, based on the information received through the senses from the environment. The result is our behavior.

So, let's review this idea: We have a body. Then when the spirit of life activates the body's abilities, it turns on the mind. Once the mind is activated, it starts to process information received through the sense from the environment. As a response to the information processed, the mind directs the body to act in a specific way. This particular action of our body is called behavior.

Now, let's see another aspect of our body.

We know that communication between humans is an important factor in our life.

But, did you know that your body also continuously talks to you?

Did you know that the position of your body affects your mental state and stress level?

How you normally walk?

Chapter 3. Human body.

How your shoulders lean?
How you keep your head?
What is the position of the muscles on your face? Etc.
Example:
If you were the president of a company with many employees, would you have an open door policy towards the employees? Would you listen to their voice, needs and ideas? Research shows that by having an open door policy, the better working environment is created. The employees are doing a better job and overall the company fairs better.
On the other hand, by having a closed-door policy, and neglecting the employee's suggestions, needs and ideas the overall situation of the company is less productive. The employees are less interested in doing their best for the interest of the company. As result nobody wins.

    Now imagine your own body as a huge company. It has a few trillions of employees. And believe it or not, all are doing pretty good job. But as in a regular company, sometimes some of the employees want to talk to the C.E.O. They might have an important message to convey. But is the C.E.O. going to listen? Are you going to listen? Yes, you the C.E.O. of your body. Do you have a habit of listening to what your body wants to tell you?
Or through painkillers or others like them, you are continuously trying to silence them?
Well, you may silence them for a while, but probably you're going to hear from them again shortly.
Later on in this book we are going to discuss the importance of paying attention to the messages that our body continuously brings to our conscious awareness, and how to properly respond to them.

    So, from this information we can see that we are equipped with a wonderful body, which has amazing abilities. Understanding its functions, and doing our best to respect the laws and regulations that govern its functions, we are able consciously to design and create our own destiny.
Now lets go to the second element, which is the life's energy or spirit.

B. Human spirit.

- The burning inner fire that keeps us all alive. -

As we mentioned before, we can safely say that the spirit is the life's energy or life's force that keeps the body alive and functioning properly. Without it, there is no mind, and the body is as good as dead.

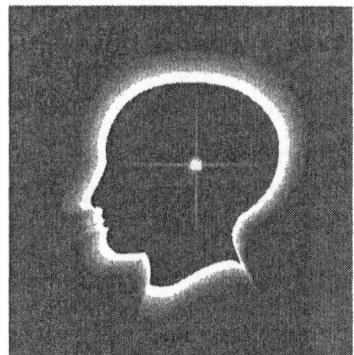

Let's imagine a nice house. It's big, luxurious and has everything that a good house should be equipped with. Like any other house, it has electric power as the main source of energy. The electric power even though enough to handle all the appliances and necessities of the house is limited by the capacity of the fuse box. As long as we use the power within a reasonable limit, nothing bad happens. But let's say that we buy some machinery or other electrical appliances that use a lot of electric power. We start using all these new energy-consuming devices. What is going to happen to the other appliances? Well, they might not work properly any longer, because heavy consumption of power, take too much energy allotted for the house.

So, it's wise to become informed about the *side effects* of these highly energy users; before we invest in them.

Now let's see what can we learn from this example related to our subject.

Our body has a limited amount of energy that it uses to maintain and accomplish tasks during our life. Among other things, the brain takes a specific limit of this energy and uses it to maintain the functions of our senses. The brain also uses energy to transform the bits of information received through the senses into electro-chemical messengers that are sent throughout the body to activate the body's muscle and bones to behave in a specific manner. The higher the intensity of the behavior, the higher the amount of energy needed.

Example: We need little energy to walk, talk, but much more to run or to sing.

Now, we know that when we get angry or are under stress, we cannot function properly. Why is that?

Well, anger, anxiety, depression, stress and other negative emotions are high-energy consumers. They are negative emotions with negative effects over our body and they are also high-energy consumers. They take more than a normal amount of energy, leaving the other functions or files with less than they need to function properly.

A prolonged stressful life as we may know, triggers a less productive and enjoyable life.

So, we have one more reason to learn how to eliminate stress.

Let's talk a little bit about another aspect of the spirit of life.

Even though it's one of the most important ingredients in the proper operation of our body, and maintains all the components of it in continuous working conditions, the spirit does not take any characteristic of the organ or component that it activates or maintains. Spirit by itself, is just a power without any consciousness of its own; similar to the electric power source in our homes. When we turn the lights on, that power illuminates the house. But the power itself is not an illuminator. It just activates the light bulb, and the transform itself in caloric energy and we see it as bright.

| Chapter 3. | Human body. |

When we turn on the TV, the same electric power activates it and helps receive the audio and video information through the antenna or cable, then transforms them into images and sounds we see on TV.
When we turn on the air conditioning, the same power makes the air conditioner produce cool air in the house.
We can go ahead and use countless example of how this energy activates different energy users, each with its own characteristics. The point is, even though all the energy consumers use energy to functions, the power itself just activates them and makes them accomplish the tasks they were designed for.
If one or more of the energy consumers breaks down, the power itself is useless. Somebody needs to fix them first, and then the power will *make them work* again.
    Basically, something similar happens with the energy power in our body.
The power activates all our senses and organs making them function properly. But it never takes any of their properties.
For example:
If somebody hurts one of his or her eyes, and the eye is damaged, what's going to happen? Even though the spirit or energy is there, because the sensor is damaged, it will not function properly. The same thing might happen with any other senses or organs. If they are damaged, the spirit of life, even though present, will not help. That particular organ has to be fixed first, then the spirit will activate it and make it function correctly.
Let's talk a little bit about an aspect of the human spirit, if understood properly, will help us do unbelievable and positive changes to our lives and others.
    Suppose you have a computer, the latest model with everything one might dream about. This being the case, the computer comes with a huge memory capacity.
When you start any project or work with any file, how much of its memory do you think the computer is going to use with each task?
Well, even though it does have a huge memory, it only allocates a small part of it to each task. If we are not aware of this and work with large files, it might slow down or even freeze on us. The more files that are working at one time, the harder it's going to be for the computer. The best advice is to divide our tasks in smaller files, and work one at a time. To improve the quality and quantity of our work, we can change the original settings regarding the capacity of the folder that contains our files. By doing this, the computer allocates more space in the memory and our work becomes easier.
    Now, let's come back to our subject; Spirit. Even though our brain has an unbelievable capacity, the power that maintains it is limited and dispersed throughout our body. Each organ of our body is allocated a specific amount of energy that keeps each of them functioning in proper order. Beside the organs that we are equipped with, our brain also allocates energy for other tasks that it has to accomplish, such as: absorbing and processing information coming from our environment, thinking, planning, sorting, arranging and classifying information in *files*, etc.
We all heard about the importance of setting goals. Now we are going to shed more light in their importance. Once we understand their importance and decide that goals should play a big role in our life, what we are actually doing is directing our minds to give priority and spend more energy in that particular goal. The more importance we consciously decide to give to it, the more energy and importance our brain will allocate for its achievement. As long as we keep it alive in our minds, the brain will continuously work on its accomplishment. This is done because we are equipped with what professionals call *Reticular-activating system*. This works much like a Priority Mail. When you send a letter to a specific destination, you got to make sure that the address is correct. If you want that your letter to get there fast, then you have *to pay* more and send it Priority Mail, or even Express Mail. By doing this, out of all the other pieces of mail; yours is given priority. Of course that doesn't come automatically; you have to pay extra for it. The same thing happens to our brain. When we set a goal, the reticular activating system is activated and gives priority to the accomplishment of that particular goal. Like a laser guided missile, it keeps following the target until it reaches it. If the target keeps moving in different directions, it also adjusts its course and continuously follows it until it reaches it.

Now having a better understanding of this fact, it's up to us to start designing our life by setting the goals that will bring us to where we really want to be. Unless we do this, we are going to be tomorrow as far away from our goals as we were yesterday.

Regarding our subject of eliminating stress forever, we are going to do what it takes to accomplish it. We start by setting a serious goal of becoming stress free. Once we do this, we want to make sure that we direct our conscious behavior in the same direction by looking for the information that will help us reach our goal.

Not only will this *method* work with our goal of becoming a stress free person, we can use it with any other goal that we want to accomplish.

Do you want to improve your family life? Or, maybe your financial situation? One of the fastest ways to get there is by using the fastest means that gets you there. And there is no faster way than this one.

Now let's go further and discuss the next secret, the *driver* of our body. The one helping us to go wherever we want, and also sometimes where we don't want to go, the human mind.

Review Question: What does our body needs in order to be able to function properly?

Answer:
- We need clean air, healthy foods and proper information in order to personally grow and properly deal with the environment.

"The quality of these three ingredients generates the strength of our spirit, the fire within that keeps all of us alive."

Secret # 4.

"Unlocking the mystery of the designer of your own heaven or hell."

Chapter 4.   C. The Human Mind.

- Mind? How many of us know we have a mind, let alone know how to control it?

Superior to any other intelligence, we have a mind over which we have a conscious control. In other words, we can choose to use our mind in the way we want to. Now, how can we define the mind?

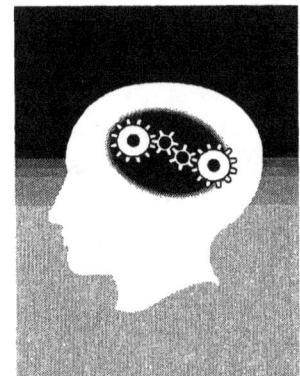

Well, first, let's see what it is not. The mind is not the brain or our body. It is not the information from environment that enters into the brain. It's not the life spirit that keeps us alive. Also, it's not our behavior.

What is the mind then?

We can say the mind is like a network of abilities or characteristics that our brain is equipped with that once activated by the life's energy, or spirit, is able to direct the body to generate specific behaviors. The behavior is influenced by the information used.

When it comes to humans, the mind has the ability to consciously accept or reject any information. Even more, it can modify or combine some or all the information that it chooses to assimilate. Once the information is assimilated, the mind has the ability to transform any information through the nervous system in a feeling or emotion that is brought to the conscious level and is felt by our body. When the information is positive, or perceived to be positive, it produces a positive feeling or emotion.

On the other hand, when the information is negative, or is perceived as negative, it produces a negative feeling or emotion.

None of the other inferior intelligences have this ability to accept, reject, modify or combine the information received.

Even though the human mind is not something like an organ we can pinpoint, in order to have a mind, we do need to have a body with a brain to process the information. Also we need the energy or the spirit to activate and maintain in working condition the abilities of the body and brain.

Now let's talk about the brain which is the organ used by the mind to manifest itself. Even though it's only about three pounds in weight, our brain is considered the central command of our body. Its functions are based on electro-chemical reactions that continuously take place inside it. Through our sensors, each bit of information that goes through the brain, produces a specific electro-chemical reaction that is felt by the body.

For example, the human eye continuously absorbs video information from the environment and sends them to the brain with unbelievable speed. It takes 200 milliseconds for the information to travel from the eye to the brain.

Now, we can spend countless hours talking about the wonders and abilities of our brain, but we'll rather look into the subject of how the mind is developed and what we can do to use it better.

The anatomy of the human mind.

- What makes us tick? -

The more science advances, the more wonders of the human mind the scientists are discovering. Many things that in the past were considered miracles today are accepted as normal functions of our mind and body. Many of us heard the expression *mind-body communication*, which basically means that our mind continuously communicate with our body, making sure that all the cells that make up our body's organs are doing their job properly.
Imagine a government in a free country. It has the responsibility to take care of all its citizens. To provide them the necessities of life, and also to provide them with security, so they could enjoy a wonderful life. That's the way we might see our mind. As a governing agency over our body, with the jurisdiction over the health and safety of its citizens.
 As conscious beings, humans are designed to have a conscious control over their minds.
We know that in order for our body to function properly, we need to feed it properly. So, if the body needs food to be able to function properly, our mind needs information as food. Without information to process and transform in emotion, we can say that our mind is dead. A live mind is one that continuously processes information, and supervises the growth and development of each cell in our body. The quality of information we decide to feed our mind with, determines the quality of how our minds work.
We have a major responsibility to make sure that we feed our mind with proper information. By doing that, we are empowering our mind to control and direct our body in such a way that we can live a joyful life. On the other hand, if we do not care what kind of information are we feeding our mind, the results could be a stressful and unhealthy body; hence, an unpleasant life.
Let's take an example to illustrate the importance of information.
 Suppose you go to a party and there are a few people enjoying the party.
Then suddenly all the sounds and people voices disappear.
Nobody is able to hear or speak, everything becomes quite. How many people would like that? None. Pretty soon, some will even start leaving the party.
Then after ten minutes, all the colors start to become black or white, like an old black and white movie. The situation becomes more unpleasant. How many will like that? None. Soon some others will leave the party.
After another ten minutes, another interesting phenomena happen. People cannot recognize each other; suddenly they are all strangers to each other. What is going to be the outcome? Well, would you like to live in such an environment?
Of course you would not. So, the point is that the more our senses are activated and continuously absorb information from the environment (audio, video, etc.) the better our mind works; creating a feeling of enjoyment. When we reduce the information, the operation of the mind is reduced, and of course the results are not pleasant. Knowing that the more we use our senses to absorb information from the environment, the better our mind works. Also we have a great responsibility of what kind of information we absorb / feed our mind with.
 As imperfect humans living in an imperfect world, many of us have a bad habit of blaming the environment for our problems. The reality is that we are the ones that are exposing our mind to unhealthy information. As a result, we have to suffer.

Chapter 4.   Human mind.

We should learn how to exercise our free will, and consciously decide how to use our mind. Once we become aware of this huge responsibility, we'll make sure that we use our mind in such a way that we benefit and as a result we live a wonderful life.

Let's see how the information we absorb from the environment is being processed by our mind and transformed to emotion. We made a little drawing to be able to visualize how this might take place.

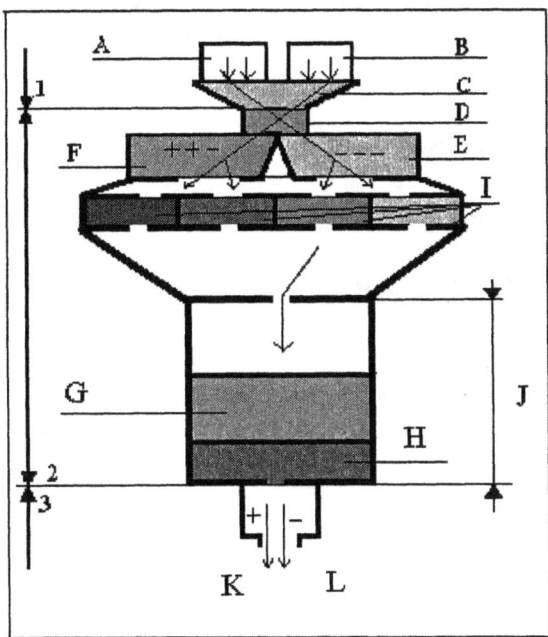

A. Information received from the environment through our five major senses.
B. Information received through the inner sensory monitoring system.
C. Our ability to select (accept or reject) the information. In other words, we have the reasoning ability, or the free will
D. Reticular system.
E. Defense mechanism.
F. Propulsion mechanism.
G. Information stored in the file
J. Memory file
H. Blueprint for the file (the summary of that file)
I. The four personality types (adaptive, aggressive, analytical and passive)
K. Positive emotion released to the body to feel it.
L. Negative emotion released to the body to feel it.

Now let's make sense of what we see in this picture, and what each represents (A, B.). We know that through our senses we continuously absorb information from the environment. Our brain stores the information in files, similar to a computer (J.). Being equipped with the ability to reason, we have the choice to accept or reject any information from the environment (C.). In our search of the environment, the reticular activating system points our focus toward the information that contributes to the accomplishment of the goals we set for ourselves (D.). Based on the meaning we give to the new information, we link it to the propulsion or the self-

defense mechanism (E, F.). Once linked to one of the two mechanisms, an emotion is attached to it. If it's linked to the propulsion mechanism (F.), it means that is meeting the inner needs of our personality type, and the emotion attached to it is positive. As a result, our body will feel a positive emotion (K.).
If the information we perceive as negative, we link it to the self-defense mechanism (E.). Being linked to this mechanism, it becomes an inner fear, of our personality type, that of course is transformed into a negative emotion that is felt by our body (L.).

In chapter 2 of this book, we discussed a little bit about some amazing abilities that we possess.
All these abilities we can display because our mind is the one to bring them into reality.
Let's review them some more.

    1. The ability to maintain oneself with life.

    2. The ability to grow, multiply and continuously develop its capacities.

    3. The ability to consciously identify, explore, absorb, enjoy and acquire ownership of the environment.

    4. Create new events and situations, factual or fiction.

    5. To store information in our memory banks.

    6. Recreate characters, events or situation from memory.

    7. Ruin our health by the improper use of our mind or body.

    8. Maintain, rejuvenate or restore the health of our body, by properly communicating with it.

    9. To consciously control and direct our life the way we want it.

Our mind is able to accomplish all these things by using two of its functions, the subconscious and the conscious functions.
So, let's go ahead and discuss these two functions.

    1. The Subconscious functions.

    2. The Conscious functions.

Let's take one at the time and see how they work and how we can benefit by knowing how to properly deal with them.

1. The subconscious functions.

After the conception of a child, starts the beginning process of cell multiplying that result in body organs. The primary subconscious functions of the mind start to develop so it can control and maintain proper functions of these organs. Once the baby is born, all the subconscious functions are already formed and working, and they keep working all his / her life.
The conscious functions start to form after the child is born, and continues to form new ones during his life.
Both kinds of functions were designed to work in harmony to maintain a proper operation of our body.

If we compare the subconscious functions of the mind with a car, we can say that the conscious functions of the mind are the driver of the car. The car is equipped with many functions and abilities, but it needs a conscious driver to make these useful. The driver on the other hand, has the ability to control and master the car according to his / her own will. But, he / she better know and understand how to properly use the car, otherwise it might become a source of pain and suffering. Same thing happens with our mind. We have a conscious control over it, but if we don't know how to use it properly, we are the ones that are punishing ourselves. And this happens too many times.

Basically much of the stress that we encounter is our own product due to the fact that our conscious part of our mind works against the subconscious mind.
Let's elaborate more on this. In order for our brain to properly control and maintain our body functions, it was equipped with a specific blueprint for each function.
If we are familiar with the way a house or a building is built, we know that the construction workers must have a blueprint or plan of that particular building in order to be able to construct it. Based on the information in the blueprint, they make the building.
Our subconscious mind works in a similar way. Having the blueprint, our subconscious mind follows it in controlling and maintaining the proper functions.
Let's take another example:
If you are familiar with a computer, you know that it has a specific program built in by the manufacturer. The program makes sure that everything is working properly. Also, it makes sure that every time we use the computer, it responds properly to our commands.
Now, there are some functions that we cannot change or modify. But with some of them, we might be able to modify. If we are specialists and know how the computer was designed to work, then we could modify some of its functions so we can use it better. But if we have no idea on how it works, and still *play* with it, we have a chance to do something wrong. Of course that particular function will start to work based on the new program. Most probably we will start complaining; what's wrong with this computer? Why isn't it working properly? There is nothing wrong with the computer, but a *specialist* has been playing with it.

Beside the original program installed by the manufacturer, we have the choice of installing new programs, or software. Based on the quality of the software, we get more or less quality results from using them. Once the software is installed, any time when we use it, it will function the same way based on the program that was built in it. If we don't like the particular software, we have the choice to replace it with another one. But, if we have the software that we do not like, we cannot expect it to get results different from the ones that it was programmed to do.

Now let's get back to our subject.
As we have mentioned before, our brain was equipped with two kinds of functions, subconscious and conscious.

The subconscious functions can be compared with the original program from our computer that was installed when the computer was originally built. The program of our subconscious mind is capable of processing more than one hundred million messages/second received from inside or outside of our body through its sensory monitoring system.
It control our heart, lungs, kidney, and all the other body organs, making sure that they are properly fed and in excellent working conditions.

We mentioned earlier that the mind stores bits of information received from the environment in so-called files. Each file contains bits of information about a specific subject.

A *file manager* arranges the files in the order of their importance; which is determined by the propulsion and self-defense mechanism. Our personality type influences the two mechanisms themselves. The personality type is influenced by what we received hereditary from our parents combined with the cultural conditioning that all of us are subjected to. Especially the conditioning we unconsciously accepted in childhood and were not aware of it. The cultural conditioning is determined by the information we are exposed to, or that we decide to expose our mind to. The file manager has authority over any other files; it could modify or change the essence of any existing file. Let's elaborate a little on this.

The file manager is composed of the blueprints of all the files from our memory in the order of their importance. In other words, our overall opinion about the most important aspects of our life. Such as, what we really believe about our existence, our family, our interaction with other people, our health, job, etc. If we have a positive outlook in life, the file manager is linked to our propulsion mechanism and reflects that over all the other files.

By the same token, if we have a negative predisposition, the file manager is linked to the self-defense mechanism, and is going to reflect this over all the other files.
That's why is very important to make sure we build a positive outlook about life.
Moving forward let's discuss the conscious functions.

2. The conscious functions.

If the subconscious functions can be compared with the original program installed in the computer, the conscious functions could be compared with the new software that is installed. We have a choice of what kind of software to get, but once installed, it will work the way it was designed to. So, we must be sure we get the right software that we need, otherwise we might get different results than expected. Now, any new software that we install, (one of our habits) will work not according to our desires, but the way it was set up to work. The reason is that once something becomes a habit, it becomes a secondary function of the subconscious mind, being triggered without conscious awareness.
But, unlike the original subconscious functions that came with the original program, we have the choice to replace the secondary functions of the subconscious mind (old formed or any other habit) with new ones.

Soon after birth, once the baby leaves the mother's womb and enters into a new environment the conscious functions of the mind start to develop. In the previous functions, the subconscious were developed based on a preset program that was transmitted genetically from the parents; so most of these functions cannot be altered or modified.
The conscious functions on the other hand are influenced by the information coming from the environment, and they can be altered, changed or modified. That's why each individual is influenced by the environment

he/she grew up in. The language, customs and personal habits differ from one part of the earth to another. Somebody who was born and grew up under the communist system will think and behave different than somebody who grew up in a capitalistic system. But, because all these conscious functions are like learned behaviors, as we mentioned before they can be changed or modified. It's a matter of being aware of this, and learning how to change.

Now let's go back to the little child which starts to develop his conscious functions.

Each of us has his / hers own individuality. In other words, every one of us has his own universe and we consider ourselves to be in the center of it. We are in charge, nothing happens, or shouldn't happen without our knowledge. We are number one priority, no matter what. This is a normal thing, because being designed as conscious beings with an inner desire to keep living our inner instinct to survive makes us to put ourselves first, and them the others. So, when the little child is born he/she is equipped with the same inner drive to keep living.

In the first years of his / her life most of the conscious functions of the body are not developed yet. Their behavior is controlled by the subconscious functions of their minds.

Of course when the parents whose conscious functions are fully developed try to reason or *make a child to behave normal* they find out that the child is out of control. The child's brain starts to be bombarded with: "NO!" Don't do that!" "Don't touch that!" "Bad boy!" "Look what you have done you…!"

All these *advices* are not consciously understood by the child because his conscious functions are not developed yet, remember? But, the subconscious functions are working and they interpret these as a danger that in turn triggers the subconscious function of his defense mechanism and the child tunes out and starts to cry.

So, the child's subconscious mind starts to form negative neuron-associations. The face of the parent, that is the video part, the voice of the parent, which is the audio part, and a negative feeling or emotion all these three form a neuron-association that is stored in the child's memory. The many of these associations are stored in his/ her memory the more the child unconsciously starts little by little to avoid the parent and starts to feel uncomfortable in their presence. That's why we see today such a big gap between generations.

Many parents are not aware of this fact and unconsciously are damaging the child's future mental development. Many specialists in child development agree that too many people spend 40 to 50 years to get over the first five years of their life.

The first five years of children's life are the most critical, because in this period the conscious functions of their mind are formed. Meanwhile their behaviors are controlled by the subconscious functions of their mind that does not have conscious abilities. It only accepts commands, and based on the information previously stored in its memory, it makes a decision. Like any other unconscious intelligence our subconscious mind does not understand a negative command. If you have a computer, do you have a command that says: Do not do this, or do not do that? No, there are no such commands. All the commands are positive, to do something, open a file, type, add, edit etc. That's the same way our subconscious mind was designed; accept positive commands, and when given a negative one, guess what? It understands it as a positive. If you tell your child:

John, you can play anywhere in the house, but in this room you're not allowed to enter, you got that?

Yes, mom, the boy says.

But what do you think is the first thought that goes through his mind?

I got to see what's in there. I got to find a way to get in there.

Now, why would a good boy like John think like that even though consciously he might have understood the command?

He might have understood it consciously, but his subconscious mind understood it as a positive command, and immediately triggered an inner desire to fulfill that command. And many times, the inner desire triggered by the subconscious mind takes over the conscious understanding of "do not do that". Once John is caught wondering through that room, his mom is wondering why doesn't this little child listen and obey his parents. She starts to punish him. By now, you get the picture.

Then what's the solution? Well, it's very simple: Always avoid giving somebody (especially to a child) a negative command. Learn to rephrase any command to make sure it's expressed in a positive way. This way, both the conscious and the subconscious mind are getting the same command, and there is no conflict between the two.

We mentioned before that each of us posses our own individuality.
Once a child is born, he also becomes an individual. Meeting basic needs and survival are the first priority. A new universe is born with him, and he is in the center of it. You might consider him as your child, but at this stage he don't have any idea who you are. When you behave in such a way that his / her needs are met, you're considered and accepted as part of his / her universe. But, if for some reason you don't meet his needs, you become the enemy and are not welcome anymore until you change your behavior. Try to take a toy away from a three-year-old child and see what happens? You become the enemy, no matter if you are the mommy or daddy. Why? Because the child's conscious functions of the mind are not developed yet so he might consciously understand your behavior. His/ her reactions are controlled by the subconscious functions of his mind.

The problem is that adults have no idea about these things, and trying to reason with the child at this age is almost as useless as talking to a wall.

Instead of taking away the toy or other things they might be playing with, bring them a different toy that is more interesting or new.

Because of an inner desire to explore and find out new things about their universe, they'll accept it. They will put aside this toy or accept the other one.

Among the first conscious functions that a person starts to develop are: walking, speaking, writing, reading, riding a bike, going through school and many other developments. Getting older he / she learns to drive a car, learn a trade, or other skills. All of these are accomplished through a simple method of repetition. Repeated enough, it becomes a habit or a secondary subconscious function, that is triggered automatically when perceived as needed. So, why do we get stressed? We repeat some negative things, or perceived some things or situations as negatives. Repeated enough, they become habits that are triggered automatically by the subconscious mind. Being negative, they also triggered a negative state of mind that was previously attached to them. And guess what? We get stressed. In other words, during our life, through repetition, we unconsciously built negative blueprints for these particular things or situations. Our subconscious mind triggers these habits using negative blueprints to accomplish whatever it was asked to do. To eliminate stress, we have to replace these negative blueprints in our subconscious mind with different ones that do not have attached to them any negative feelings. Once new blueprints are built, anytime they are triggered, there will be no more stress.

The invincible enemy, the stress that had power over us for so long, becomes powerless when we replaced the negative blueprints with new ones.

Remember: What kind the blueprints do I have that triggers my behavior? Are they the ones that produce stress? If yes, then it's my responsibility to replace them. Now, let's see the anatomy of a blueprint, and how to change an old one with a new one.

Chapter 4. Human mind.

The anatomy of a blueprint.

- Your house looks good to you, but who built its blueprint? -

As we have mentioned before, our subconscious mind has a blueprint for each file that is stored in our memory banks. This blueprint is actually the summary of each particular file. In other words it is made of a sentence that expresses our real opinion or core belief about the subject of that file. Some of our blueprints have been formed during our childhood starting from infancy. Others are formed in the present, or will be formed in the future from new kinds of information we expose our mind to.

Unaware of this fact, we keep behaving based on these blueprints and by doing that we keep reinforcing them.

Also we have mentioned before, the file manager is the one that oversees and affects the behavior of all the others. It is composed of our overall opinion about life in general. If we are an optimistic person, our file manager has much positive attached to it. Because of this, it will affect the other files in positive ways.

On the hand if we are a pessimist person, our file manager has much negativity attached to it. This will be reflected on all the other files also.

We all heard of the importance of setting goals, and stay with them until we accomplish them. When we set a new goal, we basically open a new file in our brain's memory. Once a new file is open, it also needs a blueprint for it, so the subconscious mind has a plan to use in accomplishing a task when requested. Remember, the blueprint is the summary or the essence of that file. So, instead of waiting a long time for the normal formation of the file, we accelerate the creation of that file, by consciously creating a summary for it.

In other words, we create the blueprint. We do this by using simple and concise sentences that are commonly known as affirmations. The essence of these is going to become the blueprint for the new file. Once we start to make and use new affirmations, we are strengthening the new file we just opened in our memory. Then, the reticular system in our brain starts to pay attention to these and focus on the kind of information that matches the file and we start to be attracted towards this kind of information. This way we are capable of setting goals and accomplishing them.

Beside the fact that we can use affirmation to build new files with blueprints consciously chosen, we also are capable of using affirmations to replace the old blueprints from some of the files we don't like.

Let's take an example to illustrate this:

Suppose we are a young person and have a hard time establishing a relationship with a person of the opposite sex that we like.

First, we are going to find out what's the existing blueprint. We do this by asking ourselves seriously: What's stopping me from being successful in starting this relationship?

Then listen what comes into your mind. The first thoughts are most probably the blueprint.

It might sound something like:

"You're nuts, that's why, you'll never get what you want."

"Who do you think you are, he /she is not for you, you don't deserve that?"

By getting an answer like that, we realize that in our file on how to build relationships, we don't have much positive information on how to accomplish this. Not only that, but we also have some negative information about ourselves.

Second, after we got the idea on what we have in the file, we consciously and seriously tell ourselves:
This is my old opinion about me based on the wrong information I fed my mind with. I am letting go of the past, and build a better future. The present and future is better, I am making it better.
Remember:
"Your past does not necessarily have to equal you future, unless you make it such"
Third, after we decide to change the present and the future, we start coming up with some positive affirmation about ourselves such as:
"I am a kind and loving person."
"I am capable of giving and receiving a lot of love."
"I enjoy good company with nice people."
"I deserve to find the person I can make happy, and be happy with"
By using these kinds of affirmations and really believe them, little by little they are going to override the old ones stored in our memory.
We also go a step further and start living these affirmations. We do this by asking ourselves again some questions related to our affirmations.
As a kind a loving person, how can I really do that? We are going to get some answers, something like this:
"I could be nicer to others."
"I could show more concern for my relatives and friends"
"I could understand others more, etc."
Then start applying these things in your daily lives.

By focusing our attention on these things, we are filling up the new file we just created with positive information, and of course that the blueprint will be a positive one. The more we strengthen it, the more it will have the power to override the old blueprint.

Let's see how these affirmations should be in order to be effective and get the results we want. Basically there are three important elements of an effective affirmation:
1. The affirmation should be as short and concise as possible.
2. It should contain action verbs stated at present tense.
3. It should contain words that trigger a high level of positive emotion.

Let's elaborate a little bit on these three elements.

1. The affirmation should be short and concise.

Why do we need a short sentence, and not a long one? There is an obvious reason for this. As we mentioned before, the blueprint is the concise summary of that file. Talking about only one file, we basically are talking about one subject. Having one subject, we need the summary of that particular one, and not others. The file contains many details. The summary or the affirmation contains only the essence of that file.

2. The affirmations should contain action verbs stated at present tense.

Humans are designed with an inner drive toward searching, identifying, exploring, absorbing, and enjoying the environment. To do this, we continuously have a need to do something. We don't want to sit around and not do anything. Inactivity makes us become bored. To satisfy these inner desires, we continuously set goals, even though we might not even be aware. If we want to live our life the way we want, we consciously set goals that take us where we want to be.

Why should we use the verbs at present tense? Well, this is very simple. Somebody once said:
"If you want to succeed in doing something, you should start with the end in mind."
In others words, you have to see in your mind eye the outcome of your goal, and then take the necessary steps to accomplish it. Let's take a simple example to illustrate this:
Suppose that you have to make one hundred copies of a report. You go to the copy machine, insert the original and press the start button. But before you do this, would you press the button that says make one copy, or the one that says one hundred copies? The right thing to do is to press the button that says one hundred. But, why? You don't have one hundred copies, but one. Yes, but, to get one hundred copies, you need to push the button that says one hundred. After that, the machine takes over and brings into reality what you are intending to accomplish. The same thing happens with our mind. We use the present tense because we want that particular command to be brought to reality as soon as possible. Then it's just a matter of time until our subconscious finds the necessary ingredients to bring it into existence.
Let's take another example:
Suppose you want to go in a short trip to the mountains with your family. What do you tell yourself? You start with the end in mind. What's the end? Enjoying the beauty of the nature way up in the mountains.
"I want to enjoy this weekend with my family in the mountains."
But you are still home, or at work, whatever. Consciously or not you give a command to your subconscious mind to accomplish this goal of yours. Then it starts to do the necessary things to gets you there. You tell your family members to buy the necessary items, prepare the car for the journey, and so forth.
We can see that it makes sense to believe that even though our goals might be far from becoming reality, the affirmations we make about them, should be in the present tense.
Let's talk about the third element of a good affirmation.

3. Should contain words that trigger a high level of emotion.

We know that the more we like something, the easier it will be for us to accomplish it. The less we like it, the harder it becomes for us to bring it into reality. Do you know why this is?
The reason is that our whole behavior is based on two inner drives: One towards pleasure, and the other away from pain. When we perceive something as pleasurable, we do it much easier. On the other hand, if we perceive something as pain producing, of course that the inner drive says to stay away from pain and we tend to avoid doing it.
Knowing that we have an inner drive toward things that cause us pleasure, we consciously choose words that define a high level of pleasure when we make affirmations.
We do this by using words that define as many of our senses as possible. Why should we do this?
Well, we tend to be impressed and remember people, situations or events when most if not all our senses were highly activated. Negative emotional charged - such as stressful situations, and positive charged, - such as joyful and pleasant ones. So, in our case we use positive emotional charged words.
By doing that, we unconsciously attach them to our propulsion mechanism and start to get attracted toward these particular goals.
For example: I would like to become a teacher, to teach people how to improve their life. For me to do this, I would find some affirmations that would sound like these:
"I am enjoying the satisfaction of seeing people benefiting from my teachings."
"I feel wonderful when I see that my students are using the information I have provided"
"I feel great seeing my progress in the art of teaching"
"I enjoy seeing myself a better teacher every day."

We are going to create a *movie* with these affirmations and continuously replay it in our minds until we believe it's true. Not only that, but we'll start behaving and acting like we do in our *movie*. Little by little our behavior will start to change from inside out. The motivation to become what we want is going to come from our inner burning desire to become a teacher.

We can create many of these affirmations. By continuously reliving them in our mind the *movie* we created will be used as a blueprint for our subconscious mind to follow in bringing into reality this particular goal. Now let's discuss how to set realistic goals for ourselves.

When we set goals, what actually do is, we are creating first a blueprint, and then gathering the rest of the information to fill up the file and accomplish the goals.

There are three important questions we need to ask ourselves in order to set realistic and achievable goals.
1. What do I really want?
2. Am I willing to pay the price to get it?
3. Are my actions in line with my goals?

Let's take one at a time, and elaborate a bit.

1. What do I really want?

This is a very general question, so we might consider applying it in few areas of our life. What do I want in my family life?
What do I want in regards to my job? What do I want from myself in regards of my contribution to the society I am living in?
What do I expect from my future? There are many other questions we might ask ourselves. Once we defined what we really want in different areas of our life, we go to the next step.

2. Am I willing to pay the price to get it?

Before we start to do the necessary things to accomplish any of our goals, we should ask ourselves this question:
Am I willing to pay the price to get it?
In other words, is the reward that comes from accomplishing this goal valuable enough for me, so I will be willing to pay the price for it?
Many people today set goals for themselves, but later on they find out that the reward has little or no value for them. So, it's useful to make a realistic analysis of the cost we might need to pay in order to accomplish the goals we want, before we start working on them. Once we figure this out, we get a green light to our subconscious mind to go ahead and bring it into reality.

3. Are my actions in line with my goals?

Once we set a goal, we have given a command to our subconscious mind to accomplish that particular goal. Influenced by outside stimuli we might find different ways to do it. Not realizing that our subconscious set goal does not correspond with our conscious desire to accomplish it, we find ourselves in a dilemma. Consciously we want to do something that might feel right to us, but subconsciously our body is pushed to do something else; resulting in stress. We need to discipline ourselves in such a way that we become our own friends, and not our own enemies. Let's take an example to illustrate this:

Suppose you are a sales person that makes $3,000/month. To get the $3,000 you need to make about 30 sales /month. Let's say that this month you got all the sales you need and only half of the month is gone. Having a subconscious blueprint that says you are a $3,000/month person, your tendency will be to slow down and take it easy. Even if you do more sales, your tendency is to stay around the sales you are used to. Unconsciously you want to stay in your *comfort zone*.

If the situation is the opposite, it's almost the end of the month, and you have less than half of the sales done, your tendency will be to rush and get all the sales done fast. You're out of your *comfort zone* and you'll have an inner anxiousness to get the sales done. That inner blueprint is triggering the command to be fulfilled. From here, we can see that each individual has his / hers blueprints about how much money they should be making.

Poor people have a blueprint that says it's enough if they make money to survive. In turn, they struggle all their lives to survive.

On the other hand, rich people have a different blueprint about their worth and the money they should be making. And of course their subconscious minds will focus on the things that will make this possible. So, if anybody would like to change their life for the better, the most important thing to do is to learn how to change their old blueprints about life, with new and better ones. Like somebody once said.

"It's not enough only to know more, someone must become more"

If we just hear about it, we become knowledgeable. But, to really become the person we want to be, we need to change the inner forces that make us become that person. In other words, we need to change the old blueprints that our subconscious mind uses to mold our behavior, with better ones.

     From this information, we can see that we are determining the conscious functions of our body. They started functioning from an early age and at this time we don't have enough experience to refine them. But now knowing these things, it's our responsibility to do a thorough clean up. Having much more experience, we'll be smart enough to do the right thing and remove the wrong information that we accepted during our past, and replace them with new and better ones. As a result, the life we improve is ours.

We have mentioned earlier about the three abilities we posses that create our state of consciousness.

We have called them: reasoning, imagination and finally emotions.

Now let's go and discuss these three major abilities.

The Three Major Abilities.

- Our inborn amazing abilities, -

By now we can see that when it comes to the human mind, we can safely say that we are dealing with a *very powerful live mechanism* capable of doing amazing things. This is made possible because of the wonderful way we were designed to function. Let's talk now about three major abilities that our mind is equipped with.

The first major ability is the ability of reasoning. The second is imagination, and the third one is emotion. We put them in this order because they work together in this order. First through reasoning ability, we have the freedom to consciously choose to accept or reject any information from the environment. Once we decided to choose specific information, the second ability takes this information and combines it, or processes it. Once it is processed, the third ability takes the result of the processed information and through the nervous system, is transmitted to our body to be felt as an emotion. To better understand how this happens let's imagine a three-piece chain link. Even though its made of three links the chain is still one piece.

By *Reasoning* ability, we might understand the capacity of understanding the environment or any other information that we come in contact with. Accepting or rejecting, and passing a judgment by labeling it positive or negative.

This ability is specific to humans only. None of the other life forms on earth posses this ability. Being able to reason our own environment, we can choose to differentiate between things, accepting or rejecting them based on our free will. In other words, unlike the animals that have a built in program on how to instinctively react to the environment, we have this ability to exercise our free will in deciding how to react to outside stimuli. Used properly, this ability helps us to develop into normal and successful human beings. Improperly used, it brings unpleasant consequences.

To illustrate the second characteristic, we will use a simple illustration: Visualize a calculator.

Why did you buy a calculator? Well, you trust that this small piece of plastic could do math much faster than you can. Don't you? You don't have to be shy. We all use one for the same reason. Now, how come a simple piece of plastic that can't talk, walk, is capable of doing math much faster then we can imagine?

Well, those guys who invented it, found out that there are some materials that are capable of combining numerical information, according to some specific laws that do not change, and give the right answer all the time.

Isn't that something? Yes it is. And, it does not matter how many times you use the calculator, you always get the right answers.

One of our brain characteristics is to do something like this, yet even more. A calculator needs somebody to turn it on, and to punch the numbers in order to function. Unless a human being does this, the most powerful calculator isn't worth anything. But our brain does not need a battery or somebody else to turn it on and off.

We as conscious human beings, have the capacity to combine not only numerical information, but also process all kinds of information. And guess what? Our mind is capable of giving us the best answer. Of course, the quality of the response depends on the quality of the information that we have *stored in our mind* in that specific area.

This characteristic is what we commonly call *Imagination.*

It is a property of our mind to combine any kind of information, and give us a result, based on the quality of the information that we previously fed our mind with in that specific area.

Remember the saying: " Garbage in, garbage out."

We feed our mind with quality information; we get quality results. But if we do not care what kind of information enters our mind, do not be surprised that we come up with unsatisfactory or even bad results.

An improper use of this ability is the major source of stress for most people today.

The third, but not the least ability that we have, is the capacity to consciously feel the result of the information that we previously accepted and combined; no matter if they were negative or positive.

If we have chosen to accept positive information and combined these, as a result we might feel a positive emotion. On the other hand if we accepted and combined the negative information we'll probably feel a negative emotion.

I say probably because we have the choice of giving any meaning to any kind of information no matter what they really are. The quality of the emotion depends not on the quality of the information, but on the meaning we might give to the information; which could be positive or negative. And based on the meaning we give, we will feel it as a positive or negative emotion. This ability is commonly known as: *Emotion.*

Let's take a simple example to illustrate this. Let's picture a simple radio. We know that the radio has an antenna through which absorbs from the air radio waves. It then transforms them into sounds by the use of a speaker that is built in. The vibration of the speaker with the sound produced by it is the *emotion*. The same way our body absorbs from the environment information that is combined by our brain, and then we feel them through what we call emotions. Now the radio itself has no ability to give any interpretation of the waves received. It will express them exactly the way they are. But we humans have the ability to interpret the information we absorb from the environment and give them the meaning we want. By doing this, we can change the emotion that is felt. The quality of the emotions that we'll feel is determined by the meaning we give the information, and not the quality of information. That's why there is a big truth in the proverb that says:

"Whatever you decide to believe, it becomes true for you"

Understanding this fundamental truth will help us eliminate stress, because stress is a negative emotion that is the result of our giving a negative meaning to specific information or a part of the environment. Knowing that we have the power to choose the meaning to any information, and then it's up to us to learn how to do this. Once this becomes a habit, we will unconsciously do it any time it's necessary. Of course the result will be positive, and the stress will go away. Like the other two abilities, this one when properly used, can be beneficiary to us. But, by the same token, improper use of it might result in stressful situations.

At this point, let's take each of these abilities one at a time, and see both sides. In other words, learn how by using them properly will result in a happy life, and also, the side effects, and the damage that might result from an improper use.

 Or

"Our freedom to choose"

Reasoning.

- When intellect meets the matter -

Superior to any other creature on the earth today, we humans are equipped with the ability to understand our own environment, and give a meaning to it. By having this faculty, we are able to enjoy and live a happy life. We can look around and see the beautiful earth, full of wonders that please our senses. We take these things for granted, not realizing how lucky we are, to be able to manifest this ability. Take for example, the most beautiful picture, and show it to a dog, or cat, or to a horse to see what they think. You may be amazed at its beauty, but they have no reaction of appreciation or any other, except maybe to use it to play, or even eat it.

Observe the variety of colors, shapes and forms that our environment is made of; making it possible to enjoy it through this ability of reasoning: To look at the environment, feel, smell, or taste it, and by doing that we are able to live a joyful life.

Sounds like a paradise, but then why still do we have so many problems in the world today, and talking about our subject, why is that millions of people today, are experiencing greater stress in their lives?

Now, this ability of reasoning is of great benefit to us; if we use it properly. Unaware of, many times we might misuse it and of course then the results will be different.

Let's take a simple example to illustrate this:

We all know about cars. They were designed by the manufacturers to be used by people, and by doing so, to simplify and make life better. But, did you know that cars are one of the major causes of death? Now, can we say that the cars are bad? Or, that the manufacturers of the cars had bad intentions in their minds when they designed them? Can they be blamed for the death of people killed in car accidents? Everybody will agree that's not the case. The reality is, that the improper use of automobiles, are the causes of these accidents. More than that, we all know that all cars are equipped with some safety devices, or systems that might prevent an accident, such as the brake, signal system, horn and etc.: All of these, are provided for the sole purpose of avoiding danger, and making them safer and more enjoyable. The same thing happens with this ability of reasoning. We can use it properly, and as a result, we enjoy a beautiful life. Or, we can, for some reason, misuse it, then the results are different. One of the undesired results is stress.

If we take a closer look around us, we observe that we have at least two sides in most situations. We have good and bad, black and white, day and night, right and wrong, tall and short, big and small, negative and positive, pessimist and optimist, and so on. We can recognize that these examples are opposed to each other, and by being opposed they have opposite results or effects when they are used. Every day we use our senses, and try to reason which one of these is best for us. When we choose properly, the results are positive, but, by the same token, when we choose something improper, we cannot expect that the result will be positive. It will be negative, and in many cases, will result in stress.

We know that basically, there are two kinds of people, some who are optimists, and some who are pessimists. All are going through many kinds of situations in life. But the way they go through them differs a lot. Why is that? Well, as we have mentioned before we are equipped with this faculty of reasoning, through which we are constantly selecting or choosing different kinds of bits of information. And of course, the quality of information selected influences the quality of results.

If we are a pessimistic person, we have the tendency to choose or select negative information. By doing this, we get negative results, and many of them will result in stress. If we are an optimistic person, we have the tendency to select and choose positive information, and of course that the results will be positive.

Here's the key: We need to learn this, believe it as the truth and once we do that, it will become true for us. Then an amazing thing is going to happen. We'll start to recognize negative information, and its negative results, and be able to use the faculty of reasoning to reject this bad habit of combining negative information. Step by step, our attitude will change, from a pessimistic view, to an optimistic one. If anybody makes a survey to see what kind of persons are more stressed, guess what? The reality is that all pessimists are people with a high degree of stress. On the other hand, the stress level of optimists is much lower, even somewhere close to zero.

We mentioned earlier, that our mind continuously absorbs information from the environment, and based on our own interpretation; we attach a meaning to it. We do not have to be a rocket scientist to recognize that people, who are pessimists, though they may not be aware of it, are continuously attaching negative feelings to the information received from the environment. Once they do so, these neuron associations, are placed in *storage* in their memory. When these are recalled; they start to feel the negative feelings. Unaware that this is a part of a negative association from their memory, they blame the feelings on the environment. That's why almost everybody today, believes that we get stress because we encounter stressors.

On the other hand, the optimistic ones, looking at things through a positive attitude are attaching positive feelings to the new information. The results are totally different.

Anytime when they recall this information, they are not producing any stress.

Let's take a simple example to illustrate this:

First, you are aware that you are a normal person, with a normal mind, aren't you? And, your answer will be: Yes.

Now, a normal person, with a normal mind, when asked a question, what should he / she normally do?

Answer the question in a normal manner. This is a natural reaction.

But let's say, that I ask you this question:

Please, tell my about a very positive experience you had when you were fourteen years old, and give me some details. As a normal person, you start to tell me about this exciting experience you had in the past.

Now during your explanation, what kind of state of mind do you start to experience? Unaware of, you start to feel good, and relive some of these wonderful feelings that were stored in your memory for so long; and now, even though years later, you feel them again.

Now, how come when I have asked you a simple question, it changed your mood, making you smile and feel good? When a person is asked a question, he / she should answer the question in a normal manner. Why didn't you answer in a normal manner but you started to answer in a positive state of mind and happiness?

The answer is not that there is something wrong with you, but my question triggered in your mind certain memories, that have been attached some positive feelings. You started to see in your mind's eye the people and places that you have been many years ago. Beside the video and audio information that you are reliving, you started to feel also the positive feelings that you had attached to them in the past.

Now let me ask you another question:

Please tell me about a negative experience you had when you were seventeen?

Well, once you start telling me about this negative experience, I could see how your previous smile disappears from your face. The tone of voice changes, and by the time you finished your experience, I could see that your mood is more negative, rather than normal or positive. Why is that? Is there something wrong with your mind?

No. But then why not just answer the question without the negative feelings?
See, you are still a normal person, but my question triggered this time totally different kind of memories. These memories having attached to them some negative feeling from the past, makes you start to feel them again. They are the ones that changed your mood, not the present or the environment; like most of us might think. This is basically a major source of stress: To unconsciously retrieve and relive many of our past memories, to which we have attached in the past a negative feeling. Because this process happens instantly, we blame it on the environment, as the source of stress.
Of course it does not matter how hard we work on this, we will never be able to eliminate stress because we are working in the wrong direction. What we should be doing is, accept how our mind processes information, and work in removing these negative feelings that were attached in the past to many of our memories. By doing this, anytime when we might recall any of the past experiences without a negative feeling attached to them, there is no more stress, but a memory with no negative effect over us. It is as simple as that.

As we mentioned before, people who are pessimists (or negativists), are attaching more often negative feelings to the experiences they go through, unaware of the fact that this information will be *saved in their memory banks* to be retrieved later. Of course later on, when retrieved, they have a stressful effect over them.
On the other hand, the optimists ones, or the positivists are attaching a positive feeling to their experiences, and they are storing positive feeling with these memories. When retrieved and relived, they will create a positive mood.
Now let's go to talk a bit about the second ability that we posses: imagination.

"Our right to create."

Imagination.

- Your ability to conceive and put together anything you want -

We mentioned earlier, that imagination is our brain's ability, to *combine* any kind of information, based on specific rules, and give us the right answer, based on the quality of the information that we have combined. Knowing this, we can spare ourselves much pain, sorrow, anxiety and stress, just by the simple fact of stop *combining* the information that will result in this. See, all these negative states of mind we just mentioned, come from us. Unaware of this, we keep combining wrong information, and of course that the results are negative. If you have a car that requires unleaded gasoline, and you fill it up with diesel fuel, do you think that it will work normally? Not at all. The truth of the matter is, that we are responsible for our thoughts and feelings; nobody else puts a gun to our head, and forces us to think this way. The problem is that from our early age we were conditioned by our environment to behave in a specific way. This isn't the right one all the time. Being bombarded with negative information, unaware of the fact that we should be selective in our choosing the kind of information we are feeding our minds with, we followed the way the *crowd* behaves. Naturally, we get the same results as they do. Gaining a better understanding of how our mind works, we should be smart enough to realize that it's up to us to design and create our own destiny, based on our positive goals, not on the goals of others.

Many of us are familiar with the expression, self-talk. It's like we have another person inside that keeps talking. The problem is that most of the time for many people that talk is negative. Unaware of we open a negative new file and build a negative blueprint for it. Once we open it, the reticular system starts to attract our attention towards information to fill this file. We start to be attracted and preoccupied with negative information that starts to fill up the file. Being a negative and maybe impossible goal, the subconscious mind keeps focusing on looking and collecting information to solve it. Of course that this result in a continuous negative self-talk, and eventually a stressful and a miserable life.

A few years ago I asked myself this question: Who's inside me that talks when I hear things in my head. Some say it's our little inner child that controls most of our thinking and acting behavior. Really, who's there talking?

Is there a C.I.A. agent? Or a K.G.B. agent? Or a little devil? Or a little angel?

Who's that voice from within that many times we have to fight or obey?

There are many interpretations to this, but by being realistic and understanding the way our mind was designed to function, we should recognize that it is just the work of our unconscious mind. There isn't anybody there, unconsciously we are generating this inner adviser, we are just not aware of it. But its "voice" gives us a clue about ourselves.

When we have the habit of practicing negative self-talk, it means that we have a negative file manager with a lot of negative information about ourselves. (information that we believed in the past about ourselves)

The solution is to do a self-analysis to find out where it originates from, and get rid of it; replacing it with a new and better one. In other words, we learn to combine positive information with positive results rather then acting the old way by combining negative information and of course getting negative results.

To better understand the role we play in this process of imagination let's ask our self two interesting questions:

What is more easily to do?

Convince your close relatives that they are part of your family and their behavior should reflect that? Or try to convince some strangers to become part of your family?

If you agree that the first task is easier, then you should know that it's much easier for you to start working in changing your behavior than to try convincing others to change theirs.

Now let's talk a little about the third link in our chain which is emotion.

"Our right to perceive our own creation"

Emotion.

- When we reap what we have sown. -

Simply put, emotion is our body's response to any information processed by our brain. In other words, any information that enters and is processed by our brain creates an electro-chemical reaction that in turn is transmitted to our body to be perceived.

This ability to express emotion makes us superior to any other creature on earth. Not only able to consciously react to the environment, but have the ability to feel the enjoyment through what we call emotion. This is done through our nervous system that brings about to our conscious awareness, these feelings of emotions. The other forms of life do not possess this ability of being aware of the environment, to feel, enjoy, be happy about it. We have mentioned before, that through reasoning, we consciously or unconsciously, absorb information from the environment. Through the process of imagination the brain combines them, and as a result the nervous system is activated to create a specific feeling in our body, which we call emotion. In other words we are aware of the cake, we can see it, taste it, enjoy it, and are able to express and share that joy.

Now let's go back to our subject of emotion.

As a third link in our three-piece chain, emotion is basically a flavor of our lives. We could have been designed without it and still be alive and conscious, but looks like the Master Designer had more in mind about the human race than to just be alive. And our ability to feel emotion proves that.

Now, somebody might ask; why do we have to deal with negative emotions and why are they part of our life?

Well, that's simple. We will learn later that we are equipped with two mechanisms, the propulsion and the defense mechanisms. Through the propulsion mechanism we are pushed forward to identify, explore, absorb, enjoy and own the environment. As a result, we feel positive emotions and thus we are happy and enjoy life. But, when there is a potential or a real danger, the defense mechanism takes over and through different degree of pain, (which is nothing other than negative emotion), makes us aware of the necessity of doing something about it. That's a normal thing.

Now the question comes: How about stress and depression or any other negative emotions that we feel even though there is not any danger? Well, the answer to this is that feelings of stress or other negative emotions are the result of triggering the defense mechanism when actually it is not needed. This occurs because we are not aware of how our mind works. When we feed our mind with positive thoughts, the subconscious part of our brain understands that everything is OK and we can enjoy whatever we are doing.

But, by the same token, when we feed our mind with negative thoughts, or we keep pondering upon them, the subconscious part of our brain understands that we are in danger and triggers the defense mechanism creating a negative emotion.

It's like when you get in your car to go some place and try to drive your car with the emergency brakes on.

The car might move, but there is a lot of stress on the engine and transmission.

Even though the general idea is that emotion is something that we have no control over, the truth of the matter is that, we have the power to control this feeling we call emotion. We need just to learn how.
Remember, emotion is the result of combined information selected through reasoning. So, having a choice in selecting the information we want, we could become smart enough to select and accept information that results in desired emotions, not undesired ones.
The only time when we cannot control the intensity of our emotions is when an imminent danger is perceived, and the subconscious level of our defensive mechanism triggers them. Let's take an example to illustrate this:
Suppose you are on the sidewalk and want to cross the street. Before crossing the street, as usual you look around to make sure it is safe and then you proceed. By the time you get to the middle of the street, suddenly you hear a loud noise coming from two cars crashing together, right behind you. Instantly your whole body goes through a state of intense emotion, your adrenaline level goes very high, and you become scared, thinking for the moment that your life is in danger, even though the accident have nothing to do with you.
Why did this happen? As we have mentioned before, the defense mechanism goes on as soon as it perceives a possible dangerous situation, from the environment.
The crashing sound was identified as a possible danger, so it triggered the proper response; you become instantly alert and find the fastest way to get out of danger. You start looking towards the place the sound came from and take the necessary steps to avoid any injury. Once you looked behind you, and see that there were two cars involved in an accident, the high level of emotion drops drastically. Soon you get back to normal, even though that experience remains in your memory banks.
Now, these kinds of situations shouldn't be confused with stressful situations. It does not matter how high the intensity of these kinds of emotions, they are not affecting our stress level. They are just a response to a perceived danger. In other words the defensive mechanism is just doing its job. The problem is, that most of the people do not know this fact, and unaware of this difference, they start to consciously attach a negative meaning to situations like these. By doing this, many of these situations might become a source of stress for them. We might know people that get scared very easily.
For them, right away the sky is falling, even though there might not be any real danger.

It's important to acknowledge that there is a difference between a conscious negative meaning we might give to a situation, and a proper response to the defense mechanism, when it perceives a potential danger.
The more we learn about our marvelous brain and the way it functions, the easier it will be for us to use it for our own benefit, and we could eliminate negative emotions that are destroying the happiness of millions of people.
There are billions of dollars spent today to find out if there is life in other parts of the universe.
This implies that the faculty of reasoning could be used to discover the wonders of the universe. The same ability could be used to discover the wonders of our personal inner universe. And of course that the benefits could be more appreciated by those who need to solve their own inner problems.
It makes perfect sense for us as individuals, to open our eyes and recognize that we need to learn about ourselves, and our destiny. As we all know, each of us is interested primarily in his / hers own welfare first, and then on others.
It does not matter how good others are doing, if we are miserable and in need. Or how much peace of mind others might have, if we are missing it.
Now let's talk a little bit about how emotions are manifesting themselves in our body. Based on the kind of information that is processed, we can say that our brain triggers three levels of emotions.
1. Low-level emotions

2. Medium-level emotions.

Let's take the first kind of emotions.

1. Low-level emotions.

Low-level emotions are the ones that are experienced by our body as thoughts or psychological mental states.
We can safely say that the word emotion defines movement inside of our body. The movement produced inside of our body by any information processed by our brain.
Not long ago, scientists discovered that our thoughts are the lightest form of energy. In other words when we are entertaining any kind of thoughts, these are the result of our brain releasing very light forms of energy. The same thing happens when we are expressing any positive or negative emotions. As a result of the processed information absorbed by our brain from the environment, our brain releases small amount of energy that is brought to our conscious awareness as a positive or negative state of mind or feelings. Even though these are low-level emotions, their intensity might be lower or higher based on the information processed. Being exposed to the same environment for a longer period of time and processing the same kind of information repeatedly, we form what we call thinking habits. Based on the quality of our environment, we might cultivate positive thinking habits, or negative thinking habits. So, if we see ourselves as negative thinking people, we can leave the environment that conditioned us to think negative. If there isn't any way to leave it, we are still able to improve and change our negative thinking habits. We do this by changing the meaning we give to information coming from this negative environment.
You might have heard true stories about people that survived the Nazi concentration camps, even though they were exposed to a very cruel environment. They did this by consciously deciding to change the meaning of the information coming from their environment. By doing this they were able to survive under unbelievable circumstances.
Remember we talked earlier about the fact that our thoughts control our actions, and also that we have the ability to control our thoughts?
There is a law that is called: *The law of substitution* that says that we are capable of substituting a negative thought with a positive one. Even though we might not be familiar with its name, many times we have used it, when we have replaced positive thoughts with negative ones. What we learn now is to do the opposite. Substitute a negative thought with a positive one. We are able to do this because we are equipped with free will, to consciously choose what kinds of thoughts to entertain. All of us are equipped with this ability, the only thing is that most of the time we are not aware of it, or we might forget about it. We have learned earlier of the importance of building new blueprints with the use of affirmations. What we need to do is, open new files in our mind and form the right blueprints for them using positive and constructive affirmations.
"I am responsible of my own feelings."
"Nobody can control the way I feel, but me."
"I am capable of changing my old negative thinking habits with new positive thinking habits."
Having these expressions engraved in our memory, they will become blueprints that are automatically triggered by our brain when we are faced with a situation or an environment that might influence us to think negative.
One great man that lived in the 20th century once said:

"He who cannot change the fabric of his thought will never be able to change reality."
Also, one of the greatest American presidents said:
"People are as happy as they make up their minds to be."
Taking control of our thoughts is not as hard as it might seem to be. We need the proper knowledge and our efforts to implement it. Remember: The many negative thinking habits we have, the more negative emotions we experience. On the other hand, the many positive thinking habits we posses, the better our life will be.
Remember: "If it is to be, it's up to me"

2. Medium-level emotions.

Medium level emotions are the emotions that activate the faculty of speaking. We mentioned before that some kinds of information once processed by our brain, triggers low-level emotions. Now there are different kinds of information, that once processed by our brain, triggers a higher level of emotion and is expressed by our body by speaking. In other words speaking is an expression of medium level emotions triggered by specific information that we absorb from the environment. As in the case of low-level emotions, when the information processed was perceived as negative, medium level emotions are negative. That's why people who speak a vulgar or negative language are the ones exposed to environments that cultivate negative thinking or negative behavior. The same way that we formed thinking habits, we also have formed speaking habits. Based on the quality of information that we were exposed to, we have formed positive speaking habits, or negative speaking habits. Now, if the quality of our thinking habits has an effect mainly on ourselves, then speaking habits have the same effect, but also on the persons we are speaking to.
The next time when you start speaking to someone, remember that you and the person you are speaking to are both affected by the quality of your speech. With our speech we can heal, or we can harm others and ourselves. To better understand this, compare this faculty of communicating with others with possibility of gift exchange. In other words anytime we talk to somebody, the whole content of our speech is like a gift we are giving to the person we are talking to. Now, you consider yourself a kind and generous person. Right? If that were true, what kind of gifts would you give to others through your speech? The kind they gladly accept and thank you for? Or the kind they wish you kept for yourself?
Now, can we do something about our speaking habits? Yes we can do. As in the case of thinking habits, speaking habits are triggered by previously blueprint formed in our subconscious mind. Here too, we have a choice to stay with the old habits of speaking, or by replacing the old blueprints, we actually are changing our speaking habits with better ones.
Let's go now, and talk a little bit about the third level of emotions.

3. High-level emotions.

As we mentioned before, this level of emotions triggers actions. In other words, some information that our brain processes has much effect over us that require an action from our part. It's not enough to think or speak about it, but to take an action. These could result in positive actions or negative ones. But, to implement these actions our subconscious mind has to have also a blueprint to follow in triggering these actions.
Let's go back to the example with the house: Each house or building that is constructed requires a blueprint or a definite plan. Having the blueprint, the construction workers are able to build exactly what the owner of the construction wants. The construction workers are following the blueprint exactly the way it was planed. They will never have one kind of blueprint and build a different building than the one on the blueprint.
The same way our subconscious mind (that controls our behavior), in order to implement any action it needs a blueprint of that particular action. The more clear and detailed the blueprint is, the easier will be for our subconscious mind to work on making it a reality. That's why all the professionals are telling us that in order to succeed in life, we need to set definite goals and detailed plans and to write them down.
By doing this, we basically are building a clear blueprint for our subconscious mind to follow in bringing into reality our conscious goals.
Let's see now what are some expressions of this faculty of emotion.
Well, based on their polarity, we can say that basically there are two kinds:

1. Ones, have their roots in a positive reasoning, and are expressed in a positive way.

1. The others have their roots in a negative, or absence of reasoning, and these are expressed in a negative way. We'll take one at a time:

1. Positive Emotions.

These emotions have their roots in positive information or perceived as positive.
Also, these positive emotions trigger positive thoughts, positive speech and positive behavior, or actions. They might be: love, kindness, happiness, joy, laughter, excitement, and so on. The people who manifest these qualities, aware or not, are repeatedly using their positive reasoning towards themselves or others. This happens until they become habits that are triggered instantly. In other words, they have formed a good blueprint in their subconscious mind about this subject. So, we have a choice; use a positive reasoning, knowing that this will result in a positive emotion that of course is what we ultimately want.
Now, let's go to the other type of emotion, negative emotion.

2. Negative Emotions.

Now, if the positive emotions have their roots in positive reasoning, then based on the same law, the negative emotions have their roots in negative reasoning. Like the positive emotions, the negative ones also could be short term, or long term. Do any of us like these kinds of emotions? Of course we don't. Then let's see how can we identify them, and what we can do to eliminate them.

Living in our world today, many of us are facing difficult situations, and as a result we start to feel a large variety of these negative emotions. Many of us are familiar with: anxiety, depression, anger, aggression, irritation, impatience, hostility, stress and many others.

Now, what are all of these? They are nothing else but different degrees of negative emotions. They could be short term, such as: anxiety, anger, aggression, irritation, impatience, hostility, or long term such as sadness, depression and stress. Even though some might differ from others in intensity or symptoms, all have their roots in negative reasoning, resulting in experiencing them as unpleasant feelings.

We might follow today's tradition and treat each of them individually, using the existent means, or recognize their common source and deal with it directly. As a result, all the symptoms will disappear. Let's take an example to illustrate this:

Suppose you have a tree in your back yard that you want to get rid of. What will you do? Will you keep cutting down the branches one by one, and by the time you get finished, they might start to grow again? Or, a better way is to cut its roots, and then the whole tree withers and dies.

Well, the answer is simple. Go for the roots. The same thing happens with these negative emotions that we have to deal with. Instead of spending our time trying to deal with one at the time, it's better to find their roots and work there.

Then, once starved of their source, they will disappear by themselves.

See, we know that there is a law of cause and effect, which basically says that everything is caused by something else. If we get a cold, for example, it is because we contracted a virus. The cold does not just appear from nowhere, for no reason. We might not know the reasons, but they are always there. So it is wise, to look for the reason why something happens, rather than working hard to eliminate the effect, neglecting the cause.

Most people believe that once they have finished school, learning is over but the reality is that they keep learning daily. But not being aware of this, they are not selective with the information that they come in contact with, to choose only what is beneficial for them. Every one of us is a specialist in something, depending on the work we do.

How did we become specialists? We learned. What is the result of our learning? We make enough money to survive, right? How about learning a little bit more, and become specialists in knowing ourselves. Then we might be able to get rid of stress that is producing so much misery in our lives. We do not need to go to college for many years, or spend a fortune.

Let me ask you a simple question:

In order for you to be a good driver, and benefit from using your car, do you have to know everything about the car?

No, but you need to know the most important things, and respect them. As a result, your life will be more enjoyable by using the car in the right way. The same thing happens in our case. To use our mind the right way, we need to learn the basics, and then respect these laws of the mind. The results will be amazing, almost unbelievable.

See, everything becomes simple, if we learn how properly to use them.

Remember the first time when you drove the car? Yes, it was a little bit scary, but soon after you started to master it, things changed. Now, what advice would you give to others, who want to learn how to drive?

Well, it's a piece of cake, you may say.

The truth is that it's not difficult, but relatively easy. The same thing happens with the elimination of stress.

To do this, we need accurate knowledge to use with our reasoning ability, so we can get the real results. By doing this, stress wouldn't be something that we have to live with, but just an option.

Remember: "If it is to be, it's up to me"

So, up until now, we learned that negative emotions could be controlled, and eliminated, if we do it the right way. We should stop being slaves to uncontrolled negative emotions that might make our lives miserable. Remember, there are two kinds of people today.

The ones, which do the thinking for themselves, and are called: *Leaders*. The others, who need somebody to do the thinking for them, and are called: *Followers*. Which one would you like to be? We know that our mind controls our body, and if that's so, then who should control our mind?

Should we let environment control our minds or should we learn how consciously to control our minds, thus controlling our environments? You might know the saying:

"It's not what happens to you, but what you do with what happens to you."

We all have a choice, to let the environment control us, or we could learn how to control it for our benefit. The only way to eliminate stress is by learning how to control our mind and as result the environment.

From this information, we can see that emotions play an important role in our life, because they determine our state of minds, or more accurately, they are our state of mind. Even though it might be news for us, there is a relatively easy way to deal with them. The most important thing that is required from us is to want to do something about it. It's our responsibility to do that. Unless we do it for ourselves, it will remain undone. As you may know by now, in order for anybody to do something, they need to have a desire to do that. But the desire will never come unless somebody is aware of such a possibility. Up until now you were taught, that you have to *manage* these negative emotions, for as long as you live. Now, gaining a better understanding of reality, it's up to you to take the necessary decisions to do something about it. We do that by changing our understanding of it, how it's created, and the role we play. Realizing that it's ourselves who are creating it, we are changing our behavior in such a way that the result is no more stress. In other words, we become stress free persons.

Until now, we have learned that through the ability of reasoning, we can differentiate between the information that we receive from the environment. We have a conscious choice over the information that we are dealing with. So, we can discriminate between the ones that we want to accept, or reject. Then through the ability of imagination, we have the capacity to *combine* information that we have chosen in such a way that we might get the desired results.

As the result of the activation of the first two abilities, we get the third one, the ability to feel the results that is emotion.

Moving forward, we'll talk about the next secret; human behavior and find out what happens when we start to interact with the *environment*.

Review Question: What does our mind uses to implement our behavior?

Answer:
- Like any other sophisticated accomplishments, our mind uses a blueprint to dictate our behavior.

"Through Reasoning, we choose what we accept. Through Imagination, we combine the information accepted. Emotions, are the results we feel after our mind has combined what we have chosen to accept."

Secret # 5.

"What we become through what we do. The anatomy of a habit."

Chapter 5. D. Human Behavior.

- You're not what you think you are, but what your behavior makes you to be -

Going back to our main subject, in order to eliminate stress forever, we need to appreciate the value of knowledge that will enable us to accomplish this task. Treating it as valuable information, we'll make sure that it's assimilated in a such a way that will be permanent in our memory, becoming a habit, that will be triggered any time when it's needed.
Let's see a few steps needed to get to this goal.
1. The very first step is *Awareness*.
2. Once we are aware of what is important, than we go to the second step, which is *Desire*.
3. The third step following the desire is *Decision*.
4. Once we decided what we really want, we need *Motivation*.
5. And finally, we need *Discipline*.

Now let's take one at a time and see how we can benefit by applying them.

1. Awareness.

- Knowing that we know. -

Did you ever wonder why so many people are poor today? Why many are working for minimum wages, working very hard, and barley surviving? When others are making tons of money by working easier?
If you ask somebody who works for minimum wages, "Why don't you get a better paying job"? How do you think they'll answer?
"That's the best I could find" probably will be the answer. But what is the real reason? Their level of awareness being low impedes their progress towards finding something better. If they really knew about something better they'll seek it.
Remember the blueprints that each of the file uses to accomplish a particular task? Do you think poor people already have a blueprint on how to become financially independent in their memory? Or do they have a blueprint on how to be

poor and stay that way? It's obvious, that the main reason they are poor is because they never consciously or haven't created the right blueprint to become financially independent.
Why do you think somebody wants to become a doctor, or engineer or lawyer?
Because they are aware of the advantages of becoming professionals.
That's why they take the necessary steps to go to college, make necessary changes in their lives and they know its value. Their level of awareness is much higher, so the desire comes out of the awareness. Let's take a small example:
You are driving your car with your family and you have to stop at a signal light. On the sidewalk, you see a big sign with a picture of a tasty hamburger. Once the kids see the sign, what is going to happen?
"Daddy we are so hungry" That's probably what you'll hear.
Why is that? Because they see this brand's name and the products they sell on TV. Their level of awareness is very high. They already have a blueprint about that particular fast food restaurant, so as soon as they see the sign; automatically the blueprint triggers the craving of hunger.
The brain was designed to recognize easily the information that it's familiar with. That's why in order to learn something; we need to keep repeating the same information to ourselves, until it goes in our long-term memory. It's called the learning process.
We can see that awareness is very important, and the first step in learning a new behavior.
You may wonder how somebody becomes aware and how he or she could develop a high level of awareness.
One way is to consciously look for valuable information and once we hear and believe it, we become aware of their importance.
Another is when somebody else, already aware of important information, tells us about it. Again, once we hear, we become aware of it.
Now awareness like many other things in life has a positive side and a negative one.
The polarity of awareness is determined by the way we interpret the new information.
If we interpret the information as a possible source of pleasure, the awareness is positive or constructive. If we interpret the information as potential pain, the awareness will be negative.

1. The negative awareness.

Let's see what negative awareness is and what we can do about it.
This kind of awareness has two aspects:

A. The first one, even though it is a negative awareness, it has or should have a constructive effect over people.

B. The other is very dangerous and destructive.

A. Constructive Negative Awareness.

This kind of awareness we can also call fear.
When properly understood, it is a necessary ingredient for our life.
When misunderstood, fear could be among the biggest causes of stress.

Chapter 5.   The human behavior.

There are many situation or things in life that most people perceive as stressors. Most of them originate from misunderstood fears that become the reasons for stress. These situations come from constructive fears and are a normal reaction by our body to potential dangers. To better understand this, we need to learn something about how our body functions.

Humans were designed with a defensive mechanism that has the roll to keep us away from danger. Any time that our brain senses that there is danger nearby, this mechanism turns on and acts as a protector by directing our body away from that particular danger.

Let' take an example:

You are walking on the sidewalk and you get to a stop sign and want to cross the street.

Being aware that cars are passing by, you look around to make sure it's safe to cross. You see a car coming, but it's far away so you think that there is enough time to cross. So you go ahead. As you make a few steps you hear a loud sound coming from behind you. Another car is getting close; the driver sees you and honks the horn.

What is going to happen?

When you decided to cross the street, the self-defense mechanism turned on in its first stage.

It made you look around to see if it was safe to cross.

This, we call the *Primary Stage.*

Seeing the car far away, it was not a danger to cross. Still, when crossing, you start walking faster.

This is called the *Secondary Stage.*

While crossing you heard the horn sound. Right away you turn your head to see from where the danger was coming from. In a split second, your mind analyzes all the audio and visual information and passes a judgment on where the danger is coming from. From the car coming far away, the one behind, or from where the sound of the horn came from?

This is the *Third Stage.*

Finely, after your brain senses where the danger came from, it triggers an instant command to the body to move away from it.

This is the *Fourth Stage.*

In each stage, the level of awareness is different, starting from low towards the high. The highest being the fourth.

It's important to recognize that we have a conscious choice in the first two stages, and then once we start going through the other two, we'll react instantly out of reflex or habit. At this point, we do not have a conscious choice of our actions.

We need to think twice before deciding to do something. We do not want to get involved in something and then find out that we loose the conscious control of the situation.

Getting into an experience like this, the level of adrenaline gets higher than normal. Many people interpreted this as a stressful situation.

But, as a matter of fact, even though it might look like one, it's not a stressful situation.

It becomes a stressor only when after an incident like this you develop a fear of crossing the street. Here is a very important thing to remember. After a situation like this, you should use the "Reasoning method" from chapter 11, "Solving the mystery of stress." It's important to do this because if you don't, your mind will be associate the crossing of the street with a danger. And the reality is there is no danger in crossing any street as long as you do it safely.

By using the "Reasoning method", you realize that you need to be very careful, not fearful when you cross the street.

Many times in life, we go through difficult situations and our safety mechanism turns on. Not paying attention, we associate fear from these events and negative feelings; resulting in stressful situations. Doing this, the constructive fear that is supposed to protect us from danger, becomes a destructive fear that should be eliminated.

Chapter 5.   The human behavior.

We need to learn to differentiate between a situation that triggers our defense mechanism and a real stressful situation.

The so called *stress* caused by our defense mechanism is a temporary state, it's induced for our own protection, and should not be confused with a real stressful situation.

The *Stress* that we are learning to eliminate, is the negative feelings that we have associated in the past to some things or events

Let's take another example:

We all drive cars, and know that all have gages and indicators on the dashboard. Suppose you drive your car on the freeway and suddenly the *low coolant* light turns on. What does this mean? Is the light broken? Do you need to change it? No.

This is a *warning* light. It turns on to advise you of a potential danger to the engine if you do not pay attention to it. So, the wise thing to do is open the hood and check the coolant level. Add coolant if necessary or fix the leak if there is one. You shouldn't replace or remove the light. It will not help to do this. The light was designed as a warning device, to advise and warn you.

You should not be mad or scared of it, but understand its purpose because it started flashing for your protection. "Don't kill the messenger if you don't like its message."

The problem is by not being aware, many people are associating a negative feeling to these incidents, and once they do that, any time when something like this happens again they get stressed. In the future, these incidents become *stressors* for them.

Remember:

"It is not what happens to you but your response when it happens to you."

When negative feelings are attached to this kind of situations, fear becomes destructive.

When positive feelings are attached to this kind of situations, fear becomes constructive.

It's up to us to understand and believe this, and develop a habit of linking positive feelings to these situations. By doing this, we eliminate the potential of getting stressed.

It is important because a negative awareness has the tendency to generate a negative desire and a positive awareness has the tendency to generate a positive desire.

Remember the rule:

"Garbage in garbage out" And it is just a matter of choice.

We could say that there are a few kinds of fears. Based on our personality type, we experience more or less of these fears. They have all their roots in our childhood. Unaware of them, we let them control our lives and many times they become a source of stress.

Beside the fear that is a result of our protective mechanism, we may at times, experience different kinds of fear that stops us from progressing in life.

- This kind of fear is a destructive one, and it should be recognized as such and work to eliminate it.

We are familiar with expressions like:

I can't do that, I don't know, I have no idea, impossible, no way, never, don't do that, don't touch, and so on.

From our childhood, we were bombarded with these kinds of *commands* that are affecting our thinking ability, and stopping us from progressing in adulthood.

The old saying: "Every plant has its own roots," applies to us because like a plant, these fears have roots too. To be able to properly deal with them we might consider where they come from. They all come from our childhood.

Some times in our childhood we felt rejected, we lost something, or we felt pain to a high degree. These fears leave a deep mark in our subconscious mind, and unaware even as adults, they might have a negative influence over us.

Did you ever wonder why, when children are instructed not to do something, they have the tendency to do the exact opposite?

It is widely recognized that once somebody receives a negative command, automatically they develops an inner drive of curiosity to find what's behind the banning.

Research shows that the brain of children under 4 or 5 years old, the faculty of understanding between a positive command and a negative one is not completely developed. They can't make the difference between *do it* and *don't do it*, and as a result both commands are taken as positive. And, of course they get punished for not listening. Then, they get frustrated, "why are they getting punished", because according to their understanding; what they wanted to do was good. What they get out of this is that every time they want to do something that they feel is good for them, they get punished. Then, they start developing a negative emotion toward progress and development. Once in their memory, it stays there for the rest of their lives. Even as grown ups, they still have that subconscious fear that keeps them from changing and progressing in life.

This fear is deeply rooted in their subconscious mind from childhood, and unless they learn how to eliminate it, they will have hard time progressing and the procrastination will be their good friend.

Remember, how you felt when you were a child, and you did something that you thought was good for you and your parents saw it completely different; you didn't feel good at all. You saw your parents face filled with disappointment or maybe even anger. Without realizing, in your mind you associated the desire to do something you want, with the negative emotion or pain. Any time you wanted to do something different, there was that negative feeling from long ago that comes up making you stay away from better changes.

This fear probably manifest in many aspects of our life.

It is important to understand its potential damage and find the right way to eliminate it.

Once we are aware, we develop a desire to get rid of it.

Then we make a decision, build enough motivation to keep us disciplined until it's gone.

These are the same steps we need to go through to achieve any goal:

Awareness, Desire, Decision, Motivation, and finally Discipline.

- Another kind of fear that we inherited from childhood, and we keep adding to it during our life, is fear of loss.

Do you remember how much you cried when you lost your favorite toy? How about that beautiful Barbie of yours?

You may not realize it but everything that happened in our childhood, to whom we have associated powerful states of mind negative or positive, are still deposited in our minds. It's still controlling and directing our decisions and desires.

There is a very powerful line that I learned many years ago that says something like this:

"Forget your tribulations, but never forget what they are teaching you."

The reality is that we may consciously forget all of these events that we go through during our life, but our subconscious mind retains them in our memory. This includes the states of mind that these situations were attached to. Any time we go through similar situations, we start to feel the same way. If the experience was positive, we feel good, but if the experience were negative, we feel bad.

As grownups we have this fear of loss, and because of this we may become very possessive toward other people or things that we posses.

When we become too possessive toward people, we take the risk of loosing them.

Many husbands lost their wives because they were too possessive with them.

Also, many parents lost their children, because they were too possessive with them. Somebody once said:

"The best way to control somebody is by educating them to be responsible for the freedom you give them."

Because:

"The gift of freedom becomes a curse when given without proper education."

In other words we are free to do anything we want, as long as we are aware of the effects our behavior has on others, and are responsible for our actions.

It's advisable to revise our attitude toward others, and if we see to much possessiveness, let go and learn to do it the right way.

You'll feel better if you knew that you gave somebody the freedom to leave, rather than to know that he or she left you. Beside the possessiveness toward people, we also have the tendency to be possessives toward things that are important to us. It is a good thing to know how to save, but when we become too possessive toward things, we are doing ourselves a disfavor.

There is a saying that a few people believe and really understand, but there is much truth in it:
"The more you want to hold on to what you have, the more you are stopping yourself from getting more. "
How this could be possible?

We know that consciously we can handle one thought at the time. We just cannot think about two things at the same time; it's better to take one, and then the other.

If our mind is filled with the thoughts of how to save what we have, we'll never have the time to keep thinking how to get more.

There are people who spend hours looking for a bargain to save a few dollars. The time they spent to save the buck, could be spent more profitable to get something more valuable.

This also applies to a job, or some other things.

We spend so much energy going to work in order to get paid few dollars/hour. By learning something different, a person could make much more money with less time and effort.

There is a very big difference between working hard and working smart.

- Another kind of fear that causes stress is fear of pain. Pain is a normal reaction to our body to a potential danger. Why do I say normal?

Because our body was designed with a self-defensive system, which makes us aware every time something is going wrong with our body. It's like a warning light in the dashboard of a car.

It warns that there is something wrong with the engine and we better fix the problem, not just cover the light.

The sad truth is that today most of us are covering the light on our dashboard with so many kind of painkillers. There are more that one thousand aspirin based painkillers on today's market. What do they do?

Just like their name says: *kills the pain*

A very helpful aid in coping with pain is to ask us:
"Why do I really get a headache?

If we do this, and we are honestly trying to find a truthful answer, we'll be surprised to find out that we don't need painkillers for headaches. There is another reason for it.

If you have a tree in your back yard, and after a while its leaves start to dry out and fall down, what would you do? Start painting them green?

Or, would you realize that the problem comes from its roots, and you have to do something. The same thing happens with us. We just cannot fix something right unless we find out the real cause of it. So, it's important to recognize that pain is not the problem in itself.

There is something else that needs to be taken care of, and then the pain will disappear by itself.

There is a law of cause and effect. It does not matter how many times we try to eliminate the effects; it will never work. It will be a never-ending story.

Go to the cause and eliminate it, and the effect will automatically disappear.

B. Destructive Negative Awareness.

Before we go into this subject, it's important to remember, what we do today depends on what we have learned in the past. Future behaviors will be determinate by the kind of information we accept in our minds today.

We discussed earlier, that we as humans, consciously or not, are designed to continuously assimilate information through our senses. So, it doesn't matter where we are, we are continuously bombarded with

Chapter 5.   The human behavior.

many kinds of information. A wise thing to do is to be selective in the kind of information that we let enter our mind.

Also, we learned that once in our minds, the information is going to affect our future decision process.

Let's take a simple example:

      Take a one-year-old American child to a different country. Let's say China, and let him live there for twenty years. Afterwards, try to bring him back here to America.

How do you think he will behave? Like an American? Or like a Chinese?

Who's customs will he follow? Whose language will he be spoken?

Even though the child was born here, and his parents are Americans, but because he grew up in a totally different environment, his behavior will reflect the environment that he grew up in. In other words, he will speak and follow the Chinese language and customs.

In order for him to behave like an American, he needs to learn the language and American customs. After he learns that, he might decide to behave like an American.

Why is this important for us to know?

Well, during our life we spend about 1/3 of it sleeping, another 1/3 working, and the other 1/3 trying to make it as pleasant as possible by recreation or entertainment.

So, when we sleep, we sleep. When we work, we don't have too much choice over what kind of information we feed our mind with. But, the third part is the time when we assimilate information. And, we better be careful on how we use this time because the way we spend it, will affect our entire life. Based on the quality of information we are feeding pour minds with, we could become a failure, or a success.

Let's take a simple example:

      John and Mary is a happy couple with two children and both of them work. John junior is about 13 years old, and little Henry is only four.

Every morning both parents go to work and the kids stay at home.

How do you think they spend their time? They play with toys, but probably they turn on the TV, which is widely recognized to be a *baby-sitter.*

There is nothing wrong with watching TV many may say, but the reality is that violent TV scenes may affect the future decision making process of some of the young ones.

Imagine that every movie you see is like a file you put in your computer. The more movies you watch, the more files are saved into the memory.

Then when you want the get some answers to some of your problems where do you think the *computer* will get the information from? It goes into its memory banks and seeks information related to your situation. Then selects out of them which ones fit the best your situation.

If the child watches many educational programs, the answer will be positive, but if the child watches negative programs the answer will probably be negative.

Remember the subconscious mind does not care what you plant in it, but will produce the results according with what you put in. "Garbage in garbage out"

Leaving children alone to decide what kind of programs they are watching might result in a future negative behavior. We are aware of how large this problem is today; violence among teenagers.

      Society is building more and more prisons to fill them with criminals. The public has to realize that these bad behavior starts in our homes.

We let kids fill their minds with many kinds of violent and bad things. Then we expect them to behave as normal people, with kindness and fairness, and when they don't; we punish them.

It's like you take some American students and give them a test in a foreign language. If they do not pass it, they get punished. Sounds crazy, but this is what happen with our youths today. They are exposing their fragile minds to all those immoral and violent programs, and then we expect them to have a moral and decent behavior.

The reality shows that our younger generation is deteriorating faster and faster. Today's extreme entertainment is one of the main reasons for this situation.

Chapter 5. The human behavior.

By getting used to *movies* and *entertainment*, people are not aware of anymore what kind of messages are being transmitted.

Picture somebody offering your favorite kind of food, but add a small amount of poison.

Would you eat it? Certainly you would not. But, our younger generation is not aware of this potential poison in today's entertainment, and we can see the result.

The questionable *movies* that bring millions to their producers are also one of the main reasons why the immorality and violence is skyrocketing.

When we look at this kind of entertainment, and see how people in them use violence and immorality to handle their situations, we are *feeding* our mind with them. Later when we are facing similar situations, our brain searches through our memory to find out what kind of information we already have on this particular subject. It takes whatever information it finds as a reference. Finding positive and constructive, it will direct us to react positive, but negative will direct us to react negative.

By knowing this, we need to be careful on what kinds of programs we are watching. Also, we need to be selective in what our children are watching.

Their mind is more sensitive and more easily affected by today's negative influences. You may have heard the saying:

"Buy American, the job you are saving might be yours."

So, we can say:

"Be selective in what you and your family entertains with; the family you may save, might be yours."

The destructive negative awareness is among the worst of our enemies. But unlike other enemies, this is an invisible one, like a time bomb.

Almost two thousand years ago, the most powerful empire that existed was the Roman Empire. Even though it dominated the scene of history for so many years, its fall didn't come from outside enemies. Internal instability caused primarily by decimation of the smallest cell of the society: the family, due to immorality and violence.

Something similar is taking place now. The glamour of violence and immorality is portrayed in most of the current entertainment without any responsibility toward the potential danger that this will bring to our younger generation.

Researchers show that by the time a youngster is sixteen years old, they already have seen hundreds of thousand of violence scenes. When we realize that all the visual information stays in their memories, it's no wonder that tempers are hard to control. To add, many times the way they solve problems is through violence or other negative means.

It's very important to remember that the potential danger of destructive negative awareness is great and the damages very painful for everybody.

This is not just children problems but adults as well. Preventing and make people aware of this danger should become a major goal of society

Remember: You have a choice on what you allow into your mind, but once there, the choice is gone and your future behavior might be determined by the quality of that information.

You feed your mind with positive, healthy information; you will have a positive and healthy behavior.

By the same token, you feed your mind with negative and damaging information, you might have a negative or even unhealthy behavior.

The choice is yours. Choose the right thing, for your sake and those whom you love. Moving along, we'll discuss positive awareness.

2. The positive awareness.

Positive awareness is our ability to open up to any good *information* that surrounds us even though right now we not necessarily consciously seeing it.
In order for us to do that we need to recognize a basic truth:
Nobody knows everything about everything. We may know everything about something, or something about everything. It does not matter who we may think we are, we still have things to learn. We are designed like a huge magnet that continuously look to attract information to feed itself with.
It's essential to recognize our limitations and always have an open mind toward positive information.
We love flowers, especially roses, right? They are among the most beautiful flowers.
Also, it's known that their thorns are very sharp and could be painful. Is this fact stopping us from buying roses? No. Why not? Because, we do not focus on the thorns, we focus on their beauty and aroma.
We all love mountains right? Yes. Every year folks go camping and enjoy this time spent there. They present a potential danger from wild animals but will this stop people from camping in the mountains? No. Why not?
We are focusing on the positive aspects of these situations, not on the negative ones. That's why.
From those two examples, we can see the importance of the awareness of positive things. Although we are aware of potential dangers, we choose not to focus on their negative sides, but on positive ones. By doing this, we enjoy the time spent in that *particular place*.
This is a healthy way of seeing things. It's useful to learn how we can expand the area where we can use this kind of healthy thinking.
In other words we learn how to be more aware of positive potential of things that we are dealing with.

The three aspects of positive awareness: financial, family life, and spiritual will be dealt with now.

The financial aspect of positive awareness.

If we take a closer look at today's educational system, we realize that, as good as it might seem to be, it's kind of *outdated*. We need to do something about our education, if we want to be more successful than the regular guy who is spending their lives working for minimum wage.
Going back in history we'll find out how all this came about.
We may know that before the 1900, the majority of the American economy was an agriculture-based one. Also, the main commercial centers became large cities.
The larger the cities became, the more people were needed. All of these cities started to develop and expand different industries and the need increased for a new, younger work force.
In order to fill this need, they created an educational system designed to attract the youth from countryside to the large cities. This system was very effective because both parties involved were satisfied. The manufacturers got the work force to produce their products, and the workers obtained basic knowledge. The job was providing a decent and fulfilling life style.
Since then, every body knows that they have to go through this educational system, then once they finish it, they need to get a job that will assure that they can make a living. This process went through the years up till today. The only thing is that starting with late seventy's, things started to change.
The science advanced so much that we entered a new era: "The computer era."
We all are glad that we can benefit from the advancement of science, but also we start to see its side effects.

The new computerized technology started replacing the human working force. Since then, thousands and hundred of thousands of workers were laid off. This replacement process started to develop in most areas of life. This present educational system still does the same thing it was doing in the past. Preparing the young generation to enter the work force.
But, the reality is that there are less and less jobs for most of those who finish their education.
In order to be able to survive or even b to succeed in life we need to find better ways to deal with this problem.
Remember the saying:
"If you keep doing what you were doing until now, you will keep getting what you were getting."
There is much truth in this expression.
We cannot improve our financial status, unless we keep up with the knowledge required. We need to open our minds and take advantage of today's technology and learn how to use it instead of procrastinating in our old way of thinking.
In other words: "Shape up, or ship out"
It is much better to keep looking with optimism on how can we continuously improve our education in the future. By doing this, no matter what the future may bring, we'll be equipped with the knowledge to cope with any challenges and overcome them for our benefit.
Another aspect of positive awareness is towards the way we handle our family matters.

The family aspect of positive awareness.

How can positive awareness help us in dealing with family matters?
Well, if we can accept having a miserable job, for whatever reason, we'll never want to have a miserable family life.
Positive awareness plays an important role in the happiness of our family life. Our house should be:
"Home, sweet home"
But did you know that sweet things are never made from sour things? Are you aware that YOU must be the biggest source of sweetness in your house?
Did you know that you would never accomplish with vinegar what you'll accomplish with honey?
If you ask others how they see you; would they see you as sweet, or sour?
Remember: "The one who knows better should behave better "
I think that you know better, even you recognize that.
We have mentioned earlier about roses, we love them even though after a few days they wither and die.
And we also know that: "The most beautiful roses have thorns" So, it's possible that beside our fault, in certain situations, there are other family members that might be at fault too.
Do we necessary need to focus on the thorns, or do we have the choice to look at the roses also?
Focusing on the beautifulness of the roses rather than on their thorns is very wise
People have the tendency to mirror each other.
When we get home, a choice is made to enter the house with a *rose* on our face, or with a *thorn* between our eyes.
And based on our choice, we'll get a spouse with a *rose* on their face, or one with an even bigger *thorn* on the head.
Remember, we always have the upper hand on this.
Keep in mind and never forget that even if we had a rough day at work and have a thousand reasons to get upset, there isn't any reason in the world to punish our family by bringing home the negative situations of our working environment.
Let's take a simple example:

Chapter 5.   The human behavior.

Most of us are familiar with the computer and we know that in order to properly use it we need to follow its principles and regulations. Once we have learned them, they have to be used every time.
There are many files in a computer, and we can access them any time we want.
But, we always run one file at a time. We wouldn't do a good job if we overlap many files at the same time.
So, what we do is, we work on one file, then once we have finished it, we close it, and then proceed to the next one. In our daily life, we are accessing all kinds of *computer files* from our memory.
We may not be aware of it, but when we wake up in the morning, subconsciously we turn on *the morning file*. Get up, wash, get breakfast, prepare for work, and leave the house. Once we leave the house, our subconscious mind closes this file, and once in the car, it opens another file: *The driving file*, which contains the information about driving. Arriving at work, it closes this file, and opens another file: *The working file*.
Dealing with things that are important during the working hours, our *reticular activating system* stays on and we can focus on doing the tasks required. Upon finishing our job and getting back home, *the reticular activating system* is still active. It keeps looking to find ways to accomplish the tasks required at work. Not being consciously aware of this, we overlap *the working file* that is still open with *the family file*. We might be wondering why things in the family don't go the way they are supposed to. Our mind keeps switching from one file to the other, and none are working properly. This of course many times becomes a source of stress. By now, I think you get the picture.
What is going to happen? Well, remember we cannot properly use two files at the same time. We need to close the previous file, and open *the family file*.
Forget about bringing home the *thorns*, instead bring home the *roses* by closing all the old files and open the right one; *the family file*. With a little practice and discipline, we'll be able to consciously focus and control which or how many files our mind is dwelling upon.
We can make our life much more pleasant by recognizing that it's our responsibility to do this. It should start with us.
As we mentioned before, we might not be able to change others, but we can change ourselves, and this it's ours responsibility to do so. Realizing the huge benefit of doing this, it'll become more and more pleasant. The other family members will start seeing the difference, and they will start to do their share too.
Therefore, do your share, sow the good seed and wait patiently for the great results that will come.
We have mentioned two aspects of positive awareness: The financial and family aspects, now let's discuss about the third and maybe the most important aspect of positive awareness:

The spiritual aspect of positive awareness.

Even though we live in a very advanced society where we are able to travel millions of miles through space see through powerful telescopes the immensity and infiniteness of our universe, we are still puzzled by the questions like:
Who really are we? Where do we come from? Where do we go after we die? And so many other questions that are still debated between religion and science.
During all human history, people keep asking themselves these questions. And doesn't matter how many people ask these questions, different answers are received.
Let's analyze these questions from a point of view that is generally recognized as trustworthy.
We know about something called: *Common sense*.
It does not matter were we come from, or what's our age, or affiliation we all recognize that using common sense is the simplest way to judge things.
Using the principle of common sense is a healthy way when we are faced with situations where there are many interpretations to various situations.
Some may know the saying:

Chapter 5.   The human behavior.

"If you ask ten people to answer the same question, most probably you'll get ten different answers."
But if we ask all ten to put aside their own ideas and use common sense things start to change. Step by step most probably they start to come to the same or similar conclusions.
So, the best way to approach this subject of human existence is to use the principle of common sense.
In one hand, we have religion that for thousands of years is keeping most of human kind divided into so many fractions that are fighting among themselves not necessarily a physical war, but an ideological one.
On the other hand, we have the scientific community that is trying desperate to give answers to these questions, but at the same time for some reason reject religious ideas about human existence. Sad to say, both in general left behind the law of common sense and followed ideologies that sound so amazing, but if we use common sense, we can see that many of them just don't make any sense.

     We have mentioned earlier that our subconscious mind cannot make a difference between reality and fiction, and every thing we want to believe, our mind accept it as truth.
Once in our memory, that information will be use by our brain in future similar circumstances. For example:
History says the communist ideology never worked, and will never work, no matter how good the intentions of their leaders may have been and how sure they are that this ideology is working. But could a person tell this to one of those leaders? Will they accept it?
Of course they wouldn't. But why is that?
Because, as we just mentioned whatever somebody decides to believe, it will become *truth* for him or her. It may not be for others, but for them it is *real truth*. In other words, what he / she perceives and accepts, it becomes *truth*.
The same thing happens with these religious or scientific organizations.
By perceiving their ideologies the way they do, they become truth for them. The problem is that the more organizations we have, the more ideologies there are.
 A fair and just way to get a better understanding is to always use common sense as guidance.
This law of common sense   will be a proper way to judge things.

     As h we all recognize that beside the fact that we have physical needs, such as to eat and drink and so on we also have a different kind of needs that we call spiritual needs.
 They are not satisfied only with eating and drinking but need something more; something that money cannot buy. We could call it a spiritual hunger. These physical things do not satisfy it.
This kind of hunger is only satisfied, when   the reality of the existence of mankind and us as individuals is understood, and when we align ourselves with its purpose.
In other words we become greatly satisfied when we understand who we really are, were we come from, and what is going to be our future.

     Remember the example with the two people on the boat in the middle of the ocean during the stormy weather? One of them knowing what they were going through; was waiting patiently for the storm to pass.
On the other hand, the second one was very scared; not knowing what was going to happen.
With regards to our life journey, in some way we are just like one of those two. If we know the real truth about the human existence, we can accommodate ourselves to fit that purpose, and go through it with peace of mind.
But if we do not know the truth, we will be pushed back and forth by different kinds of teachings that keep changing like the weather.
So, positive awareness plays an important roll in this matter, because it helps us to open our minds to the truth, which is refreshing. Even though there are so many interpretations of whom we are, were we come from, and were are we going, there must be a truth about our existence. We just have to keep looking for it until it's found.
The first principle of common sense that we are going to discuss is the following:
"Behind any intelligent design, there must be an even more intelligent Designer."
If you ask anybody on this earth if this is truth, all of them that are in their right minds, will agree that this statement is true.

So, let's see how this statement helps in our positive awareness.
Before we do that we need to recognize the fact that most people, if they don't like a particular outcome, they avoid the things that might lead them there. This happens very often in the scientific community also.
Let's take a simple example:
You have been driving your car for about six years. The car is in reasonable shape.
You need to fix things here and there, but over all, the car is in working condition.
Then suddenly you find out that there is a noise in the engine that might be a serious problem.
As soon as you become aware, you take the car to a repair shop.
The estimate that you will get, will depend on were you take the car to.
If you take the car to a mechanical shop, you get an estimate on the repairs of the engine.

Right?
But if you don't want to confront the reality that something might be wrong with your engine, you take the car to a body shop for an estimate. From there, the repairman will start looking at how many dents there are on your car, and how many body parts are needed to be replaced. If you ask them if you can drive the car like this with these body damages, they will tell you that it's OK. But, if you really want the car to look like new, you need to spend some money to do these body repairs.
What is wrong with this example?
Is the estimate from the body shop wrong?
No.
But, what is wrong is, to shift the attention from the real problem to a secondary one that is not so important. We can easily see that the most serious problem with the car is *the life of the car* -the engine. And once we see there is a danger that the engine is going to break down, it's wise to look up what to do to fix it before it breaks down. This is the way a situation like this should be dealt with.

Now, we come back to our subject of positive awareness in the spiritual area of life. We understand that none of us would like to die. Every other creature accepts death as a normal thing, but we don't. We want to keep living.
Did you know that a dog when is old and about to die is aware of this and goes some place away and accepts death as normal?
I remember when I was about seven years old and had an old dog. I used to play with him every day. Then one day I didn't see the dog. After two more days, I ask my father where was the dog, because I hadn't seen the dog for three days.
Then with a lower voice my father told me:

"Son, this dog has served us faithfully for so many years, but lately the dog knew that he is too old and shortly will die. So three days ago, he left the house and yesterday I found him in the back of the garden dead, and I buried him."
I started to cry because even though he was only a dog, he also was my friend. And my father told me:
"It is OK to cry, because Nero (that was his name) was a very good friend, but animals, unlike humans, receive death as being normal."

Humans differ from any other living creatures, because by being aware of our own existence, they can differentiate between past present and future through a conscious process. We are aware of the value of life and we just do not want to loose it.
Like we have mentioned before awareness produces desire.
And being aware of our own existence, we automatically develop the desire to keep living.
We also mentioned earlier that:
"Behind any intelligent design, must be an even more intelligent designer"

If we carefully examine the way the whole universe functions and analyze all the information concerning life and everything on earth, we can conclude that humans are the best fitted beings to live in this kind of environment.

Let's take an example:

Suppose you want to buy an aquarium with these little tiny colored fish. What would you do?

First you will look for the right place in the house. You will not put it in the kitchen, or in the bathroom, or in a dark place. You'll find just the right spot, with enough light and right temperature. Then, you look for an aquarium with all the necessary accessories like rocks, plants, thermometer, water purifier, and other little things that are required for the fish to have a pleasant environment. After everything is ready, you get the fish and put them inside. This is a reasonable project and those are the normal steps to follow. Now, once the fish are inside they start to multiply.

After a while, one of your enemies comes, and to destroy your project he pours a small amount of poison in the water. As a result some of the fish die, and others get sick.

Even though not all die, the poison affects all of them. Some are affected more than the others.

Now, if the fish are able to talk to each other, would it be fair to blame their bad situation on you, who built the aquarium for them?

Or, is it right to blame the real bad person who did this. I think that you'll agree with me that they should be thankful to the ones who brought them in *his house* and blame the bad guy for all the consequences of poisoning the water.

Now, in regards to the subject of whom they are and how do they got there, would it be reasonable to believe that they evolved from some previous primitive form of life?

Or, should they recognize that they were there because the owner of the house made this decision.

Let's look a little closer at this example. The fish do have some abilities or characteristics that help them enjoy their lives in the aquarium. Their bodies were designed to live under water. They are able to move freely through the water, without the need to come to the surface and get oxygen. They have been equipped with different sensors to detect food or danger. But, even though their environment in the aquarium fits them perfect, what do you think is their ability to understand and perceive the environment outside the aquarium? How much of their ability to function under water, will help them understand what happens outside their realm?

The reality is that being designed for a specific environment, their sensors are not equipped to detect the realities that exist outside their own environments. They just cannot comprehend the other worlds that exist outside. Their eyes were designed to perceive and understand the underwater environment. They are not capable of seeing or perceive outside environments. It's like you want to see a movie using your radio. It's just impossible. The radio was designed for transmitting audio information; the TV was designed for movies. And no matter how sophisticated your radio might be, it's not able to work as a TV.

So, what should the fish think about their environment?

We all will agree that they should accept the truth and be thankful that the owner did all of this for them. Also in the exploration of their world, they should give credit not to themselves, but to the one who designed and created their environment.

Now let's compare the universe, the earth, and humans on it; with the house, the aquarium and the fish. Do we see any similarities? Let's be honest and compare.

Something very similar has happened in our situation.

But we are much smarter than fish, and can come up with very brilliant ideas about the truth of our existence. We let theories, like the evolution, influence our minds when with the very use of common sense we can clearly see that this theory is just a theory, but much more than that it has no scientific basis.

Let me ask you a few simple questions:
- Does the science recognize the laws of nature?

Yes, it does.

Chapter 5. The human behavior.

- Has the science discovered, that in order to maintain balance in nature all its components, such as: plants, animals, birds, trees, insects, fish, and other live creatures, must maintain their proper place in the nature?

Yes, it has.
- Does science believe, by mass extinction of some animal species and plants this is affecting negatively the balance of nature?

Yes, it does.
- Does science recognize by destroying this balance, life itself is in danger?

Yes, it does.
- Does the evolution theory, base its whole ideology on the process of natural selection? In other words, each life form evolved from a primitive life form to a more complicated form of life, and the strongest one survived the weakest one?

Yes, it does.
- Does science recognize that millions of years ago there were dinosaurs on this earth?

Yes, it does.

If all these statements are true, how can you explain why life was not terminated when there were only two, three, four or one hundred primitive life forms?

If now there are billions life forms and let's say we eliminate half of them, we all agree than pretty soon those that have been eliminated will automatically trigger the extinction of the other half.

How come life didn't cease to exist when the dinosaurs suddenly went extinct?

If the strongest survived the weakest, how can you explain that today after millions or billions of years of evolution, there are still large varieties of weak creatures left?

How can you explain that during all these years of evolution, these defenseless animals were not extinct, but survived, even though they were relatively few compared with the other stronger predators?

Accepting the evolution theory is like somebody that takes you to a huge car lot with many kinds of cars. They will explain how many billions of years ago, there was a simple primitive car, and then after years and years that primitive car evolved into a better one.

This process kept prolonging until today, after billions of years, we have beautiful Cadillac, Mercedes, and a huge variety of other kinds of cars. All without exception came from that primitive car.

Now, if somebody tells you this kind of story, what will you believe?

Would you take it seriously? I don't think so. Right away, you will start to reason that it's just impossible. From common sense, even the most primitive car must have a designer and it was designed for a purpose.

Everybody has the right to believe whatever they want to believe, but if the question comes if this is true or not, all could agree that it's not the case.

Let's take another example:

Suppose you go to a computer show. There are hundreds of computers from the cheapest and simplest, to the most expensive and complicated.

Then somewhere in a corner you see a group of people listening to a speaker.

The speaker is explaining the history of the computer according to his understanding.

He starts saying that millions of years ago, there was this primitive computer and as time passed by, because the right environment that created itself, the little primitive computer started evolving into a better one, and so on. Today, thanks to this long process, we have the most powerful, advanced computer that is capable of doing amazing things.

What will you honestly believe about this explanation?

How about the people that keep saying that this is the truth?

This may be a satisfactory answer for people who are not interested in the truth but in science fiction.

If we really are interested in reality of human existence, we need to get to the bottom of this and find the truth. Because only by knowing the truth, we can take the right decision on what to do about the future.

Going back to the example with the car, it doesn't do any good to us to switch our focus from the real problem that the car has (engine problem) to a different that will give us a false hope. (The assurance from the body shop that we could safely use the car with the small dents on it) From these two examples, we can understand that it's important to look for the truth, and be fair with ourselves because we are talking about our own life.

Again, we can see the importance of positive awareness in our life when it comes to the subject of evolution versus creation.

An important factor that contributed to the formation of this evolution theory was the poor and insufficient behavior of religions at that time.

Throughout history, religions in general, showed too little interest in truth.

Being divided into many fractions and varieties, they were interested primarily in promoting and imposing their own ideas. Also, they competed with each other instead of looking for the common ground and uniting in truth. Most of major religions considered their traditions and customs more important than the truth. So, by trying to promote their own ideas, they contributed to the division among people.

This led to the mentality, that creation could not be possible because those who were supposed to represent the reality of creation, were to busy in promoting their own religious ideas.

This was the kind of environment that Charles Darwin, the founder of the evolution theory, grew up in. He saw the hypocrisy of most religions of his time, and even though he spent some time at Cambridge to get a degree in theology, he turned against religion and started making wrong conclusions. If the religions of his day were hypocrites, then the creation also must be false. Once he started rejecting the process of creation, the only reasonable explanation must be evolution.

In fact, if you take the evolution theory and follow its line of reasoning, it coincides very well with the bible's account of creation. If you replace the word creation with the word evolution, both have the same steps of development.

The only difference is that in the bible it is use the process of creation of: universe, planets, earth, plants, animals and finally humans.

On the other hand, the theory of evolution is used in the process of evolution.

First, the universe came about through a big bang explosion.

As a result of this huge explosion, the planets were formed including the earth and then the most primitive forms of life were evolved into plants, animals and finally humans.

For his time, these ideas were amazing for the many who were against religion. They also were hard to sway the religious leaders. They were being divided in so many ideologies that they weren't able to prove the naivety of the evolution theory.

But, before he died, Darwin recognized that he was wrong:

"I was a young man with unformed ideas. I threw out queries, suggestions, wondering all the time over everything; and to my astonishment the ideas took like wildfire. People made a religion of them."

First, he was not aware that so many people would accept his ideas, but later on in life he realized the potential destructive effect that this might have on the future.

That's why his last words were:

"How I wish I had not expressed my theory of evolution as I have done."

The reality is that this theory did unbelievable damage to humanity.

The communism ideology is deeply rooted in the evolution theory. Also Hitler and his regime used it as a basis for their ideology that German race is superior to the others and lesser breeds should be eliminated. By doing this, we're just following the normal course of nature. And we know the consequences of this kind of ideology.

In the bible, there is a parable of the gardener from which we can learn a very important lesson. The good gardener has sown the good seed. Then over night, the bad gardener came and sowed his bad seed. But then the reapers are not encouraged to go right away and pull out the wicked seeds. When they are small,

Chapter 5. The human behavior.

they are all alike and nobody can differentiate between good ones and bad ones. Only after they grow up to maturity, could a difference between them be made. The same thing happens with ideologies.
They may appear to look pretty, like little puppies, but once they grow up they become fierce and dangerous.

A similar thing happened with the evolution theory.
In that particular time of history, many honest people were fed up with false religions of their time. Trying to fight against them, instead of condemning their falsity, they wrongly rejected the account of creation.
Imagine that you take your car to the mechanic, and not being honest, they charge you more than necessary, and the car still has problems. Then you take it to a different mechanic, the same thing happens, and than to another, and so on.
Now, it's true that this is an unpleasant situation. It's not fair to start fighting against the manufactures of the car as it's their fault, not because mechanics are not honest.
The best thing to do is look for a good mechanic and recognize that the manufacturers have no fault in this. We need to use common sense.
We could spend hundreds of hours debating why it's impossible that humans are a result of evolution. The point I will like to make is, by recognizing the value of positive awareness, we could open our eyes to the most important things of our life; our future. Only by looking for the truth, finding and practicing it, will we be able to fulfill our destiny.
It's important to work, start a family and do other good things but most of all, secure our future.
Someone very appropriately once said:
"Be careful how you plan your future, because you have to spend all your life in it"
It's not enough just to live, it is important to find the real reason for living, the purpose for it. And once we find it, practice until it becomes a habit. Then we can truly say that we are living our life to the fullest.
Today there are many skeptical people who argue about the possibility that we are a product of an intelligent designer because nobody has seen this designer or creator.
For this reason, there is none. Let's again use a little bit of common sense.
We are creatures about five to six feet tall. Right? Yes.
Now, if we look around, even though we are not the biggest of the creatures, we are the most intelligent.
If we compare ourselves with insects or microorganisms, we are giants. But let's start flying one thousand feet in the air. How do the people on the ground look? Most probably, like these microorganisms. Let's go even higher, right to the moon.
How big are we then? Going even further, move out to the solar system. How big do we look now?
Move throughout millions of galaxies and again, how big are we?
The scientific community tells us that all of these planets that makes these millions of galaxies are in a perfect harmony, working like a giant mechanism according to laws of the universe.
The One that designed all those galaxies, with millions of planets and suns, is the same One who designed the earth and the human specie.
Visualize, how powerful that Creator should be, to be able to design and create these galaxies with millions of stars and planets.
Could a simple human being be able to look at him?
Did you ever tried to look at the sun without special glasses? I don't think so.
Then, how are you able to look at the one who created the sun? It's just impossible.
See, this is like a little microorganism that can be seen only with the microscope, wants to see us and understand how we function. Sounds silly, but the example is very similar.
We need to be reasonable in our expectations; otherwise we could end up believing crazy ideas that could have negative effects on our future.

Chapter 5.   The human behavior.

Looking realistic at the way the universe and the nature work, it's reasonable to believe that our earth is like a laboratory in which the human specie is tested for a certain period of time.
Once all the tests are done, *the end* will come.
That's way it is very important to look for the truth and accept it.
The ones that are really looking for the truth, they will surly find it and will change their lives accordingly.
Remember, if the designer of the universe was able to set up and assemble the whole universe and maintain it to function forever, He is able to see your seriousness and guide you to understand the truth, and teach you how to benefit from it.
There is no shame in recognizing the truth.
Would you be proud of the fact that you are closely related to the president of the country in which you are living in? Or are you ashamed of that? The Creator of the universe is much more than that. And He is interested in getting close to everyone. So, it's just a normal thing for us to do the same.
By doing this, we ally ourselves with the Master of the universe. Who could argue with that.
    As we have mentioned before it is important to be realistic about our future, because like it or not, we have to spend all our life in it.
So, be aware and pay attention to the information that will help you financially, improve your family relationships, but more important, become aware of the information that affects your future.
Remember: "You have to spend all your life in it."
We have seen the importance of awareness in our life. As we mentioned before once we become aware of something, we'll be capable of generating a desire toward that particular thing. The next subject for discussing is desire.

2. Desire.

- What the eyes see, the heart starts asking for. -

    What is desire? Well, every moment we come in contact with information from our environment. The more we are exposed to it, the more our level of awareness increases. Then our mind starts to work in finding out which information might be of benefit, or is meeting our inner needs. It automatically triggers an inner craving toward that particular information. The information could be audio or video, something we see, or hear.
    This is what we call desire.
    So, we can say that desire is an inner drive toward something that is perceive as a source of pleasures.
    As the second ingredient to the process of changing, desire is triggered by the kind of awareness we are exposing our mind too. Feeding our minds with positive constructive things, we'll develop positive and constructive desires.
On the other hand, if we keep feeding our mind with negative things and not being aware of their negativity and perceive them as good, the desires that will be triggered will be negative.
    Remember: "Garbage in garbage out"
    So, we can see that we have the choice to control our desires by being selective to the information that our minds are exposed to.
Remember: "If it is to be, it's up to me"
There are two kinds of desires:
A.   Positive desires.

B.	Negative desires.

A. Positive desires.

Let's start discussing about first category: Positive desires.
During our life, we gather many kinds of information, some negative and other positive.
All are forming the foundation of our thinking ability.
Our thinking process is determined by the quality of the information.
What make us superior to any other creatures is our faculty of reasoning and the ability to consciously decide what to do, or how to react in different kinds of situations.
So, it is important to recognize that positive desires have as outcomes positive behaviors, and consciously choose the positive desires over the negative ones.
Because today's society is filled with a variety of cultures and life styles, we can say that there are different kinds of positive desires.

a.	One kind would be positive desires with positive outcomes.

b.	Another kind would be pleasurable desires that look or feel good but have negative outcomes.

a. Positive desires with positive outcomes.

These kinds of desires help us progress and develop ourselves financially, spiritually and in family relationships.
To be able to do this we need to learn to look for information that will trigger these. By doing that, we eliminate most of the potential sources of stress and because nobody ever gets stressed when life feels good.
We start to get stress only when things go wrong and we cannot handle them the way we would like to.
During our life, we gather millions of bits of information that are stored in our memory banks. Also, every day we are faced with new and different situations that our minds deal with.
Statistics show that our reaction to the outside environment is 90% based on instinct, and 10% reasoning.
This means that many times we are reacting instantly without thinking of the new information.
Based on outside stimuli, the reaction could be physical when we go to do something, or it could be as thoughts or desires.
When it's expressed as desires, it is important to learn to examine and control desires before they start to transform into reality. If the outcomes are positive, go ahead and follow the necessary steps to fulfill them.
But, if we realize that the outcomes may be negative, recycle or replace the thoughts or desires with positive ones.
Someone once said:

"You cannot stop birds flying over your, but you can stop them from building a nest on your head."
The same thing happens with our thoughts and desires. We might not be able to stop them from coming, but we can control them, and retain only the ones that will have benefit.

Remember:
"We are not responsible for what comes to us, only to whatever we allow in."

A common problem is that many people do not know how to control their thoughts and desires. When they are entertaining positive thoughts and desires, everything is ok. The problem is, many times the thoughts and desires are negative. When this becomes a habit; it is a bad habit and a major source of stress.
That's why it's important to realize it doesn't matter how bad the thoughts and desires may be, they can be controlled and replaced with positive ones.
Once we replaced them with positive ones, the potential source of stress disappears.
Let's see how the desires are formed.
We can safely say that the desires are divided in two categories:

1. Desires triggered by outside, new information.
2. Desires triggered by our inner, subconscious needs.

Desires triggered by outside new information is our next topic

1. Desires triggered by new information.

When we were born, we could say that our memory was empty. Then, soon as we opened our eyes, we started collecting information, which is stored in our memory banks.
Based on our personality type inherited from parents, we have the tendency to be attracted to some things more than others.
This way, we are building our own personality type on the foundation inherited from parents.
Humans were design with an inner drive toward continuous knowledge that is expressed in a high degree of curiosity.
If we forgot how curious we were as a child, look at our children's behavior and we can tell that they have a high degree of curiosity. They want to know everything. If we want to go some place, they'll want to go also.
Parents want to do something children want to help.
We let them loose in the house and they go all over messing up everything.
They do all of these things because they have a high degree of curiosity.
Of course, they do not realize that their parents do not accept the mess they have made in the house.
They drop that expensive vase, and start smiling because now they have about five or six pieces on the floor. Since its much closer, they can play with it.
They have no idea that this is driving their parents crazy, and start crying, when for an unexplainable reason to them, the parent does not let them have this kind of fun.
More than that, looking at their faces, they realize that they don't want them to have fun. They start to feel frustrated. The next time, they start exploring *new worlds and new civilizations;* for some reasons Dad/Mom gets upset again but this time they were just playing in the kitchen with some *nice toys*. We know that a kitchen is not a toy room, but children do not know this. Everything for them is new, and must be explored. They cannot comprehend why parents get upset when they want to learn more about their environments..
On the other hand, the parents have a hard time understanding why children do not want to be good kids, and stop causing so much trouble.
Year after year, by this kind of *communication,* kids get the message that they should stop *conquering the world* and be a good and quiet person. They observe that when they stop exploring, their parents are happy. So, gradually the kids learn that they should stop trying to explore their world because any time they try to do this, it only results in trouble.
By the time children are old enough to go to school, they form a deep, subconscious fear of the unknown, or of exploring new things or trying new and different ways.
Once they grow up to become mature persons, they'll be very careful to stay and idle in their own position or *comfort zone,* never thinking about the possibility of changing.

In other words, the typical person, one of the 99% of the followers that are working hard to survive, never thinking that they could change for better.

Let me ask you a simple question:

Did you ever ask yourself, how is it possible that when you go to a circus, you see a huge elephant tied up with a small rope; why would the elephant listen to the trainer even though they could break that rope? ?

Let's see how this can be explained:

When the elephant is very young, the trainer ties the elephant with a chain from a strong post and keeps him like that. Now, the elephant of course wanting to wonder around, soon finds out that there is something there that is holding them back. Then they start to pull themselves out of this bondage. Pulling, and pulling and pulling, the chain being stronger does not give up. They keep on pulling, thinking that sooner or later they'll be able to get free.

So, they keep pulling more and more, but after weeks of trying and no success, they finally realize that it's in vain to try to get away. Elephants learn a habit of staying quiet in one place and not try any more to escape because there is no way to break free. Once the habit is formed, the trainer releases the elephant and uses only a small rope. Any time he / she pulls the rope, the elephant is going to obey automatically out of habit, not being aware that this is just a small rope not a strong chain.

Why do the trainers do this?

Because, they know that a very effective way to *train* an animal is to teach habits; once formed, it will last forever. The elephant like any other creature, does not like pain and will do anything to stay away from it. Any time they try unsuccessful to break free, their minds are forming associations between the will or desire to break free and pain.

And once the habit is formed, any time that they want to break free, automatically it triggers pain. That's why the trainer, knowing that with a simple rope, they keep the elephant in control and obedience.

So, this is what our parents unaware of did to us, and also not being aware of, we do the same to our children. This is wrong, it's very wrong, and understanding this reality, we should do our best to correct these mistakes. Otherwise, our kids will fill the ranks of those 99% followers that are spending their entire life working hard to survive; when they could easily change and work smart to succeed in life. Let's take another example:

We are familiar with cars. They are vehicles that we use in our daily activities. Because our life becomes more and more sophisticated, we need to travel often from one place to another: Shopping, work, vacation, here and there, etc.

In other words, the car is the means that help us to enlarge and expand our activities.

When we started to learn to drive, we were taught for the car to move forward, we needed to press the accelerator pedal. Also, when we wanted to stop, we needed to press the brake pedal. Right? Yes.

Now, we could rightly say that the accelerator pedal is the tool that triggers to movement of the car. And for our safety, in order for us to stop the car, we also have a protective system, the braking system.

The system was design as we just mentioned to help slow down and stop the car depending on our necessities. So, we can see that these two systems are opposed to each other. If we want to go, accelerate, but if we need to stop, we have to use the brakes.

Piece of cake you may say, everybody knows this. That's why I choose this example. All of us know these things about cars.

Now, let's see how this example helps in our subject:

If we take a closer look at the way our body functions, it's easily realized that we were designed with the capacity of continuous learning.

In other words, as long as our eyes are open and we are awake, through all our senses our mind absorbs audio and visual information from the environment.

After the information is processed, it goes into our memory and becomes a reference for future decisions that we might have to make.

Chapter 5. The human behavior.

So, we have an inner drive toward new information. This inner drive we might call it desire.
And we could compare it with the accelerator pedal that triggers the movement of the car. The same way our desires triggers our movements or activities.
Also beside this, our body is equipped with a safety mechanism that was designed to perceive any danger and trigger a reaction to stay away from any potential dangerous situations.
We could compare this with the brake system that prevents the car from potential danger by slowing it down or even stopping.
Now, as in the case with the car, both systems are important and one should not eliminate the other. But they should complement each other. The same thing we should do with our body.
When we need to learn and explore new things, we trigger the desire mechanism.
But when a potential danger is perceived; it automatically triggers the safety mechanism.
Now, how far do you think you can go with your car if you for some reasons develop a *strange habit* of pushing the brakes too often? Probably you would move very slowly, if you move at all.
On the other hand how safe would it be if you develop a *strange habit* of always stepping on the accelerator? You would put yourself at a great risk.
So, we all see that we need to balance the two. When we need to go, we step on the accelerator. When we need to stop, we do just that by stepping on the brakes.

Now, let's go back to our example with the little child. Before they start walking, there're flooded with hugs and beautiful smiles, getting all the attention. But once they begin to walk, things start to change.
Born with a powerful desire to know and learn, children explore their surroundings. For them, everything is a new world to be explored.
But, in their conquest, they don't realize that their parents have different opinions. Parents would rather want them quiet, and stay in one place, not wondering all over like a *loose cannon*. So, very soon children start to realize that their desire to explore, are triggering a painful reaction from their parents, who before this stage, would do anything to please them.
Now, when the children finally are able to explore the world by themselves, they find out that a lot of their wants, has a negative effect on parents. These adults seem to be against their exploring desires.
Children just cannot understand why parents don't want them to be happy anymore, because almost everything they do is perceived as bad.
They like to run all over the house, getting into everything. They get a little hammer and everything around them becomes a nail. Hammering then becomes the next logical step. They have so much fun doing this but for some inexplicable reason, parents do not feel the same way. Many times, the children get punished for doing these behaviors.
That's a very interesting behavior from the parents. It seemed to them, that they don't want them to be happy anymore. Inch by inch, their desire to explore diminishes, until the kid becomes *a good kid*.
In other words, the kid becomes a person with low self-esteem. A person who doesn't believe much in progress or individual initiatives. Does this sound familiar? Yes, maybe too familiar. Depends on which side of the *tracks* we grew up.
Many of us went through these kinds of treatments and as a result, we became persons not too much interested in changing our lives for the better. We would rather work harder on the job we got, instead of recognizing that we could do better only by learning something that is better.
So, it is wise to recognize that we need to replace this tendency to have a negative attitude toward change with a positive one. Once we do that, our mind will open to information that will make us aware of how to change.
Then, aware of the possibility of getting better, we'll develop a desire to change. And of course once we have a desire, we will take proper action.
Remember: "A positive desire is born only from a positive awareness."
Always keep an open mind toward the things that have real value because that's the only way to progress.

Chapter 5. The human behavior.

"Desires triggered by our subconscious needs " is our next category.

2. Desires triggered by our subconscious needs.

Even though we might be able to satisfy our physical necessities we have in life, such as eating and drinking, we still have other kinds of needs that are not satisfied by food or drink. These are called *inner needs* and are triggered by our subconscious needs.
Let's see what these needs are, and how they express themselves in our life.
All of us have the inner desire or need to live. And not just live a monotonous life, but as wonderful as possible.
To fulfill these inner desires we *are conditioned* to behave in a specific way. We always want to be happier; so things that might make us happy attract us. On the other hand, we want to stay away from pain, or things that might be the cause of it.
We learned earlier about the two mechanisms, the propulsion and the self-defense. The propulsion mechanism is design to help us to live a joyful life. In other words to identify, search, explore, absorb, enjoy and own the environment we live in. The self-defense mechanism is designed to make sure that in our quest towards happiness, we won't hurt ourselves. It is a protective system that keeps us away from things that might cause us harm.
These two mechanisms continuously generate inner desires toward things that produce pleasures, and also toward things that keep a person away from danger. So, we can say that there are two kinds of inner desires:
   1. Inner desires toward pleasures.
   2. Inner desires to stay away from danger.
Earlier, we discussed these two kinds of inner drives or needs.
We have seen that the inner desires toward pleasures could generate personal needs, and also could generate universal ones. Our personality type determines our subconscious personal needs.
Also we have learned that the inner drives that keeps us away from danger could be determined by the information coming from our own body, or by the information coming from the environment.

Until now, we have discussed positive desires with positive outcome. Now let's go to the second category:

b. Pleasurable desires that look or feel good but have negative outcomes.

This is an interesting way to put it you may say, but if we take a closer look at our problems, failures or other negative outcomes, we might be surprised to find out the reasons for them. We know the truth of the saying:
"Whatever somebody sows, he also shall reap."
Nobody wants negative outcomes, but then why do we get them?
The main reason is sometimes we just do not pay attention to what really is behind things. The reality is many times we do not make the distinction between what we really want and what we think we want.
An example:
Suppose that I am about thirty pounds overweight. What do you think I want? I want to loose thirty pounds. Right? Yes. I really want this. But also I might like to eat a lot. Now, what can I do about this? Well, I need to learn to verify my desires by looking at what kind of outcomes they might produce.

If I like the potential outcome, then I should maintain these desires and reinforce them until they become reality. But if I do not like their outcome, I need to learn self-discipline to let them go, because sooner or later, they will produce the negative outcome that I don't want.

We all are aware that in today's society, there are many kinds of problems.

We have crimes, violence, robberies, and many other negative situations that make life unpleasant.

Where do you think these situations come from?

We learned earlier that when children are born there is nothing negative in them.

Then where do the bad guys come from? Someone once said:

"A genius is made, not born."

If the genius is made, not born, the bad also is made not born. Now, is there anybody that intentionally wants to be bad? Not too many.

If you pay a visit to a jail facility, and ask inmates why are they there, most of them will tell you that they didn't mean to do it. They thought that the outcome of their actions would be different. But, now they realize how wrong they were.

So, what we need to do is learn a habit of verifying our desires to make sure that we will like the outcomes, and then go ahead and fulfill them.

The negative outcomes of certain desires have two important stages that we need to mention:

1. Primary stage.

2. Secondary stage.

1. The primary stage.

In this stage, we have to deal with negative consequences of a particular situation that might be more or less damaging to us. These are temporary consequences. They come and go. Let's take a simple example:

You just got your paycheck, and on the way home you remember that you need to buy yourself some clothes. So without any hesitation, you decide to make a little stop at your favorite store that just happens to be in your way. You need only some small stuff, so it won't take long.

But, once in the store you forget about all the other things. You remember that you also need other items, and after a few hours has passed, with little money left in your wallet, you go home happy.

Once you get home and look at the mail, you remember about the bill that supposed to be paid last month but you postponed it until this month. When the reality sets in, you remember that this will cost you a late payment on your record.

But every body makes mistakes. So, the next time you'll be more careful.

This is a typical example with little negative consequences. But there are others with much more damaging effect.

2. The second stage.

This is a more dangerous stage. Because it has long term negative effects over us.

Let's take an example:

If you are familiar with the bible, you might remember the story of Judas Iscariot.

He had a reasonable desire to prosper. He wanted to change his financial status, so he started thinking which is the fastest way to get a lot of money. In that period of time, thirty pieces of silver were a sizable sum of money, and it didn't require much work.

So, it sounded reasonable for him to get the money this way. This is what he really did. He forgot to check what was the outcome of such a desire. He found out later that he became a

Chapter 5.	The human behavior.

traitor to get the money. Trying to repair his mistake, he went to return the money. When he realized that they wouldn't take the money back, he threw them away. But, even doing this, didn't change the fact that he became a traitor. So he went and hanged himself.

What can we learn from this example?

"It is wise to check in advance what you might become in the pursuit of your desires."

Why is a thief a thief? Were they born a thief? No. Not being careful on what kind of desires entertains them, he / she follows wrong desires, thus becoming a thief.

Why is a criminal a criminal? Because, the means they use in pursuing the fulfillment of their desires, makes them become a criminal.

Both didn't pay attention to the potential consequence of wrong desires. They had to find it out later, when it was too late to change what they had become.

Now let's talk a little about some of these desires, that even though might not make us a thief or a criminal, do have an important impact in our lives.

Many parents because of economical difficulties, or other reasons, have children that spent most of their time outside their parent's presence. This sounds like a normal thing. What's bad about this is the mentality that parents should be parents and kids should be kids. What do I mean by this? Well, the parents should be parents, and the children should be children, but more important parents should also be their child's best friends.

Lately, there exists a big gap between generations.

For some reasons children start breaking the relationships with their parents, and find themselves on their own, not necessarily physically, but emotionally and intellectually. As a result, many parents suffer from not being able to understand why their children have such a rebellious attitude towards them. Well, if we are honest, the major reason is that parents were not aware on building a parent, child relationship. More important, they are supposed to build a strong friendship with their children also.

See, if you want to be in good terms with somebody and maintain a good relationship, it's enough if you make known to the other party the rules and regulations that should be respected so a positive climate would be maintained. But if you want to build a lasting friendship, things are different. Just by keeping a good relationship where everybody follows the rules previously established, is not enough to build a strong and enduring friendship. It needs much more than that. Remember, children don't know how to build a friendship, but they copy and mold their behavior from their parents. They need to be taught how to build and maintain a strong friendship. That requires the first steps to be made by the parents. In other words, parents have to lower themselves to their kids level, and start building a friendship on their kid's terms. The kids were never parents, so there is no way that they could lift themselves up to their parents level and build a friendship according to their parent's expectations.

Being very busy with work and other parental duties, parents neglect to make the building of a strong friendship with their kids a first priority. In their thirst for love and affection, children start to develop friendships with other people, especially peers, unconsciously excluding their parents from their inner circle of friends. By the time they reach their teen years, they realize that they can find faster, easier love and understanding outside of their family circle. Going through their teens, their bodies are also going through important changes; making them much hungrier for love and affection. By not having experience in this new territory, they find themselves the puppets of the entertainment industry that glamorizes violence and loose conduct. Then the parents, observing their behavior, try to advise them in proper directions. But, whom do you think the teens are going to listen to? To these people who call themselves parents where there is no strong friendship between them. Or, to the others whom the children have established a good or even a strong friendship? Well, the reality proves that kids move farther and farther away from their parents, unconsciously building the huge gap between generations. The more the parents try to discipline their children, the more rejection they receive.

The major reason for this is that in pursuit of their personal goals, or to be the perfect parents, many parents miss the most important thing. The foundation of a great parent child relationship is a strong friendship. So, remember the price others are paying for not building a strong friendship with their children.

There is another danger we need to discuss that we call: "The time bomb."
Let's take an example:
We know that some countries use land mines around their borders, or other places. These land mines are like time bombs that are designed to explode when somebody mistakenly steps on them.
Left alone, they do no harm, but when somebody steps on them, they go off; destroying everything around.
For somebody, who is not aware of a land mine field, this could be a potential disastrous situation.
Well, sad to say in today's time, we are faced with many of these kinds of time bombs.
Many that are going off today, were planted years ago. And unaware of, we keep planting others today that will surely go off sometime in our future.
Let's see what these time bombs are, and what can we do about them.
We mentioned earlier that:
"Whatever one sows, they'll shall also reap"
Our life is full of activities, and beside the work we do to make a living; we also have the need to relax. We want to enjoy our life as much as we can.
This is a normal desire and there is nothing wrong with it. Now the way we do that is important. Because, as we mentioned earlier the things we desire might have a positive outcome, or might have a negative outcome.
Now we know that there is a pretty big difference between adding and multiplying.
If we add ten plus ten, it equals twenty.
But, if we multiply ten by ten, the result is much higher, it is one hundred.
Let's see what this has to do with our subject.
Somebody once said:
"If you want to get food from your soil, you have to work or cultivate it, but if you are looking for precious metals, you have to dig much deeper."
When it comes to our desires, it is advisable to check them for their outcome, but it's much more important to dig even deeper to see if any of them have a time bomb hidden.
If that's the case get rid of them, even though they may look harmless now, because they might come back and bite us later.
So, we can use the adding process and look superficial at our desires, or we can use multiplying process and look much deeper into our desires to find out if they might have a negative outcome.
One area in which we should be more careful is, in the family environment.
In many families today, one of the spouses, or maybe both, forget about loyalty toward each other, and start looking in different direction for their personal needs. It might look like there is more excitement with other people rather than their spouse. This looks like a common thing today. If you look at the movie industry, the so-called *new life styles* are seen as something normal because almost everybody does it. You might know the saying:
"The grass looks much greener over the septic tank"
What was viewed, as exemptions years ago, today became the new normal. We take these things for granted, but the reality is that we are paying, and will pay a big price for these things that we take lightly now.
All of them are like these time bombs waiting to explode in the near future. We are wondering why fifty percent of the marriages today end up in divorce. We forgot that we are slowly indoctrinated by today's entertainment, how sweet it is to fool around, to violate others rights to happiness. Also, we find it acceptable that our children to be taught by *the modern day baby-sitter,* that life has no value and violence is an easy way to solve our problems.
We see all these things in abundance around us, and being so use to them, are not aware of their future effect on our children.

They really are like these time bombs hidden under ground, which could have a disastrous effect on the young generation.

So, next time when you turn on the TV, remember what kind of gift you give to your children. Will there be something that they will benefit from, or will it be another piece of a large time bomb hidden waiting to explode in the near future?

We know about the disastrous effect that cancer has on peoples. Did you ever ask yourself why so many people die of cancer? The main reason is that people find out too late about it. And at that time it's too late to cure it, so the only option is to live with it as long as possible. But, if the cancer is detected early in life, it might be treated and cured.

The same thing happens with these *time bombs*. If we are smart enough to detect them early, we could defuse them. But, if we do not pay attention, and let them to multiply, the time will come when we just have no more control over them. Of course, that will result in a negative and unpleasant outcome. Let me tell you a little story from which we have a lot to learn. It's called:

"The little Prince story"

Once upon a time, there lived a king in a distant land. He was the wisest king on his time. And he had a son, a little Prince that he loved dearly. He would do anything for him. Beside his mighty army, the king also had a mighty float of sailing ships.

The Prince loved the sea very much, so one day he asked his father if he might have his own sailing ship to wonder at the sea in a long journey.

"I love you, my son." The king said to the Prince.

"And I will give you the best one."

Then one day, the prince wondering around, found himself in a place where many sailors meet and party. They were having a lot of fun, talking about their adventures at the sea.

The Prince started listening, and soon was very excited of what he saw and heard. So, he made a custom of going and listening about these fascinating stories told by sailors.

Not long after that, he decided to take the sailing ship given by his father and start exploring the seas. And who others than his *friends,* the sailors and storytellers, could be his crew. So, he invited them to go along with him in his journey. All of them started sailing the seas. They had many adventures together. But after a while, his friends started to change their attitude from nice and friendly to rude. Not long after, they took over the sailing ship, and started pirating the seas.

The Prince had no choice, but to submit to them. So, pretty soon, people started to hear that the Prince and his crew became pirates.

The news saddened the king's heart and sent words to his son to abandon his friends and come back.

"Come back my son, come back, come back..."

And even today, people who understand the reality of human existence, can still hear the king voice,

"Come back my son, come back, come back..."

If we take a closer look to the human specie we can see that something similar has happened with us. We left the truth, common sense, justice and love and divided ourselves into different nations, political parties, religions, different kinds of other ideologies, forgetting that we are only one family; the human family. We opened our eyes to new ideologies without seeing the harm that these would produce in the future.

And, now when we are not able to control ourselves, we are the victims of our own mistakes.

And unless we turn back and recognize the real truth, we are destined to struggle and live in misery far away from the potential for which we were designed.

This story of the little prince, should serve as a reminder that we are responsible for our own destiny. We need to be careful of what kind of information we are feeding our mind with.

Because sooner or later, these will take control of our life, and if they are positive and constructive, we will enjoy a positive life, but if they are negative and destructive, this is what we will get.

So, we can see from this information that it is wise to think what effects will it have in the future on the things that we accept and feed our mind with.
Because later on, we will reap whatever we have already sown.
We have discussed in this chapter about positive desires. We found out that these desires might have positive or negative outcomes. Now let's go and take some time with negative desires.

B. Negative desires.

We consider ourselves as good and decent people. Right? Well, if that is the case, why do we have so much violence and badness in society today? We turn on the TV, or radio to listen to news and what do we hear? Bad news. We want to see a movie and what do we see? We see bad news, violence, immorality and any other form of negative conduit.
And many of us are aware of the destructive effects that these have on the young generation. But what do we do about them? Not much. Then what do is expected? It's like somebody gets sick and instead of taking care of his health, does nothing to cure it, and wonders why they have these kinds of health problems.
When children are exposed from infancy to negative things, they get so much use to them and then it becomes a normal thing. Once they grow up, many have no more respect for life, morals, dignity or positive behavior.
And of course that many develop negative desires, not knowing to differentiate between good and bad. Even the vicious criminals were once sweet little children with a bright future. For different reasons, they were exposed to much violence and negativity. Over time, they started changing from innocent children, to rascals, then to teenage problems, and finally to criminals without regard to law and order.
That's the result of not being aware of potential dangers that negative information might have over people.
The subconscious mind does not differentiate between good or bad, right or wrong. Any information that is consciously accepted in our minds becomes a database for our subconscious thinking process. In other words, when we are faced with a decision, the subconscious mind goes in our memory to find out what kind of information is stored about the subject that it has to make a decision on. Based on the information found in memory banks, it makes a decision. So, by not being aware, we are filling our memory banks with negative information that of course will be used in the future. And who is going to suffer first? We are, and also those around us.
That's why it's wise to be careful and analyze our desires by looking at what kind of results they might bring in the future. What happens after we desire something strong enough? We want to make a decision.

3. Decision.

- The ability to choose to act. -

The third element in the formation of a new habit is decision.
After we developed a desire toward something that is wanted, we have to go to the next step in our process and make a decision. To make a decision is much easier said than done.
Today indecisiveness is the root of many of our problems. It's important to realize the role that decisions play in our life. The process of making a decision consist of two steps:

Step one: Theoretical decision.

Step two: Practical decision.

Let's take one at the time to see the role each of them plays in our life.

Step one: Theoretical decision.

We call it theoretical because this decision is made in our mind only. It's like an advance stage of desire. But we are not taking any action to really materialize it. Most of these kinds of decisions go without ever becoming a reality. Reasons for this might be:
1. They might have a weak foundation.
2. We might be the type of person who likes to dream a lot without ever intending to make them come true.
3. We neglect to follow the necessary steps to turn them into reality.

1. They might have a weak foundation

Exposing our mind to exciting new information causes these kinds of decisions, but unfortunately, they don't have a solid root in our mind.
We have mentioned earlier that there are four different personality types and every one is based on our personal needs. We have the tendency to accept and behave toward the fulfillment of these inner needs.
So, also the decisions that we are making are influenced by our inner needs. If the new information is perceived as useful for fulfilling our needs, we'll decide to accept and follow through. But, if the information is not useful to fulfill our needs, even though we will make the decision, it will probably never become a reality. They do not have a solid foundation.
Let's take an example:
John has an aggressive personality, as many others in this category. He has the inner need to be in control. Having a responsible position in the company he works for, he finds himself in the position of not being able to handle his job any more, because it's too much work for one person.
It's suggested to him to hire another manager to take over some of the responsibilities. Even though this sounds like a reasonable suggestion, this idea it's not welcomed by John; who feels that this is undermining his authority. To solve this problem, he'll focus in directing others better. He feels that other employees' behaviors have contributed to this situation. This kind of situation happens quite often: To focus on the

decisions that meet our inner needs, and to be reluctant on deciding towards things that might trigger our inner fears.

2. We might be the type of person who likes to dream a lot without ever intending to make them come true.

Many of us retain a childish behavior of being dreamers with a vast imagination, but with no desire to do something about it. It is a good thing to be a dreamer, because every discovery started with a dream. Anything we do is the fulfillment of our dreams, even though we might not be aware of it.
The best thing to do might be to learn how to direct our dreams toward our purposeful real needs.

3. We neglect to follow the necessary steps to convert them into reality.

Not having a strong root and loosing focus of our dreams of course we will neglect the necessary steps that follow the decision process.
This is seen very often in the family when the parents tell the kids to do something. Many times the kids accept the decision to do it, but soon after that they *forget* and end up not doing it. So, it is recommended that parents be aware that it is not enough to tell the kids to do something. This does not mean that the kid will do it once he says:
"Yes, I will do it"
It's better that the kid understands the reason behind it, what they're going to gain or loose if they don't follow directives.
By doing this, they become aware of the responsibility toward that particular thing and will do it freely.
Now let's discuss about the next step: practical step.

B. Step two: Practical decisions.

These are the real decisions because they are the ones that follow through. Like desires, decisions are divided in two categories:
1. Positive decisions.
2. Negative decisions.
We call positive decisions the ones that have a positive outcome, and negatives the ones that have a negative outcome.

1. Positive decisions.

Everybody would like to make only positive decisions, but for some reason we find out that many of our decisions were not as good as we thought they might be.
It is important to learn to focus on the advantage and reward of good decisions, and view the negative decisions as learning experiences.
The most experienced person has to learn and practice in order to become a good decision maker.
There is no such thing as born wise man or born genius. We all know that success and failure are both learned behaviors.

Chapter 5.   The human behavior.

Nobody was born successful and also nobody was born a failure. In order to increase the percentage of good decisions, we need to learn to practice decision-making process. The more decisions we make, the more experienced we become.

In sports, the best-paid athletes are the ones that excel.

The secret to their success is that they are the ones that practice the most. That's why they score the most points. They become better because they are practicing more than the rest. This is valid in any area of life. The more positive decisions we make, the better we get at it.

Our willingness to make a decision is influenced by the kind of situation we are dealing with. The more the situation meets our inner needs, the more we are inclined to make such a decision. The more the situation triggers our inner fears, the more we'll be reluctant to make such a decision. So, everything boils down to our inner needs and fears. Based on this, one might or might not make that particular decision. That's why it's important to know our personality type and become aware of our needs and fears.

This is a universal law that applies to every human. Be aware of this principal and consciously control it. It will set us apart from the average person, with the ability to master many of the situations that might seem impossible for others.

A major obstacle in our process of making a decision is procrastination. Much harm is done by this negative *quality* that we call procrastination. Somebody in a funny way called it:
"The ability of stopping yourself from making a decision."

Let's examine why we really procrastinate and what can be done to overcome it.

There are a few major reasons for procrastination:

1. Unaware of dealing with a decision that triggers a subconscious fear.

2. Conscious decision does not meets our inner personal needs.

3. Decision "constipation"

1. Unaware of dealing with a decision that triggers a subconscious fear.

Many times we are faced with making a decision. For some reason, we feel an indisposition toward a particular decision, like an inner fear that tries to stop us from making that decision. If this is the case, we need to analyze the decision to see if it's triggering an inner fear of our personality type. Because, as we have learned earlier, always when we are faced with something that might trigger an inner fear, our brain will automatically take us out of that particular situation.

In other words, we get the feeling to stay away or not get involved in it.

Many times this inner fear works for our own good, but sometimes it might be stopping us from developing and progressing in life.

That's why it's important to know us and keep in mind what our inner needs and fears are, and learn to use them as our allies in our progress. This way, we eliminate many of potential stressors.

Many people stress themselves to the max because they want to do something, but are not aware that it may cause an inner fear. So, they work hard to accomplish something that they later find out is a source of stress. That makes them even more stressed. For example, you have a person that is an apathetic or passive type and you try to put them in a position to take the lead and control in a situation. What's going to be the result?

First of all, they won't like to be in control, and even if they'll accept the position, their ability to function, might be limited. This is not because they're dumb or crazy, but it's not something they feel freely doing.

Even worse, their inability to work at the level required by that particular job will be potential stressors.

To avoid procrastination, it is wise to keep in mind that rather to just appoint somebody, we should make sure that the chosen person has the personality type required for that situation or job.
Doing this, they will be able to successfully fulfill their responsibility, without procrastinating or under stress.

2. Conscious decision does not meets our inner personal needs.

Earlier we saw that procrastination is triggered by our inner fears. Now, beside the fears, we have inner needs that unconsciously need to meet.
When these are not met, we are not attracted toward that particular decision and most of the time will not take it.
Let's take an example:
You have an adaptive or assertive personality type. One day your boss at work calls and offers you two choices:
One: To take the manager's place that just called in sick.
Two: To take the place of the secretary from customer service department.
Which one will you choose?
Probably you will refuse the manager position and will accept the other. Why is that?
Well, by now you know that being an adaptive personality type, your inner need is to please others, not to control and make decisions. You will seek the position that will meet your inner needs, and reject the ones that will trigger your fears.
On the other hand, if you are an aggressive personality type, you will never want to accept the secretary position, but proudly go for the manager's position. You will not want to do secretary work, to have somebody tell you what to do.

3. Decision "constipation"

We call it decision constipation, for the simple reason that when this happens, we unconsciously are stopping the decision from forming. Let's see a little about how this works.
Let's say that you want to buy a house. For many to buy a house is a major thing. It requires important decisions to be made for this to be achievable.
Most people do not own a house because they believe they cannot afford it. But the reality is that this is not necessary true. Well, you don't necessarily need money to buy a house (we can substitute knowledge for money).
But, because we do not have the money, we fail to decide to buy it. In other words, we become *constipated* about that decision. We might consider thinking a little bit different:
First, we decide if we really want it.
Second, we need to see what this mean to us, or how important it's for us to purchase it.
Third, we look for the options in getting the money to buy it.
Fourth, we do the necessary steps to get the money.
Fifth, we buy the house.
The decision constipation happens when we change this order of process, by putting the fourth step right in the front. And of course, many times we just don't have the money that will result in our indecisiveness.
Taking one of these steps at a time, in this order, we'll have many more chances to make the decisions about buying the house.
Do we really need the house? That's number one.
To own a house is a privilege. We could deduct the interest paid on the house. We could do any improvements to the house because it is ours, and so on. That's number two.

Well, we may not have money now, but we might sell one of our cars and use it for down payment. Borrowing some money from relatives is another option. Going to a seminar that teaches us how to buy property with no money down is something else we could do or we could look for a house to buy by taking over payments. Government auctions, and government financing could give us our goal. If we keep looking, we might find other ways to come up with the money. That's step three.

If we need to sell the car, go ahead and do that. If we find a special program, go and do anything that is required to get it. That's step four.

Finally, after all those steps are taken, we are in position of buying the house.

So what can we learn from this?

"Where there is a will, a way to accomplish it, is not far away."

"When the student is ready: The master appears."

Now, let's go to the next category of decisions, that is negative decisions.

B. Negative decisions.

Much like negative desires, negative decisions are the result of exposing our minds to negative information, which might result in negative desires; triggering a host of negative decisions. It's like a chain with many links connected together. One holds the other and so on. Most of our negative decisions are made without unawareness. We find out later on about them, when we are faced with the consequences of these decisions. The best thing to do is to learn from them, by seeing them as learning experiences. Looking at negative decisions this way, we become aware that these are not the best decisions, and we'll make sure in the future that we will not repeat them again.

Now somebody might ask:

If we are equipped with such a powerful brain, with such unbelievable abilities, why is our brain letting make so many wrong decisions? Well, understanding the way our reticular activating system works, we can easily answer this question.

This system is designed, among other things, to help us accomplish our goals. It directs our focus toward the things that we need to bring these goals into reality. The problem is that this system does not pass a judgment over the quality of our goals. It doesn't do that; it's up to us to consciously decide if we are setting positive goals or not. It maintains our focus toward the things that help us accomplish them. If we are not careful and set negative goals and desires, it starts to be activated and direct us towards these things, even though these desires or goals will have a negative effect over us. So, this system is very good in what it does, as long as we are careful of what kind of desires we start to develop. But if we do not pay attention, and start desiring wrong things, this system might become an enemy, because we might have to suffer the consequences of some negative goals or desires.

So, until here we discussed the first two steps: awareness and desires. Now, let's go to the next secret that will keep us focused on our goal of becoming a stress free person, Motivation.

Review Question:
What is our behavior the result of?

Answer:
Our behavior is the result of our continuous interaction with the environment that we are exposed to. Based on the existing blueprints in our minds, our subconscious mind responds to the environment through what we call behavior.

Review Question: What are the first three components of creating and changing our behavior?

Answer:
- Awareness; the first step in perceiving what happens around us.
- Desire, once the level of awareness increases to a specific level, it triggers an inner craving or desire toward that specific information or away from it.
- Decision, when the awareness gets to higher level, the desire becomes strong enough to condition us to make a decision.

"We all were born as wonderful human beings. What we are today is what we made ourselves through our behavior."

Secret # 6.

"The hidden reasons behind our actions."

Chapter 6. 4. Motivation.

- You can take a horse to water, but you cannot force them to drink -
- The strong reasons that keep us acting-

    Motivation is among the most important ingredient in the process of forming a habit. Because, even though we make a decision, if we don't have enough motivation to finish; we end up back where we started from.

    If we look at the root of the word motivation we can see that it is made up of two words put together: motive, and action. Motivation is the invisible motive that helps us keep working in whatever we plan to do. It's like a continuous renewal of the original desire until we completely accomplish it.

    There are many ways that people use to motivate themselves or others. Some of them are reasonable, but others are not so, or we can say unfair.

    Basically the motivation techniques have their motives in two major mental states:
1. Fear driven motivation.
2. Pleasure driven motivation.

These two basic motivators could be recognized at a very large scale. In today's world there are two kinds of systems:
Ones that have fear as the basis for the way it motivates people in general.
 Here we find the communist, the totalitarian, and dictatorial societies.
Others have pleasure as the foundation in the way they in general motivate people.
Here we find the capitalistic democratic societies.
The ones that use fear are inclined to keep its people in submission through a subconscious fear of authorities. People are relatively obedient to them out of fear. In this kind of country when people hear about: "Gestapo", or "K.G.B." or "Security forces," or "National guard" or other different names, they are automatically inclined to be obedient out of fear of punishment. This kind of motivation is very efficient, but the side effect is there is no real loyalty toward the government except imposed by fear. Also the level of stress in these countries is very high, because when fear is the only motivation, it results in a high level of stress. On the other hand, in countries where the basic motivation is pleasure, the things are much better. The system is designed to keep its people in subjection because of the multiple possibilities of enjoying life. Also, the side effect is that people are used to taking things for granted, not knowing how to appreciate their real value. In some countries, we have too much *education* and no freedom. In others, too much freedom and not enough *education.*
It would be wise to balance those two in such a way that one will help the other not exclude each other.
Now let's get down to a personal level and discuss the first major basis for motivation.

1. Fear driven motivation.

This kind of motivation is very effective on the spot, but it does have an unpleasant side effect.
In many families today, without being aware of, some parents use this kind of motivation. The child basically conforms up to a certain age. Then, they learn that they have *more rights* than they thought, and start to rebel against their parents. The *battle* between generations starts, and children start to leave their families and try to live separate lives.
The parents are suffering and try any way they can to *help* them out, but in many cases, their efforts are in vain. The real problem is the parents were never taught how to rightfully teach their child and based on their own upbringing they did what they thought was right.
As we see today, there is a huge gap between generations, and not too many are able to find a solution.
The only way to correct this is for the parents to learn how to properly deal with their children. Hopefully, children would respond accordingly.
Many times we expect children to act and behave normal in spite of not having the right model to follow. We wonder why they don't listen and obey us? You may remember the saying:
"Children don't do what the parents tell them to do, but what they see their parents doing"
It is wise that parents make sure that the methods that they are using are the ones that will result in what they want from their children.
The sooner they do this the better, because statistics show in today's world, the tendency of our youth is to drift farther from the way adults are use to.

Some call the time we live in a *New Era*. But if we are honest and try to look in the future to predict how the world will be in next ten or twenty years, we'll be surprised to find out most things will change for the worst, even though technology keeps progressing. We might have a modernized society but the family environment is degrading more and more. Children are not motivated any longer to stay attached to the family; spouses see no reasons to be loyal to each other. And the main reason for this is the fact that they are missing the right motivation to keep them united.

Beside the family environment, this fear driven motivation could be seen in business relationships and also in a spiritual realm. Many people at work are subjected to this kind of treatment and are motivated to work by fear of loosing their jobs. Also in the religious area, there are many religious ideologies that are motivating people to be obedient by fear of punishment such as hell fire, or others.
Many people fall for it and out of fear; they accept and follow set guidelines.
One negative effect of this kind of motivation is that it sets up a stage, when the one who motivates is in a higher position and authority, and the other is always pushed down making them feel inferior.
And once somebody gets used to being motivated this way and changes the environment where there is no more fear based motivation, people just don't know how to react when given a choice. They expect somebody to decide for him / her. It's like a child who never learned to walk, who stayed crippled in bed for ten years, and then suddenly is asked to run. Even though he is ten, he needs to learn to walk first, and then he might start running later.

Another side effect of this kind of motivation is it lowers the level of self-esteem of the person. These kinds of people have the tendency to be more negative oriented.
As a result, they are in a position of getting stressed much more easily than others.
Let's see how we can recognize when somebody uses these kinds of motivations, and how we can deal with it.

Chapter 6. Motivation.

1. When punishment is the result of nonconforming:

In the family:
"Listen child, unless you do your homework within one hour, you are in deep trouble."
"You will be grounded and will be in trouble if I don't find your room clean when I come back home"

How about a more constructive approach:

"I know how much you like to play Nintendo and as soon as you finish your home work, I'll gladly allow you to do play it."
"A clean child like you likes to live in a clean house, right? I knew that, and I believe that you don't want me to ground and punish you for keeping your room messy? So you'll remember to make sure that your room stays clean all the time. Right?"

What has been done here? Basically, we send the same message but in such a way that is more accepted by everybody.
There is no fear of punishment, but instead the children are positively motivated to do what is required from them. Using this kind of approach, we increase the chances to build a positive relationship based on friendship that will result in a better communication.

In business:
"This is the third time you are late, one more time and you are fired."
"These files were suppose to be ready two days ago, if they are not ready today, you will be penalized."

How about something like this:

"You know that one of the rules in our agreement is that all of us need to be at work on time, and we risk the possibility of loosing our job if we keep coming late. So, please remember that we want you to work with us, not work for somebody else."
"Many times we have a lot of work to do in a short period of time, that's why we should keep in mind to do the most important things first, avoiding being penalized for not doing our job within the time required."

As we can see, we send the same message to the employee but in such a way that's more acceptable, without motivating them to do their job out of fear of punishment.

2. When guilt is use to motivate:

In family:
"If you really love me, you will buy me this toy."
"I don't know what's wrong with you, because I told you many times to do this and it is still not done."

How about this:

"I know that you love me, and you know that you make me happier by buying me that toy."
"We all know that some things take more time to be done, but for a smart child like you, this is a piece of cake. Right?"

What have we done? Well, we did eliminate the guilt and motivate in such a way, that the person to whom it was intended feels free to respond positive to our motivation. Proceeding this way, we increase our chances to motivate and communicate with others.

In business:
"Why is it only you who cannot do this job right? Everybody else is doing it right"
"You are always behind in your work. You're supposed to be ready a long time ago."

Let's try a different approach:

"We all know the importance of quality in our jobs. Most of us are doing well on this. What do you think you'll need to bring your work up to the quality required?"
"We know that some tasks take more time than others, and some times we get behind with our work. But when this becomes a habit we need to improve ourselves. What kind of improvement do you think you'll need to make sure that you finish your job on time"

We eliminated the guilt and rephrase the idea in such a way, that the person is more motivated to see reality, and take the necessary steps to improve its working habits.
So, from these examples, we can see that it does make a difference in the way that people are motivated. Using a proper method of motivation might result in a more positive outcome.
In order to do this; we might consider differentiating between an individual and their behavior. We can say that he or she is bad when they keep practicing a bad behavior. But when somebody just makes mistakes from time to time, it's better to look different at them.
We are all imperfect human beings and many times we fall short. This does not necessary mean that we are all bad. As we mentioned earlier, our habits are learned behaviors that could be changed.
So, we might consider to verify and change if necessary, any of our behaviors if they do not produce the results we want.
The right way to motivate is to accept the person in the way they are, focusing in his/hers qualities and clarify to them, what are the consequences of a good behavior and what are the consequences of a bad one. Also, an environment that will motivate them to do the right thing should be created. Once this is done, we recommend them to act in such a way that their behavior will result in positive consequences; and it's up to them to act accordingly.
Now let's discuss a little about the pleasure driven motivation.

2. *Pleasure driven motivation.*

Opposite of fear driven motivation, the pleasure driven motivation encourages a person to do a specific task for a reward.
This kind of motivation is also effective, but many times is a short-term motivation.
The potential side effect is that the person, to whom it's intended, might form the habit of doing things only for a reward. When the reward is missing he / she does not feel that they are under the obligation to do something.
Let's take some examples and see what can be learned:

In family:
"If you behave better this week at school, I will buy you that toy you have been asking for."
"If I find your room clean when I come home from work, I'll let you play with your Nintendo."

Now this kind of motivation works good, and many parents use it but by proceeding this way they need to keep rewarding children in order for them to obey.
We can rephrase the same idea with something more long-term motivation.

"I think that you are smart enough to understand that you should behave good not only for others but for yourself at any place. I have the confidence that you'll remember that and as a proof that I do trust you, I will buy you that toy you were asking me for."
"I believe that a clean child like you, would like to live in a clean room no mater if you play Nintendo or not. I do agree with this and I am proud of having an intelligent child who knows how to appreciate it."
By rephrasing the same idea, we replaced short-term motivation with a longer-term motivation in a way that is acceptable by anyone to whom it might be intended.

In business:
"Unlike other companies, we pay 2 % commission for any sales you make over the minimum required."
"And, if you keep working hard, after six months, we'll give you a raise."

This is a pretty good way to motivate, but it could be improved by focusing in on long-term motivation.

"Our main goal is to maximize your potential and build a habit to be the best salespersons in this line of business. As an incentive to you, we will add 2% commission to the minimum required."
"We are looking for individuals that are interested in becoming top producers in our company. For these kinds of people, we have an incentive program to reward their efforts."

So what have we done here? We redirected the short-term reward to a long-term commitment. Also, we made them understand that we appreciate and reward those who are exceeding in their efforts to excel at what they do.
If we review these examples, we realize it's much better to use long term motivation by teaching them to form a habit of doing things the right way. As a result of their good behavior, they'll be rewarded accordingly.
There is a wise saying that says:

"Do not give a fish to a hungry man, because tomorrow they'll come back for another one, but teach them how to fish and he'll feed himself forever."
For the process of motivation to be properly applied and understood, we should keep in mind that there are a few important factors that build powerful motivation:

1. Emphasize the fact that it's up to us to exceed in our deeds.

2. It is more important to become better and stay that way, rather than to exceed from time to time. In other words, develop a habit of doing the best we can. Like they say: "It's not enough one to know more, he /she must become more."

3. There's always somebody who appreciates good qualities.

4. The best are always respected and rewarded for their efforts.

5. Awareness of the disadvantages or even negative consequences of procrastination, which is the biggest enemy of motivation.

6. Find out the persons personality type and link their inner needs to the motivation in order to accomplish the task.

Now, after we saw the importance of motivation, let's go forward to the next step, and talk about discipline.

5. *Discipline.*

- Staying with the goal until it gets accomplished. -

Discipline is an important factor in the habit-forming process, without it, all other work done previously might be in vain.
We could say that discipline works on two levels:

1. Mental level of discipline.

2. Physical level of discipline.

1. Mental level discipline.

We know from our own experiences, before we could physically accomplish something, we have to plan it in our minds first. After thinking enough about it and considering it necessary, we start to physically accomplish it.
In other words, everything we do starts with a thought first.
The same thing happens with discipline. In order to physically accomplish it, we need first to

Chapter 6.   Motivation.

do it mentally. Now you may ask: How can we do that?
Well it is not as difficult as it may look. There is something called: *mental rehearsal*
In other words: a mental repetition of certain information that we need to learn.
There are many ways to do that. When we were in school, we were taught to do our homework and had many things to memorize.
What have we done? We went home and started studying. We had to read the material many times until we really understood it and started to remember it. Once we understood it and were able to remember and could repeat it to others, our studies were finished.
So what is the key? Repetition. How much repetition? Until we understand it. In other words, repeating in our minds the same idea until familiarity sets in. To do this properly, we need to keep in mind how information that we assimilate is stored in our memory. We can say that there are two stages of our memory:

a. Short term memory.
b. Long term memory.

a. Short term memory.

Let's suppose that you have a computer and you log on the Internet and start browsing.
You find a large variety of information in many areas of life. Now, after you finished looking around, you turn the computer off. What's going to happen with all the information that you previously have looked at? Are they still in your computer? No, unless they triggered your interest and you copied or saved them. If you didn't copy or save, they are not in your computers memory. So, the next time when you want to see the information again, you need to log on the Internet and keep looking until you find the same information. It can be said that the information is in your *short-term memory*. It's gone and not stored in your long-term memory.
But, if you go again on the Internet, and you do copy or save the information on your computer, and as a result it will stay in the computer's memory. Any time you want to review the information, you don't need to go to the Internet to retrieve it, just pull the files from your computer that contains the information. The information is in your *long-term memory*.
This is basically what happens in our brain.
During our life, people see and hear a variety of information.
Some of the information is not important and it comes and goes in our short-term memory. Soon after, we do not remember it anymore. We need to see it again to remember it.

b. Long term memory.

Now, there is another kind of information that is perceived as important and for some reason it's remembered long after a person encounters it for the first time. This kind of information went in our long-term memory.
For example:
We learned to walk and since then it's done automatically. We learned to read, and since then, we can always read. We learned math, and since then can solve any math exercise. We learned about colors, and since then could recognize any color so on. Now, if we look careful at these examples, we can find out that we had to practice for a while to master these skills. If we would try them only once, then probably that we would not be able to remember them later.
Any information that is repeated enough and develops into a habit is going to pass from short-term memory into long-term memory.
And once it is there, people can retrieve it any time when needed.

Now knowing this, we can consciously decide what kind of information we might need in the future and make sure that we learn the information in such a way that it goes into our long term memory.

Repeating to us the information until it becomes a habit, and once placed into our long-term memory, it can be retrieved any time in the future.

This is the mental level discipline, our willingness to work on assimilating information in such a way that it becomes a mental habit.

The physical level is our next topic.

2. Physical level discipline.

When a mental level of discipline is developed, move to the next step in discipline; physical level.

After it's understood on what to do now, we start physically doing it and keep doing it for as long as necessary.

The key is to do it for as long as it takes to become a habit.

Many people start doing things, but after a while they stop. It takes discipline to succeed. As in the mental discipline, the key factor is repetition.

During our life there are many things that is learned and become a habit. Learning to walk, and since then we do it automatically. Learning to ride a bike, we do it any time we want, learning to drive a car, we can drive any time we want, and so many other similar examples.

Resembling mental discipline, the physical one takes practice and we have to do it more than once, until it becomes a habit.

Remember how many times children fall down until they finally can walk?

For some reason, they keep getting up until eventually they stay straight and walk. Even though they are very small, they sense the advantages of being able to walk and keep trying until success. Knowing this, we can consciously set goals to learn habits that are self-important and discipline ourselves in repeating the necessary things until they become habits.

Scientists say that if a person does a certain thing for about 21 days in a row, most probably it'll become a habit.

An important thing that we need to keep in mind is that once we learned a habit of doing something, basically we are half way from benefiting from this habit.

The reason is, even though we might know mentally and physically how to do something, we'll still need to want to choose to do that thing consciously.

It is true that once it becomes a habit, it'll be triggered 90% of the time by our subconscious mind. In some cases when there we have more than one habit for the same thing, we need to consciously choose to do it.

And to do this, we need to attach to it something that is valuable to us; that could be pleasure, or a high moral value. When we do this, then automatically we will tend to choose the one that is perceived to be the most beneficial for us.

So, knowing the way this process takes place, we can consciously set goals to achieve, and follow the same steps so they become habits from which benefits are gained.

After understanding this, we can say that discipline is our ability to keep directing our actions in such a way that they become a habit. Then we consciously or not choose to do them for as long as it takes to get the full benefit.

We need to use discipline in all areas of life. By doing this, we are able to build a better and fruitful life. Also, we avoid many things that might be a source of stress.

It might be very useful if we start to make a priority list of things in life. Many times, by not having a good plan, we find ourselves working hard on things that are not so important. Some times we ignore doing things that are more important. You might know the sayings:

"By failing to plan, we plan to fail"

Chapter 6. Motivation.

"The ones that have no plans, end up working for those who do."
Let's look at a simple exercise to clarify these statements:

Take a piece of paper and divided it in four columns. In the top of the first one you write: *Things that are important, and urgent.*
On the top of the second column write: *Things that are important, but not urgent.*
In the top of the third one you write: *Things that are not important, but urgent.*
And finally on the top of the fourth column you write: *Things that are not important and not urgent.*

Then you start to fill out all these columns with the things that you have to do in your life. After each task using capital letters, you write the benefits or rewards of getting them accomplished. Also the inconveniences, pain and stress resulted from not accomplishing them. Then take a few moments to reason with yourself what's better: To reap the benefits and rewards by doing what's necessary to accomplish them, or can you afford to suffer the consequences of neglecting them. Ponder a little bit upon these facts. Once you have finished the list, make sure that you keep account of their priority and take one at the time and stay with it until it's totally completed. Do not go to the next one unless you have finished the one before it.

Do the same exercise with your daily activities following the same process.

Doing it this way, you can maximize your time and efforts and can see a major difference in your life towards the better.

Once we know which task is the most important, it's wise to look and focus on the benefits that will be attained. By doing this will help make a positive association between the task and the positive reward, which will help us to accomplish it much easier and better.

Doing things that we like is very rewarding.

We have mentioned earlier that our thoughts control our actions and we have the power to control our thoughts. So, it is wise to remember that discipline starts in our mind first, and once we are able to control our minds, then it will be much easier to control our actions.

Also it's important to differentiate between tasks that really have value for us rather than the others that don't. Once we know to do that, we will focus after the ones that have real value for us, and as a result, our life changes towards the better.

Remember the first rule that we mentioned in the beginning:

"The ones that knows the rules of the game can play the game the way they want."

See, our main goal from this information, is to learn how to eliminate stress forever and in order to do that we need to get familiar with the rules of this game.

Once we know them we can really play this game the way we want it and win by learning how to eliminate stress.

Until now we have learned that the first step is to expose ourselves to right information from which a person can see that they do have a choice in their fight against stress.

We are able to do more than manage stress; we're able to eliminate it. Being aware, we go to the next step, which is to develop a desire to get rid of it.

After seeing the advantage of being stress free, we make a decision to do it. Knowing that a desire, without motivation, will never accomplished anything; we look for the benefits we get from this and motivate ourselves enough to keep disciplining ourselves until it's mastered as a habit. Finally, we keep choosing to eliminate the stress by following these steps we learned.

Since we learned that 90% of our reactions are habitual, we have a 90% chance to automatically eliminate the stress from any situation that might have a stressful effect over us. The other 10% of our reactions are the result of analyzing the situation and then reacting to it. Here also we have the upper hand. Becoming familiar with the idea of eliminating stress, we use our reasoning abilities and consciously decide to solve our stress problem by taking the necessary steps required.

Chapter 6. — Motivation.

Now, let's go ahead and discuss an important characteristic that we need to develop to discipline ourselves, Self-control.

Self-Control.

- Knowing when the right time is. -

Self-control is our ability to restrain ourselves from doing something until we consciously decided what's the best way to respond.
In other words, our ability to deal with the events in our lives in such a way that they result in a pleasant environment. It's our responsibility is to recognize the course we should take, and direct our energy toward that pleasant climate.
This requires us to identify what are the things we should be doing, and what are the things we should not. And choose the ones that we should.
Basically, we all have experience in self-control. We do it every day. The only difference is that we are not aware of the importance of applying the same thing to other situations where self-control is badly needed. For example:
Most impatient people still deals very well with self-control but in certain situation only.
When they drive to work, nobody rushes to get there one hour early. They patiently stay in their cars and drive to work. Going home and patiently start to eat, one bite at a time they'll never try to eat everything at once. They take their time. When they shower they never get out only halfway clean. They practice patience and self-control until they're ready; then they get out.
We could come up with hundreds of examples to show that anybody could control him or her and has enough patience to finish what they started.
The only thing is that they are not aware that the same self-control that they used to do these kinds of things, they could use on other more important ones.
In other words, there is no shortage of self-control, but it's a shortage of managing the self-control in a more fruitful way.
Let me tell you a joke to illustrate this point:
Once upon a time more then a hundred years ago, there was a servant that was working for a rich man. The rich man was a nice man, but his wife didn't like the servant very much.
One day in the morning, she tells the servant that she didn't have time to get breakfast for him, so in the evening he will have to eat his breakfast, lunch and also dinner. After a hard day of work our friend comes back and he is invited for dinner.
The rich man had already eaten, so our friend was to eat alone. Knowing that after a hard working day, the servant must be very hungry, the rich mans' wife brings him a huge bowl of yogurt.
The poor man starts to eat and eat, until he filled his stomach with yogurt.
Once he finished, the lady asks him if he would like some more.
"No" he replies, "I ate enough."
Then she comes back and brings him some soup.
"O boy" he says: "let me try to eat a little bit more."
He tries, but very little he could eat. After that the lady comes back, bringing a plate full of barbeque steaks. The poor man almost goes crazy. He looks at the steak, barely touching it, but it's too late, he wishes that he had eaten the steaks first, not last.
The next day in the morning, the rich man asked him if he liked the food last night.
With sorrow in his voice the man says:

"You know, your wife makes excellent food. The only thing is that she does not know how to arrange it. Had she first brought me the steaks and soup, who in the world would still eat that much yogurt?"
This is a funny story, but the truth of the matter is that many times we are like this lady.
We have the self-control and know how to use it, but many times we are not aware that we should use it in other more important situations.
And as result, we might miss a big opportunity, or even put ourselves into a dangerous situation.

If you go and visit a prison and watch the inmates inside, you realize they are well behaved. They are peaceful and look like they are thinking a lot. They do not look bad. They show a lot of self-control. The only reason they are there is they fail to show self-control when it was badly needed. That's why they have to pay a price for it.
They wish to turn back the time so they could control themselves and act differently but it's too late now.
This could be a lesson for us, because now we still have a choice of deciding to manage our self-control.
Remember, we all have self-control, it is not in short supply, and it's our inability to use it at the proper time.
So, we need only to learn how to manage it better.
To better manage self-control it might be useful to understand that self-control has three components: Responsibility, Courage and Consistency.
Let's take one at a time, and see what can we learn from them.

1. Responsibility.

- The ability to respond accordingly. -

Usually, by nature we are used to dividing things into two categories:
Things that we think are our business or responsibility, and things that we think are not our business or responsibility. We do this as a habit, not being aware that the word *Responsibility* has also a different meaning that we might think. If we really want to know what the word *Responsibility* means, we need to go to the root of it. Take a closer look at the word and see that it's made up of two words: Response, and ability. In other words, our ability to respond to a situation.
So, the next time when you are faced with a decision to do it or not, think of it as your ability to respond and if it is, then respond. In case that we do not have the ability to properly respond, it might be better to restrain ourselves, because it might result in a potential stressful situation.
We all have our limitations, and we cannot do everything we want. The more we are aware of this, the easier it will be to protect ourselves from getting hurt and getting involved in something that was out of our reach.
You might remember the sayings:
"Think twice and do it once."
"The tailor cuts his material 3 times and the material is still too short."

All of us respond to our environment in one way or the other. The question is: Do we respond properly to that specific situation? Or, it doesn't matter to us what the results might be.
Well, it should be of our concern the way we choose to respond. Probably it's going to affect us sooner or later. The way we respond to our environment is an important factor in eliminating the potential stressors from our lives.
Remember:
"It's not what happens to you, but what you do with what happens to you".
We could be the ones that through our responses accumulate and increase the number of stressors or reduce and eliminate them.

As mentioned before, we can respond to a situation by reacting under an old and improper habit that will trigger a stressful situation. Or, we can learn new habits that will be triggered in our minds before we

Chapter 6.   Motivation.

start to get into a *stressful situation*. Being warned in advance about a potential danger, we could consciously decide to act in such a way that we are eliminating potential stressful effects.

We all know that once we are into a stressful situation, it's very hard or even impossible to think clearly. The decisions that we make under this kind of state might not be our best. By learning to recognize our ability to properly respond to situations, we can consciously control our behavior in such a way that we might benefit.

       Now going back to self-control, let's ask a simple question:

Do we have the ability to control ourselves? We should, and if we do not, then we could learn how to do that. Why? We are the first beneficiaries, and of course for the benefit of others.

Remember, there is a great difference between people who know how and control themselves and people that for some reason do not know, and are controlled by others, or by the environment that surrounds them.

That's why we have in our society, a small number of people that are leaders; they take the lead and are aware of their capacities. They use them well, and as a result, make it big.

On the other hand, we have the great majority are the followers, who are waiting to be controlled, and depend on others for directions. Not being aware of their own capacities so they could use them for their own benefits, they work for the leaders.

Remember:

"If you don't have plans, you will end up working for those who do."

They stay at the bottom of the society, working hard to survive, not being aware of the fact that if they'll do something about their situation, they could improve their life. From working hard to survive, to working smart thus being able to succeed. Now going back to our question:

"Do we have the ability to control ourselves?" The answer is: "Yes we have."

Let's see how.

       Technology advances every day and people benefit. But what does this really mean? Is the technology advancing by itself? Or, are there people who are using more of their capacities and discovering these new technologies? The high level of awareness of people interested in technology makes it possible for the technology to advance rapidly. Knowledge itself exists already, and based on our interest in it, becomes more available to us. The more somebody is interested in looking for it, the many chances they have to find it. That's way we are taught the importance of setting goals. Once a goal is set, *an order* or *command is given* to our brain to look for that kind of information. Now, the brain as long as it feels that we consciously still want the information; it keeps looking for it. If for some reason, we start to give other commands that override the first ones the brain will stop looking for the information requested. That's why we are taught that once a goal for ourselves is set, it's important to stick to it until it's completed.

       Understanding and believing these important facts, we can realize that the self-control process works the same as any other goal that we set.

Properly understood and followed until it's completed, results in positive outcome.

Misunderstood and done half way, it'll result in frustration and eventually in stress.

Now, let's see what are some of the *ingredients* necessary to master responsibility:

1. Awareness of the positive results out of it.
2. Awareness of the fact that we are in control of ourselves, and our actions will determine the results.
3. Appreciation and love for ourselves enough to motivate us to make the right choice.
4. Appreciation for the rights of others to benefit from our actions.
5. Realization that the well being of all involved should be more important than the well being of one.
6. The rewards come only after the jobs are finished.

Let's take one at the time and see how all these could be accomplished.

Chapter 6. Motivation.

1. Awareness of the positive results out of it.

Most things in life have two opposite aspects. We have black and white, small and big, sweet and sour, good and bad, positive and negative and so on. People have a choice of selecting any of these that might fit certain situations. Some of these are done consciously, and others unconsciously. People have a choice to randomly do these things, or think purposely and choose when it's better to do or not. Knowing this, we can do it purposely, and we can benefit in other areas of life in which we need to improve and change towards better.

In our case, we can use the same freedom of choice to choose to see what is the benefit of learning to use our ability to respond. By deliberately doing this, we highly increase the chances to succeed in what we are planning. We can learn the habit of looking for positive results that we might get from being responsible, and focus on them.

By doing this, we increase the areas of our lives where we can show responsibility of handling the situations with courage and dignity.

2. Awareness of the fact that we are in control of ourselves, and our actions will determine the results.

When we were children, we were taught to depend on our parents, which is a good thing because this is true. But, for some reason, some of us still maintain this depending attitude and many times feel that, what they do and how to do it, depends on others.

Unconsciously they look for others approval when they do something, and are not aware that there childhood time has gone long ago, and they are now the ones that should be in control of their destiny.

Having this kind of dependency attitude, they restrain themselves from exercising their responsibility. That's why it's important to learn to grow up. See, this inner fear of doing it wrong is misleading. When we were children, we didn't have the necessary experience in many things and that's why our parents made many decisions for us, but now time has changed.

Ready or not, we are in control of ourselves and also we are the ones that are paying the price for this.

The major problems come, when we give control to others so they influence our decision-making process. So, if you think that others are controlling your life remember this:

"Somebody will control your life to the degree that you allow them to do so."

Believe it or not, you have the authority to decide to whom, and how much you let them control your life. As a result, you are responsible for the outcome.

If you think that you can be responsible, you'll become responsible but if you think that you cannot be responsible you'll become irresponsible. It's always your choice.

3. Appreciating and loving ourselves enough to motivate us to make the right choice.

We might know the biblical advice:
"Love your neighbor as yourself."
We believe that this is good advice, and we should pay attention to it accordingly.
But let me ask a simple question:
Do we know how much we love ourselves, so we can love our neighbor in the same way?
This question might surprise you, but it's a very valid one. We need to know and appreciate ourselves to the right value, and then do the same thing with our neighbor.

Chapter 6.   Motivation.

Do we appreciate ourselves, our body, our way of speaking and acting, our rights and of course our obligations? Are we doing these things in excess, or are we neglecting ourselves because we're too busy to please others?

By learning to have a balanced view of the love for ourselves, this will create motivation for us to develop our ability to respond to the outside environment accordingly. You may know the story about the goose that lays the golden eggs.

For the goose to lay a golden egg everyday, the goose has to have care. As a result, the goose is able each day to reward its owner with a golden egg. By neglecting the goose, we are jeopardizing the source of golden eggs.

4. Appreciate the rights of others to benefit from our actions.

What do you mean? There is no such thing as a *free lunch* somebody might say.
Well, it depends on whom you ask. We know that each of us is responsible for our own well-being. Now, let's pay attention a little to what happens continuously around us. Let's see if we can learn a lesson from our *Mother Nature*. When was the last time when you paid anything for the sunlight that you daily enjoy and benefit from? Or for the rain that cleans the air you breathe, make you flowers and vegetables grow so beautiful? For all the nature's beauties that you enjoy every day or when you go on a vacation? We continuously benefit from many things that are taken for granted. We receive them as gifts, without having to pay for them. Isn't this a wonderful privilege? What's your opinion about *Mother Nature* that supplies us with all of these things? Would you say it's a kind and generous person? Yes, of course. If we show similar qualities toward others, how are we going to be viewed? That's a good feeling to be perceived as a kind and generous person. Then, remember:
Others perceive you by benefits that they enjoy from your actions.

5. Realizing that the well-being of all involved is more important than the well-being of only one.

What would you think is more valuable: A complete car, or some of its components like the engine or transmission or any other part? Even though each part has its own value, we can recognize that the car as a whole is more valuable than any of its parts. Well, we are living in communities that involve other individuals. Our family is a community. Our work place is also a community. Our neighborhood is also a community and so on. If that's the case, it's just fair to understand and realize that we are responsible to a certain degree, not only about ourselves, but also for other members of our community. Thinking this way, we are able to better exercise our ability to respond to any situation or event that we have to deal with daily for the concern of all involved.

6. The reward comes only after the job is finished.

Now, let's talk about the next ingredient that keeps our desires alive, because as we have learned, there is a positive sweet reward, once we finish the job.
It is important to always have in mind the reward, because this will be a powerful motivation for us to stick to the job until it's completed.
Remember, our brain makes any decision based on the two inner drives: Toward pleasure, and away from pain. Associating in our minds the objective we desire to accomplish, with the feeling of getting rewarded for doing it automatically, will increase our inner drive to complete this.

Chapter 6. Motivation.

One day I was talking to a friend, and he was telling me that his job was getting harder, and he lost the motivation to do it. As a result, he started having a hard time in dealing with this. We were walking in a parking lot, and there were many cars parked next to each other.
Looking at the row of cars in front of us, I told him:
"How hard is for you at your age, to go under these cars, and start crawling from one end to the other?"
"That's impossible he said. I will not be able to do that; it's too hard for me."
Then I turned to him and smiling said:
"What if at the end of the cars, there will be a briefcase with a million dollars?"
"Would you do it?"
"Of course I will do it, anybody will."
See, I said, the bottom line is not really if you can or not, but if you have enough strong motivation to keep your desire alive until you complete it.
That's what you have to work on. You might consider looking at your job from a different point of view. Once you change your point of view, or your attitude towards your job, it'll become more pleasurable, and you could accomplish it better.

Remember that during our past, we have associated negative feelings by the expression, *hard work*. When we have a job to do, and we call it *hard work* we basically bring back that memory and of course that we start feeling that negativity that was previously attached to it in the past. Looking at the job from a different point of view, the benefits or the rewards for having it, things will be different. When we think this way, our brain will trigger a memory about benefits and rewards. Then we'll start feeling good, motivating ourselves to finish the job soon, so rewards can be enjoyed.

By having the right positive attitude towards the rewards that comes from getting the job done in time and properly, we are supplying ourselves with enough energy to take responsibility, and accomplish goals that are being set. Seeing things from this point of view, we will eliminate many of potential stressors that might otherwise have a negative effect.

Proper understood, responsibility will help to eliminate another category of potential stressors. So, let's focus a little bit on our personal life.
By interacting with other people, many times we feel that others do us wrong, and as a result we are going through stressful situations. Sometimes the more we try to repair the situation, the worst it gets. Properly understanding the role that responsibility plays in our life, we could eliminate these potential stressors. Let's see how it can be done.
An important thing always to remember is the fact that we and only we are responsible for our feelings. Most of us are use to looking for outside factors that determines our feelings.
We were wrongly taught that the outside environment is responsible for our feelings.
What do I mean by this? We commonly accept the idea, that around us life is full of stressors that might have a negative effect over us.
Getting used to this idea, we tend to blame the environment for our feelings, and try to change it, so it might cause us pleasure instead of pain.
There might be nothing wrong with this, if the source of stress is really the environment.
But the truth of the matter is, that environment has little or nothing to do with our feelings. We decide consciously or not, to feel the way we do. Eleanor Roosevelt once said:
"No one can make you feel inferior without your consent."
Also, one of the greatest American presidents, Abraham Lincoln said:
"People are as happy as they make up their minds to be."

Upon deciding to give a specific meaning to the environment, the brain will bring from its memory associations from the past with that particular situation.
And when to these memories were associated negative feelings, unconsciously we feel these negative feelings again.
Not being aware of this, we blame the environment for our negative mental state.

So, by understanding this reality, we can start to learn how to remove these negative associations from past experiences and also learn to consciously decide how to feel about these situations.
Understanding this important fact and acting accordingly, we are eliminating potential stressful situations, that otherwise might have a negative effect.
Remember, there isn't anything in the world that could force you to feel negative, unless you decide to do it, consciously or not. Basically, we are responsible for our happiness. If we are not happy, the first place to look is to ourselves.

Another important factor that we might keep in mind is the realization that there is a big difference in outcome between wanting to be right, and wanting to be happy.
If we are the kind of person that always want to be right, we are setting ourselves up for stressful situations. We'll always find people that might strongly disagree and many disagreements will result in stress.

We live in an imperfect world, and we have to deal daily with imperfect people. Everyone is looking for their own good, and less people are looking for the truth in any situation.
Not being aware of this, we are going to put ourselves in stressful situations, because there isn't any way to act perfect in an imperfect world.
 The best thing to do is to learn to change focus, from wanting to be right, to wanting to be happy.
If we realize the advantage of wanting to be happy, rather than right, we will drastically reduce the chances to encounter stressful situations.
In trying to do this, it's useful to remember, we'll never accomplish with vinegar what we could accomplish with honey.
Now, let's talk about the second ingredient of self-control, beside responsibility, courage.

2. *Courage.*

- Letting go of fear. -

As a part of self-control, courage plays an important role in our life. Let's see how we can define courage:
We can safely say that, courage is our ability to change from an idling state, into a more active one towards a specific goal. In other words, to get out of the normal conformity or comfort zone, and accelerate towards a goal. Basically, we all have courage.
The problem consist in our ability to manage it in such a way that we could fully benefit.   Let's take an example:

Suppose, we drive on the highway at 65 miles/hour. From the opposite side are other cars coming at the same speed. So here, we have two automobiles coming toward each other at a combine speed of 130 miles /hour. And what is separating them? A double yellow line that can be crossed over in a second.
Did you ever stop to think how much courage is required to do this? Well, it takes a lot of courage to do that. But why is it done? We train ourselves to stay on our line, and we are assured that even though the danger is very close, we just pass by it, and most probably nothing is going to happen.
 Even though we occasionally hear about a head on collision, we still have the courage to drive. We can think of many examples to illustrate this. The point is that like any other ability, we need to manage it the right way, so that we can benefit. The major problem that exists today, and is stopping people from exercising courage, is that because of an old habit of looking at it the wrong way thus determining many not to exercise it properly.
Courage requires action, and action means change.
And we were wrongly taught that change produces stress. If that were the case, why in the world would somebody do something that they know will result in stress?

So most people prefer to be inactive, or idling in their comfort zone, instead of having courage and doing something to change their situation.

The truth of the matter is that not any kind of change produces stress; it only raises the level of awareness.

When we talk about things, not people, we can say any change produces stress, but in our case the situation is different. Being aware of our own existence, we have the faculty of giving a meaning to the changes that affect our body. If we call them stressors, they will become stressors, but if we call them different than stressors, they'll not become stressors. So, it's up to us, to want to be stressed or not. If we are honest and look at the environment, we might consider it a source of pleasure because its known that nature makes us feel good.

That's why we all are anxious to take a vacation to relax and enjoy nature.

The stress starts to bother us, when some of the elements of our lives get out of control and feel that we cannot handle them any more. That's when we start to associate negative feelings with these particular elements, and as a result we start to feel stressed.

When we face new changes, our brain starts to compare new information with old ones from memory. Once a match is found, the brain brings it to our conscious level and we remember these past situations. But, because in the past we have associated a negative feeling to these particular situations, automatically we will start to feel the same feelings that have been previously attached to them.

That's the real stress that is felt, not the new situation. This is the truth that people today are missing. Because of this misunderstanding, many people are mismanaging courage, thinking that by bringing change, it also brings us stress.

Take a closer look at this information, because you could gain a great benefit from it. Stress basically is not the *stressor* itself, but the negative meaning that we are presently attaching or have attached in the past to these changes. And we have a choice to do this.

Take courage and learn how this works properly, and by doing that the sky is your limit.

Now, after we learned about responsibility, as the first component of self-control and courage as the second, let's see about the third component; consistency and persistency.

3. Consistency and Persistency.

- Positive "stubbornness." -

In order for us to manifest self-control, we need to be aware that we are responsible for doing this. Once we are aware, we need the courage to take action.

After we get enough courage to do it, we need to be consistent in doing it, so the process of self-control is completed. Let's see what consistency and persistency are.

We could safely say that it is an ability to repeat the same thing until the particular goal is accomplished. In other words, staying with the task until is completed. Consistency has to do with staying with the same task and not deviate from it. Persistency has to do with the length of time required to stay with the task until is completed.

This is very important, because we all know that if we just start something, and do not finish it, it'll have little or no value. We've just wasted our time and energy with it.

In order for us to be consistent, we might need to understand the way this works.

We could say that it works in two stages:

1. Theoretical stage.

Chapter 6.   Motivation.

2. Practical stage.

1. Theoretical Stage.

In this stage we learn, and are convincing ourselves that we need to do this to be really consistent.
This is very important because, unless we truly believe in our hearts that this is true, and the need to do it, we will not be able to keep doing it. The length of the persistency is related to the degree of our belief that we need to do it. We might know people who have the custom of saying:
"I know, I know" even before you have finished what you were about to say. Then when they are in the situation to do what they were required, they found themselves going:
"I don't know." And their ability to do it becomes close to zero. Why is that? Because, they didn't theoretically understand it properly. They rushed to go to the second stage of practical doing it. They found them unable to be persistent in that particular situation. , The more we learn theoretical, the easier it'll be for us to do it practical. It's like any other task that a student must learn.
If the teacher gives them some homework to do, let's say learn a song, which student do you think will know the song better? The one that reads it once, or the one that reads it five times? Of course the one that reads it five times with the intention of understanding it?
The same thing happens when we learn to be persistent. Once it becomes familiar and we understand it, then we can practically do it.

2. Practical Stage.

We saw from the first stage that the more we understand it theoretically, the easier it'll be to do it practically. By practical stage, it means the action itself that repeats itself many times over until that particular goal is achieved.
This stage also is important, because unless action is taken action, we didn't accomplish it. Remember the biblical advice that says:
"Faith without works is dead in itself."
We basically all have this ability, but like courage and responsibility, we might need to work on managing it. Let's take an example:
You might have heard about traffic jams, especially early in the morning or afternoon towards evening. Do you know why we have traffic every day, except weekends? Because there are thousands of people on the roads, going to work exactly at the same time, every day. They are driving to work in traffic every morning, and then back home in the evening. They do it consistently every day without question. They might not like it, but they surly do it. There are many other examples in which people show consistency.
So, what we basically might need is to learn how to manage it better.
By properly understanding these two stages of consistency and persistency and the need to better manage them, we could apply them in various activities. Soon, we'll realize that we are able to achieve many other things, much faster than before.
By doing that, we are exercising a self-controlling attitude toward the environment, and as a result we can eliminate many potential stressors. In the past, these had a negative effect over us, because we weren't able to properly control ourselves.
From past experiences, many times after a person did something wrong under stress, they realized that they were suppose to know better. They had to control themselves to avoid a particular situation. This is what we are learning here: To build a habit of better managing the ability to control ourselves. Once we have this habit firmly implanted in our mind, every time when we are facing a situation that requires self-control, the brain will trigger this habit in our conscious mind. We will remember that self-control is needed.

Chapter 6. Motivation.

This will happen before we get into a situation, when the mind is clear, and we consciously make proper decision. Let's take another example:

There are two drivers: One has one year of driving experience, and another just got their license, with no experience at all. Whose reactions do you think are more proper in a difficult situation? And why? Well, we all should agree that the one who has more experience could react better, because they have driven many times more than the one that just learned how to drive.

He / she had more experience in controlling the car, and could understand the road condition much better and how to react to them. Does this mean that the other driver cannot become experienced? Not at all.

By driving, they could get enough experience to properly handle the car. In no time, they'll be able to master the ability to control and use it for their own benefit.

So, we have seen the importance of learning how to master self-control in such a way that we can properly deal with any situation.

We understand that we can do this, by being responsible for our actions and feelings, and by manifesting courage and consistency.

Going back to our main subject from this chapter, we realize that it's possible to direct the flow of information that enters our mind and channel it in the direction of our planed goals. Once we have learned and do it as a habit, the response to the outside environment will change dramatically. We will stop being the victim of our environment, and we'll become the ones that control it toward our goals.

It may sound complicated but actually is not difficult at all. We basically are doing this every day but with other things, not with our purposed goals. Let's take an example:

Most people have a job, whatever it is. They go to this job every day and once there, obey all the rules and regulations that the job requires without question. Why is this done?

The first time when we got the job, people disciplined themselves.

They were taught that if they want to keep this job, these are the requirements. They have learned that at work, there is a certain behavior that is permitted. Their minds should be preoccupied with things pertaining the job.

A person could not come to work and start thinking and doing different things that wouldn't help to do the job. During this time when they are working, they focus their attention and energy towards the purpose of the job. People know that by acting this way, they could keep the job, and be recognized as a person who is doing this job properly. Appreciating the value and importance of the job, they have learned and formed the habit of respecting the job rules, knowing that only by obeying them there is a benefit.

So, the same principle can be relevant in our case. We need to stop letting the environment control our thinking, and start being selective in information that we get. Being selective, we eliminate many potential stressors. Also by learning to give the right meaning to information that we need to accept, we also reduce the potential stressors that otherwise might affect us. Basically it's just a matter of choice. The major problem is, that people are not aware that they have a choice. That's why we need to learn, and update our thinking ability with right information about this subject.

Remember, all over the world people are taught that change produces stress, and our inner inclination is to stay away from change.

But also remember what we have learned earlier, that this inner inclination is not a natural one, but come from many rejections we get when we were children. Even though we are adults now, we still have these fears of change in our subconscious mind.

So, it is up to us to decide to take control of our life, or like before, let it be controlled by the environment.

Remember:

"If it is to be, it's up to me "

"The one who knows the rules of the game, plays the game the way he wants to"

Now let's go further and talk a little about the next two secrets, the two major mechanisms that each of us is equipped with.

Human beings were designed with conscious minds whose priority is to identify, explore, absorb, understand, enjoy and own the environment that they are living in.

We call this: "The Propulsion Mechanism."

At the same time, in order to do this, we were designed with another mechanism to protect us from any kind of danger that we might face during our life.

We call this: "The Self-defense Mechanism."

Let's take one at a time.

Review Question: What is the fourth component of creating and changing our behavior and the driving forces behind it?

Answer:
- The fourth component is motivation that usually is driven by fear or pleasure.

Question: What is the fifth component of creating and changing our behavior and what's behind it?

Answer:
- The fifth component is discipline. The factors that dictate it are: Self control, responsibility, courage, consistency and persistency.

"Through these five steps, awareness, desires, decision, motivation and discipline, we can keep ourselves slaves to the merciless environment, or we can free ourselves from the bondages of stress."

Secret # 7.

"Who's behind our inner drive for happiness and pleasures?"

Chapter 7. The Propulsion Mechanism.

-The cravings of your heart-

As we have mentioned before, this mechanism has the role of identifying, exploring, absorbing, understanding, enjoying and owing the *environment* we live in.
This means that we have the inner desire to know and experiment with new things. We also have the inner desire to look for things; situations and people that make us feel good and happy. In other words as many specialists have put it, we have the inner desire toward anything that brings us pleasures.
Being equipped with the propulsion mechanism it creates in each of us an individual inner need to fulfill a specific emotional quota each day. It's just like a bank account in which you have to make daily deposits. When the deposits are insufficient, there's the risk of overdrawing. To be able to function properly we need to have a specific amount of information to feed our mind with, which of course will create the quota of emotion.
Most information that we are feeding our mind with is negative. From this we can conclude that we are making negative deposits in our *bank account*. As a result, one feels negative emotions and stress. People make these kinds of negative deposits daily and aren't aware of this. The stress that is encounter daily is nothing else but the result of negative deposits a person is *saving* in memory banks.
By being aware of this, it's realized that's the wrong thing to do. Instead of making wrong negative deposits, we educate ourselves in feeding our mind with the right kind of information.
The first time when we heard about stress, a new *file* was opened in our memory. During our life we have deposited all the related information about stress in this *file*. Guess what is the dominant idea is? Stress cannot be eliminated.
What kind of *blueprint* unconsciously we have made about this *file*? One that says stress cannot be eliminated and. Having this kind of *blueprint*, all behaviors are going to be directed by it.
Now, in order to learn how to eliminate stress, we need to open a *new file*, with a totally different name, and fill it up with information that helps accomplish this. Of course a new *blueprint* will be formed. The new information being superior to the old one will create a superior *blueprint* that's going to direct our behavior in such a way that stress will be eliminated. This will come from inside out, not from outside in. Then the propulsion mechanism is going to push forward in exploring more of this subject until we have completely benefit from it.
We have learned earlier about the role that our habits play in our life. We mentioned at the beginning of this chapter that the role of the propulsion mechanism is to identify, explore, absorb, understand, enjoy and finally own the *environment* we live in.

Chapter 7. The propulsion mechanism.

So, the end result of the activation of this mechanism is ownership of the *environment*.

Now, this *environment* could be: things we like, people, (spouse, children, relatives, friend, etc.) situations or events, or even the environment itself. Beside all of these, there is something else that qualifies as environment, our own *habits*.

Once we fully developed a habit, it becomes part of us. We own it, and of course we wouldn't like to lose it. The problem occurs when we form negative, bad or harmful habits. They too become ours. And unconsciously we live with them not being aware that they don't bring us any pleasures, only discomfort and pain.

Now, let's go forward and see how the two levels of this mechanism work, the "Conscious level" and the "Subconscious level"

A. The Conscious Level.

The conscious level of the propulsion mechanism starts to develop after a child is born. Basically it is part of the conscious functions that each child starts to develop in the first few years of life.

The conscious level of the propulsion mechanism has the role to continuously looking for things, situations, events, or people that help us to be happy. We call these *wants* or *desires*. People want to have nice cars, big beautiful houses, and other luxurious things. Most are under the impression that if they get these things they'll be happy. Don't get me wrong, they do play an important role in happiness, but they're not the most important ingredients in our happiness.

Actually, happiness is an end to a means. To be happy, we first have to consciously identify, explore, absorb and understand and own the *environment* we deal with. Again by *environment* we mean everything that surrounds us: nature, places, people, events or situations.

Now, if each person is consciously looking for things that drive them toward happiness and positive feelings, why is there so much pain and sorrow around. ? Most of us are not aware of how our mind works, and many times choose to explore and absorb information that don't result in happiness and positive feelings. Instead the exact opposite; pain and sorrow. Once we started to identify, explore, a particular kind of information, like a roller coaster, our minds unconsciously starts going through all the other stages. The results of this process are the emotions that our body feels either as positive or as negative feelings.

We have the ability to use free will in choosing to accept or reject any information from the environment. Knowing this, it becomes our responsibility to learn to differentiate between the kinds of information that we decide to absorb. Not any kind of information will result in positive feelings or pleasures that a person seeks.

This is why we have so many problems with stress today.

Just like happiness, stress is also an end to a means. People have to do something specific to stress themselves. Stress doesn't just happen for any reason. No, people are the ones that *work* hard to create it. Of course we might not be aware of this important fact, but we do it to ourselves. We are the creators of our happiness, but by the same token we also are the creators of our stressful *environment*. In order to get stressed, a person have to look at things, situations or people and interpret them as negative, bad, painful etc. Many do not mind *working hard* at this. There are so many reasons to justify behaviors.

"Our job is too stressful." "Dealing with family life is too stressful." "Balancing the checkbook is too stressful." "The situations I am going through are too stressful." "Dealing with these people is too stressful," and so on. Nobody ever says life is just like a beautiful rose. But the reality is that when it comes to stress, we are the creators of our stressful *environment*. Not knowing, or being aware of the way the mind processes information, we are absorbing information that we interpret as negative. Many of us give a negative meaning to many bits of information, and as a result it becomes negative emotions or even stress.

Being equipped with this propulsion mechanism, which continuously generates inner desires to explore, identify, absorb, understand, enjoy and own the environment, we are faced with the responsibility of using free will in choosing carefully what kind of information our mind is focusing on. As we all see, there is too much pain, sorrow and stress and most of these are the results of focusing in the wrong direction.
Mark Twain once said:
"I have lived a long life, with many problem and tribulations, most of them really didn't happen."
So, we can make many things happen, and if we are not careful and selective with the information we are absorbing from our environment, we might be the ones that are creating and maintaining a stressful *environment*.
Now let's go and talk a little about the next subject: the subconscious level.

B. The Subconscious level.

To better understand the difference between the conscious and the subconscious level of the propulsion mechanism let's consider an illustration. We know what an airplane is. It is very complicated machinery that can fly, and passengers are transported from one place to another much faster than they could with an automobile. We also know that there are people with specialized training who are able to control and fly these planes. They're called pilots. More than that many of these airplanes are equipped with another kind of pilots. These are not human pilots, but computerized equipment that is able to fly the airplane. We call them autopilots.

Both, the pilots and the autopilots have the ability to fly airplanes. The pilots fly the airplanes consciously. They are continuously aware of what happens around them, and based on the information gathered, a conscious decision on how to maneuver the airplane is made.

The autopilot by being a computerized machine, makes decisions not on conscious awareness of what happens in the environment, but on the program already stored in its memory and new information obtained through its sensors. The autopilot constantly receives information from the environment that is analyzed instantly and compared with previous information that was already stored in its memory and a decision is made. All of this happens in a split of a second.

The pilot is in control of the airplane all the time. But there are some exceptions. For example, if for some reason, the pilot is not in control of the airplane, the autopilot takes over and controls it until the pilot turns the autopilot off. Another exception is when the pilot turns the autopilot on, to relax; not being under obligation to control the airplane. The autopilot dictates how the airplane is flown.

Going back to our subject, the conscious level of the propulsion mechanism is the pilot, who consciously flies the airplane. The subconscious level is the autopilot. When we use our conscious level of our propulsion mechanism we generate what we called *wants*. On the other hand, when the subconscious level is used, *inner needs are generated*. These needs come from inside us and have a strong influence over our behavior. They are almost uncontrollable.

Chapter 7.   The propulsion mechanism.

Because these inner needs keep passing from the subconscious level to the conscious level they create what we call habits of thinking.

As a general rule, we can say that the conscious level controls our behavior, but when people do something as a habit, they basically are switching the control from conscious level to the subconscious.

The subconscious inner needs are manifesting themselves in two ways:
1. As subconscious personal needs
2. As subconscious universal needs.

Now, let's consider our subconscious personal needs.

1. Subconscious Personal Needs.

-What makes each of us unique? -

If we take a closer look around at things that are not man made, commonly called *Nature* or *Universe*, they are functioning together like gigantic machinery that continuously follows certain specific laws and regulations. The basis of this machinery we can say that are four major qualities that are expressed by its *designer* throughout nature and the whole universe.

One of them is power, another is wisdom, the third one is justice and finally the fourth one is kindness or love.

What do I mean by this? First of all, for somebody to be able to set up such a complex universe, with millions of stars, that person must be very powerful. We also learn from science discoveries that this universe functions like a perfect watch in which all the planets follow strictly their own orbit.

On earth, the nature's laws all work perfect and in harmony. This requires a lot of wisdom from the One who designed and set them up.

Beside the power and wisdom we also can see that all of this complex giant mechanism is built in a just and fair way. There is nothing in the nature that is unjust or unfair.

Everything in nature is built to complement each other, and because of this we are able to enjoy our life here.

We know that out of all the creatures on this earth only humans have the capacity to be aware of their own existence. Many scientists realized that people were designed with a life span much longer than what we are experiencing. For some reasons our life span is much shorter than should be. By looking at the way our body is designed, anybody could see that people should keep on living and not die at all. The purpose of nature was designed basically for our enjoyment. None of the other creatures could enjoy the nature to such degree like humans can.

What would you think about a person that comes to you and gives you a huge home for free? The house is fully loaded with all the necessary things for your enjoyment. Free rent, free heater in the winter, free air-conditioning in the summer. A large variety of foods, all free, and beside these a beautiful garden with anything that you could imagine. All of these for free, plus many others. Would you say that this person is very kind and good to you?

Well, if we look around us, this is what we exactly get for free. The huge home is our earth with all the vegetation that grows from the ground. The sun to keep us worm, but not too hot, so we might die. Each year, we have a cool and snowy winter to refresh our souls, a warm spring when all the flowers blossom and then a beautiful summer to enjoy the beaches, the lakes and forests during our vacations. The autumn with the falling leaves and all the fruits and vegetables ready for harvest. We have all these plus countless other, all for free. We have a big and generous *Mother Nature* that provides all these free of charge.

If we want to be realistic and look around at the beautiful nature that surrounds us, we have to recognize that whoever created these, did so with a positive intent in mind. We are the only kind of living creatures that are able to comprehend, feel, and enjoy everything that surround us. From the beautiful smell of a tiny rose, to the majesty of a night full of stars.

So we can recognize these four major qualities that are the basis of this giant design that we call our universe.

People also have these four qualities within themselves.

Based on our development, these qualities are more or less visible. All the other qualities a person poses derive from these four. The desire to power is important to many of us. Some of us spend years and years trying to show wisdom by making new discoveries. In other words, we put our wisdom to work.

People want to make sure that justice prevails. They also build sophisticated systems of justice that has the intention of establishing justice for all, even though sometimes it needs improvement.

Finally, more than anything else, we all have this quality of love. We love dearly our spouses (at least on the honey moon), children, relatives, pets and so on.

Based on this understanding, we can say that there are four major personality types:
1. Aggressive personality type.
2. Assertive or adaptive personality type.
3. Analytical personality type.
4. Passive personality type.

There are more than six billion people on the earth, everybody no matter what nationality they are or where they live, has one of these four personality types as a dominant.

In other words we can divide the entire world population into these four categories of personality types. Being equipped with all four one of them is more dominant than the rest.

We mentioned earlier that humans function on two basic inner drives:

The inner drive toward pleasure, or things that are pleasure producers generated by the propulsion mechanism.

The inner drive away from pain, or things that are pain producers generated by the self-defense mechanism.

Since we were designed to be continuously conscious, we have this inner drive toward things that makes us feel good. In order to continually achieve this state, the other inner drive has the role of keeping us away from pain. In other words we have needs that we perceive as pleasure producers, and subconsciously we have an inner drive towards them. We also have fears that we perceive as pain producers and we have a subconscious inner drive away from them.

It is very helpful to know what is our own personality type, to be able to consciously choose things that fulfill our needs and stay away from things that are our potential fears.

Every one of these four personality types has their own needs and fears. It's important to recognize what kind of personality types the people we are dealing with have. Knowing this we can avoid things that may trigger their inner fears, and to approach them with things that fulfill their inner needs.

That's the whole secret of a good relationship or a good communication, in all aspects of life: financial, family relationship and many others.

Now, let's take one at a time:

Chapter 7. The propulsion mechanism.

The aggressive personality type, the director, or the controller.

- Let me teach you... -

People with aggressive personality types have a subconscious desire to develop and strengthen their power, to have control over their life and others.
They need to have the last word in any situation, they feel that everything evolve around them, they must be the main event. They want to know everything and have the need to be in control to exercise their power in almost any situation.
On the other hand, these people have a deep fear of loosing control.
They cannot accept second place and they cannot afford to loose an argument; it's too painful. In all their decisions, they're always looking for ways to fulfill their controlling attitude. Their personality type is expressed by the way they think, talk, and dress, the cars they drive and so on. In any situation, these people will look for opportunity to get control, and most probably panic anytime danger of loosing power or control is presented.
The positive aspect of this personality type is that these people when they are well trained they make strong and dedicated leaders in society.
Setting high goals and fulfilling them, driven by ambition are the major characteristics. They're not intimidated by challenges. On the other hand, when not properly trained, they make very good dictators and troublemakers. They are less incline to back off; they rather step on you than move aside.
It is wise to adapt our behavior accordingly to what is known when you are dealing with this kind of personality. It's to our and others advantage. Doing this one can eliminate a potential source of stress.
Remember: "The best way to avoid the casualties of war is to avoid getting involved in a war"
If you are dealing with aggressive types, it's better not to start arguing with them. The more you want to impose your view, the more they will get *stubborn* in their ideas.
When they feel that might lose an argument, their nervous system goes in alert because it perceives a treat to their inner needs. They will do anything to win the argument, which puts them in a stressful situation, from which nobody wins.
We know that this is not only a local problem, but affects the whole world.
Nations are fighting against nations. In the same country different political parties are also fighting each other for power. In the same cities, neighborhoods are fighting each other. Family members are fighting one another. The cause of all these fights is to get more and more power. Almost everybody wants to control the other. As a result, people get into stressful situations, and become stressful people. The solution? A person needs to learn how to lose a battle in order to win the war.
Let me ask you a simple question:
If the German government would have known in advance before they started World War II, they would lose the war, and their country be humiliated and almost destroyed; do you think they would have started the war? This is an important lesson for people. Many times they have the inner desire to manifest aggressive personality and forget this might bring unpleasant consequences. It is important to ask ourselves what price do we might have to pay for it, if we want to fight this situation. If the outcome is worth the price, then it's wise to do it. On the other hand, if the outcome isn't worth the price, we better back off and control ourselves.
Someone once said:
"It's O.K. to be aggressive when you have adaptive people around you, but it's wise to be careful when there is another one like you around."
See in advance what the outcome might be, and then prepare yourself to deal with it accordingly.

Chapter 7.   The propulsion mechanism.

Remember the saying:
"There is a time to speak, and there is a time to listen "

The assertive, supportive, or adaptive personality type.

- How may I help you? -

Opposite to the aggressive type, the adaptive or the assertive ones are the ones that feel good to please others.
They do that out of an inner desire to be accepted and recognized.
They are interested in other people's needs and shows caring and kindness. They identify themselves with the ones in need. They feel the others pain, and make themselves available to fulfill the needs of others.
They are not used to saying no to others, and because of that many times he / she set themselves up for failure for not being able to please everybody every time.
On the other hand the adaptive types fear rejection. They just cannot stand to be rejected and will do anything to be accepted. They are easygoing, sociable, getting along with almost everybody, and do not have that controlling attitude like the aggressive ones.
They are less stressed than others, but their major source of stress come from failing to please others. That's why it's important for the adaptive ones to learn that they have limitations and just cannot do everything they want to. But if they do as much as they can, that alone is enough.
Remember: It is noble to "Love your neighbor as yourself" but you have to love yourself first, and then show love to others.
On the other hand:
"A blind man cannot lead another blind man" It must be a balance because none of the extremes are good.
Therefore, it's important for the adaptive or the assertive type ones to remember that it's wise to control their attitude by learning when it is really needed to be adaptive. We know that many people like to take advantage of people who are easily controlled.

The analytical personality type, or the thinker.

-It's exactly that much... -

Totally different from aggressive or adaptive, the analytical or the perfectionists are the kind of people who have an inner desire to know about details in all situations that they are dealing with. For them, everything must be in perfect order. They are not satisfied with general information; they go deep into the situation and are careful not to miss any of the smallest details.
In other words they seek perfection.
On the other hand, they fear general things, or missing details.
In all of their conversations, they use details and expect others to respond accordingly. It's important to keep this in mind when we are dealing with an analytical and provide them with as many details as possible in our communication.

| Chapter 7. | The propulsion mechanism. |

They make good engineers, lawyers, architects and accountants.
They are prone to get stress more often, especially when they sense that details are missing.

The Passive personality type.

-Leave me alone please...-

Totally different than the other three personality types, the passive ones are the kind of people who have an inner desire to be left alone. They find pleasure in being alone and usually are introvert or private people. They don't like too much company. Indifference is pretty much known to him / her. Their basic fear is to get involved. They'll rather listens than talk and are much quiet than the rest.
Knowing this, we can learn how to deal accordingly with them in fulfilling their needs. Doing this, a person can improve communication thus eliminating potential causes of stress.
If we are aware of these four categories of personality types, it's important to learn how to properly deal with each individual type. If one would like to improve the relationship with them, it's wise to fulfill their inner needs and avoid bringing them things they fear. Once they sense the fear, their nervous system goes on alert and the first reaction will be to defend themselves.
Once the nervous system goes on alert, the thinking ability is reduced, and the reaction will be defensive.
Let' see how we can recognize each personality type and what's the best way to handle them.
First of all we need to find out about our personality type and recognize our inner needs and inner fears. By doing this we will be more careful not to set ourselves up for failure by unconsciously avoiding things that are fulfilling our inner needs Or even worse, by stumbling on the things we fear, which will result in a potential source of stress.
 Once we know exactly which type we are, it is also wise to find out as quickly as possible about the people we are dealing with, especially family members, friends, and coworkers. The sooner we know their type an edge is gained in tailoring our behavior to fulfill their inner needs, and also to avoid things that triggers their inner fears.
We eliminate many potential sources of stress by doing this.
We are aware   that all around the world, people are fighting every day. Not only in wars but also in families, among friends, relatives and so on.
The basic reason for these fights are, being unaware, they trigger each other's fears by not knowing how to communicate properly. As we mentioned before, once the fears are triggered, the defense mechanism goes on and the person isn't in the position of thinking clearly.
Their first priority is to defend themselves. They perceive any information as a treat and respond by rejecting information and fighting back.
This is why it is important to learn these things in advance and form a habit of recognizing their needs and fears before interacting with them. Once we become aware, we'll be more careful in the way we talk and act towards them.
Let's take a simple example:
After a hard day at work, John comes home and finds out that his wife didn't fix any food for dinner, because she was busy with other things. He gets upset, leaves the house and goes to a fast food restaurant to eat. Now let's see how each of the personality type interprets this situation. They all see the same thing, but the meaning given to the situation differs from one to another.
The aggressive one:

"Poor John, he is not respected in his own house. His wife is not appreciating him. John needs to teach her a lesson. First, she has to make sure that the food is ready for him and then do the rest of the things."
Here, we can see that the aggressive one sees that his needs are not fulfilled and his first reaction is to find the fastest way to do this, no matter what.

The adaptive or assertive one;
"O boy, John is tired and hungry, he must be feeling bad not finding the dinner ready. Poor Mary, she had so much to do today that she didn't realize how fast the time pass by. Now she might feel bad that she was not able to fix some food for her husband. John is supposed to understand her and they should go together to eat out."
The adaptive one on the other hand starts to feel sorry for both of them. And right a way he tries to find the solution to accommodate them both.

The analytical one:
"These two people need to learn time management. You don't just do things. You need to make a list of the things you need to do in the order of their importance and must strictly stick to it no matter what. Mary is spending too much time on unimportant things. John on the other hand needs to learn how to handle his wife. If he has a problem, he should face it not run from it."
Different than the first two, the analytical analyzes and gets to the bottom of the situation. He is not superficial but gets directly to the point.

The passive one:
"No big deal. He should go out and enjoy his favorite food without anybody bothering him. She could do her own things. Every body should be happy. No harm to anybody."
The passive one feels O.K. about the situation as long as one leaves the other alone.

We can use many other examples, but basically every personality type will react in a similar manner. Each of the four personality types unconsciously will look to fulfill their own inner needs or desires. And at the same time, try to stay away from things that may trigger their inner fears.
Being aware of this fact we can make any situation better by learning how to adapt to it.

Imagine you are driving a stick shift car. Which gear are you going to start with first? The third gear, then second, first, and finally fourth? No, you start with the first gear, which is the lowest. Once you pick up some speed, you switch to second, then third, and so on. In other words you switch gears according to the situation. You are not going to drive on the freeway on the first gear, are you? Of course you're not. Understanding this in order to benefit from using the car, you have to adapt your driving habits to the terrain, and then it becomes a normal thing.

Let's see how we can benefit from knowing these things.
We have mentioned earlier that awareness triggers desire. By knowing this, we realize that we have a choice of what kind of information we are exposing ourselves to. Knowing that exposing our mind to positive information eventually will result in positive desires, we can do this consciously by directing our behavior according to a pre-established plan, or goal that we would like to achieve. This is the way the TV and radio commercials work.
They have pre-established goals in mind to sell products or services.
They look for the best information that will trigger desires toward these specific products and services. Once they run these ads on TV or radio and other means of advertising, people see them and develop an inner desire toward them. If they keep watching them, eventually many will buy the products and services.

Having a better understanding of these four major personality types we can learn to develop the ability to self-actualize them. In other words, even though these personality types are the inner force that drives our behavior, we are able to control and use each in the right situations. This is done by setting a goal to become self-actualize. By doing that we are now opening a new *file* in our memory: "The self-actualizer file."

Once we set this goal, the reticular activating system will start to focus our attention towards the things that will help to accomplish this goal. Soon, we will start to master the habit of self-actualizing, which put us in a much better position to deal with everything in life. We will start to understand when we should be aggressive, or assertive, or analytical, or passive. Little by little we can see how our life will change for the better. Do not believe the idea that you must be close to the end of your life in order to become a self-actualizer. The sooner you understand how this process works, the faster you'll be able to accomplish it. The only one that could stop you from doing this is you, and no one else.

Going back to our subject of our inner personal needs, we are aware of the importance of fulfilling our inner needs to eliminate potential stressors. We are also aware of the fact that we can prevent going into stressful situations with other persons by fulfilling their inner needs and eliminating their inner fears. By doing this we are able to eliminate most of the potential stressful situations around us.
 Knowing our personality types, and the ability to self-actualize them, we all able to handle others and ourselves in such a way to avoid and eliminate stress.
From this information we gain a better understanding of how to approach any situation and have control over our feelings and desires thus eliminating the way many potential stressful situations start.
Another important thing we should pay attention to, is the fact that based on each individual upbringing, each type could be an introvert, or extrovert. The introverts are the type of persons that during formative years for some reasons may have not been encouraged to express themselves. As a result, they tend to keep things inside instead of expressing themselves.
On the other hand, extroverts are people that don't keep things inside but immediately express them verbally. The adaptive and the aggressive types tend to be more extroverts. The analytic and the passive tend to be more introverts. Of course there are exceptions from these. We all manifest some or all of these personality types, but one tends to be more dominant and affects behaviors in a positive or negative way. Therefore we should remember the more we learn to self-actualize ourselves, the easier our life will be.

Now let's go to the next set of needs that a person has, universal needs.

2. Subconscious Universal needs.

- What all of us have in common. -

Universal needs are the second category of our subconscious needs. They are called universal because they are found in all humans that ever lived or are living on earth today. The only difference is the level of awareness and the cultural conditioning that each individual has based on their own upbringing.
To better our understanding of these needs, we need to discuss the relationship between humans and their *environment*.

We all know that there are things on our earth that we see daily, but we are not necessarily aware of their purpose, or how they originated. We just take them for granted. But by doing this it doesn't change their role in nature or our life.

Have you ever seen a very expensive piece of artwork, like a painting that does not have the author's signature at the bottom or the back?

Every well-known painter makes sure that they sign their signature on paintings. Do you know why?

Well, it is not difficult. All artists would like to be recognized as the author of that painting. They don't want their efforts be in vain. He / she wants to be remembered by those who saw the art. For their own recognition as an author and master, it was signed.

If we take a closer look at the human race, we can conclude that there is indeed somebody's signature on it.
Like any other artwork, we can safely say that usually the artwork is a material representation of some of the master's inner desires or intentions. For example:
A poet usually writes in verses about his / her own inner needs and desires. A painter will also express their own inner desires or aspirations through paintings.
Now, let's look at the marvelous human body and see what was the intention of the designer. Let's take a simple example to illustrate this point:
We all are familiar with cars. We use them every day. There are small cars, medium size ones and full size cars. Common sense tells us that the smaller the car the smaller the engine, the bigger the car the bigger the engine. Nobody puts a huge engine into a small car for no reason.

Not long ago, I watched the Discovery channel and saw a very interesting documentary about the brain. What amazed me the most, was when the reporter asked one of the professionals how soon he thinks that we'll build a computer as powerful as the human brain? The answer amazed me.
"We are about two or three centuries away from building a computer comparable with our own brain" he answered.
I couldn't believe my eyes! I knew we had a powerful brain but with all of today's technology, humans are still very far away from being able to build such a computer. This made me thinking:
Now, if we were designed to live for seventy, eighty or maybe ninety years, why in the world were we equipped with a brain so powerful that in our life span; we use so little of its capacity?
Most probably the Designer's intention was that our live span to be much longer than it is now.

Humans are superior to the any other creatures on earth. Unlike the others, we are consciously aware of our existence. Our genetic code inherited from parents, gives us the ability to decide which programs we want our minds to work with. In other words, we have a choice to respond to the outside environment, to accept or to reject any outside stimuli. This makes us much superior of any computer that must be programmed and doesn't have its own conscience. What does all of this have to do with the designer's signature?

Well, looking at the way we were design to function we understand that we have an inner need and desire to work accordingly with the original desires of the Designer.

Let's take an example to illustrate this:

There are cars that are designed to work with super unleaded gasoline, others with unleaded, and some still with regular. Suppose that you have a car that requires super unleaded gasoline, but you keep using regular. If the car would be able to talk, what do you think it will tell you? It'll tell you that it runs with this gasoline because it has no other choice and it wishes to be filled with super unleaded. Then it'll be very happy and function at 100% of its potential. The same thing happens with people. They live their life, some better than others, but unless they understand the purpose of their life; humans function on *regular* only. We have an inner need to find out what our destiny and future are. Until we find the real truth about the existence of our human specie, we are living only a small part of our potential.

Today there are many rich people that have everything they could desire but still are not happy. Some even commit suicide. Why is that? Because they are not satisfied with *all* they have. To fulfill the inner desire, money and other things can't help.

We learn from physics that people, like everything else in the universe, have the same atomic structure. More than that the quantum physic tells us that a person is all energies that vibrate at different frequencies and what they see with their eyes is the manifestation or interpretation of these forms of energy.

There is a law that says: "An object in motion tend to stay in motion."

In other words, once these energies are programmed by the designer to work at a certain frequency, they tend to do that. As a matter of fact, we are aware of all the laws of nature and recognize that all these laws function perfectly. All the planets constantly follow their laws. They keep obeying the programs in which they were intended.

The way humans' function is a bit different. We were designed with the ability to choose whether we obey the laws or not. We need to be aware of this important fact and learn the truth about human existence. By doing this we can choose to obey the laws that help us to live properly according to the original design.

In conclusion, we can say that the inner universal needs are:

To understand and follow the real purpose of life, the reason we are here for, our own personal destiny, and universal destiny as humans.

We know that today there are so many categories of ideologies and religions that give different interpretations about the human existence. Not all are correct or possible. We just can't be created and at the same time came out through a process of evolution. One ideology must reject the other. Two plus two cannot be three, four and five. There is only one right answer; in this case, it's four.

The secret of human existence is like a puzzle. Unless we find out the real truth, we can't solve the puzzle.

Let's take an example to illustrate this:

You are the King in your kingdom and you have lots of subjects. To test their loyalty, you write a book with all the rules and regulation that you require from them in order to be accepted as loyal subjects. You use a certain secret code for the message in the book. In other words, the message of the book is not literal, but somebody needs to find the real meaning of the message in order to understand it. What do you think is going to happen? Well many of them will believe one way, others will believe different. Based on each individual level of knowledge, everybody has their own interpretation.

What's the truth then? Are all of them right? Well, no. Who could be right and who could be wrong? It's not too difficult if you know the truth.

We can safely say that the one that will humbly go to the King and ask for the secret code are the ones who could find the real meaning of the book and have chances to obey the rules and regulations of the book. The rest are following their only own interpretations. Some could be better than others, but none are based on the truth because they just do not know the truth. They follow their opinions. This is what is happening today. We are bombarded with so many kinds of ideologies and it's not easy to find the one based on the truth.

Chapter 7.   The propulsion mechanism.

As we saw in the previous example, the truth should be with those who are going to the originator of the universe and seeking it.

The fact that somebody comes with an ideology and he finds people to believe in it, does not necessarily means that it is reliable and based on the truth.

We all know from history, people were wrong in their ideologies and sometimes it took hundreds of years to prove these falsehoods.. Not long ago, people believed that the earth was flat and considered heretics those who thought different. But now, we are realizing that this was a big mistake and we might laugh at past generations; thinking how narrow minded they were.

But for them, the idea that the earth was flat sounded good, and believable. Once they accepted and believed it became true for them. They proceeded to teach it as the truth, even though it started as somebody's opinion. .

Going back to our subject about the inner universal desires, we can safely recognize that we are an intelligent design or product of an intelligent designer.

Unknown to most people today, the *Designer* left his signature on his design. That is an unconscious inner drive towards fulfilling the purpose for why we were created. Every living human on earth today has this inner drive. Most people don't know how to fulfill it and are working hard in the wrong direction trying to fill up this emptiness that they feel. Most of them live and die without finding out how to fulfill their inner drive.

The first wise step that we might make is to honestly look around. As an old writer wrote about two thousand years ago:

"From the beginning of the world, men could see what God is like through the things He has made."

We are all familiar with the expression: *Mother Nature*. What do people mean when they use this term? Do they mean that the nature has a mother? Or do they mean that the way the *Nature* behaves toward our environment and us is kind like a mother and for our benefit?

I think we all agree that *Nature* has so many provisions for our good and happiness on earth. That's why people came with this term; *Mother Nature*.

Since when is it possible that *nothing* becomes *something*, and programs itself to work as billions of different and sophisticated intelligences? Not only that, but the programming is so sophisticated that it's able to build in a multiplication system so that each of the billions of intelligences are able to reproduce themselves. Even more, all the billions of intelligences are harmoniously and synergistically perfect working together so the entire universe works as a whole. To believe that all of this just happens to happen the way it does, it's too much of science fiction.

People might think that they are alone on this earth and can do everything without any consequences. That's not true. Humans are here for a purpose and the purpose is great. We just honestly have to look for it.

Many years ago I heard a story that I think might fit here. It starts like this:

One day a student ask his teacher what is the truth and how somebody can find it. The teacher asked back:

"Do you really want to find out the truth? "

"Yes." The student said. So the teacher took him to a nearby lake and told him:

"Follow me."

Both started going in the water. When the water was up to their shoulders, the teacher grabbed him by the neck and pushed him under the water. The student started to panic and wanted to escape but was hindered. . The teacher's hands were holding him down. After a few seconds of no air, the teacher pulled him out and said:

"Son! When you look for the truth as much as you were gasping for air when you were under water, then you'll find the truth."

Even though this is just a story, it is very true for us today.

We're too busy with many other things that life has to offer. We don't pay attention to the real value of looking for the truth of our own existence.

We are satisfied with many things others are offering but this might be a big loss for us. It doesn't matter how busy we'll be with all these things, they'll never fulfill this universal inner desire.

All of us are proud of our parents and are not ashamed of them. Especially when they are in a high social position. How proud will you be if your father is the president of a company or even of a country? You will be proud of that and not be ashamed to tell others about him.

Since our common parents are not the monkey, but an intelligent and powerful creator, shouldn't we seriously look to get to the bottom of this truth? Find out who we really are and where we came from? He is more that a president of a company or a country; He is the Designer and Creator of the whole Universe. We should be proud of that, not ashamed to recognize this fact. Take some time out and honestly look for the truth about the human existence, you may be surprise to find how valuable it is.

Now let's go and discuss next secret, the second mechanism that we are equipped with:
"The self-defense mechanism."

Review Question: What is the propulsion mechanism, and what kind of needs does it trigger?

Answer:
- The propulsion mechanism is the figurative engine that continuously generates inner drives to identify, explore, absorb, understand, enjoy and own the *environment* we are surrounded with.
  It works at the conscious and subconscious level, and it generates our personal and universal needs.

"We can use our propulsion mechanism as the best tool in our journey to freedom from stress. It will generate all the motivation that is needed to finish the race and win it."

Secret # 8.

"Your invisible protective guardian."

Chapter 8. The Self-Defense Mechanism.

- And you thought you were defenseless-

If the propulsion mechanism could be compared with all the good things that a society provides for its citizens, so they could live a beautiful and prosperous life, the self-defense mechanisms can be compared with all the arrangements made for the safety and protection of its citizens. These arrangements include protection from within the society, but also protection from outside sources that might intrude and jeopardize the peace and harmony of citizens. We all are equipped with this kind of system. Being equipped with such a mechanism, we realize that in our quest for happiness and a better life, not everything around us contributes to our goals and aspirations. Many things might be harmful to us, so for our protection we were designed with such a protective mechanism. Understanding the way it was designed, its rules and regulations are the basis of its functions we can live a joyful and happy life. On the other hand, not being aware of its existence and the way it functions, we might cause ourselves much pain, suffering and stress.

Our brain activates the self-defense mechanism in a few stages based on the potential danger perceived.

1. Stage one. **The primary stage.**

In this stage, the self-defense mechanism is continuous on, but only for the maintenance of our body functions.

2. Stage two. **The alert stage.**

In the alert stage, the brain receives information that is perceived as potential danger, and activates the self –defense mechanism to check if it's real danger or just a false alarm.
Warning signals are sent to our conscious awareness to do something about the situation. These signals usually are in different degrees of feelings of discomfort, fear or pain. Not being aware of this, many people are using pain- killers or other *medication* to get rid of them, which of course isn't the best response. We might consider paying attention to this *language through which our body talks to us* and try to find out what is causing the pain and eliminate this cause. Once we do that, the symptoms will disappear automatically.

3. Stage three. **The fight or flight stage.**

In this stage, the brain decides to fight the danger or to stay away from it, and activates the self-defense mechanism to take the necessary steps to deal with the perceived danger. If an outside source hurts our body, the self-defense mechanism will start to fight the *intruder* until it gets rid of it.
If the brain perceives a potential life-threatening situation, the self-defense mechanism instructs the body to avoid and stay away from danger. In other words, it orders the body to flee from danger.

4. Stage four. **The regeneration stage.**

In this stage, the brain understands that the danger has passed, and instructs the self-defense mechanism to go back to its original stage, the primary stage.
If some damage was done to the body, the self-defense mechanism will start the process of repairing or healing that particular damaged part of the body, trying to restore the balance and health. If the damage is minor, the repair and healing is going to restore balance and health to the body.
If the damage is serious, the healing and repair process might be only partial.
Let's talk a little bit about an interesting aspect of our self-defense mechanism.
Beside the fact that was designed primarily for our defense, it also is responsible to *defend* everything that we possess and we might perceive as belonging to us.
We mentioned earlier that the propulsion mechanism has the role of identifying, exploring, absorbing, understanding, enjoying and finally owning *the environment* we live in.
The end results are to get ownership over *the environment* that causes us pleasure.
Once we get ownership of any part of this *environment,* (things, people, situations, events, etc.) it becomes ours. Then the self –defense mechanism takes over and get jurisdiction over them, protecting them as its own. This is where the fear of loss comes from.
We all know that we don't feel good when we lose something that belongs to us, and will do anything to protect our assets.
Beside the assets we mentioned, we have different kind of assets that we don't want to lose, or get rid of. These are called habits.
Once we fully develop a habit, it is quite difficult to get rid of, and it might be a good thing if the habit is a good one. The problem is because of cultural conditioning, or other factors, we sometimes develop negative or bad habits. Guess what: the self-defense mechanism designed for our protection becomes the one that stops us from getting rid of these bad and harmful habits.
Understanding this important fact, we can consciously work on letting them go. Of course that our first reaction will be not to do that, but realizing the principle: "Short term pain for long term gain, instead of short term gain for long term pain," we discipline ourselves and take necessary steps in getting rid of them.
Like the propulsion mechanism this one works on two levels: the conscious level, and the subconscious level.
Remember the example with flying the airplane? The airplane could be flown by the pilot, and by the autopilot. Something similar happens with the defense mechanism. A warning to our body to take a protective decision could be triggered by the conscious level, when we consciously decide to avoid certain things, situations or people that might present a danger. When danger is perceived at the subconscious level, it automatically triggers the proper response based on the information previously stored in its memory about that kind of perceived danger. The self-defense mechanism uses different levels of pain to bring to our conscious awareness the existence of a potential danger. There are two kinds of pain that are triggered: psychological and physiological pain. Even though many people are not aware of it, the psychological pain is a warning from our brain that something is not right. Not knowing how our defense mechanism works, the mistake people make is they try to eliminate this pain through treatment, such as pain killers, instead of

looking to find out what's the reason our defense mechanism triggers this kind of pain. Understanding the way this mechanism works, we are going to become our own doctor, knowing to behave in such a way that we will not trigger the self-defense mechanism at the wrong time, so it might cause us pain, anxiety or even stress.

Let's move to the subconscious level of self-defense mechanism.

1. The subconscious level.

Our nervous system plays a major role in the proper functions of our body. It also is the instrument through which the self-defense mechanism brings to our conscious awareness that we are in danger. Based on the gravity of the danger perceived, it triggers a specific level of fear or pain.

The subconscious level of the self-defense mechanism is triggered by two kinds of information that it receives.

One kind has to do with the information received from inside the body.

The second one has to do with the information received from the outside or our *environment*.

A. Inner information

We all know, that our body is made up of a number of organs and all contribute to normal functions. We also know, that each of these has a special role to play and all have to work in harmony, for the whole body to work properly.

Many times, we might remember that we have experienced different kinds of pain. Sometimes we might have got a headache, or chest pain, or back pain, etc. All these feelings of pain are nothing else but warning signals from our nervous system, that something is not right, or does not function properly in that specific area, where the feelings of pain came from. We should pay attention, and do something about them.

The mistake people make is that they use painkillers, which are doing nothing else but numbing the pain, while the cause of pain is still there.

If you look on the dashboard of a car, you'll see many gages and indicators. You may see some red lights that might flash some times. Suppose you are driving your car, then suddenly a red light goes on, and when you look closely, you'll see it's the oil light. Would you stop the car and check the oil level, to make sure that is O.K. or you take some masking tape, and tape over the light so it won't bother you anymore?

Well, obviously you'll be smart enough to stop and check the engine, instead of covering the light. It might surprise you to find out, that every time somebody uses painkiller, without trying to find out the cause of their pain, they are doing nothing else, but *covering the light*. By doing this, they will prolong the problem causing it to get bigger, instead of eliminating it.

The subconscious level of the nervous system goes on alert any time it perceives that one of its body components might not function properly, and a conscious decision needs to be taken.

B. Outer information.

Beside the information received from our own body components, the subconscious level works with the information received from the environment. To illustrate this, let me ask you few simple questions: When do you eat or should eat? When do you drink? Why don't you use the same wardrobe in the summer, as in the winter? Why do you sneeze? Why do you wear sunglasses? We do these things, and are familiar with them. But did it ever cross your mind on why people do these things? The answer is that our subconscious level of the protective mechanism based on the information collected from the environment, triggers these actions for our protection. When a person feels hungry, or thirsty, that is the warning that the body needs to assimilate food to maintain its proper functions.

When the temperature changes, the same thing happens as we're warned by the feelings of cold or heat to take action.

If we obey these warnings, things are going to be fine, but if we keep ignoring them, or overreacting to them, two things might happen:

1. The warning signals become more accentuated, until we do something about them.
2. We might alter our response to the environment into a positive, or negative way.

In the first case, the worst that might happen is that a person might require medical attention to resolve the situation.

In the second case, if a person alters their response to the information from the environment, this might be a major source of stress, if they do it in a negative way.

We might know people who get scared very fast, and many small things are major challenges, or problems for them. They have this so called quality *to major in minor things*, when it comes to their reaction towards these events. You might know someone who has the habit of saying:

"Don't worry, nothing bad could happen." Soon after that, they suffer the consequences of their negligence.

These people, have unconsciously altered their proper response to the environment in a negative way, and many times for them, this might become a source of stress.

As we have seen from this information, the subconscious level of our protective mechanism goes on alert, and if it's not properly understood, it might be considered a source of stress. The reality is it's just doing the job for which it was designed. We are the ones that don't know and misunderstand its functions.

Let's go further and see how the conscious level of our defense mechanism works, and how it might help us eliminate many potential stressors.

2. Conscious Level.

Beside the subconscious level, which reacts to the environment without our conscious awareness, our defense mechanism goes on alert also when triggered by the conscious level.

Let's use an example to illustrate this.

Suppose that you just bought a new car, a nice sporty one. One day, coming back from work, just before you get into the freeway, one of your high school friends passes, and right when you are side by side, tells you:

Hey John, nice car, but you're still slower than me. Let's see if you can catch up with me, and he speeds up the freeway.

Now, this incident might bring you past memories about your adventures during the high school years, and the tendency is for you to go for it. But that time has gone, and who's first is not so important to you anymore.

You start thinking about potential negative consequences that your actions might have, and you decide to control yourself. Your safety is more important than a game.

This is a simple example, from which we can see how the conscious level of our defense mechanism works. We consciously use this level every day, with any information that comes from the environment. Any decision we make is based on two questions that we consciously or not, ask ourselves:

Does this bring me pleasure, or is it going to bring me pain? These questions are the works of the conscious level of the self-defense mechanism.

Chapter 8. The self-defense mechanism.

There is a very important question that we need to ask:
What is the standard used for comparison when we make a decision, to identify something as good or bad?
Well, let's take an example to illustrate this:
Suppose, there is a family of immigrants coming to America from, let's say China. There are two parents, and four little kids. When they arrived, for some reason, only two kids came with them, and the other two remained with their grandparents. They were two and three years old. The ones that came to the U.S. are four and five years old. Now they all were born in China, and started to learn the Chinese language and customs. What do you think is going to happen after ten or twenty years? Well, the ones that came here, even though they were born the same place as the other two, will change completely. They will speak a totally different language, and their customs might be different than those of the Chinese people.
Why does this happen?
When a person is born, their brain is like a huge and empty library. Soon after birth, they start to fill up this library with all the information that is absorbed from the environment. They might think that the past is gone, but this is true only for the conscious mind. The subconscious mind thinks there is no such thing as past, present or future. Each bit of information that is entered is still there; ready to be retrieved when asked for. People might not know how to retrieve it, but it's still there. All the information that has been absorbed during an entire life becomes the database for the thinking process.

To answer our earlier question about the standard used for comparison for deciding what's good or bad, we can say that: All the decisions that people make concerning the conscious level of the defensive mechanism are made based on previous information that's contained in ones subconscious mind about a particular subject. How could this be? Well, first we should know that there is a relationship between the conscious level and subconscious level.
Anytime when we talk or ask ourselves any questions, we are sending a signal like a command to the subconscious mind to find the answer.
Soon after, a thought comes in the mind that is the answer from our subconscious level. Many times a negative or wrong answer is received and you might say: Why is that?
Well, there is a simple explanation.
We have asked ourselves wrong questions. That's why unpleasant answers are received.
Remember, the subconscious mind does not pass any judgment over the information it receives as good or bad. It accepts it as truth as long as the conscious mind does so. That's why, even though all four kids from our example, born by the same parents in the same place, after ten or twenty years, they will be totally different people. Two of them, will speak and behave like Chinese people, and the other two, will speak and behave like Americans.
Now, what has this to do with stress? Well, here is the secret.

We all grew up believing that there is no solution to eliminate stress. Learning that and believing it, what will be our attitude about stress? We must live with it. All our conscious decisions we have made in the past reflect our thinking. What we need to do is to *come to America,* so to speak. Like the two kids that came to US with their parents, they had to learn the new language and new behaviors if they really wanted to integrate themselves into this new society. The same thing happens with us. We want to eliminate stress? It's just impossible to do so with our old *language.* We need to know the new one, and then we might be able to practice it. It's simple as that.

Up until now, we have learned that our brain as the central command of our body, functions based on two mechanisms.
One, *The propulsion mechanism,* that helps to identify, explore, absorb, understand, enjoy and own the environment.
The other designed for our protection is: *The self-defense mechanism.* Both of these mechanisms continuously work together in finding the right solution to the information that is attained by interacting with the environment. As I mentioned before, people use the previous information *stored* in their memory banks as reference to any decisions that are made. Now, how many people are aware of this so they can learn how

to use them properly, and have the desired results?
The reality is that our parents didn't know, because their parents also didn't know. They have done what they thought was good, which was not necessarily the best thing every time.
Like they did, we are also probably trying our best.
But, like the twelve years old kid from our example, we might *wreck the car* not necessarily because we are bad people, but just because we do not know how to properly use it. The good news is, that we all can learn the proper way. Once we understand how these two mechanisms work, we will be smart enough to use them in such a way that they'll complement each other, instead of misusing them, and get stressed.

Let's say that you buy an expensive and complicated computer, or another piece of electronic machinery. Without the owner's manual, it's very difficult, maybe even impossible, to operate it. If the company that sells you the product gives you the right manual, it's a matter of applying the rules and regulations shown by the book, and everything becomes possible. The machine works well. The same thing happens with humans. Once they know the way the body was designed to work, and how these two mechanisms work, it just a matter of following the instructions.

All the stress that has to be faced daily, is caused by the improper use of these two mechanisms.

Imagine how easy it would be for your car to go forward if you keep stepping on the brakes, or if your emergency brake is engaged at all times? There is a lot of stress on the whole car if it has to run like this. This is what people basically do all the time when they unconsciously trigger the defense mechanism at the wrong time, and then have no success in going forward. Consciously, they want to go forward, but subconsciously trigger the defense mechanism, and want to stop. The result is what is called stress.

Do you still want to live your life, as a stressful one? Keep doing what you were doing, but if you want a life free of stress, then the solution is simple. Learn these simple things about yourself, and then apply them daily, until they become habits. Once they are habits, you will do them as a normal thing.
Remember:
"If it is to be, it's up to me." I need to do it for me, and for you, the only one that can do it, is you.

Getting to the end of part one: "Who really are we?" by now we have acquired a better understanding about ourselves and about some amazing abilities we were equipped with. Indeed each of us was born as a wonderful human being with the right to live a stress free life. Not only that, but nobody is entitled to take our right away from us.

Now, let's go forward and discover the next secret, by finding out who's really responsible for one in getting stressed. Who are the so-called *monsters that are playing with our mind* and driving us crazy?

Chapter 8.   The self-defense mechanism.

Review Question: How do you describe the self defense mechanism and what are the factors that activate it?

Answer:
- If the propulsion mechanism would be the *engine* that generates our inner driving force, the self-defense mechanism would be the *breaking system* design to protect us from anything that might cause us harm.
- This system works at conscious and subconscious levels and is activated by information coming from inside of us and from the outside environment.

"Getting a better understanding of our protective guardian, it will stop being a source of stress and become a helper on our journey to a stress free life."

Part 1. Review Question: After we got to the end of part 1, "Who really are we?" what can we say about ourselves? Who really are we? Are we still *a three dollars* valued old violin? Or does the message of this part help us understand that the dust has been cleansed, the loose strings were rightly tuned, and we are ready for a sweet and pure melody.

Answers:
- As the story of the old violin goes, by now we got enough information to understand that we too as wonderful human beings equipped with amazing abilities, are deserving to get a chance of living a stress free life.

- By changing our paradigm of stress from stress management to eliminating stress, we learn to use our body according the laws and principle they were designed to and then the impossible becomes possible.

- Acquiring knowledge will make us knowledgeable people. Acquiring accurate knowledge and continuously applying it will help us to win the game of life.

- We are not just human beings. We are wonderful human beings designed with amazing abilities.

- The quality of these three ingredients, clean air, healthy foods and proper information generates the strength of our spirit, the fire within that keeps all of us alive.

- Through Reasoning, we choose what we accept. Through Imagination, we combine the information accepted. Emotions, are the results we feel after our mind has combined what we have chosen to accept.

- We all were born as wonderful human beings. What we are today is what we made ourselves through our behavior.

- Through these five steps, awareness, desires, decision, motivation and discipline, we can keep ourselves slaves to the merciless environment, or we can free ourselves from the bondages of stress.

- We can use our propulsion mechanism as the best tool in our journey to freedom from stress. It will generate all the motivation that is needed to finish the race and win it.

- Getting a better understanding of our protective guardian, it will stop being a source of stress and become a helper on our journey to a stress free life.

"Indeed we all are wonderful human beings, equipped with amazing abilities, and deserving to get a chance of living a stress free life."

"…….But no, from the room, far back, a gray-haired man came forward and picked up the bow;
Then, wiping the dust from the old violin, and tightening the loose strings,
He played a melody pure and sweet as caroling angel sings………"

Part. 2

What Are We Dealing With?

Part. 2

What Are We Dealing With?

Secret # 9.

"The 'monsters' that play mind games on you."

Chapter 9. Who Really Are The Stressors?

- It's not what happens to you, but what you do with what happens to you -

People's minds in many ways are like a computer. It doesn't care what you put in. It will process any information that's put in according to the same laws and regulation that governs its functions. You might know the saying:

"Garbage in, garbage out "
What makes a person's brain superior than any other computer, among other things is that besides the sound and picture, it associates also a feeling which they have a conscious choice to define it as positive or negative. In other words, it continuously produces neuron-associations between pictures, sounds, and feelings that are attach.

The secret of eliminating stress is to learn how to become aware of the things or events that we perceive as stressors, and replace the negative feelings previously attached to them, then associate something different that doesn't cause any stress. By doing this, we eliminate the so-called *stressors*.

We can't call a car an airplane, because it's a car, everybody knows this. But, someone who seems to be an enemy we might call him friend, or something similar.

We do this not necessarily for them, because they might be not worthy, but we do it for ourselves and for our own protection. In our memory, we have only good feelings associated with the word friend. This is what we feel when somebody is called a friend.

By the same token, we have only negative feelings in our memory about the word enemy.

A negative state of mind is what we are going to feel when we call somebody our enemy. Let me ask you a simple question:

Suppose you have two choices: One, you get $5000, but you have to give away $2000 to your enemy. Second, he gets nothing, and you get nothing.

Which choice will you choose? I know that you would like your enemy to get nothing, but because you get much more than they get, I think you'll be smart enough to choose the first option. By changing our opinion about them, we might do them a favor. It's much smaller than the one that we'll do ourselves when this is done.

No wonder Jesus Christ considered by many the wisest man that ever lived, taught his people to love their enemies.

If we think a little bit, is it possible that He might have asked his own people to do something wrong? Or maybe He knew long before us the way our mind works, and how it processes information.

In order for us to be happy all the time, we might need to take in consideration of the way we look at things. Looking at them as being our enemies or as friends, because based on our decisions, we are the ones that are determining the way we feel, good or bad.

Now the big question is:
Who are the *stressors*, and why do we really get stressed?
There are few basic reasons why we are getting "stressed" and we'll take one at the time to discuss and clarify.

1. Things we give inappropriate meaning to.

2. Things that are unchangeable and we try to change, also things that we are supposed to change and we don't do it.

3. Things that are unsolvable, and we try to solve, and also things that are supposed to be solved and are not. .

4. Unrealistic expectations about our future, or unfulfilled dreams.

5. Unfulfilled subconscious needs, and unaware of dealing with subconscious fears.

6. Dwelling on things from the past.

These are the six important areas we are dealing with, that are the so-called *stressors*. Or, in other words, these are the roots of potential stressors.
By learning how to change these from old interpretations to new ones, it will result in different outcomes; ones that do not produce any stress.
You may think that this is a difficult task to do, but let me put it this way:
If you go back in your past during your childhood and adolescence, you went to school every day for so many years. You had to study daily, pass many exams, and follow so many instructions during all those school years.
Now, why did you do this? To be able to get a job, (j. o. b. just over broke) then once you started working, you are every day subjecting yourself to your boss and working between 8 to 10 or even more hours/day.
Daily you spent much energy in doing your job, just making enough money to be able to live. In order to keep doing this you know very well that you better stay healthy; otherwise the cost of medical bills could drive you to poverty. As you may probably know already, most of our medical problems have their roots in stress. No wonder it is called *the plague of our generation.*
Instead of spending huge amounts of money during your life to fix all those side effects of stress, you'll be smart enough to take the necessary time to learn these things. Once you have learned, they will become habits, and then all these side effects will disappear.
This is the whole secret. You need no college degree or other sophisticated studies. This is a regular learning process of information. Only the benefits are unbelievable. Try to imagine getting rid of so many problems with such a simple method.
Remember; you learned to write, read, and many other habits, like: driving a car, or maybe fly an airplane, play a musical instrument, work on computers, or other sophisticated machinery. You learned these things and many others, you know how to learn, and it's not something new. You went through these steps of the learning process, and like everything else have learned, at first maybe you were skeptical, but then you felt better afterwards.
Remember how you learned to drive a car?

In the beginning you were afraid, but then step by step started to handle it, until you came to the point of doing it without fear, and now you look back and smile: It was a piece of cake.
You are going now through the exactly same process.

Do you remember the good feelings you got after you have learned something new?
Imagine how your life, your relationships with your family and friends will be, and how easier you could handle any other of your tasks. This might be the best thing that ever could happen to you. You need no special education, no special skills, or expensive treatments. No thousands of dollars in equipment, or anything else, but your burning desire to learn to love yourself enough to believe that this is possible. Once you believe it, you're in the right path toward becoming a stress free person.
Remember: "To play the life's game the way you want, you need to learn the rules of the game."
Once you know them, they become habits.

You must know that your thoughts, consciously or not, control everything you do. Your thoughts control your actions. It is up to you to believe and take the necessary actions to get familiar with this information.
It's well worth it to make a small sacrifice for such valuable benefits. Most of these things you know already. You just need to learn and follow the rules and regulations and the way they work. It's like a child's puzzle, you have all the pieces, but you need to know how to put them in order so they make sense.
Remember it is your responsibility to take charge of your future. Nobody can do it for you; you have to do it for yourself. If it is to be, it's up to you.
Now let's go and discuss about the first category of potential stressors.

1. New Dictionary.

Things we give inappropriate meaning to.

- Help keep the environment beautiful; clean up your speech -

First of all, people know that in order to communicate with each other, they use sounds that are called words. Each language has its own dictionary of words. So what is done, early in life, a person learns these words and their meanings and uses them in every day living. This is normal, because people from all over the world do the same thing. Up to this point everything is very simple. Now, we're going divide the words we use in communicating with others into two major groups:

A. Words that define something specific and is universal recognized.

B. Words that do not define something specific, and are open for interpretation by the one who speaks or hears them.

A. In this category we find words such as:

Numbers: 1 to 10 or any combination of 2 or more of these numbers.
Names of objects or things like: tables, cars, houses, books, electronics, etc.
Names of: plants, vegetable, fruits, trees, etc.
Names of: animals, birds, fish, insects etc.
Names of: people, and many other things.

All these kinds of words are recognized as having a constant meaning, there isn't much room for interpretation. Every body recognizes a flower always will be called a flower; nobody will call it a cat, or a tree.

B. The second category:

Words that do not define something specific, but general, and are open to interpretation. We will focus our attention on this category, because these words, being open to interpretation, people have the freedom to give them any meanings they want. This fact has a good side, but also has a bad one.

The good side is a person has the choice to give them the meaning they want according to their pleasure or understanding. On the other hand, the bad side is if attention is not given, many times people can give an inappropriate meaning and they may become stressors.

In communicating with others a person uses sentences, or phrases, and if not careful, can attach a more powerful negative meanings that have a more destructive effects. Can you imagine if one negative word had a negative effect over us, then the more negative words we use in our vocabulary creates more negative states of mind.

Did it ever cross your mind to stop and think what kind of reaction your words trigger within the person you are talking to? Can you see that the more you talk to somebody, the more that person wants to listen to you, or do you see the opposite?

Every day we use our speech ability in order to communicate with each other. Sad to say, we have to recognize that communication is a very misunderstood process. Why am I saying this? Because we all know, that there are many problems in this world today due to poor communication, or because people just don't know how to communicate properly.

They use their thinking ability to make plans, and then based on ones vocabulary, express these plans or information through words that are transmitted to others.

The others hear these words and based on their own vocabulary, give them their own meanings.

The meaning they give to information may be the same, and they could be communicating properly or the meaning could be different. This will result in a misunderstanding, which could be minor, or could result in a potential stressful situation. We know that many times people put themselves in difficult situations because of misunderstandings in communication. That's why it is very important to realize that we need to master the art of communication for our own good, and also for those we communicate with. It's true that every body knows how to talk, but to properly communicate we need to know more. We need enough appreciation for people we are dealing with and use our speech to make friends through our communication not enemies. Many times we forget the negative effect words could have toward the people we are dealing with, and then we wonder why we do not have enough friends? This starts with family members, our friends, and us.

Let me ask you a small question:

With whom do you have the habit of talking nicer? With family members or, with other people?

Imagine this scenario: Some of your family members start *communicating* with each other by yelling, using improper words and gestures, and then suddenly the phone starts ringing.

Then, one of them pick's up the phone and with a totally different voice:

"Hey, how are you, …oh, me? I am doing great, how about you?" and so on.

Does this sound familiar to you? See, many times we forget who we are talking to, and let our ego control us. We forget that our family members should be our best friends. And no matter what, we should treat them like wise. Next time remember:

"If your spouse, children or parents are not your best friends you might very well be a very poor person."

Never make the mistake in considering other people better friends than your own family members.

Always remember the words you use with them will prove how much you love them. The more you love your friends, the nicer you will talk to them. And the nicer you talk to them, the more love you show towards them.

So, remember who your first friends should be, and how to communicate with them.

Now, let's take the first category of words that could have double meanings.

1. Family circle.

The first category of words that an improper meaning is given is to our closest family members such as our spouse, children, or parents. We need to look at them as our best friends and should always be careful to communicate words that produce a positive state of mind. By doing this we are eliminating the possibility that any of them might become stressors. Now, if we learn to extend our circle of friends we reduce the risk of getting stressed.

So, let's start by learning a new habit of looking at our family member as friends.

And as soon as we master this habit a wonderful thing will start to happen: Members of the family that were previously perceived as stressors will cease to be, and they'll no longer be a source of stress for us. Once we don't feel any stress coming from them, our reaction towards them will be more positive, and they'll be more positive toward us, and so on. It is the same process when two people are fighting; they fuel each other's anger, and the fight keeps going on. The only difference is the energy is not negative so it will produce anger, but it's positive and as result, it produces a stronger relationship between the two. See, we almost never get tired of good friends and always enjoy good company. So, by doing this, we eliminate the potential of getting stressed from family members. Because we all know that the worst pain is the one coming from somebody close to us. And a large part of our stress today we could say that it comes from our family members. By learning the habit of looking at them as friends, we can eliminate some of the most painful sources of stress.

The next step is to enlarge the circle of friends, adding to them your neighbors, coworkers, and any other person that might be possible stressors.

Now you may ask: How can a stranger, neighbor, or coworker be your best friend?

Well, I am not telling you to make him or her your best friend, if you don't want him or her to be your friend. The point is not who they really are. The point is how you look at them, because your feelings are not determined by who they are, but by the way you see them. We are talking about how to protect yourself from getting stressed, not who they are.

Let me give you a simple example:

Not long ago, I once operated an Auto Repair Business. One day an old charming lady came to me with her car to do some work on it. She was driving an old Cadillac. She wanted me to change the engine on her car. I looked at her and I asked if she was aware of how much it's going to cost to do this.

"Yes," she said.

But, with this money you can buy another Cadillac, in much better condition, I told her.

This is my car. It's like my baby. I have had it for so long and I am not going to get rid of it, no mater what, She replied.

First, I was very surprised to hear that, but then I realized that for her it did not matter the condition of the car, but the fact that it was hers and in her eyes this old and broken car had more value than any other in a much better condition. So, it's not important the item itself, but how we look at it. Do you remember the old sayings?

"It's not beauty what it's called beauty, but is beauty what you like."

"The beauty is in the eyes of the beholder."

The thing itself does not trigger any reaction, but the meaning we give to it, is the one that will trigger a positive or a negative reaction in our mind. Let's take another example:

One day you go, as usual to pick up the mail, and among the letters you find one that comes from a foreign country. You open it and try to read it, but because you do not speak that language, you do not understand its message. Why? Because not knowing that language, in your memory there are no associations with these kinds of words. So, you have the choice to ignore it and throw it away, or you can go find somebody who understands that language and try to get the real message from it. You could have decided to throw it away and it's meaning becomes worthless but you didn't. You found somebody who speaks that language and after they finished translating the letter, you realized how important the message is. You feel very good about what you have done and you want to make sure it won't get lost.

In other words, you start associating in your mind a positive feeling to that particular letter, so the next time when you get another one, you'll make sure that you get its message translated. People know that this is something normal and it's true; every person knows this. What's important for us though, is that these associations take place according to some laws and regulations. Becoming aware of this, we can consciously choose to associate positive feelings to the things we want. Also we can remove the old negative associations we got in our memory from the past thereby eliminating this way the real causes of stress.

Remember, people have a lot of positive feelings associated in their minds toward things that are liked, and also have a lot of negative feelings associated towards things disliked or hated.

At any time, when people give a negative meaning to something they are associating that particular thing with a negative state of mind. By the same token, when given a positive meaning to something, they associate it with a positive state of mind. It's their choice, and also it's a matter of a habit to learn how to do this.

From all these examples, we can very well see we really have a choice to decide if we want to help ourselves, or we could keep blaming others for our situations and problems.

You may know the saying:

"Somebody fools me up once, shame on him. If he fools me twice, then shame on me."

When we don't know, we have an excuse, but once we know then, with knowledge also comes responsibility. So, it's our duty to learn how to master and control our state of mind in such a way that we could eliminate stress forever.

It might seem impossible because nobody came with this idea until now. All the other programs are teaching people how to manage their stress, but as we can clearly see now eliminating it, it's really true and possible. It takes a little time and discipline, like any other program but the rewards are unimaginable. Remember, it's up to you. Because you are the only one who can do it. YOU, and nobody else.

If we can say that the most painful stress comes from our family members, then the simplest solution to fix this is to learn a new habit of looking at them, not just as to a mother or father, or children or any other

relatives, but look at them as our best friends too. By doing this, we eliminate the possibility of getting stressed. Because by dealing with our best friends we never get stressed. But, many times some of our *relatives* might become sources of stress.

Remember, the subconscious mind has a blueprint of our real opinion about family members and this blueprint dictates our reaction or behavior towards them. If we know that some of our family members are becoming a source of stress for us, or we start to feel uncomfortable when dealing with them, it's a sign of having a wrong blueprint about them. Therefore, we need to change this blueprint from our subconscious mind with a better one. That's why we need to learn to look at them as our best friends. By doing this long enough, we're replacing the old blueprint with a new and better one. Once the old blueprint is changed, automatically it'll trigger a new, better behavior, for our own good and the good of ones we love.

Now, let's go to the second category of words that has a stressful effect over us because of the wrong meaning we have given them.

2. Bills and payments.

Now beside words that define people, we deal daily with words that define things. Many of these words can have a stressful effect over us. To eliminate the stressful effect they may have over us we'll start with things that are found around the house that could stress us. Bills, mortgage, credit card, insurance, car payments, and many other similar to these are all well known to us. The problem is that for many, these have become a source of stress. First of all, we know that these words have a stressful effect only when we are not able to fulfill an obligation towards them. If we have enough money to pay them in time, it's just a matter of writing checks, and there is no stress is attached. But when there isn't enough money, things change and we start getting stressed. One solution is to solve the financial situation.

Some times we just keep coming up short of money and many times this becomes a reason for stress. In other words: "We have too much month left at the end of the money."

Another solution is to learn how to eliminate the stressful effects these words have over us. Remember we get stressed not because these are stressful words, but because sometime in the past we associated in our mind negative feelings toward these words. What needs to be done is, to find a way to remove these negative feelings associated with these words and all stress will disappear.

Remember:

"It's not what happens to you, but what you do with what happens to you."

Do you remember after you bought the house, or the car; how proud you felt in writing the check for their payments? There was a time when these bills were not stressors, but just bills that needed to be paid. They became stressors after a while when little by little we associated negative feelings to them. So, what is needed is to get back to the *good blueprint* we had about them and replace the existing one in our subconscious mind.

The third categories of words that have a stressful effect over us are states of minds or feelings.

3. States of mind or feelings.

The third category of words that might have a stressful effect over us, they are the words that define states of mind or feelings. So, beside the words that define people and words that define things we also are dealing with words that define states of mind or feelings. These words also could have a stressful effect over us if we give them an inappropriate meaning.

Such words could be words like: bad, stupid, critical, foolish, ugly, moody, stingy, clumsy, hate, rotten, tired, sloppy, mean, and many other that are commonly use by many people. Just by hearing these kinds of words one starts feeling negative.

Why is that?

Because to all of these words, we have attached in the past negative states of mind, and any time when we use them, we feel to a certain degree their negativity.

The best thing to do, if possible, is to avoid using them, and learn to rearrange sentences in such a way that they can send the same message without using these kinds of words.

They have a negative effect to those directed too but also to those who are using them. People have learned to use these words from others. Once it's realized that they do more bad then good, we should show love and appreciation for others and ourselves. Replace these negative words with better ones that do not have a stressful effect towards us, or to the ones being communicated with.

Many times in dealing with others, things don't necessary go according to wishes, and with the tendency to accentuate ideas people get tempted to use this kind of vocabulary. They learned this from childhood of course, back then the vocabulary was more limited. Now many more *new expressions are used.* So, a person has to keep in mind that the more these kinds of words are used, the more they can hurt others and themselves. .

Humans were designed to react to outside stimuli like a mirror. If somebody smiles at you, you will have the tendency to smile back. If somebody looks at you with a mad face, you have the tendency to look back the same way. They have a subconscious tendency to mirror each other.

The nicer the language that's used in communicating towards others is, the more positive their reaction will be. On the other hand, the more negative language in use, the more negative reactions will happen. And of course their negativity will affect us too. It's up to us to control the situation by choosing words that have positive effects.

Let's take an example:

Many times if something does not go according our wishes we have the tendency to call others *names*. Something goes wrong and: "You must be very stupid to do that" or you may say:

"Are you crazy? What's wrong with you"

How do you feel when somebody talks to you like that?

You most probably don't feel good. And your tendency will be to give them the same kind of answer, or something similar.

But what is the result? Nobody likes it. Not you, nor the other person. You could learn to rephrase these kinds of expressions with something like this:

"Intelligent people do this things this way, and I have no reasons yet to believe that you are not one of them."

Using this kind of expression you subconsciously condition the other person to accept what you are saying, without them contesting it. They'll accept your advice much easier, and the line of communication stays open.

So, by understanding words that define feelings or states of mind that have negative meanings that'll trigger a negative state of mind, we should avoid using them as much as possible. By replacing them with other words or expressions, this eliminates potential stressful effects they might have over us. .

4. Verbs with negative meanings.

The fourth category of words that might have a stressful effect over us is verbs.

There are a variety of verbs we use in our daily life that also could be a source of stress. And like other words, we have discussed earlier, these too have attached negative feelings to them. Some of those verbs might be: to work, to do, to exercise, to discipline, to help, to clean, to manage, to study, to learn, to train, to read, to change, and so on.

Even though these verbs don't have any negative meaning by themselves, sometimes, because some of our past negative experiences we associated negative feelings to some of them.

And unless we remove these associations, any time we use them we are experiencing the negative feelings previously attached to them.

So, it is important to find out which one of these are having negative association attached, and use one of the methods we'll learn later on to remove these negative associations.

Let's take a simple example:

For some reason your job start to be less and less pleasurable.

So, any time when you see that you have to go to work, you start feeling down and you would rather stay home instead of going to work. What do you think would happen if you start to ask yourself these kinds of questions?

"What's the worst that could happen, if I will go to work, and can I do something about it?" or

"What's good about going to work?"

"Am I benefiting in any way by going to work?"

By honestly answering these questions, you are removing the negative feelings, and once you found something positive, a positive feeling will be attached to them. Then you'll start to feel different the next time when you have to go to work.

Remember how excited you were when you got this job? How happy you were to have your own money, control your life and realizing dreams and all of these were made possible because of your work.

In the past, you had different feelings about your job. What are causing you to think different now aren't the job itself but negative feelings you have previously attached to it.

Starting to spend more than you were making resulted in financial difficulties. Unaware of, you are blaming it on the job. And little by little you started to associate negativity with the job, and eventually it became a stressor for you.

Let's take another example:

Let's say that I am a little overweight and it was recommended that I exercise. But you know, I would rather stay in front of the TV and watch a movie. When I hear I have to exercise, I feel bad, why me? Maybe I'll start tomorrow. Again we start asking the same questions:

"What's the worst that could happen? And what can I do about it? And of course:

"What is good about it?"

Well, by now we can see that in all these situations we'll find something good that we can benefit from. And again doing this we remove the negative feelings toward exercising, and attach a new and positive feeling.

Recognizing the verbs that have a negative feeling attached to them and by using these simple methods learned earlier, a person can eliminate these potential stressors.

Even though we live in a very *stressful world,* always remember that it's up to the individual to define what is, or what's not a stressful situation. We are the creators of our inner world.

The way we make it, that's the way we'll live in it. We all have a choice about this. It is our responsibility and nobody else. Take the time that is required to learn how to master your own destiny.

Now let's go to the next category of so-called *stressors*

2. Unchangeable Versus Changeable.

Things that are unchangeable and we try to change, and also things that we are suppose to change and don't.

- You may want to change the world, but the world might not want to be changed -

More than fifty years ago, Reinhold Neibuhr, wrote what today is commonly known as: "The Serenity Prayer"
During all these years, this little prayer has inspired millions of people to think about what's the best way to deal with their lives. With its simplicity and deep meaning it stands as a powerful tool to use in our life today.

"GOD, Give us grace to accept with serenity the things that cannot be changed, courage to change the things which should be changed, and the wisdom to distinguish one from another"

What can be learned from this little prayer? People can learn some very powerful truths. First of all, accept the idea that there are things a person didn't make them. The best thing to do is to accept their existence. Once this idea is accepted, people need the wisdom to make the difference between those who are unchangeable and the others who really could be changed. Nature has many laws, and people have many governmental and local laws.
It's wise always go along with the laws by knowing and respecting them. When somebody tries to fight against them, they're the ones who are going to loose.
We all know what could happen if we do not follow the laws of nature, or the laws of the land we are living in. Keep in mind that we cannot change other people, among these are included:
Family members, such as: spouse, kids, parents, and other relatives. Then we have neighbors, friends, coworkers, strangers, enemies, and so on.
We just cannot change any of them and it doesn't matter how much we want to. It's like fighting a losing war. So, forget it, and focus on other things; the ones that can be changed. See, anybody can change himself or herself and it's their own duty to do that. What we can do for others is to make them aware of the fact that they have freedom to stay the way they are, or to change themselves. Also, we might create an environment that helps them to change and once done it is up to them to change. Many people are stressing themselves by trying to change others. The husband wants his wife to change. The wife wants her husband to change. The mother wants her children to change. The children want their parents to change, and so on.
What is the result? They stress themselves without any positive results.
Why? Because they are trying to change things that could not be changed, or at least the methods used are not the proper ones.
What we really can do is change our attitude toward them. Change ourselves first, and then they may change themselves seeing that we are different than before.
Remember we mentioned before that we humans have the tendency to mirror each other. We may know the saying:

"Kids don't do what they're told to do by parents but rather what they see their parents doing." This has been learned from childhood and tends to continue as adults too.

If you have a problem with somebody, see what you can do to fix it, do your share first, and then expect others to follow the example.

Now, let's focus on the things that we really can change: Ourselves, and our attitude toward other people or events.

Why in the world should we change ourselves? Do we have any reason to do this?

Well, if our life is perfect and we have no problems, then it's fine the way it is, and the need to change isn't necessary. But, if we have problems and difficult situations develop, probably an improvement is necessary to make our life better.

Also we should not forget the fact that we all make mistakes and need to constantly learn to adapt to new situations. Our life is a journey, and consciously or not, we are learning all the time. The difference is those who are aware of this are selective in the information that they feed their minds with. On the other hand, people who are not aware of this cannot protect themselves from the *garbage* that our societies have. Then it's wondered why they're in situations that cannot be handled? Why does this happen to them?

Remember that our mind is like a computer and it doesn't care what you put in it. It'll give out what you put in: "Garbage in garbage out."

The human mind was designed to constantly process billions of bits of information that's absorbed from the environment. After birth, a person starts collecting information that is processed by the mind. During life, our brain stores these bits of information in our memory banks.

When people need to make a decision, the brain goes back in its memory to find the best solution from the information that's stored in the past. Based upon what it finds, a solution is given.

In the case of we are poor learners the brain will have less information to compare with. But for those who are good learners and appreciate the value of knowledge, the decisions will be better.

No wonder people with less knowledge are part of the 99% followers; barley surviving.

On the other hand, people who appreciate the value of knowledge and progress are among the 1% of leaders who are succeeding in what they are planning.

So, we have seen that is wise to distinguish between things that we can change and things that we cannot and do our share in working with the ones that we could change.

Now, let's go and discuss a little bit about next category of so-called *stressors*.

3. Solvable Versus Unsolvable.

Things that are unsolvable that we try to solve and also things that we are suppose to solve, but are ignored.

- Not every thing that's impossible could become possible -

Many times in our life we get faced with tasks that we need to accomplish. In our desire to solve them, we are faced with ones that are our responsibility to do. Beside these, we are also faced with some that are not our responsibility to solve. Not being aware of the importance in differentiating between the two, we end up spending unnecessary time and effort trying to solve the ones that will never be solved. These are unsolvable and by not being aware, busy trying to solve the ones that are unsolvable, we do not focus on the ones that are our responsibility to solve.

In both cases, there is a great potential in getting stressed.

See, the problem is our focus is shifted in the wrong direction that makes us unable to do what we should. And we want to solve the wrong things that of course might results in stress.

What is needed is to make sure that precious time is spent on right things needed to solve, rather than on the things that cannot be solved.

Let's see some of these, and what we can do about them. In today's world, we are faced with many crises and worldwide problems such as violence, immorality, and many forms of lawlessness.

There are different government agencies and organizations or groups that are spending huge amounts of money and resources to fight these problems. Some times these situations are affecting many lives and people feel obliged to do something about them. When some of these situations happen in our life they bring a great deal of stress. The idea to do something is good, but the question is:

What is the right way and how to do it?

Spending a lot of energy into the wrong direction and we could be thinking that we are working hard toward something of value, but we might be wasting time on something that will never be accomplished.

And this will happen not because we are not capable of solving problems, but because we are working on the wrong task, an unsolvable one. We could be facing a difficult situation in the family caused by unfortunate circumstances. And of course we would like to do something about it. Are we working on things that really matter? Or do we start to fight in the wrong direction. A common mistake that people make in this kind of situation is that try to find out:

"Why has this happened to me? Why me? Why now? Why did you do that?" and so on.

This might seem to be reasonable questions, but they can also be a potential source of stress.

Things good or bad, happens to everybody and many times we just cannot protect ourselves 100%. Now, there are situations in which it's necessary to find out the reason for that particular situation and how to prevent it from happening again. But, some times there are situations that we just cannot control, and we might fall victim to some circumstances and bad things. Trying to answer why, we are putting ourselves into stressful situations. Because any time when we ask ourselves a question and we are in an emotional state of mind and do not have enough information about that situation, we'll experience a state of stress.

We mentioned before that stress is like an overload of energy on an electric circuit. It tends to overheat the circuit and eventually the circuit will short out. Something similar happens with our brain.

When we ask ourselves a wrong question and our brain does not have enough information to answer, it keeps looking back in our memory for the necessary information. Not finding it triggers a stressful state. Unaware of, we keep asking ourselves the same wrong question, thereby it keep triggering a stressful reaction.

That's why it's very important to learn to ask questions that'll trigger a positive feeling.

We should be aware of the fact that any time we talk to ourselves we actually give a command to the brain to find answers to our questions. If we ask the wrong questions, we'll end up stressing ourselves.

We might have a problem at work, caused by factors that are beyond our control. Many times we might ask ourselves the same wrong questions. The results of course will be the same, stressful situation. What can be done about it?

Well, instead of stressing ourselves by asking wrong questions we better look for real solutions that will help prevent this from happening in the future.

We cannot change something that already happened, but can prevent it from repeating again in the future. Instead of focusing on the event that is already gone, change your focus towards preventing it from happening again.

You might know the saying:

"Forget your tribulations, but never forget what they teach you."

We need our energy to be spent on the things that have value and on something we can control. By learning to leave the unsolvable alone, we do us a great favor, eliminating many potential stressors that make our life less unpleasant.

In other words, we become aware of the fact that our previous blueprint formed in our subconscious mind about these things is not the best one. It's our responsibility to substitute it with a better one. Then our attitude about these kinds of situations will change, and we'll find ourselves dealing the proper way with them.

Now, let's go and talk a little bit about the next category of so-called *stressors*.

4. Dreams Versus Reality.

Unrealistic expectations about the future, or unfulfilled dreams.

- Anybody can dream, but wise people dream achievable dreams. -

Another category of *stressors* that plays a major role in our life is: unrealistic expectation and unfulfilled dreams.
If we go back to our childhood, we can remember our many dreams. We wanted to do so many things and our imagination was running wild. As time went by, some of us forgot about these childish dreams and the reality of life made us to look at life in a more realistic way. But, others are still enchanted by childhood wild dreams and are still affected by them. These situations are seen more often with people who as children were ambitious dreamers, but for some reason, life for them was not as pleasant as it was supposed to be. Now, the truth of the matter is that the dreamers are the ones that have more chances to become somebody in life, rather than others who are not. But a dream without the necessary steps to fulfill it remains just a dream. If we start to become a negative inclined type of person, soon we will find out that we have one extra reason to get stressed more often. So, is there anything that can be done about this? Well there is, and it's not difficult to do. The first step in solving this is to make a list of our most desirable things that we want to do. Then take another piece of paper and divide it in two columns.
In the top portion of it write:
    1. Achievable now.
    2. Not achievable now.
Now take column 1 and divide it in two and again on the top portion write:
    A. Of value, and worth achieving.
    B. Of no value, and not worth achieving.

Than take the column 2 and divide it in two and write on the top portion:

    A. Achievable in the future.
    B. Not achievable in the future.

Now take the column 2.A, and divide it in two again:

1. Achievable in the future and of value.

2. Achievable in the future but not worthy, with no value.

Now once you finished with this list you can see by yourself that there is a certain logical order that you should follow. The reason that many people get stressed is because of unrealistic expectation or unfulfilled dreams that they don't follow the right order of achieving or fulfilling their dreams.

If somebody works hard to fulfill a dream that is not achievable now, they're just stressing themselves.

As we can see, it's not enough just to dream, we need more than that: To make a plan to fulfill these dreams in the right achievable order needs to be done. Otherwise they'll become a source of stress, when we see that the more we dream about them, the farther away they get from us.

Going back in our past again as a child we were so impatient about our dreams. We wanted them to be fulfilled right away. We felt bad when we didn't get them right a way and started to cry; we wanted them now. After many years, these associations are still in our memory and we still have these wants. As adults we might not cry to get them, but the feelings of urgency are still there.

Now, there is nothing wrong with a feeling of urgency in doing something. The problem is that when the focus is in the wrong direction and dreams are not achievable, this sense of urgency becomes a powerful source of stress. It's advisable first to make sure that the dreams we are holding dear in our minds to fulfill, are really achievable and worthy of our time and efforts.

See, it's not enough just to work hard, but more important to work hard on the right dreams.

Most people are hard working people. But, what they are working for so hard? Sometimes they work hard for something of little, or no value. That's why we see so many people that are hard working, but they are still broke. For some reason, they do not progress in life, even though they spend a lot of time and energy on their jobs. The same thing happens with unfulfilled dreams or unrealistic expectation.

Unless a person makes a list to determine which ones are achievable and worth the time, and stick to the list, they'll keep finding themselves working hard in the wrong direction. This will result in time lost frustrations and eventually in stress.

Learn the proper way to deal with these unfulfilled dreams and unrealistic expectations. By doing this, we eliminate potential stressful situations that these might create for us, and of course at the same time improve our life too.

Remember, we have an old blueprint in our subconscious mind about how to deal with these kinds of situations. Unless we consciously exchange that blueprint with a better one, our behavior will stay the same.

Now let's see the next category of potential stressors, and how to deal with them.

5. Inner Needs And Fears, Sources Of Stress?

When our best allies become our enemies.

- Fear; friend or foe? -

We have learned earlier about the two mechanisms: the propulsion and the self-defense mechanism. The first one produces inner needs, and the second produces inner fears. Not being aware of how these two are working, many of these inner needs or fears might become a source of stress. Let's take one a time and see what we can do about them.

1. Unfulfilled Subconscious Needs.

As we have learned earlier, there are four major personality types and each of them has two basic characteristics:
One is a positive drive towards fulfilling the inner needs that is triggered by the propulsion mechanism. And the other is a negative inner-drive away from things that might produce a danger triggered by the self-defense mechanism.
Now, how many people really know these things today, so they can plan their life in such a way that they can work towards fulfilling their inner needs and not against them? Let' me ask you a little question:
There are two drivers. Both of them have a driving license. But one of them is aware only sixty percent of the driving rules and the other is aware of all the rules. Now, what would be the chances for the first one to cause an accident, and what would be the chances that second one would be? The first one, by being aware of only part of the rules, could apply only part of them. On the other hand, the one that knows all the rules could apply them all. The same thing might happen with us when we are dealing with subconscious needs. Not knowing some of the rules, the first one has more chances to get involved in an accident. By not knowing, we cannot be aware. By not being aware of, we could put ourselves into a stressful situation.
So, it is wise to appreciate the value of knowing these things and by applying them we could very well eliminate many potential stressors.
Different from unfulfilled dreams, the subconscious needs are more powerful and our mind perceives them as a must, or we put ourselves in dangerous situations.
What we could do is to identify our own personality type, and based on that, we find out which our inner needs they are. Then once we know this, we learn a new habit of recognizing in our life what the obstacles are and circumstances that might cause us to not be able to fulfill these inner needs.
Knowing that, then we can do something to modify these circumstances so they'll result in fulfillment of our inner needs. In case we cannot modify the circumstances, we could reason with ourselves consciously about the length or duration that we might have to exercise patience until we will be able to fulfill them. Let's take a simple example to illustrate this:
Let's say that you are an aggressive personality type. Of course that your inner needs are to be in control of everything that happens around you. Now, at home because you are the *boss*, your inner needs are fulfilled pretty easy.

The company you work for sends you to a different city for some special project, to help another team of specialists for two weeks. Upon arrival at this location, you *observe* that many things should be done different and the other team members seem to be not aware of this. They keep working hard, but they are missing important things that make the job nonproductive. Of course you see yourself as the one that should be in control, and to direct everybody in the right direction.

The only problem is that you are not at home, and you are sent as a helper for the team, not as a leader. You try to advice some of those who are on the same level of authority as you are, but one of them tells you:

"Listen my friend, we have a boss who does the thinking. Our job is to do what he says."

How are you going to feel about that? That's very tough talk, and for you, who have the need to be in control, it's a big blow. You feel the need to do something about it, right now.

Now, many people not being aware of the fact that they are dealing with an inner need start immediately to take steps to fulfill their inner needs, regardless of the consequences. By doing this they'll probably put themselves into potential stressful situations that could have negative effects over their lives.

Now, because one is dealing with an inner need, they have the impression that the situation is in a critical stage and action is needed now, no matter what. If this happens, this type of person might do more damage rather than correct the problem.

The right way to solve this kind of situation is learn to recognize the difference between an inner need and a situation that really needs to be corrected. In our case, this person has both an inner need and a situation that needs to be corrected, which determine one to do something about it now. If people follow their inner habitual instinct, they might do more damage than repair. In this case, they need to exercise patience. But this is something that might be missing in an aggressive personality type.

By learning a habit of reasoning, that'll be triggered by the brain before our inner needs, it'll transform that inner energy triggered by our inner desire into motivation. Having enough motivation we can take the real necessary steps to be effective in solving the situation.

See, the secret is that, when without a right habit formed, the inner desire triggers the instant habitual reaction to the situation and then reasoning capabilities diminishes until it becomes zero. A person reacts to the situation and if the situation does not change according to their inner desires, it may very well become a stressful situation. But, if people learn a new habit of dealing with these kinds of situations, and when they approach a situation like this, a new habit kicks in. With the right habit to deal with these kinds of situations, the results are positive and the potential stressful situations are eliminated. Then, follow the normal steps that are effective because they are not taken under a previous habit, but under a new one that promotes thinking first, and then action. As a new thinking habit, they can use something like this:

"Is it worth dying for?" or

"First thing first." or

"There is always tomorrow." or many others like these.

By learning these expressions, what actually happens is, they form a blueprint in our brain's memory and our brain will trigger it any time we are getting close to a potential situation that has to do with our subconscious needs. Once it's triggered, these questions are brought up to the conscious level, so we understand the things needed to be done. These expressions are attached to meanings that are totally different from our old habit.

When anybody hears: "Is it worth dying for?" or "First things first" or "There is always tomorrow." What do they understand about them?

Well, it doesn't matter how urgent and difficult or important the situations are, our lives and health are more important. No matter how soon these need to be accomplished, the right and most productive way to deal with them is to start to do the first thing first. Also, it doesn't matter how urgent it could be, if we cannot do it at one time, there's always another day tomorrow.

By having this kind of information in our mind before we get into a stressful state, we consciously take the necessary steps to do things in a right way. Proceeding this way we become more productive and also eliminating any possible stressors that could make our life difficult.

Going back to our example, if you already have learned this new habit of dealing with inner needs, the situation is still the same, but your attitude is different. You'll still see that this situation needs to be dealt with, but the approach you are going to use is different. Having the habit already formed, it'll trigger these expressions in your mind:

"Is it worth dying for?" or "First things first" or "There is always tomorrow"

You still understand the urgency of the situation, but that inner need to be in control will transform itself in motivation, that'll help to take the necessary steps towards helping the situation to improve. And because "There is always tomorrow" and "First things first", you'll develop patience, understanding that there is no way to solve this situation right a way. It'll take a little time, but with determination, you'll be able to successfully accomplish it.

See, we are all capable of reasoning and following the right steps to accomplish something, but the only problem is if don't learn the habit of thinking first and then act, we will deal with the situation based on old the wrong habit of reacting under the impulse of the moment. Most of the times this habitual impulse triggers fear or anger, and they stop us from reasoning the right way to deal with the situation.

Let's take an example to illustrate the difference between an old habit that we unconsciously formed in the past that might have a negative effect, and a new one that we learn and could control for our benefit.

You walk on a street and you see two houses, one next to the other. In their back yards, there are huge gardens. One of the owners is a gardener and the other one is not. You take a closer look at their gardens and see a big difference between them.

One is nice and clean, with many kinds of flowers and vegetable grown in a professional manner. But the other looks like nobody ever did anything to it. The grass is way over grown, the weeds looks like they are the king, because they have grown way above the other plants and vegetables. In other words, the garden needs somebody to take good care of it. Now, both owners want to benefit from their gardens.

What will be the difference in benefits between them?

Well, we could agree that there is a big difference. Why do you think that there is such a big difference?

The main difference is that the owner who appreciating the value of his / her land, learned the necessary procedures that enabled them to use the potential of the land for their benefit. On the other hand, the other owner, unaware of the potential of the land, and too busy with other things; left the garden to develop by it. And, of course we have two different kinds of results.

Now let's change the word garden with the word mind. We have two different people, one that appreciates the value of their mind. Knowing this, they learn how to use the mind, and cultivate only things that will benefit them. . Also, he / she takes care of potential "weeds" that might want to grow in his *garden*. On the other hand, the second one, not being aware of their responsibility to control what is *growing* in the mind, and what kind of seeds are being planted, lets their mind be controlled by the outside environment. Of course by doing that the results are totally different from the previous one.

Going back to our previous example with your job, now you can understand that unless you take care and clean up your mind of anything that does not belong there, you have to put up with all the old *weeds* that have grown in your mind in the past, when you were not aware of the fact that you should be selective with information that enters your mind.

Once you understand this necessity, and then most probably you will be willing to take the necessary steps to change the situation for the better.

If we are honest with ourselves we might recognize that's more important that the results of our actions are positive. We need to do whatever it takes to learn to change our behavior rather than hold on to our old habits that are not able to solve situations the way they should.

By doing this, we'll be able to eliminate the potential stressors caused by having to deal with inner needs.

So, what we are basically doing is replacing the old blueprint that was formed in the past in our subconscious mind, with a new and better one. Once the new one is firmly established, our subconscious mind will use the new one, so our behavior will be different.

Now, let's go and see what we can do about the inner fears that might be a source of stress.

2. Unaware Of Dealing With Subconscious Fears.

Now, beside inner needs, we also might have inner fears as sources of stress. These might constitute an even more difficult challenge for us, because subconscious fears trigger feelings of danger resulting in more powerful potential stressors.

We have learned earlier about the self-defense mechanism. When we link any information to it, it becomes active and creates a negative emotion in our body, as a signal that we need to do something about this information because it might present a danger. Basically, it's doing its job. It's our mistake when for no apparent reason we trigger it into action. Remember, we mentioned earlier that the self-defense mechanism could be compared with the braking system in a car. It's very important that this system to be in working condition. But, if we step on the brakes at the wrong time, it doesn't know that we made a mistake, it'll start working; doing its job. It's up to us to use it at the proper time.

Many times in life we get into different situations, start to worry, get scared easily and realize that stressful situations are close by. Worry might transform into stress that stops us from being able to deal the right way with the situations. But, if we reason a bit, we just have no specific reason on why we're worrying.

In these kinds the situations we might have been dealing with an inner fear that we might not be aware of. And, of course we feel their negative effects over us. The main reason for these kinds of situations is that we are unaware of the importance of being selective in what we should let enter in our minds. In the past, we accepted information that trigger these inner fears at the wrong time; when they are not suppose to.

It's like when you are riding in a bus to work, and for some unexplained reason the driver pulls the emergency brake. What do you think is going to happen? Every body on the buss will go through unpleasant experiences with negative results. Now, the emergency brake is a system that works for the safety of the passengers, and should be used in proper situations. If it's used in improper situations this system, design for protection, will be the one that'll produce damages.

As mentioned earlier, humans are designed with a self-defense mechanism that goes on when they get close to a potentially dangerous situation. This system is design to work in two stages:

1. First stage, when our subconscious mind triggers the command to act, and it's an unconscious reaction, based on previous experiences with that particular situation.
2. Second stage is when we consciously plan and decide to avoid potentially dangerous situations.

Let's take on the first one:

1. First stage.

In this category we have to deal with two kids of situations:
1. When the danger is imminent.
2. When we are approaching potential danger.

1. When the danger is imminent.

In this category we have situations when we have no warning in advance. Everything is fine, then suddenly something goes wrong, and we are facing a dangerous situation. In this case the protective mechanism triggers the proper reaction that it could find in an instant moment, so we can be protected by the perceived danger. This is an instinctive reaction based on previous experience with this kind of information. For example:

You drive your car on the freeway minding your own business, when suddenly out of nowhere somebody cuts in front of you and steps on their brakes. You just don't have the time to analyze and make the right decision. You just respond instinctively based on what you learned in the past to do in case of a situation like this or similar: step on the brakes, and try to avoid a collision. Now this is a normal reaction to a situation like this. But, here is a very important thing that we need to pay attention to. The more time our subconscious mind has to decide what reaction to trigger, the less intensity of the emotion we feel. The less time it has to find the right decision, the more intensity the emotion is felt.

So, when the situation is critical, and the subconscious mind has very little time to analyze the right response, we feel an intense emotion, we say that we got scared, or some things like that.

Now, unaware of, we associate a negative feeling with these kinds of situations. That's why, the next time in the future when we are going through similar situations, we will feel the same negative feeling that we previously attached to these situations. These negative feelings are potential stressors that need to be taken care of by learning to disassociate them from these particular experiences.

It's very important to determine the difference between normal reactions of protection with high intensity due to the shortness of time for our mind to find the right reaction to that particular situation, and the negative state of mind that we unaware of associate with these kinds of situations.

The high intensity feeling is a normal reaction, and should not be eliminated, but the negative state of mind that we have attached to it after this happens. As a matter of fact, even if we try to eliminate this normal reaction, we will not be successful, but will result in getting stressed.

If you remember in the past about one of these situations, you will realize that at that particular moment you were going through an intense feeling, but only a little bit later you started to get scared and be afraid. That's when unconsciously, you attached a negative feeling to the situation, so the next time when you go through a similar situation, unaware of, you will trigger the same negative feeling, that could become a potential stressor. Let's say that when this situation happened, you had two of your young children with you. Probably they took it totally different than you. For them, it was an amazing experience, something they'll want to brag about to all of their friends. When they'll do this, you can see that there isn't any fear in their explanation, but only an excitement for the event that they went through. Why is that? Because for them, it was a sensational experience, not a fearful one. In their mind, there are no negative associations with this kind of situations, so they didn't perceive it as a dangerous one. But, as mature persons, being aware of the potential dangerous situation, we see it different and attach to it a negative feeling.

So, it's wise to recognize when we are dealing with these kinds of situations and, we need to remove these negative feelings that were previously attached to them. By doing that, we can eliminate the potential stressors that we encounter when we go through these kinds of situations.

Now let's see, about the second category of situations.

2. When we are approaching a potentially dangerous situation.

Now, all of us know that the more we do something the easier it becomes for us to do it later. In other words, we learn and master our habits by repeating them many times. This principle works with any habit, good or bad. So, when we know how to do something well, we say that we have experience in that particular case. The more experience we have, the easier we could find a way to accomplish it.

There are many times in life when we have to deal with potentially dangerous situations. Having experience in this area, we see potential dangers in advance, but unaware of we might attach them to a negative feeling.
And this is what we commonly call *Worries*.
May sound unbelievable, but this is the truth about worrying. It is nothing else but negative feelings that we have attached in the past to certain situations that were perceived as potential dangers. In other words, we keep recycling negative thoughts. And by doing this, we are putting ourselves into stressful situations.
What is stressing us is not the situations themselves, but the negative feelings. If we remove these negative feelings away from situations, we will realize that, we are moving towards potential stressful situations, but once the negative feelings are not there, we are able to think clearly and take necessary steps to avoid or eliminate the potential stressors. See, we're capable of reason and finding solutions for our situations.

What keeps us *worrying* is not our incapacity, but that negative feeling that makes us lose control and concentration. Once we lose control and concentration, the intensity of the emotions with the negativity of feelings are the right ingredient that result in worries. So, it's wise to learn to recognize when we are facing these kinds of situations and remove the negative feelings, before they become too strong and develop in stress. When we are in a stressful situation, it's almost impossible to control ourselves and try to remove these negative feelings. That's why we learn the habit of recognizing these kinds of situations in advance, so when we approach them, our brain will trigger caution and not fear. Not being under stress, we can consciously take the necessary steps to eliminate potential stressors. It's like, when after you got used to driving the car, your reactions to protect yourself from an accident will improve very much, if you are aware when a potential dangerous situation could happen. Because you have increased your ability to prevent potential accidents, the chances of getting involved in an accident are lowered. The same thing happens with worries. The more we learn to eliminate them, by recognizing that the negative feeling are responsible for the worries, and not the situation itself, the less chances we'll have to get into a stressful situation. Remember:
"We are not responsible to what comes to us, but only for what we hold on to."
"If it is to be, it's up to me"
What we basically need to do is change our old blueprint that our subconscious mind uses in these kinds of situation with a better one. Once done, our behavior will be controlled by the new one that will not create stress anymore.
Now, let's progress to the second stage and see what we can do about when we consciously decide to avoid a potential dangerous situation.

2. Second stage.

In the first stage, we couldn't consciously do something about the situation, but reacted based on the habits that were previously formed. In this second stage we have the choice to consciously do something about it, or even plan ahead on how to deal with potential stressful situations. When this is done, we are avoiding many potential stressful situations, because as we have mentioned earlier, the more we are prepared in dealing with a situation, the easier it'll be for us to go through it. This works in two ways:

We can have the good habit of thinking of how to consciously deal with a particular situation.
Or, we can have a bad habit of *thinking* of how to deal with a particular situation.
Humans, were design to continuously absorb outside information through our senses and as somebody once said: "Our mind is incapable to rest per say." As long as we are awake, our sensors are in working conditions, and we continuously absorb information from our environment. We can compare our mind to a microphone that is on all the time. It'll pick

up any kinds of sounds that are found around it. The same thing happens with us; we can absorb any information that the outside environment is bombarding us with. Now, we have two choices: We could accept all of them without discrimination. Or, we could learn to be selective, and accept only the information that might benefit us now and in the future.

As mentioned earlier, consciously, we can handle only one thought at the time. We have a choice to consciously keep our minds busy with positive constructive thoughts, and as result we will live a healthy life. Or, we can keep our mind busy with negative thoughts, and of course by doing that we setting ourselves up for failure, leading to an unhealthy lifestyle.

We have mentioned earlier about worries. Let's take another example to better understand what worries are and how to deal with them. We are all aware of the fact that people are benefiting of the services provided by banks. We also know that people put their savings in the bank. So, in other words, they save their money for the future, when they could use them in time of need.

Now, is there anybody that might save something of no value? Let's say just regular pieces of paper? No, nobody would do that, because these regular pieces of paper have no value at all. Is there anybody that might consciously save something that will cause them pain in the future? I don't think that anybody will do that.

See, when we keep thinking positive thoughts, we basically put in a saving box, positive feelings for future use. But by the same token, when we keep thinking negative, we are putting negative feelings in the saving box for future use. These are going to become potential stressors.

What we do today, by thinking positive thoughts, or negative ones, we basically save them and they'll become a memory for future use. Then in the future when they're remembered, they'll be relived.

Therefore, remember when you start to worry again, you basically start feeling these negative feelings, but more than this, you save them for later use. If you like that, then keep worrying, but if you do not like it, you better stop. You have the power, the choice and also the responsibility to do this.

We know that as long as we are alive, we use energy to function. No matter what we do, good or bad, we have to use energy to accomplish it. Now, let's say that you were given a pleasant assignment to do. What will be the state of mind that you'll have during this period? For sure that it will be a positive one, and you'll be able to accomplish it very well and easy.

But let's say that you were given another assignment that's very unpleasant. What will be your state of mind in this situation and how easy could you accomplish it?

Well, if you are honest, you could recognize that this situation is exactly the opposite. The assignment will be much harder to do, and you will feel that the progress is very slow in accomplishing it. Of course, that your state of mind will probably be a negative one. So, if somebody else forces us to accomplish an unpleasant assignment, we will feel that he / she is not our friend, or they do not care for us, right? We could say yes. But, what do you say if, unaware of, we do this to ourselves by choosing to think negative?

This is exactly what we are doing when we keep worrying or thinking negative.

See, it takes energy to succeed and it also takes energy to fail. It is wise to learn to make the difference between the two. Once we are aware of the fact that we are responsible for ourselves, we consciously could choose to dwell on the positive thoughts, rather than on negative ones.

We are familiar with the expression: *Negative self- talk*, or *negative thinking*.

We have mentioned earlier that during our life we learn many kinds of habits and one of them is to consciously plan ahead about the future. Now, we can spend energy thinking on positive terms and get positive results. Or, we may spend energy thinking in negative terms, and of course we become the creators of our own stressful environment. So, stop blaming it on others, because we can safely say that there are no stressors out there, but only the ones that we create for ourselves. Remember:

"It is not what happens to us that stresses us, but what we do with what happens to us."

We might have not been aware of this before, but now since we became aware of, it becomes our responsibility to do something about it. Since at all time we use energy to do things, why not use energy to do them right? Why should we do them wrong first, and then spend a lot of time and energy to repair them and do them again? It makes perfect sense to do them right the first time. By thinking positive we stop being our own enemy, and start becoming our own friend. By doing this, we eliminate many potential stressful situations.

If a person looks around, they can see that everything in nature works in a harmonious way. In other words, everything follows certain rules and regulations and by doing that the harmony is preserved. We could learn from nature and plan our life ahead keeping in mind that the way we plan it's the way we live.
"Remember how you're going to plan your future, because you will spend all your life in it"
Way too many people today, plan to fail by failing to plan. It's like you get into your car parked in the street, turn the engine on and then leave it alone. What do you think is going to happen?
Nothing, because there is no driver to control it, eventually it'll run out of gas and dies off.
The same thing might happen with our life, unless we take control of it and plan positive actions instead of negative ones. Remember the next time when you find yourself thinking negatively; you're working hard to create your own negative stressful environment. If you really like it, then keep doing it, but for sure you will not like the results and remember that you always have a choice. It's nobody's responsibility but yours.

So, in this chapter we have learned that during our life we formed a blueprint on how to deal with these kinds of so-called stressors. When we encounter them, their old blueprint dictates our behavior. We need to recognize this fact, and if we do not like our behavior, we need to replace the old blueprint with a new and better one. Once we replaced it, of course that our behavior will change for the better. The so-called stressors have no more stressful effects over us.
Now, let's go further and discuss about the next category of so-called stressors.

6. Is The Past Really Gone?

Dwelling on the things from the past.

- Where am I really living? The present or the past? -

To better understand this, let's take an example:
In many ways, our brain works similar to a computer. In the computer, we put in many kinds of files. We can design these files at our own discretion by putting information audio and visual together and of course we have to put a name to each of these files. Once saved in the computer's memory, any time in the future we want we can retrieve these files by typing their name. Instantly, the whole package of information appears on the screen so we can start working with them. After finish working, we have a choice to put them back the way they were, or make changes by erasing or adding some information to these particular files.
The difference between a regular computer and our brain is that in our case beside the audio and visual information, we unconsciously attach a mental state or feeling to each file.
Based on our previous experience with that particular situation, we might attach a positive state of mind, or a negative one. All these go into the brains memory.

When we remember things from the past, it's exactly like when we type the name of a particular file that we want to open. Automatically our brain will bring to our conscious level, the type of information that is wanted. Of course, we'll start to feel whatever feelings were attached to them, positive or negative. This process of remembering is very useful, but also misunderstood, and has a very stressful side effect.

Because when we remember unpleasant things from the past, we put ourselves in the situation of reliving these negative feelings that were associated with them.

So, an important thing for us to understand is that in our memory, these neuron-associations that we formed every second are made not only of audio, and visual information. They are coupled with a mental state or feeling that as we mentioned before, could be positive or negative based on our experience with the information. All this happens automatically in a split of a second.

When we remember some things from the past, we unconsciously bring back these neuron-associations at conscious level. Many people have the habit of *living the past*, and unconsciously keep relieving the same negative feelings that they have attached in the past by these situations.

Also the negative self-talk that many people have the habit of using, has the same negative effect over them. Unconsciously they keep retrieving files from their memory that contain negative feelings attached to them, and of course by doing that they are exposing themselves to these negative feelings.

They have in their minds situations or events that were not handled properly according to their satisfaction, and are unconsciously having a priority in their thinking. But since they are gone, there is no sense to keep trying to change the past. It'll not happen. It will just create a stressful state of mind.

They do this because in the past, they have formed a blueprint in their subconscious mind that says it's OK to keep thinking about negative past experiences. Not being aware of the way their mind works, they do not see the necessity of changing their mentality about this. But, the only way to stop living in the past is by changing the old blueprint with a new and better one.

Now, realizing that by *living in the past* we are the ones that are punishing ourselves, and knowing how to create a new blueprint, it's our responsibility to do something about it. Otherwise we keep living our life like we did before and it wouldn't be a pleasant one. We should remember that:

"If you keep doing what you're doing, you'll keep getting what you're getting."

"Be careful with the way you plan your future, because you'll spend all your life in it"

So, until now we have seen the major sources perceived by us as being so-called *stressors*. We perceived them this way because of our old blueprints that were formed during our life. And, of course having these specific blueprints, our behavior was dictated by them. As long as the old blueprints are still there, our behavior will remain the same. But, understanding the way our mind works, and who dictates our behavior, each of us has the opportunity to change the old blueprints with new and better ones. Once we do that, our behavior will be different. We stop seeing these so-called *stressors* as *stressors*, and start to see them into a different light that does not causes us to get stressed anymore.

In part one of this book: "Who really are we?" we have learned that we all are wonderful human beings that already posses the ability to live happy and a stress free life. Coming to the end of part two: "What are we dealing with?" we are getting a better understanding of what stress really is, where it comes from and the role we play in its creation. Now, let's reveal some secrets that'll help us combine the new information about ourselves with the new understanding of what stress really is, in such away that we too can live a stress free life. The next secret will help us understand that we need to free ourselves from the past in order to live better today.

Chapter 9. Who really are the stressors?

Part 2. Review Question: What are the six major groups of the so-called stressors, and what can we do about them?

Answer:
- Our vocabulary plays a major role in the quality of *food* our mind digests. The quality of our speech reduces and increases the emotional quality of our life.
- The uselessness of knocking on locked doors. Before you start to work hard, you should make sure it's in the right direction.
- Some things no matter how much we want still are impossible to solve.
- Dreams are the first steps in accomplishing any great thing. The best dreams to dream are the achievable dreams.
- Our inner needs and fears. Are they our friends or foes? The inner drivers of our behavior let us have them as our best friends.
- Our past is no more a major negative factor in our stressful life, but is just a reference guide.

"If these six major group of stressors would be a monster with six heads, what would happen if one by one we are to cut down all of its heads? The monster will have no more power over us."

"……The music ceased, and the auctioneer, with a voice that was quiet and low, said;
"What am I bid for the old violin?" And he held it up with the bow.
"A thousand dollars, and who'll make it two? Two thousand! And who'll make it three?
Three thousand, once, three thousand, twice, and going and gone," said he……"

Part 3.

When The Impossible Becomes Possible.

Part 3.

When The Impossible Becomes Possible.

Secret # 10.

"Free yourself from stress, start enjoying a better today and an even better tomorrow."

Chapter 10. Solving The Mystery Of Stress.

-Without education the gift of freedom becomes a curse. -

By now, we have a reasonable understanding of how our mind works, the laws and principles that govern its functions and the way our brain processes information. Also, we have seen things that used to trigger a stress response from our body. Now, we can go forward and learn some simple ways to eliminate stress.

We have learned previously that during our life we continually interact with the environment and absorb information. To each bit of information we give a meaning and we unconsciously link it to the propulsion or to the self-defense mechanism. If it's linked to the propulsion mechanism it produces a positive emotion that is felt by our body. On the other hand, if it's linked to the defense mechanism, it produces a negative emotion that also is felt by our body. Based on its level of intensity, we might experience different levels of pain.

From the previous information we learned about our old blueprint from the file *how to deal with stress*. That old blueprint says that we cannot eliminate stress. As long as we live, we have to put up with every kind of stressors.

By the way we have been dealing with stress in the past, we have realized that this blueprint has to be replaced with a better one. Yes, we can eliminate stress. One that says we are stress-free persons. Stress isn't our cruel invincible enemy anymore, but an option. It's up to us to live a stressful life. Then our behavior will reflect the new one. We are going to create a *new file* and a new blueprint for it.

Once a blueprint is created, the new file needs as much information as possible to override the old one. Also, we are going to create a new and better *file manager* that is going to affect our overall behavior. We don't want the old file manager to contradict the new stress free file.

An important thing to remember is that once we start to get into a *stressful situation,* it's difficult or even impossible to get out of it before it takes its course. We need to be prepared in advance on how to learn to deal with it. By being prepared in advance, our subconscious mind will bring this to our attention before we get into *stressful situations*. Being warned in advance, we could take the necessary steps to eliminate the stressor(s) that we might have to encounter. This is what we were going to do. We are going to prepare ourselves in advance so when the time comes to implement the knowledge we acquired, we'll be ready. Let me ask you a simple question to illustrate this point.

Why doesn't the army do a very intensive and continuous training with its soldiers?

Why not just recruit, arm them with the latest technology and let them wait until a war starts. Afterwards, tell them to do their best under the circumstances and get some training while they are fighting the war. How many army commanders will do that?

Nobody in the right mind will!

Why not?

Because for the soldiers to perform well in a war, they need to be trained even before the war starts. All the training is continuously done for this simple reason; to be prepared and ready when the time comes.

The same principle applies in our case. In order to win the war on stress, we need to train our mental and physical powers before we get into stressful situations, not waiting until we get there; then trying to make the best out of it.

Now, let's see how we can accomplish this.

The first step in eliminating stress is to get yourself a notebook or something similar.

By now, you have a lot of knowledge about the way your body and mind works.

Now it's time to find out what's inside of your *stress file*.

You're going to do a *brainstorm session*; put on a piece of paper everything that you know about stress. Not only your opinion but also as many stressful situations that you have encountered during your lifetime. Go back to your childhood and remember the most stressful situations that you went through. Even though they happened long ago, they still might be a source of stress unless you do something to *heal the past*.

Then you arrange these items in a specific order; for example, number one, two, three….

The ones that you believe are your worst stressors; put them near the top of the list.

By doing this, you have the major information from the *stress file* of your memory.

This file, like any other, has a blueprint that when activated, directs your behavior in a stressful situation.

What we need to do is replace the file with a better one. When it's new blueprint is activated or triggered, it will direct your behavior in such a way that you will enjoy a stress-free life.

Before, when you went through stressful situations, that old blueprint that you were not aware of was the major factor that directed your behaviors. Replacing it with a better one gives you the power to direct your behavior toward the direction you want it to go.

Now, let's go ahead and see how we can apply what we have learned. There are two ways that we get stressed. One, by the new stress that we create daily; secondly, by relieving the old stress that was stored in our memory. For some reasons, we bring it back to the present and relive it again. We are going to start with the first on and learn how to stop producing new stress.

"Closing the doors on stress."

1. Stop Producing New Stress.

-People are as happy as they make-up their minds to be. -

Now, understanding these things, anytime you have to deal with situations that have previously caused you stress, ask yourself: What would be a better blueprint for these types of situations? Think deeply about a better blueprint you can make for your subconscious mind.

We have seen in the chapter: *Who really are the stressors*? What their major *sources* are. The reason that these stressors are major *sources* of stress is because we have a negative blueprint in our subconscious mind about them. Anytime when triggered, they will have a stressful effect over us. Knowing this, we will change the blueprint with a better one. Once the blueprint is replaced in our subconscious mind, the old one with negative feelings attached will be gone. We learned earlier that we are going to use *positive affirmations* as the foundation for the new blueprint.

Now, let's take each of the major sources of stress from our list and find a positive affirmation.

In the past, not being aware how our mind processes information, we have used all kinds of words and expressions. Now, knowing better, we form new positive and constructive affirmations:

"I am smart enough to use positive and constructive vocabulary, enjoying the positive state of mind resulting from it".

Now, being aware of the fact that it is useless and stressful to preoccupy our mind with things that we cannot change or solve, we have a better affirmation:

"I am smart enough to preoccupy my mind with things I can change or solve, knowing that I am capable of accomplishing them and at the same time enjoying the positive results".

Realizing that even though the past is gone, we can recall from our memory banks positive or negative memories and relive the feelings previously attached to them, now we choose to dwell on positive memories:

"I choose to dwell on positive memories from the past, enjoying the feelings attached to them."

Understanding that it makes no sense to keep dreaming about unrealistic dreams, we get more realistic in our dreams and get a new affirmation:

"I am a realistic person, distinguishing between possible and impossible dreams."

Learning about the negative effect that some inner needs and fears might have over us, we come up with a new affirmation:

"I am a kind, lovable and peaceful person and I'm always ready to help others by meeting their inner needs; avoiding triggering their fears."

These are a few new affirmations that by really believing and firmly implanting them in our minds will replace the old, stress producing ones. Once we do that, our subconscious mind will have a new and better blueprint to follow. We incorporate all of these with this statement:

"These are better affirmations for me and they will form a better blueprint for my mind to follow. By doing this I am becoming a stress free person; bringing more happiness in my life."

Now, beside these new affirmations that will replace the old ones, we are going to make a habit that each morning, we look in the mirror and tell ourselves:

"I am responsible for the way I feel and today I am deciding to be a stress free person; with positive, constructive behaviors."

In the evening, we do an analysis of that day. If we did improve a little bit we tell ourselves:

"I am getting better and better every day."

Now, if during the day we went through negative or unpleasant situations, we need to make sure that we resolve them in our minds before we go to sleep. We do this by finding a better blueprint for them.

By doing these simple things, we become aware of the importance of the role we play in our happiness and recognize that it's up to us to behave in such a way that we become stress-free persons.

We are all familiar with money. These are pieces of paper each have different value. $1, 5$, $20, $100, etc. Even though they are all the same size and shape, there is a big difference between them. For example, I would rather have one $100 bill, than eighty $1 bills.

Similarly, the *value* of our words and affirmations has *value* over our behavior. Positive words and affirmations will have positive effects. Negative ones will have negative effects.

What we have done is replaced the old words and affirmations that had a negative effect over ourselves with positive ones. By doing this, the results are positive.

Now, let's go ahead and talk a little bit more about some steps we need to take to stop producing new stress.

A. Avoid stress before it happens.

- The best way to win at war, is not to start one -

Now, let's see how our own body can help us avoid stress even before it happens.

We have learned earlier that there is a strong relationship between the physical behavior of the body and its mental or emotional state. We are all familiar with movies. We all know actors / actresses learns the script in order to make the movie.

So, what does an actor do? How do we know if he /she is a good actor?

Do they continuously look in the mirror to see if their facial expression corresponds to the script? No, they know how to portray the image required. Inside their minds, they create the states they want and automatically their bodies reflects these expressions.

Unconsciously or not they know that there is a relationship between the inner state of their minds and the posture of their bodies.

When we look at the posture of an actor's body, it tells us how they feel and the meaning of the character(s) they want to portray. The actor associates himself or herself to the role that is being portrayed and by doing this, his / hers body reflects their inner state of mind.

When people look at their performances, it looks real. If they didn't absorb themselves into these roles, everybody will realize that they are lousy actors.

Becoming consciously aware of this important fact, we start to pay attention to our body posture by making sure that it's set in the right position for each particular situation.

By doing this, automatically the state of mind will reflect that we are in tune with the situation.

We have learned earlier about the process of association and disassociation. We do this every day, we are just not aware of it. We are going to learn to *disassociate ourselves* from potential stressful situation or events and *associate ourselves* with pleasant situations or events.

When we are getting close to a stressful situation, we are going to *disassociate ourselves* from it. By doing this, we are not going to internalize its emotional charge. We are just spectators, not getting emotionally involved in it. By not associating with the stressful situation we can maintain a positive state of mind and not get stressed easily.

By disassociation from the old stressful situations or events, we remove the previous links to the self-defense mechanism. We all do this process unconsciously many times in our life. Now it's time to do it consciously in such a way that we become able to live a joyful life.

A major tool in learning to eliminate stress is to start consciously doing what we unconsciously used to do during our childhood.

By learning to practice this we are going to make our life less stressful and more enjoyable.

Let's take a simple example to illustrate this:

One day you get home from work and before you enter the house, you smell the yummy, delicious odors of food from the kitchen. You didn't taste or even see the food but by smelling its aroma you realize that there is something good for you inside. We can learn to develop a sense of *smell* and get a pretty good idea of what's going to follow. Well, we can use the same principle when it comes to stress. We can develop a sense of *smell* when we approach a *stressful situation*. Once we smell one coming, we *disassociate ourselves* from stress. By doing this, we are not feeling the negative nature of it, we are just spectators without getting emotionally involved.

B. Learn to create positive new events or situations factual or fiction, by giving a positive meaning to the environment.

- Dream long enough until your dreams become reality -

Humans are creatures of nature. In other words, we like the peace, tranquility of nature. We anxiously wait for our vacation time to spend it going to the mountains, lakes or other places in nature. Spending few days or weeks in the outdoors gives us more energy and zest for life.

Now, we are going to do a simple exercise, but before we begin, it's helpful that we find a quiet place where we cannot be disturb. Then to calm ourselves down and bring ourselves to a state able to accept suggestions, we start to imagine a wonderful nature scene. By doing this, we are able to switch our brains activity from the left side that we use in general, to the right side of our brain that controls our subconscious behavior.

Now, let's do the exercise:

Imagine that right in the middle of the wonderful nature scene, there is a movie theatre. You get in and start watching the movie that is playing, which happens to be your life's movie three years from now. Being just an observer, and not a participant, you *disassociate* yourself from what's happening on the screen. By taking this position, you understand what's going to happen to you but you are not part of it yet. You didn't do anything about your stress problems and you could see yourself living a miserable life full of stress and unsolved problems. Many family problems are caused by stress. Working environment is stressful, friendships ruined, etc.

Do you like what you see? Well, if you don't want this movie to become reality, you have a choice to do something to stop it.

Now come back to the present, breathe easily and be thankful that it was just a movie; not reality.

Imagine now again that you are three years in the future. This time you *associate yourself* to this movie. For three years you live a stress-free life. See yourself as a new person, with a new flavor for life. Your family situation improved beyond your wildest imagination. The relationship with your spouse and children is very good. Your house becomes again a *sweet home* where you are welcomed and are anxiously waiting to come back. Your workplace became a pleasant environment where your boss sees you as an asset to the company.

Your friends see in you as a fun and wonderful companion to be with.

By doing this exercise, you are creating new positive memories that are stored and used in the future by your subconscious mind.

Imagining three years in the future living under stressful conditions, we actually link these events to the self-defense mechanism. Doing this, our brain will tend to keep us away from such things that might cause harm. When we imagine ourselves three years in the future living under stress-free conditions, we link these events to the propulsion mechanism. By doing this, we are going to be attracted toward these events so we can bring them into reality. By repeating in our minds the movie of living a stress-free life, we are strengthening the *new file* about *stress-free life* and at the same time we are reducing the power of the old negative file.

Practice this as often as possible, the more you do this exercise the faster you build the new blueprint and at the same time diminish the power of the old one.

Now, let's go and talk a little bit about how to stop depositing negative information in our mind.

C. Stop depositing negative info in your mind.

- Never save fake money, it won't help when you are in need -

During every day of our lives, we go through many kinds of situations and events. Through all our senses, the brain absorbs bits of information that make up these situations / events; stores them in our memory banks. Over the night when we sleep, these bits of information are selected, arranged, stored in specific *files*. In order to stop our brain from storing negative information in our memory files, we are going to modify the negative ones right before we go to sleep. By doing this, we avoid depositing negative information in our mind that later on could become sources of stress.

Therefore, before you go to sleep, make sure that all negative situations or events from that day are *repaired*. By doing this, you are not storing any stress producing information.

Every evening before you go to sleep, do a summary of your daily activities and *repair* any unpleasant situation or event that were stressful. Doing this, you stop your brain from filing these unpleasant experiences that could have been used in the future to produce stress. Also, when you close that *file* for the day, next time when you open it again, you'll find what you left last time attached to it.

Let's see how can we do this:

Suppose that we had a fight of words with another person that created a negative atmosphere. Nothing was solved and even worse we all left blaming the other for the trouble.

Now, it's evening and we are ready to go to sleep. We are going to ask ourselves some simple questions:

"If we would've been at fault; would we like to be forgiven by others?" Of course, we would. Now, if the other person would be willing to forgive us; that would be nice. Right? Yes, it will show that they are kind and understanding.

But, only they are kind and understanding people? How about us? I think we are too.

Even if it would have been their fault, we think that we are kind and understanding enough to forgive them. We do this first to protect ourselves and to protect them. We protect ourselves by forgiving others; thereby creating a new solution for a new situation. Overnight our minds will store the new meaning we gave to the same situation. In other words, we stop depositing negative information that will later on become a cause for stress.

This is just a simple example to illustrate our point. The basic idea is by using our reasoning ability we can modify any negative experience(s) we went through; thereby turning it into negative free ones.

Now, let's go and discuss about another step we should take to stop producing new stress.

D. Make your own body a helper in stopping the production of new stress.

- Your body, your best friend -

Did you know that your body continuously talks to you?
Did you know that the posture of your body affects your stress level?
Understanding the important relationship between the position of muscles in your body and our emotional and mental state, we learn to position our body in such a way that helps maintain a positive state of mind.
How you normally walk?
How your shoulders lean?
How you hold your head?
What is the position of the muscles on your face?
How do you breathe? Etc.
Example:
If you were the president of a company with many employees; would you have an open door policy towards your employees? Would you listen to their voice, needs and ideas?
Research shows that by having an open door policy, a better working environment is created. The employees are doing a better job and the company fairs better.
On the other hand, by having a closed-door policy, neglecting the employee's suggestions, needs and ideas; the overall situation of the company becomes less productive. The employees are less interested in putting forth their best for the interest of the company. The result; nobody wins.

Now imagine your own body as a huge company. It has a few trillions employees. Believe it or not, all are doing a pretty good job. Just as in a regular company, sometimes some of the employees want to talk to the C.E.O. They might have an important message to convey. Is the C.E.O. going to listen? Are YOU going to listen? Yes, YOU, the C.E.O. of your body! Do you have a habit of listening to what your body wants to tell you or through pain killers or other medicines like these; you are continuously try to silence them?
Well, you may silence them for a while but probably you're going to hear from them again shortly.

A simple but important way to help us keep healthy is through breathing exercises.
Well, everybody breaths you may say. Of course we do, that's why we are alive.
How do you think your car runs if from time to time you fill it up with a better grade gasoline? It will run better. If it could talk it would most probably say: Thank you!

Something similar happens with our bodies. Because most of our cities have a high rate of pollution, the air we breathe has more than normal level of pollutants. When we do breathing exercises we are helping our body to give an extra dose of oxygen to all its cells. Also, our circulatory, nervous and immune systems work better. So much gain, for so little effort. The breathing process is very simple: breathe in slowly until your lungs get filled with air. Then hold in the air about fifteen to twenty-five seconds. Then slowly breathe out. In the beginning you may not be able to hold the air for that long but with practice you will gradually increase it. Do this ten times in a row, when you wake up in the morning and also before you go to sleep.
Learn a habit of doing these breathing exercises. You are going to be pleasantly surprised to find out how much more energy you get by doing them. Not only that but your overall health could improve.
Remember you are the C.E.O. of your body. If the C.E.O. of a real company gives a sizeable raise to all its employees; do you think they will show appreciation and work harder for their boss? Probably yes. When you practice these breathing exercises, you are giving all the cells of your body a sizeable *raise in their salary*. You, the C.E.O. will get a great reward; a healthier body!

E. Avoid Thinking About The Past.

- Stop opening old coffins. -

Our past could be our friend but also our enemy. We all have the capability to remember and bring back so many beautiful moments from the past. We can recreate by going back in our memory and relive them again and again. On the other hand, this might be a cause of stress if we are not aware of what kind of information we bring back from the past.
Let's take an example to further understand this concept.
Suppose that you were working for a big company. One day, after you got to work, a terrible accident happens not far away from you and a few people died. This was a very frightening experience to see these people dead and so much damage done to the building because of this accident.
Now, does it make any sense that you should go back to the place of the accident many times so you can revisit these frightened experiences? I don't think so, because anytime you go there, you are the one that goes through a negative experience again and again. It's better to let the past go especially when it produces negative emotions.
One simple way to eliminate much of the stress that we encounter is to avoid thinking about negative past experiences.

Remember what we have learned earlier about the neuron-associations that are stored in our memory? Knowing that negative experiences from the past are associated with negative emotions, what's the use of recycling them over and over so that we can get stressed anytime we do that? We need to let them go; they are gone unless we bring them back for our own discomfort and stress. Until now, we were not aware by reliving these negative experiences we were punishing ourselves. Now that we know better, don't you think its time to behave better?
Remember, "If it is to be, it's up to me."
By reasoning this way and really believing these things, you are basically helping replace the old blueprint from your subconscious mind with a new one. Once the new one is firmly defined in your subconscious mind, it will be triggered anytime when needed in the future. Also remember, with free will, being exposed to new information, you might replace the new blueprint again with another one. That could be better or worst. Pay attention to what kind of information you let enter your mind because much of it will do more harm then good.

As we have mentioned before, if we are thinking about positive experiences from the past we are bringing back positive neuron-associations from our memory banks that were stored there long ago. If we are thinking about negative experiences, we are bringing back negative neuron-associations from the past. As a result, we are reliving the negative state of mind that was associated with those negative situations.
Remember, in the earlier example with the computer, we mentioned that in many ways our brain works as a computer does. In the computer we input many kinds of files. We can make these files at our own discretion by putting audio and visual information together; giving each a file name.
Once saved in the computers memory, we can retrieve any of these files by typing their name. Instantly the whole file appears on the screen so we can do what we want with it. After we have finished working with it, we have a choice to put it back the way it was for future use or we might erase or add some information to that particular file. The difference between a regular computer and our brain is that in our case, beside the audio and visual information, we unconsciously attach a mental state or a feeling.

Based on our previous experience with this particular situation, we might attach a positive state of mind or we might attach a negative one. All of these are going into the brain's memory.

When we remember things from the past it is similar like when we type the name of a particular file that we want to open. Automatically our brain will bring to our conscious level, the information we wanted. Of course, we will start feeling whatever feelings were attached to them; positive or the negative.

After we have *relived* the information, we have a choice to erase the feelings attached to it or just put it back the way it was. Not being aware of the choice we have most of the times we just store back all the information we have *relived*.

An easy way to deal with the past is to learn to avoid thinking about negative experiences from our past.

Remember, you have a blueprint in your subconscious mind that says it's OK to think about negative experiences from the past but you were not aware of the damage you are doing to yourself. Now understanding reality better, you need to replace that old pain-producing blueprint with a new one.

The new one says:

"I am responsible for the way I feel. When I think about the past, I choose to think only about positive experiences."

"There are always chances for a better future for me and I feel good when I am taking these chances"

Once this new blueprint is firmly established in our mind, the subconscious mind will trigger it anytime it's needed. Of course, instead of pondering on negative experiences from the past, we see ourselves dwelling on the positive experiences. Anytime in the future, when we start thinking about any negative past experiences, our subconscious mind will automatically remind us about these expressions of the new blueprint.

Once these come into our minds, then we agree with them and repeat them again to ourselves. By doing this, we are reinforcing this new blueprint.

The more we practice this, the easier and more effective these expressions will be. In short time, we will realize that we lose that *burning desire* to think about negative past experiences.

We will start focusing on positive experiences and truly the future will become much better than the past. To better illustrate this let's take a simple example:

We are all familiar with cars and sometimes in the past we have learned how to drive one. Since then we drive as a habit.

Now, let's say that you drive your car on the road toward your workplace. Everything is fine for a while and then suddenly you see the cars in front of you are breaking hard; then a loud noise. What's your automatic response? Your first reaction will be to step on the brakes because an accident probably has just happened. When you hear the noise and see the car in front of you breaking, you step on your brakes and instantly look for the best move to avoid the accident. Why do you do that?

Nobody wants to get involved in an accident. Right? So, like any other normal person you also want to stay away from getting involved in an accident. Now my question is:

"Why did you step on the brakes immediately when you became aware of the fact that an accident might be ahead of you?"

The answer is that once you learned the habit of driving a car, unconsciously you programmed your brain to be vigilant and anytime it perceives danger it makes you more alert and triggers the proper reaction so you can avoid dangers. In other words you built a blueprint in your subconscious mind about what to do in these kinds of situations. You react this way any time when you get close to a potentially dangerous situation. Your brain goes on alert and triggers the reactions that you need to get out of trouble.

The brain acts as soon as it perceives the potential danger.

The same thing happens with any other habit. Once the habit is formed, the brain will trigger any necessary reactions that are needed to protect us.

Chapter 10.   Stop producing new stress.

When you learn the habit of treating the past as past and the future as different than the past, the affirmations you have learned will automatically come into your mind and you will start thinking what you can do right now to make sure that the future is better.

We have mentioned earlier that there are two things that happen when we get stressed: We loose control and concentration.

If we are already involved in a stressful situation, it's almost impossible to start reasoning and avoid it. If our brain triggers a warning signal before we get involved into a stressful situation, we can easily and consciously take the necessary steps to avoid getting into it.

This is the same type of response as our accident example.

We become aware that something happened in front of us and we take the necessary steps such as slow down, stop, and proceed with caution.

Acting this way we are staying away from a potential accident.

To protect ourselves, by acting before the situation happens, is just a matter of learning a habit that will be triggered by our brain any time that we get to a potential stressful situation. Once we are warned in advance it is easy to take the necessary steps to avoid it.

If we ask anybody that has problems in dealing with stress, after they got back to normal, if they have a second chance to go through the same situation, will they act the same way or will they act different?

Most of the time, they will tell you that they would act differently. They should have known better and avoided the stressful situation. They should have controlled themselves better in that difficult and stressful situation. Remaining calm and controlling themselves, the situation would have turned out more positive.

This is what we offer, that second chance to learn how next time to be equipped with the tools necessary to be able to stay calm, in control and eliminate the potential stressful situation.

Let's take another example:

Walking down the street you get close to an intersection with the intention of crossing to the other side. Would you just start crossing the street without looking around to make sure that there aren't any cars coming? I don't think so. Why is this?

A long time ago, when you were a kid, your parents taught you that it is very important to cross the street when the signal is green and only after you made sure that there weren't any cars coming.

In other words, you made a blueprint for your subconscious mind to know how to react in situations like these. This works like a learned a habit of protecting yourself so any time that you are thinking about crossing a street; automatically in your mind comes the warning:

"Look around for potential danger and cross the street only when it is safe"

Once you build this blueprint, it will stay forever in your memory, waiting to be triggered any time that you feel you are being exposed to a potentially dangerous situation.

By obeying this inner advice, you are protecting yourself from potential danger. You do this with many other things every day and by following these warning signals you keep away from trouble.

The same way you have built these blueprints for other things, you could build one more, a blueprint that says:

"Thinking about negative things from the past is a pain producing habit, I just don't need it, so cancel, cancel".

"I am a positive thinker. Thinking positive makes me feel better about myself and others"

Once you formed this new habit, your brain will trigger it automatically, any time you want to start thinking about the past.

Being aware of this, before you start to feel the negative associations from the past experience, you are still in control and can change the line of thought with a different one that helps to make the future better.

Let's always remember:

"Our past does not equal our present or future. The present is getting much better than the past. We have the right to live it and enjoy it. We stop confusing it with the past"

Now let's see another very important way to stop producing new stress, by talking a little bit about the *Power of Humor*.

F. *Get yourself a strong ally: Humor Power.*

- When life gives you lemons, go in the lemonade business. -

We know there is so much power in the world. We hear pretty often about atomic and nuclear power, electric power, political power, will power, physical power, the power of stress, etc. But how often do we hear about the humor power? Yes, what is humor power? Well, if the word stress has the power to destroy the happiness and joy of millions of people's lives, then humor has the power to restore and bring back joy and good feeling like a welcomed rain on a dry land. Humor has such a powerful positive charge attached to it that it's able to transform a person; bringing tears of joy to a sad and unhappy face. More important, it can undo some of the negative effects of stress. If stress affects negatively our immune system, then through laughter, humor strengthens it. If stress has the power to shorten ones life through its negative effects, humor through laughter and good cheer, beautifies our lives and even contribute to longevity. If stress is known to contribute to heart diseases or even heart attacks, humor stimulates our cardiovascular system; improving the flow of oxygen throughout our bloodstream. If stress is the root of many of our illnesses, humor not only promotes mental health, but even physical health by encouraging healing. If stress is responsible for low morale and productivity, humor is an effective and inexpensive way that could boost morale and productivity. If stress increases tension, humor does just the opposite; it diffuses tension. If stress impairs ones creative abilities, humor enhances creativity and problem solving.

But where do we go to tune the humor in our minds? How can humor become a part of our life?
Well, in order for humor to become and stay a part of our life, we need to understand how humor can be developed and continuously maintained. What kind of foundation is needed so humor could flourish and make our life more beautiful. By understanding this, humor could become part of our life, not just a cloth that is worn from time to time. Actually what kind of life is that where there is no joy, happiness and humor in it?

Now let's see something we need to understand and also what we can do to make humor part of our life:

1. Humor, the necessary ingredient to a beautiful life.

Even though it's missing from many people's lives, humor is an important ingredient. Because of a failing economy, family problems, insufficient financial ability, stress, etc. our lives tend to become dull, routine, and without flavor. We should always keep in mind and never forget that humor could rekindle our zest for life. It's one of our big mistakes that unconsciously we might not mind to keep humor out of our life.

Many years ago when I was in school, I heard a story about the mother in law with three daughter in-laws. One day at dinner, the mother in law asked her three daughters in-law how much do they love her.
The first one said: "Mom, I love you like the sun in the sky."
The second one answered: "Like the gold that shines."
The third one after thinking a little bit said: "Like salt in a tasty meal."
"What, only that much?" the mother in-law replied. Since then, she started to develop negative feelings toward her youngest daughter in-law. After a while the mother in law falls sick, and had to stay in bed for a few weeks. One by one the daughters in-law brought her food. When the youngest one prepared the food she added no salt to it at all. The food looked very well done but it didn't taste good. It was salt less.

After start eating from it, the mother in law understood what happened, and she called her youngest daughter in-law and said.

"I am sorry my dear, now I do know and understand that you really love me."

Yes, like salt that gives flavor to our food, humor is the one that bring zest to our life. It's a normal part of it. Some foods require less salt, some more. In the same way, humor, sometimes less, sometimes more, based on the necessity of the situation.

2. There is always something good in every situation.

How can such a statement be true? Do you remember watching little kids eating only the cream from the cookies? Yes, even a child already knows how to choose what's best for them. When did we start to forget to choose the best thing in every situation?

Somebody might argue: It's easy to find the good out of a positive situation, but how do you find something good out a bad or even tragic situation? Well, the reality is that we are too anxious to see the good right away. When the situation is positive, we could see the good right away. When the situation is the opposite there is still something good about the thing is that we might not see it right away. But by exercising patience, we come to the realization that you can identify something good from it. Let's take one of the worst scenarios: Suppose somebody close to us dies in an accident. This event is not a pleasant one and it brings tears and sorrow to everybody involved. What good thing can come out of such a situation? First of all, we recognize that we cannot change what happened. Since it did happen, should we just let it go by, or at least get something positive out of it? But what positive can we get? Well, when we lose somebody close, we start to look at our life a little more seriously. Then, we might start evaluating our relationships with others. Are we appreciating them enough? Are we spending enough time with them? Are we showing them enough love and caring that they deserve? Are we doing our best to make them happy? These are questions that we could ask ourselves and learn from them. By doing that we too could find something good out of a tragic situation.

3. Do we deserve to be laughed at?

If you don't learn to laugh at yourself now, you have nothing to laugh at when you get old. Who do you think you are? Like everybody else, just a drop of water in a vast and turbulent ocean.

Did it ever cross you mind to ask yourself why some people find it difficult to laugh at themselves and others don't? The more somebody has an inner balance and at peace with himself / herself, the easier it will be to laugh at their own mistakes. Fear is the major factor that blocks somebody from seeing himself / herself in a comic way. If we take a closer look at the way the world is governed by its rulers, we can say that there are two kinds of rulers. One kind of rulers is where people have the right to speak their mind freely without fear of persecution. And the other kind of rulers is where people cannot speak their minds freely. What's the main reason for this difference? Fear, yes this is the decisive factor in somebody's behavior. When somebody whose behavior is controlled by fear, he /she creates an environment where fear dominates. If we look at those countries with these kinds of rulers, we can see that they try hard to "protect" themselves with highly paid security forces that instill fear among their population. None of these rulers allow anybody to make fun of them or say something derogatory. That's considered treason and they have to be harshly punished. By having this kind of "arrangement", these people live a suppressed and stressful life not being allowed to become what they want to be.

On the other hand, the other kind of rulers, where fear is not a motivating factor, they are not afraid of being laughed at. Their people are not afraid to speak up their minds. By creating an environment like this, everybody gets the opportunity to develop and become what he or she really wants to be. The result is that everybody prospers.

Now, imagine that we are rulers that have jurisdiction over our environment. What kind of rulers we might want to be viewed as? The kind of rulers whose entire behavior is controlled by fear? Or the other kind? Think a little about this.

Now, if we are just like a drop of water in a vast and turbulent ocean, what about others? Who do you think they are? Just like us, a drop in the same vast and turbulent ocean. Now, I am not trying to say that we have a green light in going out and make fun of everybody around us. As we mentioned earlier, salt is very good, but too much salt also could have a negative effect. Some people are more sensitive than others and could feel hurt by our out of line humor. There is a healthy humor when everybody enjoys it, and unhealthy where some might feel offended or even hurt. If we are not sure, we should restrain ourselves from using humor at others expenses.

4. The most beautiful roses have thorns.

Did it ever cross your mind why do roses have thorns? There may be many explanations to this. My personal opinion is that these thorns are like the stamp "fragile" on a package that contains sensitive staff. It means, "handle with care." By doing that we could really enjoy their beauty and aroma. But by not paying close attention we might get hurt. The same thing could happen with humor. Misused could hurt very badly. So, we need to be careful not to abuse it, thinking that as long as we feel good it's ok. It might be ok for us, but how about the others that might be affected by our sarcastic humor? Remember salt is very good but use it in proper amounts.

5. Looking at humor as part of a bigger picture.

Why do you thing somebody will build such a grandiose project like the universe, and forget to make humor a major part of the lives of the most important tenants of this grandiose project?
Humor ranges from a simple smile to a soar stomach-causing laugh. All these degrees of humor have a positive effect on our bodies. When we laugh our whole body invigorates itself. As a result, all the functions of our body work better. Did you know that the international sign of friendship is a simple smile? How much does it cost? Nothing. Try this exercise for a while: Any time when you go to work or school or come home or into a store or any other place where there are people, when somebody approaches you, look in their eyes and give them a nice friendly smile. See what happens after a while. First of all you are going to see them in a different light; for some reasons they *seem to become friendlier*. You will start to feel at ease when dealing with them. The whole environment changes for the better. Remember, even though your life might have been in the past like a garden without gardener, where no flowers were growing, you have in yourself all the qualities of a good and kind gardener. You just need to become aware of this, and gradually work on building a wonderful garden, for yourself and others around you. Everybody enjoys looking at a beautiful garden. A simple way that some found to be very effective is to learn a habit of asking yourself some questions every morning right after you wake up. Such as: How can I have a great day today? What do I need to improve today to enjoy every moment of this day? What do I need to let go off today, so my relationships will get better? Since I have to live every minute of today's journey, why not make it a pleasant one? Who could stop me from having a great day? Who's responsible for my own feelings?
Once we asked ourselves these kinds of questions, wait awhile and find out what kind of answers come to mind. If any of the answers are not the right kind for the question, we cancel them by telling ourselves: That was part of the past, but now by knowing better, I am behaving better. I am going to enjoy every moment of this day.

Doing this simple exercise every morning we are laying a positive foundation for our mind to work. Having this kind of programming early in the morning becomes a positive *file manager* that influences the rest of the *files* that our brain is going to work with during the day. This influence is a positive and constructive one.

In the evening before we go to sleep, again take a few moments and do an analysis of the day. Did you make any progress? Do you have anything to *redo* before going to sleep? Do you have anything to erase, so they will not be stored in your memory banks? If you made some improvements, then congratulate yourself for the good work, saying something like this:
"Yes, I knew I can do it, and I am getting better every day."
If we did something that was wrong or negative, we could use our reasoning ability and find a better solution for the situation. We recognize that was a mistake, forgive ourselves and accept the new solution, so next time we know how to behave better.

We have learned that the first step in the process of eliminating stress is to stop producing new stress. We have seen the importance of avoiding stress before it happens. We learned how to give a positive meaning to our environment. We understood the importance of not letting out brain be a garbage can where anything could be dropped in. We realized that our body is one of the best allies in stopping new stress from growing roots in our mind. Then we learned that it does not do any good to ponder upon past negative experiences. And finally we understand the power of humor that enables us to bring zest and flavor to our lives.
Now, let's go and talk about the next secret; the second step in the process of eliminating stress that is needed in order to become stress free!

Review Question: In order to solve the mystery of stress, what is the first door we need to shut and how do we implement that?

Answer: The first door is to stop producing new stress. We implement this as follows:
- The best way to win a war is not to start one, so we avoid stress before it happens.
- Every great thing accomplished was started with a dream in somebody's mind. By creating positive new events and situations, we start dreaming achievable dreams long enough until they become a realty.
- Becoming aware of the uselessness of saving fake money, we stop depositing negative information in our mind.
- Regardless of how we used our body in the past, now we get a new ally, our own body.
- Realizing that by opening old coffins we do ourselves a disfavor, we avoid unnecessarily thinking about our past.
- Finally, when life gives us more lemons than we actually need, with the help of humor power we add sweetness to them and go in the lemonade business.

"If these six areas would form a six layers body armor, wouldn't it be wise for us to wear our armor all the time?"

Secret # 11.

"Eliminating stress from negative past experiences by erasing the negative feelings previously attached to them."

Chapter 11. *2. Healing the past.*

- Are the peace-makers really happier? -

Healing the past? Why would we mess with something that is already gone?
Well, when we are healthy our body is in a state of balance and harmony. If for some reason we get sick, our body goes out of balance. Basically, healing is a natural process instilled in our body. The body itself, if left alone has a tendency to heal itself.
Example: You cut your finger. What's going to happen? Immediately, the brain sends to that location specific messengers, some to fight the outside invaders and others to start the process of healing. Pretty soon, the wound is a thing of the past with no signs of injury, if it was a minor cut. If was a major one, the wound still heals but maybe you are left with a little mark; a reminder that you should be more careful next time. To heal means to bring back health to our body, to restore the original balance and harmony.
Now, how can we heal the past?
That's a good question but even though the past is gone, its memories are still stored in our brain. For our subconscious mind that continuously uses information stored in its memory, there is no such thing as past or future. Everything that is stored in is at present tense. That's why we need to do some changes in our memory banks. Remove the negative feelings that we have attached in the past to the so-called *stressful people, events or situations*. By doing this, anytime we consciously or unconsciously retrieve any of these memories, they won't have any stressful effect on us.

We know from our own experiences that most of the things that we put together; we might be able to take apart. Every second our brain is working in forming neuron associations between the video and audio information, our sensors are continuously absorbing from the environment. Even more than that, based on the meaning we give to the information, we associate this with a mental state or feeling. As we said before, this mental state might be positive or negative.
Since we are the ones that form these associations, we should be the ones that are capable of changing them according to our conscious desire. In other words, we made these neuron-associations; we also could break them. Let's see how we can do this.

We have mentioned earlier that our mind works very similar to a computer. In the computer, we can store many different files and have a conscious access to review, erase, replace or update any information we choose from these files. We could do something similar with the *files* from our brain.
We know that we can learn anything if we put our mind to it. More than that, we have the ability to consciously remember things from the past. Also, we know that we consciously change the information that has been stored in our memory, by adding or erasing the ones that we like.

Chapter 11.   Healing the past.

In this chapter, we are not interested in erasing audio or visual information but only the negative feelings that are attached to them.

Because, as we mentioned earlier, the things that have a stressful effect over us are not the video or audio information but the negative feelings that we previously have attached to them.

These negative feelings must be erased or replaced; afterward the stressful effect will automatically disappear.

We are going to look at two methods that could be used in erasing the negative feelings from the neuron-associations formed in our memory: The reasoning method, and the substitution method.

Let's take the first one and see how can we benefit from using it.

A. *The reasoning method.*

- Thinking ability is what makes humans superior to any other creatures. -

This method is very useful because learning a habit of asking us a few simple questions could easily eliminate stressful effect. This method could be mostly used when the so-called *stressors* are people, places or things.

We have learned earlier that our brain stores the bits of information received during our life in files, each file dealing with a specific subject. For example:

We have the health file. In this file are stored all the bits of information that were absorbed during our life about our health and our own opinions about our health.

We have the family file. In it, are stored all the bits of information about our family. All the family members, and specific things related to them. Of course, our opinions about them are also stored in it.

Then we have the working file and so on.

What are we going to do? We are going to take one file at a time and get rid of all negative associations that were stored together with this file. Once they are free, next time we access them they won't have a stressful effect over us.

Once we take a file for reviewing, we ask ourselves a few questions:

What is it that I could define as the most stressful item from this file? Write down on a peace of paper the name of the person, thing, situation or event that comes to your mind. Then take that item and consider it as the manager that will give the meaning of the whole file. Imagine that the item is in front of you; you look at it, then make peace with it, realizing that you do this for your own good. Imagine that it responds positively to your action. After you finished this process, imagine that item again and see what kind of feelings you have towards it. If it's a positive one, the file is done. Go to the next file. If you still have negative feelings, redo the process again, until there are no more negative feelings left. By doing this process, we are removing the link between the item and the self-defense mechanism. Hence, there is no negativity attached to it anymore. By redoing the file and saving it in our memory, next time when we open the same file, it will contain new information we put there last time. It will become a new and better one.

Remember: We have learned previously that our subconscious mind has already formed blueprints for every file in our memory. Some of these files contain so much negative emotions, that the blueprint generates anxiety or stress when they are triggered. What we need to do is to find a way to change that blueprint with a better one that doesn't have negative emotions attached to it. In other words replace the negative feelings associated to that specific *stressor*.

Now, are you going to live your life the old way? Or will you decide to make the necessary changes to get the desired results. I think it's about time *you make peace* with yourself by stop being the first stumbling

block on your journey to a stress-free life. Not only that but also to make peace with the *environments* that shaped us the way we are today.
We have mentioned before that so-called stressors could be: people, places and situations.
Let's take the first category of stressors, people.
This category we are going to divide in two separate parts: ourselves, and our neighbors.

1. Make peace with yourself.

- Stop being your own enemy, peace among people starts from within. -

This may sound like an interesting statement but many times we get stressed because of our own opinion we have about ourselves. We have mentioned earlier that our subconscious mind has formed a blueprint for any file that is stored in memory. Beside these files, it also has a blueprint about us as individuals. In it is stored all the opinions that we have accumulated from others about ourselves. Based on these, the subconscious mind made the blueprint.
This blueprint is made up of different kind of words that has many negative emotional charges attached to them. If this is true in our case, we are going to replace it with different a one; one whose words are positive emotional charged.
Let's take a simple example to illustrate the emotional value that words can have.

We know that many children like to play games with fake paper money. Let's say that we have five kids playing games with real money. And none of them is aware of the fact that not all bills have the same value. Even though they are the same size, their value is based on the number written upon them. So they keep trading their bills not being aware that they may trade a $20 bill for $1 bill. Or even the opposite, a $1 bill for $20 bill. Now let's say that one of them learns the real value of each bill. By having that knowledge, do you think he can benefit from it? Of course he will. Becoming aware of the value of each bill, right the way he will start trading his low value bills for others high value bills. Now, in the case with money, they have no negative value when we get them. The more we have, the easier we can solve our problems. But when it comes to words, some have high positive value, but others high negative value.

Now, let's apply this to our situation in dealing with stress. We all use words in communication. But, how many of us are aware of the positive or negative emotional value of each word we use? Being like these kids who have no idea the value of the bills they are playing with, we are not aware in our dealing with others what kind of emotional effect our words really have over them. But now after we become aware of the importance of the kind of words we use in dealing with others, and the emotional charge that they contain, we know better and use this knowledge to improve our life and also to eliminate stress from our life.
We learned that many words have positive emotional charge and many others have a negative emotional charge. So, what we are going to do is use this knowledge with the reasoning method. We are going to use questions whose answers are composed of words that contain high positive emotional charge. By doing that they will have a strong positive effect over us, becoming the foundation of the new and better blueprint about ourselves.
We do that by asking ourselves some simple questions:
"Who really are we? Or even more intriguing "Who really should we be?"
"How we should see ourselves."
Based on the scientific evidence of the wonderful body we are equipped with, and the way we were designed to function, we have to say that we are wonderful human beings designed with the right to enjoy our life to the fullness of our abilities.

Chapter 11.   Healing the past.

So, by recognizing what we really are, we are going to build a new blueprint about ourselves, one that empowers us to live a stress free life and enjoy our life to the fullness.

"I am a *wonderful* human being and *deserve* to live my life *to the fullness, without* any *stress.*"

Now, what can we do in order to *become* a wonderful human being?

One important thing that many of us are missing is enough self-esteem to believe what we want to really become. See, the reality is that each of us is born as a wonderful human being, but during our growing up, the *environment* made us what we are today. We all had a beautiful start, but somewhere in the way, things changed and we got where we are now.

Most of us are honest human beings, and to enjoy anything, we first want to have the feelings that we deserve it before it is to be enjoyed. So, in order to get the feeling that we are wonderful human beings and deserve to live a stress free life, we need this new blueprint.

You might have heard the saying: "Positive things happens to positive people"

So, what's is going to be? You're going to live your life the old way? Or decide to do something about and get the best out of it? I think it's about time to make peace with yourself and stop being the first stumbling block in your journey of a stress free life. Remember, no matter what others may say:

"I am a *wonderful* human being and *deserve* to live my life *to the fullness, without* any *stress.*"

So, next time you look in the mirror, what are you going to see? The old you, or a wonderful human being who deserves to live a stress free life? This doesn't depend on anybody else but you.

Now let's embark in a little journey and find out how and why we become what we are today. Let's discover "The secret of the child within"

The secret of the child within.

- The baby who never grows up. -

You have probably heard people using the expression" *the little child inside of you."* You might have wondered what do they mean by this statement. I heard this expression many times and even though it corresponds pretty much with reality, I could not believe that there is still a *little child* who affects our behavior when we are adults. I decided to do research and find out what does *the child within* means.

We are going to embark into a journey of your life starting from the beginning. By doing this, we are going to solve the mystery of the *child within.*

You know that there was a time when you weren't human; one year or more before your birth you didn't exist. Through a miracle of nature, your mommy and daddy found a simple way to bring you into existence. In your mom's womb, you were provided with a perfect environment where all your needs were met. Your mother's resources were at your discretion and your safety, and well-being was a priority for her. Then the time came to leave this environment and get into a new one. With you coming in this world a *new universe* was born. Guess who's in the center of it or its master? You!

Even though you didn't understand who are you and what you are doing here, the new *universe* continued to provide a pleasant environment. Once outside of the womb, you started to develop new abilities. You started to observe what's around you. The new information that your brain started to perceive was the smiling faces of some *giant people.* Did you know who they were? You had no idea. Your conscious abilities were not developed yet, but you are equipped with two very important mechanisms. To be able to rule your own universe, you are equipped with *the propulsion mechanism* that enables you to search, identify, absorb and enjoy and own your own universe. Also for your protection, you have *the self-defense mechanism*, which is designed to make you aware of possible dangers and help you to stay away from any potentially dangerous situations.

Even though they are huge and giants compared to you, your parents made you feel comfortable. You started to develop your first links between them and your propulsion mechanism.

"These giants probably are my servants; they are here to serve and take good care of me. They are the obedient servants of my universe."

You were right. They were there to take a good care of you and make sure that your needs are met. Even though these giants are your servants, they sometimes do not obey all your requests. And you needed to remind them of their *conduct* by waking them up in the middle of the night to come to you and attend to your needs. For you it wasn't a problem to wake them up. You learned fast on how to make them obey your requests. You linked your state of discomfort to your self-defense mechanism; cry and they would come to the rescue.

For you, it's easy to do this but for some reasons these servants of yours did not like it too much. That's OK with you because you had no idea what they were doing all day long.

In this period of time, when these giants were meting your needs, you started to reinforce your links between them and your propulsion mechanism. The more obedient they became, the stronger these links got. Pretty soon, you develop new abilities; you started to talk, crawl and eventually walk. Once you started to walk, a new side of your universe was opened. Your propulsion mechanism started to be activated and an inner desire to search was born inside of you. You got to explore it but also you wanted to make sure that this part of your universe was in your subjection. You needed to explore all open doors. You needed to find out what's on the table and how all these objects could be useful to you. Seeing some interesting little holes in the wall, you tried to see if your little finger would fit in there.

By now your servants had provided you with many toys and you wanted to know what's inside them. You started to take them apart to see how they function. You got your little plastic hammer and started to hammer plastic nails even though some of them broke in many pieces. The more new things you saw around you, the stronger the propulsion mechanism pushed you to explore them.

Once you started exploring this new side of your universe, a very unpleasant thing starts to happen. These giants' servants of yours started to disagree with you. They started to change their attitudes towards your explorations. Instead of smiling faces, they started to give you an unfamiliar look and sometimes a frightening, scary one. For the first time, you started to hear a new word: *NO!*

You never got this kind of behavior from these servants before and this started to puzzle you. They begun to disobey you and the looks on their faces were scary; you needed to teach them a lesson. Feeling threatened, you unconsciously started to develop stronger links between them and your self-defense mechanism. Seems like a war might break out between you and your servants. So, you did what you knew best – cry.

Even though sometimes they did not behave the way you wanted them to, they still took care of your needs. They used to obey all your requests but now they took advantage of their size, strength and obeyed you less and less. Not only that but almost anytime when you wanted to explore new areas of your environment, they seemed not to like it. Their angry faces scared you and you decided more and more to stop exploring the new world ahead of you. They were bombarding you with some words you just didn't understand.

"No! Don't do that! Don't touch that! Bad boy! Don't go there!"

"How many times I told you not to do that!"

You didn't get the meaning of these words. The more they told you not to do something; the stronger an inner desire was developing to disobey.

By the time you were five or six years old, many changes took place in your surroundings. The attitude of these giants was changing dramatically. The giants' behavior was becoming very weird. On one hand they provided you with food and clothing but on the other, they kept stopping you from exploring your own universe.

Pretty soon, the links between their angry faces and your self-defense mechanism started to get very strong. When these links got to a specific point, a blueprint was formed in your subconscious mind about their behaviors and the way you should handle them. This blueprint was affecting your attitude towards them based on their behaviors towards you.

By the time you started school, you found out that there are many others servants in your universe. Some of them were bigger like the giants you knew, others much smaller; about your size. By dealing with them and trying to convince them to be in your subjection, you found out that the bigger giants wanted to take over your environment. The ones your size were so much easier to deal with. Little by little, you gave up control of your own surroundings to these giants that were intimidating and controlling you. In other words, you became less interested in exploring your own universe, even though you saw it expanding more rapidly. You started focusing on keeping a good relationship with the ones your size. While the links between the giants' servants and your propulsion mechanism were still strong, the links between the self-defense mechanisms were getting powerful. You had no idea what that meant. You felt like you were not loved in the same manner. These giants were called your parents and were developing different behaviors towards you. They seemed much busier with other things; jobs, each other, and things. They bought you TV's and video games and gave you permission to spend time with these devices.

By the time you became a teenager, you realize that these giants started to grow smaller and you were getting bigger. Also, they didn't seem to know everything. As a matter of fact, they didn't know too much about adolescence because many of their opinions differed from yours. What do they know anyway?
Over time, you learn that you could survive without them; they were losing control over you. You were born as the owner of your own universe, but they made you their subject. That wasn't fair at all.
All the experiences you went through were affected by previously blueprints formed in your subconscious mind. These experiences were reinforcing or weakening these blueprints depending on their polarity. If you had more positive experiences, they strengthen your positive blueprints (the ones made to the propulsion mechanism). Consequentially, if you had more negative experiences and no one helped you cope with them, you were weakening the blueprint made to the propulsion mechanism thereby strengthening the self-defense mechanisms. By doing this, you tended to become a more pessimist person and your attitude towards life became more negative.

By the time you reach your eighteenth birthday, you were realizing that these former giants were not as smart as you thought and many of their opinions were outdated. Who were they kidding?
New experiences were influenced by the old blueprints formed in your past subconscious mind. Your behavior started to follow certain paths drawn by these blueprints. You already formed new blueprints about dealing with persons of the opposite sex and the old ones influenced this.

By the time you reach your thirties, you started to realize that it's possible that you might have made the wrong assumptions. These parents were not as bad as you thought; they actually were smarter then you thought. Your life seemed to follow certain patterns but you felt things should've been different. You could have done many things different in your past. For some reasons, some of these came and interfered with your life. Unaware, you kept adding to previously formed blueprints. You felt that you should do things differently but it appeared you were trapped into a certain mold to behave this way.

By the time you reached your forties, your life taught you many lessons. You agreed more with your parents and you started to miss them. By now, you realized that many things in your life went through trial and error. You follow others advice and felt things could have been better with your life. Even in your forties, there was still time to do a thorough self-analysis and take necessary steps to improve your life. By now you realize that it's your responsibility to find a better way to improve your life. One improvement was to learn from successful people and follower their advice. You realize, by doing the same old thing, you are conditioned by these childhood blueprints formed in your subconscious mind. By learning to exchange these with better ones, the whole structure of your behavior will also change. Realization sets in that it's not the environment that caused the situation that you are in but your own reaction to it. Not being able to change the *world* you decided that things would get better if you changed your attitude towards it. You arrived at a better understanding of reality and realized it's your responsibility to do something. It's not anyone's fault; it's yours. It's better this way because you cannot change them but you certainly can change yourself. Once you come to this conclusion, you realized that the blueprints that are affecting your present behavior came from the ones formed in your childhood; when you didn't have enough knowledge and experience to form better ones. All your life, you have been affected by these but not anymore. Being aware, you start searching for information that helps you replace old blueprints with new and better ones.

Now you can speed up this process by learning from an early age on how your mind works. Do something about your life, slow down and realize that it's you who should control it. You are the CEO; it's still your own universe! Even better, you are much more capable now to govern it and influence those significant others.

We can see that the old blueprints influences people to have childish behavior. By not having enough experience we built and reinforced those old, behavior blueprints. They might have been appropriate in childhood but not as adults. Until we die, they will continue to shape our behaviors unless we start to remove them and replace them with more effective, new ones. The polarity of these blueprints determines our level of self-esteem. It's important to take a look at us and see how much our level of self-esteem is affected by stress. Once we make this self-analysis, we might find out that having a low level of self-esteem has a negative effect on our bodies and the way we deal with environments. You might remember the saying:
"You must love your neighbor as yourself"
Well, to be able to love our neighbor as ourselves, we need to see how much we love ourselves. What are the love and attitude we have about ourselves? Most of us need some improvement in this area. In other words, we have to make peace with ourselves. Let's see how we can do that.

Many times we make mistakes by thinking, speaking or through behaviors. How do we see ourselves when we become aware that we made a mistake? Do we recognize, that due to our imperfections, we fall short many times creating learning experiences? Or, do we keep punishing ourselves for these mistakes by dwelling on negative self-talk about ourselves? I think it's enough that by making mistakes we are causing some discomfort and pain. We do not need to make a bad situation even worst by continuing negative, self-talk or by asking ourselves wrong questions.

You might remember when you did something wrong, you have asked yourself:
How could I have been so.... to do that? Or, Why do I always screw up? I can't do anything right.
I knew that this was going to happen. No good things ever happen to me.
This kind of attitude about ourselves is the result of the kind of blueprint we have developed. We might consider exchanging the old blueprint with a better one.
"Even though I am not perfect, I am a kind and worthwhile person"
"I will continually increase my level of self-esteem for my own sake and for the sake of those around me"
"I am careful for the way I behave, learn from my mistakes, and see them as learning experiences."
"I am a wonderful creation and I take good care of my mind / body. They are the most precious gifts that I could receive."

Repeating these statements to us and by believing and having faith, the old blueprint will be replaced with a more effective one. Once the new blueprint is firmly established in our subconscious mind, our whole life will change for the better. We will start to see everything in a new and better light.
To help you to do this, I have some news.

The good news is that as you are reading this book, it will reveal your own stress research. The professionals in stress management taught you that the best you can do about stress is to learn how to manage it. They made you a manager over something you hate; your stress!
You know you are responsible for the way you manage your stress and don't need permission from others to do something about it.

Even better news is by learning and applying the principals you gain from this book, you have a chance to become stress free person. You don't have to manage something that you hate anymore; now you can eliminate it. Once you learned these secrets, use your managing abilities to manage and improve your life.

Basically, we need to understand that even though we might be grown-ups now, our behaviors are still shaped by the blueprints we formed during childhood. Not all of us had a perfect childhood; many of these blueprints were not the right ones. Realizing this, we need to do a self-analysis of our lives.

From this point, we can see what blueprints triggered the behavior we want and which ones didn't. Knowing that these outdated and wrong blueprints are making us unhealthy, we are smart enough to replace them. Once replaced, our entire behaviors will change.

Now let's go to the next category of people we need to make peace with.

2. Make peace with your neighbor.

- Your neighbors; friends or enemy? It's up to you. -

Once we have changed the old blueprint about ourselves, a very interesting thing will start to happen. We start to see our neighbors in a different light. Raising our level of self-esteem will help to develop a better relationship with them. When we say neighbors, we mean anybody around us, family members, relatives, friends, accountancies, coworkers, next-door neighbors, or any other people we are dealing with; including those who are creating our stressors. By understanding the principal that we are all equals on this earth, born / made the same way; it will become a little easier to "love our neighbors as ourselves."

On the other hand somebody might ask: Why would we want to make peace with some people especially with those that are not our friends but more like our enemies?
Is that a smart thing to do?
Well, as we mentioned before, when we give a negative meaning to any kind of information that enters our mind we actually link it to the defense mechanism. By linking this, based on its intensity, we are attaching a specific level of negative emotion or pain. The specific level of negative emotion is felt by our body and not by the other people. By giving negative meanings to any neighbors or to the information that comes from any source, we are punishing ourselves. We are the ones that feel that negative emotion by giving a negative meaning to it.
You might know that Jesus Christ considered by many The Greatest Man that ever lived, told his disciples to love their enemies. Did it ever cross your mind why would he say such a thing?
Well, if this were true, we can theorize, that he knew how our mind works and how to provide protection from stress and other negative emotions. He knew that by considering some people as enemies they would build a blueprint that contained negative emotions. Anytime they had to interact with these people called *enemies,* the disciples would be the ones negatively affected; because they felt the negative emotions attached to this blueprint.
To change the blueprint, it's not necessary to go to the enemy and try to convince them to be your friends. No, we do not need to do this; we need to change in our minds the way we look at others.

Remember, that anything that was accomplished on this earth started with a thought first. Before we accomplish something physically, we first have to conceive it. Once conceived, the subconscious mind goes to work to transform this thought into reality. The others still remain the same; we are not changing them. We are, however, changing the way we view them by making peace with others and ourselves.
Now, these people could be our enemies or spouses that we got angry with, children who are not behaving the way we want and even parents who are interfering.

| Chapter 11. | Healing the past. |

I have a simple principle that I believe in and use in my life.
"The one who knows better, should behave better"
Probably, after you have learned so many new things about human behavior, you are becoming more knowledgeable than others. In other words, you know better.
Remember that you are expected to behave better than the rest. By doing this, the lives that are improving are yours and those around you. As the new blueprint about you says:
"Even though not perfect, I am a kind, capable and worthwhile person". Why not start being a kind, capable and worthwhile person?
Remember: "Every thing that we consciously accept and believe to be true, it will become true for us"
If we do that for a period of time long enough, the subconscious mind makes a blueprint, which in turn will trigger this kind of behavior anytime needed.
Let's take another simple example:

You are driving your car going to work. Driving in a residential area your speed is relatively low, maybe 40 miles / hour. On the sidewalk some kids are having fun, then suddenly one of them jumps towards your car.
What's your first reaction? Of course, out of reflex you step on the brakes.
A normal reaction, right? Yes, but the question is why did you do this?
In the past, when you learned how to drive, you were taught that any time you wanted to stop the car, you needed to apply the brakes. You believed this and started practicing until it became a habit; doing it automatically without thinking.
Now, any time you approach a situation that requires the use of the brakes, you do it as a habit or reflex. Once you acquire this habit, you will never forget.
Remember, your subconscious mind made a blueprint for these kinds of situations.

Let's take another simple example to illustrate the difference between having a good blueprint based on accurate information and having a blueprint that contains wrong or insufficient information:

Suppose you observe a boat in the ocean with two people inside. Their hands and feet are tied up, heads covered so they can't see anything. Both of them are lying down in the bottom of the boat and a powerful storm is tossing the boat in every direction.
Now, one of them doesn't know where they are, what's going to happen or if they will survive. On the other hand, the other person is thinking differently. He knows that this is just another challenge and pretty soon this situation will safely end. Remaining calm, this individual is having positive thoughts; waiting for the storm to pass. Let me ask you a simple question:
Which one of these two would you like to be? Would you like to be the first one or the second? The answer it's obvious. Nobody wants to be the first one.
With regret, I have to say that today most of the people feel like they are in the place of the first one. Their situations looks similar to the on whose thought processes are negative. This is the difference between knowing how to deal with stress and learning what it takes to eliminate its negative effects.
See, the secret is not in trying to change the situations because many times we just cannot do that. What we can do is manage our state of mind. The situation itself does not cause stress. It's the fact that we give it a negative meaning, thereby triggering the formation of stress. Remember:
"It's not what happens to you but it's your response when it happens to you"

Going back to our subject of making peace with our neighbors, we realize that we know better and it's our responsibility to make the necessary corrective step. The other people around us, impressed by our positive behaviors, will start to follow.
The process of making peace with our neighbors develops in two stages:
The first stage is the changes that must take place in our mind.
The second stage is the one that takes place in our attitude and communications with them.
Once we made positive changes in our mind, our attitudes and the way we communicate with others will start to change.

Remember, we have learned before that our subconscious mind makes a blueprint for any file in our memory banks. We do have a blueprint about the attitude we have toward others and about the way we communicate with our neighbors

Now let's take the first one, attitude, and see if there are any necessary changes to do in our attitudes blueprint.

1. Attitude.

- The first step in the right or wrong direction. -

Let's examine what attitude is and how it affects our life.
To understand this better let's give an example:
All of us are familiar with freeways. We know that these are large roads built between cities, states and even countries. Drivers use them to travel from one place to another.
Let's say that we are in the Los Angeles area. There is a California freeway called Interstate 5 that travels from north to south.

Now, if we get on the Interstate 5 northbound from Los Angeles to Canada, we'll find many cities. Also if we get on the southbound going towards Mexico we'll find many cities too. Now, if we want to go to a city that is 100 miles away from Los Angeles; will it make any difference if we go north or south on the freeway? Of course it would.
If we take the 5-freeway northbound and drive about 100 miles, we'll find one city, let's say, Bakersfield. If we take the 5-freeway southbound and drive 100 miles we will find a totally different city, let's say, San Diego.
What is the point you may ask? It is very simple and very important. We need to be careful which direction we take when we go on the freeway. One little misunderstanding between north and south could lead us to a totally different destination.
The same thing happens with attitude.
If we are the type of person that has a positive attitude, we end up in one place, psychological speaking.
If we are the type of person that has a negative attitude we might end up in a totally different place, psychological speaking.
So, we can say that attitude is our mental capacity to instantly understand and react to the information from our environments in a specific way.
Some of us have the tendency to understand and react negatively to our environments and they can be labeled as having a negative attitude.
Others have the tendency to understand and react positive to our environments and they can be labeled as having a positive attitude.
As we have seen from the previous example, attitude is the first step we take towards one kind of consequence or in the opposite direction; with totally different kind of consequences.
It is very wise to learn and develop a positive attitude. We are empowering our brain to process the information freely, so it's able to come up with much better results than when we had a negative attitude.
We can safely say that there are two kinds of attitudes:

1. Positive attitude.
2. Negative attitude.

1. Positive Attitude.

- The first step in right direction. -

Positive attitude is very healthy in that it helps us to face situations and challenges in a constructive manner. The human body was designed to function on positive information and commands. By having this kind of attitude is like using a machine properly and within the normal parameters. Our brain is very capable and powerful enough to solve almost anything but it needs to function within the parameters it was designed for. So, when we have a positive attitude we are creating a normal environment for the brain to function normally.

It is like a computer that you give a positive command. What will the computer do?
It will process that information and give you the results.

Anybody knows what a calculator is. Right? If we had one handy and took a closer look we could see that it is a little piece of machinery and by pushing some buttons it does all the calculations instantly. Why is this? The reason is because it was designed for that purpose.

As long as it has power and we use it according to instructions, it will give correct answers to our problems.

The same thing happens with our brain. It is a powerful computer that is able to solve the challenges that it faces as long as we use it within its parameters.

Specialists in the area of human behavior, tell us that in our reactions to the environment, there is a 90/10 rule that always applies. This means that 90% of our first reaction to the information is an instant habitual reaction based on past experiences with that particular event or information.

Only 10% of our reactions would be utilized in the process of reasoning the situation or event.

Knowing this, means that our attitude is determine by personality type; combined with past experiences with that particular event or situation. In other words, the old blueprint formed in our subconscious mind about the situation controls our attitude.

Let's take some examples:

A person with an aggressive personality type grows up in a good and positive environment and finds easy ways to meet his inner needs. What kind of attitude is this person going to develop?

A positive one, of course. This person has a bright future in becoming a leader in society or in the company that he might own or work for.

Let's say that the same person grows up in a negative environment and has a hard time meeting his inner needs.

What kind of attitude will he develop?

A negative one, of course.

This kind of person might very well become a stubborn and negative person. He has the inner need to be in control but his negative attitudes will stop him from advancing in life. Furthermore, these kinds of people have many problems in working and family environments. Each of them has the inner need to control others and this result in very stressful situations such as fights.

It is wise to recognize this and raise your awareness about the possibility of learning new habits that could change the situation.

The truth of the matter is the one who becomes aware of this principle has the responsibility to do something about it.

Remember the rule:

"The one who knows better, should behave better."

Knowing better, we change our behavior first. Then we try to help others understand reality by providing information that will help them become more aware and realize that they have a chance to change.

The problem is that many times the first one that is made aware of this is trying hard to change the other. This makes it impossible because an aggressive personality type has the need to control; not to be controlled. When somebody wants to control another, they go on alert and start to fight back. Instead of communication, we would have an argument or even a fight.
Remember:
"Understand others first and then expect to be understood"
We can see that attitude determines the future outcome of many situations. A positive attitude helps and directs efforts in a positive, constructive manner; thereby resulting in positive outcomes.
Somebody gives you a task to do. If your attitude is positive, it will be much easier to accomplish it. On the other hand if your attitude is negative, the accomplishment of the task becomes more difficult.
Some people have the habit of answering, "I don't know" most of the time when they are asked about to respond to a question or statement. It's true that is better to say, "I don't know" when you really don't know. It's much better to have a positive attitude and see if you are capable of finding the right solution to the situation.

Many times we might not be aware at that particular time about the answer but if we start thinking you'll be surprised to find out that we could solve the situation with a little more thought. The reality is that when we said: "I don't know", what we basically did; we told our brain to stop thinking about this subject. Guess what? We just don't know.
Putting it a different way, we could say: "Let me see what I can do about...." or something similar. What we actually are doing is giving a command to our brain to start looking for an answer. Believe it or not, most of the time, we will soon come up with a very good solution.
"The right attitude is everything."

We can see our personality type, combined with the information coming from our environments, influences that attitude. The more we are aware of our personal inner needs, the more we can expose ourselves to right information that will help us meet these needs. The information that is coming from the environment will give us a choice in giving positive meanings resulting in positive effects. We could give negative meanings but then the results will be negative.
Remember: "If it is to be it's up to me"
By learning to develop a positive attitude, we eliminate a great deal of stress from our life.
A positive attitude is characterized by expressions like these:
"Yes I can." "Yes, I will." "Yes, no problem." "Of course." "Yes, I will do it." "Yes I understand." "That's easy." "Yes, right away," and so many others that triggers positive actions.

2. Negative attitude.

- The first step in the wrong direction. -

Opposite of positive attitudes is negative ones, resulting in negative results. Somebody put it in a comical way: "Negative attitude is one's so called "quality" to fool himself and asking who did it"
Now let's go back to our example with the computer. We have seen that asking the computer a positive question; it will produce a correct answer.
What do you think will happen if you ask the computer a negative command? For example you type:
Please do not open this particular file.
What is the computer going to do? It cannot process the command because it doesn't understand. There are no such commands on the keyboard. All of the commands are positive; none are negative. The same thing happens with our mind when we have a negative attitude.
Unconsciously, we give a command to our brain not to look for any answers for that particular situation. Guess what? We really have no answer to the situation unless we ask ourselves how we can do this or that.

Chapter 11.   Healing the past.

Remember the example with the freeway? Well, if we planned to go 100 miles north of Los Angeles, we should enter the northbound freeway. If we enter the southbound freeway, we would get lost and wouldn't find our destination. This is the same situation when we show negative attitudes.
We might have a conscious goal but by maintaining a negative attitude, we are stopping ourselves from going towards that goal; going in the wrong direction.
Then, how can we change from a negative attitude to a positive one? Well, we need to go through the same five steps that we mentioned earlier:
First, we need to become more aware that we have a negative attitude.
Secondly, we need to develop a desire to change from a negative to a positive attitude.
Thirdly, we make a decision to become a person with a positive attitude.
Fourth, we look for things that will motivate us to change the negative attitude with a positive attitude.
Fifth, finally we discipline ourselves to choose in the future to be a person with a positive attitude.
Once we follow this process and apply its principals, it will become a habit .As was mentioned earlier, the 90/10 rule says '90% of our reaction is a habitual reaction'. By learning these steps, we form the habit of becoming a person with a positive attitude. Anytime that we are faced with a situation in which we have to do something, our first reaction will be habitual, the 90% new habit of having a positive attitude.
Believe it or not, we will automatically react with a positive attitude.
By following these easy steps we have basically replaced the old blueprint with the new one that says; we are persons with positive attitudes.
It is as simple as it looks, but remember:
"If it is to be, it's up to me"
Now, once we developed a positive attitude towards our neighbors, let's go and see what we can do about the second element, communication.

1. Communication.

- Stress, the most communicative " disease." –
- You learned to talk early in life, but when did you learn to communicate? -

Communication is a key factor in our success in life. If we really understand and apply the best techniques of communication there isn't anything we can't do.
There is no door that will not open to a good communicator but there are many closed doors in front of those who are poor communicators. Somebody might ask why do we really need to communicate?
Well, the major reason is that we want to get a specific reaction from the people we want to communicate with. All of us want a positive reaction from them. We want to be accepted and loved by our friends and relatives. Also, we might want to get something from people we are working with. Approval, rewards from the employer and coworkers are some examples.
We might want to achieve some goals and require need the help of others. For all these things, we need to communicate. Remember what we are basically looking for when we communicate: to fulfill some of our desires or needs. This means that we have the responsibility to make sure that the way we communicate will result in the fulfilling of our desires and needs.
Now, let's see how can we define communication.
We can safely say, that it is a process in which we are transmitting information to another person, who receives it and clearly understand its intended meaning. Getting

the meaning intended, they might be able to respond the way we expect them to.
This is one of the most important things in communication. The person we are communicating with is getting the same meaning that we are trying to convey. Each of us has our own plans, goals, suggestions, commands and so on in our mind that we want to communicate to them. Based on our vocabulary, we put these in words that we think they will convey them. Others don't hear our thoughts or intentions, and what's in our mind, but they hear just the words we are using. Hearing the words, based on their vocabulary they translate them in their own thoughts. Having different backgrounds and mentalities, they not necessarily give the same meaning as we do to our words. The meaning could be identical, close, fairly accurate, different or even totally opposite than our thoughts. Once translated in their own thoughts, they get the meaning of what we supposedly wanted to convey. Not being aware of how this takes place many of us are under the impression that because we are familiar with our own thoughts, and by expressing them through words, others must have got the same meaning as we intended to give. The fact that people in general have a communication problem proves that that's not necessarily the case. Unless this process is properly understood and applied, the communication fails to attain its purpose.

Many people today are going to great lengths to communicate with others but it never crosses their minds to make sure that the other party understands their meanings when they gave them the information. They are always wondering why they don't get the expected responses.
There is a big difference between talking to others and proper communication.
Any body can talk but to properly communicate, we need to keep in mind a few steps that we should always follow.
Let's take an example:
Suppose that you are a general of a mighty army. You have 100,000 soldiers under your command. You want to move your troops from one place to another but there is a large river in your troops way. If you don't care about your soldiers, you could give them the order to cross the river. Out of 100,000, some of them will make it across the river but most of them will not.
If you do care about your soldiers, what would you do first?
You'd probably build a bridge. After you are sure that the bridge is strong enough, you give a command ordering your troops across the river. This is a very simple example but we can learn a lot from it.

The same thing happens when we need to communicate.
Our messages represent the 100,000 soldiers that we need to send safely across the river. We need these soldiers on the other side. That's our main goal: To accomplish something with them on the other side of the bridge. So, if we don't want to loose them in the unsafe river, we would need to build a *bridge* that will enable the troops to cross safely.

This necessary bridge that we need to build, is a common ground that we need to establish between the person(s) we are trying to communicate with and ourselves. In other words, a line of communication that is traveling freely, understandable to all parties; without changing its meaning. If we do that, we can say that we are good communicators and there are no misunderstandings in communication.
On the other hand, unaware of it, we might trigger the protective defense mechanism on the other person's mind. They are not in position to receive the information as we intended. They go on alert; perceiving the information as a threat and start to defend against it.
In order to avoid this, we need to keep in mind some information that will enable us to communicate properly.

1. When we know the person we are communicating with.

A. Find out his or hers personality type and put the information in such a way that it meets their inner personal needs. In other words, try first to understand the person you are dealing with; then precede to communicate with them.

B. Avoid using information that will trigger their inner personal fears.

C. Recognize and focus on their positive qualities instead of lowering their self-esteem by bringing up their faults.

D. Focus on the positive reward that might result from the communication.

E. When using positive examples, put the other persons in the example and when you use negative example, put yourself in the example. By doing this, you'll make them feel free to communicate without feeling guilty.

F. Awareness of possible loss or even negative consequences of a miscommunication.

These are some important factors to remember when we want to communicate with others.
Of course, we might not be able to use all of them at once but it's important to keep in mind that the more we follow these guide-lines, the better communicators we will become.
By following this guideline, we'll make sure that the message that we are transmitting is properly understood and can be understood by others.

2. When we don't know the person we are communicating with.

A. Try to establish a positive, common ground for communicating. Find out their personality type and communicate in such a way that you meet their inner needs.

B. Use the right tone of voice.
Remember: "You will never achieve with vinegar what you will achieve with honey."

C. Make the other person feel at least equal with you. If necessary, lower yourself to their level.

D. Be willing to listen without interrupting.

E. Show interest in their opinions.
Once you use these guidelines, other people will feel free to communicate and accept your information without any fear from you.
This way the line of communication stays open and the exchange of information flows freely.
Let's take some examples to see how this could be done.
Suppose you meet John and you know that he is an aggressive type. Knowing this, you make sure that the way you approach him will make him feel in control.
If a difference of opinion arises and you really want to have the last word, the line of positive communication will be interrupted. From this point on, the discussion will transform into an argument.
Therefore, make sure you understand what's most important to you: To maintain an open line of communication or for you to have the last word?
What if John is an assertive personality type?
Well, we learned that this personality type has the need to be recognized and accepted. If we really are interested in a productive communication, we will keep in mind his needs. Recognize and accept his efforts by praising.
Proceeding this way, we certainly got his attention and the line of communication stays open.

In case John is an analytical personality type, we will make sure that we use details and precise information to meet his inner needs. Also, we will not forget to avoid generalities that would make him feel uncomfortable.

If John is a passive type, we will remember that he has fear of involvement and we must deal with him in a way that he doesn't feel obligated.

Doing this, we could succeed much better in communicating with him.

The success of a communication depends on the original intention of the communicators.

It might be helpful to compare a communication process with the drawing of a nice picture.

First of all, we want to draw a nice picture.

Second, we should look for the right tools needed to draw the picture.

Third, we need to take the necessary time to finish the nice picture.

First, we should appreciate the difference between any picture and a nice picture. We would like a nice picture not just a regular one. The same thing happens in communication. We should look for a nice and productive way to communicate; not being satisfied with just regular communication. We know that there are different results between a regular communication and a nice or productive one.

Second, we need right tools to draw a nice picture. Now, to draw any picture, we could use almost anything. To draw a nice one, we need more than that. This require us to do something more than just the norm. The experts in this area have discovered that there are three components of communication:

1. The words we are using in communication.
2. Our facial expressions and tone of voice.
3. Our opinion about the persons we are communicating with.

Surprisingly, the words we are using account for less than 10% of the value of communication.

Our body language, which is our body, facial expression tones of voice; accounts for about 60% of the value of communication. Did you ever heard the expression:

"Your face is yelling so much at me, I cannot hear a word you're saying."

The opinion we have about the persons we are communicating with accounts for about 30% of the value of communication. An important thing to keep in mind is that all three elements of communication should complement each other. Otherwise, the meaning of the message changes to reflect the most predominant component of the communication.

Third, if we are interested in a good and productive communication, we should keep in mind our role we play in maintaining it. By continuously keeping in mind the purpose of our communication, and the results that it might produce, we discipline ourselves to maintain a positive attitude during the entire process of communication. By proceeding this way, we will do our utmost in keeping the line of communication open and the results will be very rewarding. Let's take another example:

We know that for some reason we are attracted towards some people and for others we feel the opposite. Enjoying the company of people that we are attracted to and avoiding associating with people we don't feel good about seems to be basic human nature. Have you ever asked yourself why is this?

Unconsciously, the faces or names of those we are attracted to, triggers a positive reaction in our minds. This means that sometimes in the past we have dealt with some similar faces or names that resulted in positive associations towards them. Anytime when we see or hear them, it triggers pleasant feelings.

The same process happens when we encounter faces or name of persons that we have the tendency to avoid.

Let's say that in the past we had some problems with John that caused us a great deal of pain.

Now, after a few years you received a phone call from him and he tells you that he has some business to discuss with you. What is going to be your reaction soon as you recognize his name or voice? Probably a negative reaction.

Chapter 11. Healing the past.

This is normal for us to feel this way because usually everybody has the same reaction. Once we understand how our mind works, I think that it does not matter the situation we go through, we protect ourselves by the negative state associated with these particular situations. What is important to understand is that we should make a distinction between the situations that we are going trough and ourselves.

Many times, we punish ourselves to feel bad because the situation itself is bad. That's wrong and we should learn to differentiate between the negativity of a situation and our own state of mind.
Most people unconsciously identify themselves with the events they go through and so when things go better they feel good. When things go sour, they also feel sour; which is an improper way to deal with this kind of situation. By acting this way, we are conditioned by the outside environment and it is the one who is dictating the way we feel, not us. What we need to understand is that we have a choice to separate ourselves from the outside environment. Choosing how to feel regardless of polarity of the situation we are going through could make us feel well inside, even if an outside storm passes.

Going back to our example, we have a choice to believe that the past will repeat itself or chose to learn from it.
Our main concern in this situation is not to choose if we want to communicate again with this person. It is to remove the negative feelings that we have previously attached to them.
Once we do this, then we can decide if we want to communicate. Every situation is different and it's possible that we might go through the same negative experience as we went in the past. It's also possible that in past experiences, we were at fault but we failed to realize this. This negative feeling toward others will impair reality.

To clearly see the reality, we should erase the negative feelings first and then with a clear mind; determine whether it's important to open communication again.
There is a very simple saying, with a powerful truth behind it that says:
"Forgive all your tribulations, but never forget what they are teaching you." This is a very useful and important advice. By forgiving all our tribulations, what we actually do, is we erase the negative feelings attached to them. Then with a clear mind we can learn how to change the future so it will be better than the past.

By using the reasoning method, we can erase any negative association from the past experiences.
Once they are erased, next time we think about them, the negative feelings are gone. Doing this will enable us to decide what to do free from the tendency of rejection caused negative feelings attached to past experiences.
Let me ask you a question:
If you or anybody else made a mistake in the past and paid for it; is it fair to be punished again?
I don't think so, and neither do you.
Well, when we did something in the past and we felt bad, was that bad feeling a gift? Or was it a punishment? You'll probably agree with me that it's a form of punishment.
Now, if we went through this in the past and got punished for it, is it fair get punished for the same old thing in the future?
I don't think so, and neither should you.
What we basically do when we start thinking about past negative experiences is we are punishing ourselves again. We do this by bringing in the present, to relieve the negative feelings from past experiences, that don't have anything to do with the present.
Remember:
"It is not what happens to you, but what you do with what happens to you"
When we think about past negative experiences, there are still negative feelings attached to these memories. The wise thing to do is to erase the negative feelings. Next time when we start to think about the same past experiences, there will be no more negative feelings to cause stress.

Chapter 11.   Healing the past.

Until now, you didn't know the truth about this but once you have learned it, it's your responsibility to do something. As you can see, it's not a difficult thing to do.
Take responsibility about your feelings and treat yourself the way you would like others to treat you.
Remember; Communication, among other things, is an exchange of opinions (like a gift exchange). You could gladly accept it and unconsciously associate with it. Or, politely reject it and disassociate from it.
"Thank you for your opinion" you may say. The results are totally different.
    Now, after we have seen how to deal with people that might cause us stress, let's got to the next category: places and situations. We will analyze these together, using the same method of reasoning.

3. Make peace with your environment.

- Peace is more than just absence of war... if it is to be it's up to me. -

    After we have made peace with ourselves and with our neighbors, I think it's only reasonable to go forward and make peace with our environments. By environments, we need to understand places or situations that might be considered stressful.
We can do this in two ways: One; learn how erase the past negative feelings associated to these and the other way is to make a list of these possible stressing places or situations. Take them one at the time and erase the negative feelings previously attached.

    A. Erase the past negative associations one at the time, as you happen to think about them.

    We have learned earlier about the 90/10 rules, which stated that any experience that we might encounter in the present is 90 % of the time a habitual reaction. Only 10% of the time we start to analyze the situation and then act.
Let's see how this 90% habitual reaction takes place. When we go through a particular situation, our brain instantly receives the audio and video information. It automatically goes back in our memory and tries to find a match to the new information.
There might not be a perfect match, so, the brain starts to look for a partial match. Then the brain very easily finds a match. This process is very similar with the way you could find the address of a person from a Yellow Pages book. You could look for the name of the person and find their address or you could use their phone number to find the name and address. You could choose one of these two ways.
    In the same way, our brain tries to find a match by looking for memories that contain the same kind of sound for audio information or from the memories that contain the same kind of images for video information.
Soon as a match is found, the brain triggers a reaction that corresponds with that particular information founded in the memory.
In other words, the new information we just received reminds us of something from the past. If the past experience had negative feelings attached to it, we will start feeling it's negative feelings.
The intensity of the new feelings depends on the intensity of the old ones. Let's take an example to illustrate this:
    A few years ago you went shopping and spent about two hours inside a store.

After you finished shopping, you left the store to go home. Going back to the parking lot, you find out that your car has disappeared.

"O boy, that's impossible" you might say, "I left it right here."

You call the police but the car cannot be found. You suffer the loss. It doesn't matter how much you wanted to get it back; it's gone.

Of course, this experience brought you a great deal of pain. Unaware of, you have attached negative feelings or pain to this experience.

Now, after a few years, your boss asked you to accompany him on a business trip in a different city. He wants you to drive your car to the airport and leave it there for few days until both of you come back. At the end of the business trip, you will have transportation to get back home.

Soon as he asks you to do this, what comes right to your mind?

"O boy, not me again. I will never leave my car unattended, especially for few days."

Right away, you start to feel the same kind of feelings you felt when the other car was stolen.

So, what has happened?

When the boss asked you to do this, your brain started to automatically look for a match in your memory. By having a bad experience with parking your car, you start feeling the same way when you attached the past to a present situation.

Now you may ask:

Why does the brain find the negative match and not a positive one? Surely, you have parked your car many times.

The reason is that, at the basis of any decision we make, there are two motivation factors. One is towards pleasure that is triggered by the propulsion mechanism and the second one is pain that is triggered by the defense mechanism. We have learned earlier, the information that enters our mind is stored in our memory banks as files. In our case the file, *Car parking,* has been associated in the past with a lot of negative feelings. Once this file is opened, those negative feelings will come up again; even though the original situation happened a long time ago.

What we need to do is to use the reasoning method to erase those negative feelings. Once erased, this particular memory will not create any negative feelings. We do this by asking ourselves some simple questions:

"Should I let my future to be like my past?"

"My future is not my past. My future is always better"

"It's up to me to decide how to create my future"

"I live in the present, because yesterday is history, tomorrow might be a mystery, and today's a gift, that's why it's called the present."

"Does it do me any good to keep these negative feelings attached to this memory? Or is it better to get rid of them by emptying this file of all negative contents?

"I decided to remove these negative feelings attached to this file, so next time when I will open it, will be free of negative feelings. This experience will be just an old experience from when I am learning to be careful on where to park my car."

Using this line of reasoning questions and statements, we are actually erasing the negative feelings previously attached to these situations. In other words, we are replacing the old blueprint with a new and improved one.

Now, going back to our example, when the boss tells you that you should leave your car at the airport, the first thing that will go through your mind is not to do this.

Now, let's say that your boss is going to insist that you should leave the car at the airport.

How are you going to feel during this period?

This will cause stress because the past might repeat itself and you might be left without this car too. Not knowing how to eliminate stress, this period will be stressful until you come back and see that your car is still there.

Chapter 11. Healing the past.

By learning how to deal with negative things from the past, you already have learned and became familiar with the habit of reasoning. In other words, you have a new blueprint in your subconscious mind about this subject. Soon as you start to think about all the negative things that might happen to your car, your brain will automatically trigger the reasoning method.

Being equipped with free will, you have the choice to erase the negative feelings from this past experience or ignore it. Still you are left with these negative feelings attached to them. If you do ignore the reasoning method, the next time you will relieve them again.

I think that you will be smart enough to make the right choice and erase the negative feelings attached to the past experience. Once you have erased them, they will cease to be a source of stress or pain.

By using the reasoning method, we basically are convincing ourselves that the past is gone and the situation from the past was different than this one. So we have no reason to worry.

Remember:

"If it is to be, it's up to me"

From this point we learned that we could get rid of the negative feelings that are attached to the past to some unpleasant experiences. We can do this as we start thinking about them.

Let's see now another way to deal with negative past experiences.

B. Make a list of all the past negative experiences you could remember and erase them one at the time until you finish them all.

In our daily activities, we know that is useful to make a list of things that we need to accomplish. Establishing a priority, we start to take one at the time and try to accomplish them in order of importance. This is something that we are familiar with and we know that proceeding this way we have better chances to accomplish more in less time.

To erase negative associations from past experiences, we can use the same principle. We can find some time and make a list of all the negative experiences that we went through during our life. If there are too many, simply divide them in two, or even three lists. Then we take one at the time.

Let's take an example:

Suppose that a few months ago, one of your friends was involved in a car accident and died. This is a traumatic situation for anybody. This accident took you by surprise and since it happened, any time you think about this, it causes you to feel bad. You just do not understand why this happened to your friend. Why do bad things happen to good people? How can you deal with this kind of situation?

Well, as we mentioned earlier, the negative state of mind that we feel when we think about this situation is part of the neuron association that unconsciously is formed when first heard about the accident.

Since the past is gone and we cannot change it, we might consider stop punishing ourselves by reliving again the same pain that we felt in the beginning.

Unless we do something about it, we will go through this kind of pain every time we think about this situation.

It does not mean that we are selfish, if we learn how to stop punishing ourselves for something that was not our fault and by not feeling pain repeated for something that we have lost in the past.

Do we like it when we feel this pain?

No.

Can we change the situation by reliving the same pain again? No.

Can we function 100% in this state of pain?

No.

Then, we should all agree, that it's better to live in the present and do not confuse it with the past.

We are talking about things that happened in the past; they are gone and we just cannot turn back the time to change them.

We have to realize that life goes on and we need our strength and abilities to deal with present situations. By relieving the past, it keeps us in a stressful state that might have a negative effect on our present life.
What we need to do is use reasoning, thus, the negative feeling attached to this situation is reduced to zero. Then, any time in the future when we start thinking again about this situation, we remember it, we feel sorry for our friend but we don't feel the negative state of mind any longer.
If, in some situations, the intensity of the feeling is very high, we might consider repeating this procedure. After we are done with the first situation from our list, go to the second, third, etc. Once we finished, we can deliberately test the method and start to think about one of these situations again. We will be surprised to find out that we no longer feel the negative feelings that we felt before. Remember:
"The one that knows the rules of the game, plays the game the way they wants to"
We learned that the best way to deal with negative past experiences is stop punishing ourselves repeatedly and erase the negative feelings previously attached to these situations. By doing this, we do not have to keep reliving the original pain.
Once we do this, any time in the future we think about these past experiences, we are free of unnecessary pain that caused us stress. We might remember the powerful saying:
"You will know the truth, and the truth will set you free."
Before we knew the truth in this matter, we were slaves to the things that we were not able to overcome. Once we understand how these habits control our life, we can do the necessary things to become free.
Remember that being equipped with free will, we have a choice in this matter. We could still act the same old way and support the consequences or knowing the truth, we use it to free ourselves from the habits that are a source of stress.
So, once we know remember this:
"If it is to be, it's up to me"
Now, let's go forward and see how we can make peace with the C.E. O. of the Universe: Our Maker.

4. Make peace with your Maker.

- Getting a better relationship with the C. E. O. (Chief Executive Officer) of the Universe. -

Now, after we have made peace with all the others including ourselves, let's see if is there anybody else left out.
Well, the word Maker means different things to different people. Let's be a little bit honest and realistic when we pursue this subject. The bigger a Company is the more it needs to have a C.E. O. If that's the case, what about the biggest *Company* we may call Universe? It runs better than any other Company that we know of. Shouldn't the Universe have a C.E.O.? That's a good question we all should reflect on.
If there is no Maker, there is no reason to go find a way to make peace with Him. But what if there is one? Yeah, what if the Universe really has a C.E.O? What's going to be the loss or the gain by making peace with Him? Basically, the answer to these questions lies in the realm of religion. This book is not intended to be of religious guidance. Still, we are going to touch a little bit on this subject. It's too important to leave it out.
Imagine you go fishing in the ocean. For some reason, you get lost and after a few days you end up on an island in the middle of the ocean. There aren't any people but to your amazement, you find a beautiful, huge, modern house. Everything inside is in excellent condition and everything works very well. The heater,

air conditioning, kitchen appliances, bathroom, plumbing, electrical system, etc, are all in perfect condition. Next to the house, you see a nice garden with all kinds of fruits and vegetables.

You go in and start to make yourself comfortable. You live there for a long time and after a while you got very used to this house. It feels like you have own it forever. Yes, the house is yours. Who else could it be? There is no other owner around.

You may be right. But are you?

Now let's say that after a while, some other people get lost in the ocean and they end up on the same island with you. You start sharing everything with them and in the beginning they are thankful. After a while, small differences start to arise and a spirit of rivalry develops between you. Who's the rightful owner of the house? Is it you, or they are?

The situation becomes even more interesting when you find some messages on the island. They seem to be intended for the inhabitants of the island and claim to be from the real owner of the house. What are you going to do?

Intensify your fight to acquire the ownership of the house like the others do? Or try to find the real owner and thank him for the beautiful house that was built?

Well, this is a tricky question but also a very serious one.

Do you think that this house you are occupying could have been the product of a blind evolution or it must have an owner?

Let's look at both sizes of the coin.

1. Suppose that this house just happen to evolve from some other inferior thing.

If that's the case, what else should we expect to find beside what we already see?

Well, the evidence of that evolution.

Do you think it's possible that something inferior evolved into an intelligent product and all the steps of evolution of the product disappeared without a trace?

We know that if we left alone any man-made product, no matter how sophisticated it might be, in time the product will eventually be eroded and destroyed by the environment.

If a product cannot resist or at least to stay the same way, how is it possible that something very inferior, survives and stays the same? If that is not possible, how can it even evolve to a more sophisticated state?

If you believe that this is possible, I might still have some ocean front property in Montana to sell you.

Let's not kid each other; let's become realistic.

A complete house, a sophisticated electrical system, plumbing, air-conditioning system and all other fixtures are somebody's design. The fact that we might be in darkness regarding the owner or we don't like the idea of an owner; doesn't mean that one isn't in existence?

Any intelligent product, more or less sophisticated, has to have an even more intelligent designer.

2. Suppose the house has a builder or owner.

Now, how can we prove that the house has an owner when the inhabitants of the house do not see him around?

Well, how many of you drive cars?

How many of you have seen the people who build these cars?

You live in a house, right? Chances are you never saw or even don't know who built that house.

The fact that you never physically saw the owner doesn't prove that they don't exist?

None of us see the electric current either but we all benefit from its effects.

How many of us have the courage to ignore its power or to mess with it without proper protection? Well, not too many.

Now, how can we prove that the house has an owner or a designer if we cannot see them?

Chapter 11. Healing the past.

Well, it's not difficult to do that.

If we look at a car, examines its functions with all its fixtures, what can we say? Can we say that this car had an intelligent and careful designer who cares about people? Of course we can. That's a normal conclusion.

Then, what we can say about our house? It's simple; we can say the same thing.

Now let's go back to our subject.

Taking an overall look at earth, we can say that it is like a huge house. We have the summer as the heater, and the winter as the air-conditioner system. We have a large variety of vegetables, fruits and animals and food to satisfy our hunger. We have a crystal clear water system to satisfy our thirst.

We have snowy mountains to enjoy their serenity and beauty.

We have sunny beaches where we tan our bodies to swim and enjoy the waves of the seas or oceans.

We have a wonderful human body with all its sophisticated abilities.

How amazing is it to have the ability to reproduce, to love, feel loved, enjoy music or any other art, etc.

What else we have?

We need to make another book to list all the things we benefit from on this earth.

How much rent do we pay for these items? Last time I checked, we haven't written a check.

Remember, we cannot see electricity but we acknowledge its existence because we can see its effects. We can't see the Maker either but we can look at the worldly creations and recognize that some powerful force is behind them.

How can we humans, see the powerful forces in the universe such as the sun, earth, moon, stars and not recognize that there must be a creator? Are our eyes powerful enough to see?

It might be wise to start taking this subject more serious because all things in life depend on this. Maybe, just maybe, one day the owner will come and ask for past rents. It might be wise to be prepared.

If there is a Maker, who was powerful enough to build such a wonderful earth, it wasn't done so we could have a short and painful journey; rather I think a much larger scope was planned.

Open a new file in your mind, call it: *My honest search for my Maker* or something similar.

You made peace with yourself, you neighbor and the environment. Now it's time to make peace with your Maker.

If this Creator really exists, and you will honestly search for the truth in this matter, you might be surprised to find out that he will let himself be found by you. If it doesn't exist, you haven't lost anything.

Remember: "If it is to be it's up to me."

We are going to look at a little hint that I think will help in getting a realistic view about this subject.

We do this by asking few simple questions:

Even though we might be able to use calculators when it comes to solving math problems; we still know basic math.

We have 10 numbers starting from the smallest to the greatest. Like 1, 2, 3, 4, 5, etc.

We know that 4 is bigger than 2, and 6 is larger than 4. This is true, everybody agrees. If that's the case, then 6 must be greater than 2 also; it cannot be smaller, right?

Now let's take another example:

Try to imagine the evolution of the computer. During the 1970's, the computer was in its beginning stages. It took up a lot of space and its abilities were much inferior than of the ones that followed. After 1995, once Windows, arrived on the market, the computer became a necessary household item; at an unbelievable affordable price. It's capacity increased enormously and its physical size decreased drastically. Now, why did this happen? A blind evolution or did this happened because of the works and invention of an intelligent designer?

Why wasn't this possible 50, 100, 1000 or even 1,000,000 years ago?

These are silly questions you might say. It was impossible, that's why.
Why was it impossible I am going to ask you .At that time, people's knowledge and means to accomplish these kinds of projects were none existent, that's why.
The more we go back in history, the harder it would have been for those living to accomplish these things. We all agree with this, right?
If we built the most powerful computer but neglected to maintain it by leaving it alone for 10, or 20, or 100 years, what do you think is going to happen?
Will it evolve into a better, more powerful and sophisticated computer? Or will start to deteriorate to an unusable product?
I think we all agree on the answer to these questions.
Now, do you know which is more complicated and difficult to create? A very powerful computer? Or the human brain?
We might be able to build the most powerful computer but according to scientists, we are still far away from being able to build a computer as powerful as the human brain.
In conclusion, we are light years away from building a human brain or something comparable. How was it possible, millions of years ago, for the same brain to come in existence by itself?
Remember, if 4 is bigger than 2, and 6 is larger then 4, then for sure 6 is greater than 2 also.
If humans were not able to build a computer 50, or 100, or 1,000 or 1,000,000 years ago, how was it possible that the human brain (not to mention the whole earth with everything on it) evolve itself without any help from an intelligent source?
If you think that was possible, I still have some ocean front property in Montana for sell if you are interested!
So, if we really want to be realistic, we can see that there are some good reasons to look for making peace with our Maker.
If you move to a different country and were told that the president of that country might be one of your close relatives; would you be afraid or ashamed to find the truth? Would you will gladly search to find out if this is really so? Think about that. On the other hand don't you think that it would be a miserable and stressful life to live ignoring and neglecting the greatest relative that you could have, the C.E.O. of the Universe?
  Now, after we understood the necessity of making peace with ourselves, neighbors, environment, and the C.E.O. of the Universe, our Maker and took the necessary steps to implement this, we can honestly answer the question we asked at the beginning of this chapter: Who are we really? We can honestly say:
"I am a wonderful human being deserving to enjoy living my stress-free life to the fullness."
Who can stop you now from accomplishing your goal? The only one that could do that is you. You could make it happen or you could stop it from happening.
Remember: "If it is to be, it's up to me."
Now, let's go to the second method of erasing the negative feelings from our past; that is the substitution method.

B. The Substitution method.

- Trading the bad for the good. -

  Beside the reasoning method, there is another method that works effectively in removing the negative feelings that we previously have attached to certain words or situations. This method is very simple and it requires very little time.

To better our understanding how this works, it might help to take an example:
Suppose that there is a football game going on between two well-known teams and you are invited by your friend to party at their house. There are a couple of your old friends; they're all having fun watching the game. Some of the people are fans of one team and some of them of the other.
Even though you like football neither team is your favorite. For you, it doesn't matter who wins or looses. Unlike the others, you are not emotionally attached to any of them.
Now, during the game, everybody understands the events of the game from their own point of view depending on which side they were on. When a situation happens and things are not clear as to whose fault it is, everybody is blaming the other side. Why? By being attached to their favorite teams, their emotions stand between them and a clear reasoning ability.
In your case, not being attached to any of the teams, you could see and understand clearly what's happening and who's at fault even though some might not agree with you.
This is a normal situation and we expect people to react like this. The real reason is that being emotional involved with one of the teams, they cannot see clearly what happened and have the tendency to blame the other side even though the reality might be different.
The same thing happens with us when we are emotional involved in situations. We tend to see things from our point of view, neglecting to be objective and realistic and get wrong conclusions or results. Not being aware of this, we attach negative feelings to many words or situations. Later on, when we remember them, we will again feel the negative emotions previously attached to them. Now let's see what we can do to remove these negative feelings so we don't have to relive them any more in the future.
There are a few variations of this method of substitution that if properly understood and applied, could help us. Let's take one at a time and see how we can apply them for our benefit.

1. The switching position method.

As we learned earlier, we might be under the impression that we consciously control our behavior but our subconscious mind is the one that implements our conscious desires and goals. In order to do lasting changes in the way we deal with our life and in our case on how to deal with past negative experiences; we are going to learn how to directly *talk* with our subconscious mind. A simple way to do this is by *turning off our conscious senses*. First, you need to find a quiet place where nobody can disturb you. Then close your eyes and relax for a minute by breathing deeply in and out slowly a few times. In this calm and peaceful state of mind, go back in your memory and take one of your negative or stressful experiences. Slowly, try to relive it like a movie clip, only this time, you exclude or pull yourself out of it. Put somebody else in it; let's say one of you best friends. By doing this, you are no longer involved in the situation but become an observer of the movie; not being emotionally attached to it. Run the *movie clip* a few times slowly in your mind, asking yourself a simple question: What's the best advice I could give my friend who's going through this difficult situation? As an observer, with no emotions attached to the situation, you can see better what's the right advice to give your friend in this difficult situation. Once you do this, you can clearly see the reality of the event and the real action that needs to be taken. Finding the right decision that needs to be taken; the situation is half solved. Then after you do this, pull the other person out of the movie clip and put yourself back in. Now, slowly precede again the new movie clip eight to ten times in your mind; seeing yourself acting the right way. After each time you replay the movie, imagine all the positive results that come from being able to do this. Honestly express your inner joy at being able to accomplish this huge change in your life.
"Yes, I can do it, and I am getting better and better at doing it."

By doing this, we are removing the negative emotions that we felt by previous decisions, replacing them with new positive emotions.

Let's take an example to illustrate this:

Let's say that you go to a party with your friend or your spouse. While having fun, something happens and you respond improperly. This causes the person you came with to feel embarrassed. After this, you see that even though you would like to continue the party, your escort felt hurt and wants to leave. You try to convince them to stay and have fun but they do not want to.

"Well it's their problem and if they cannot take a joke" You might say and you continue with the party. After the party, you go home and realize that this person was really hurt, and does not want to communicate with you any more.

Well, even though you feel that you didn't do anything wrong, this starts to bother you, and you start to feel badly about the whole thing. You try to do your best to make it up, but nothing seems to work. You start to develop negative feelings about this person.

"How could they do this and it's not even my fault?

If that's the case, I'll forget about them and I'll go ahead with my life."

Every time you think about this incident, it makes you feel bad especially when you are not aware that you were at fault.

Having knowledge about the substitution method, you could easily fix this by using it to find out what's the best solution for this situation. It will not be difficult at all to do if right a way you recognized who was at fault and what will be the best solution.

We cannot change the past but we can change the kind of emotions or feelings we previously have attached to it. By replaying the new movie clip in our mind, we are overlapping the new movie clip over the old one reducing or even eliminating all the old negative emotions. By removing the negative feelings the next time when we think about the same situation, we do not feel the negative feelings; only a positive or just no feelings at all.

Remember what we learned earlier about the reticular activating system? We saw that it was designed to help us in accomplishing our goals that we set for ourselves. Knowing now that we have a choice in designing our own future, we will set goals to become stress free persons. Once we do that this system, we start to move towards the things that make this possible. By setting goals to master these methods of eliminating stress, we build new blueprints for our subconscious mind to follow when we face situations that used to be stressors. Also, we should always remember that being equipped with free will, we could choose to follow the old blueprints or follow the new ones.

Now let's learn about the second variation of the substitution method, the disassociation method.

2. *The disassociation method.*

Earlier we learned about consciousness and saw that during our life we continuously switch our state of consciousness from active to passive. Based on our interest in what are we dealing with, understanding the opposite effects that they have upon us, we can consciously decide when is the best time to associate ourselves to events or situations or to disassociate from them. By using the same process of disassociation, we are also going to be able to remove old negative feelings that were previously attached to some stressors.

Our subconscious mind cannot differentiate between real or fictional information. Knowing that, we are going to do some changes at subconscious level on the *stressful events or situations* that have a stressful effect over us.

Again, to use this method, find a quiet place where nobody can disturb you. Then close your eyes and relax for a minute, by breathing deeply in and out slowly a few times. In this calm and peaceful state, go back in your memory and take one of your negative or stressful experiences. Like in a movie clip, watch yourself in the stressful event. By doing this, you are disassociating yourself from it. You become just an observer not feeling the negative emotions attached to it. Seriously try to see yourself reliving this experience starting with some moments before you got into the stressful situation. Then just before you get into it, imagine that the rest of the picture starts becoming blurred and impossible to recognize what's going on. Or, you can change the picture from its original colors to black and white, then gray, then completely fade it. Repeat the experience a few times until you are not able to recognize the stressful ending to it. Once you do this, open your eyes and try to remember the whole experience. When you come to the stressful part of it, you won't feel the negative feelings any longer.

Through this process of disassociation, you create a new *situation* over the old one. By overlapping them, the negative feelings from the previous ones are removed, so the situation is no more a stressful one.

This new *situation* becomes part of that particular file where the old one was stored. When we do changes and save them in any of our files, the next time when we open the same file; we are going to find whatever we put in it the last time.

Once we have done these changes and closed the *file*, the new information will override the old one. The next time when you reopen the same *file*, you won't feel old negative feelings; they'll be gone. Since the negative feelings are gone, now you consciously decide what's the best thing to do. Choose to let them be gone forever, realizing that from now on, you are not going to let the past affect negatively your present and future.

Now let's see how we can continue on the road towards a stress free life by using the third variation of the substitution method.

3. The nail painted method.

Do you remember when you received a nice gift from somebody you love and how good you felt? Every time you look at it, brought back beautiful memories of that person. How about your childhood toys? Can you still remember how real and pleasurable they were and how much you enjoyed having them around? How about your little gifts you received in school from some of your best friends? If you are married, how about your wedding ring? When you look and meditate about it, what kind of memories come into your mind?

Well, even these little things continue to have a powerful emotional influence on us.

How come all these *little things* are able to bring so many joyful memories?

We have learned earlier about the neuron-associations that continuously are formed in our minds. When we come in contact with a part of one of these associations, the mind brings to our conscious awareness whole associations; whatever we have attached to them in the past. In our case, that little gift, we attached positive feelings. Anytime we see it again, we *relive* the positive feelings previously attached to it. That little gift becomes like a positive *trigger object* that is capable of bringing instant positive feelings to our conscious awareness.

Knowing this principle, we can make a simple positive *trigger object* that will have the same positive results; by associating it with the *file* "Living a stress free life."

You know that most women have the habit of doing their nails in different sizes and colors. This is normal nothing unusual. Take a color of our choosing and apply a dot over your thumbnail.

Then imagine the new blueprint you formed in your mind about you being a stress free person. See it with all the bits of information that teach you how to accomplish this how they are entering through a funnel into that dot of paint on your thumbnail. Picture all the pages of this book, one by one, are entering that little dot on your nail. The whole book has been absorbed by it. Visualize each page of each chapter with its secrets, one by one, entering that small dot of paint. Imagine knowing that our life's game has its own rules and by knowing them, you are able to play the game the way you want to. Envision by being aware of the importance of your body, spirit, mind and behavior; you are more careful on how to properly use them for your benefit. See also, how understanding the importance of the two mechanisms, you are able to direct your life the way you really want to. Imagine that now you realize who are the sources of so called stressors, and who's responsible for their creation. Even more than that, you are equipped with the tools that help stop producing new stress and also to remove the old stress stored in memory banks. In the past, you had no idea on how to properly deal with stress. Imagine the importance of living a stress free life; not just a Sunday cloth that is put on and off. Enjoy the new beautiful feelings by being a stress free person. Yes, you too can do that! This is not a bedtime story; it's real as the sun on the sky.

See clearly in your mind how this happen. That dot now contains all of the information from this book. Again, once the book enters the dot, imagine the unbelievable burst of positive feelings that overflow your body realizing that finally you are now a stress free person; enjoying your life to the fullest. It's up to you to stay this way. You are not any longer at the discretion of the stressful environment that used to be merciless toward you.

Now, any time you look at the dot on your nail, you will remember that you are a stress-free person and have the knowledge to accomplish this. The more often this is repeated, the easier it will be to convince yourself that this is an easy task, and pretty soon a normal habit easy to accomplish.

So, remember, this is such a little effort, for such wonderful results.

Let's review some items we learned in this chapter.
In few words, we are going to set a goal of becoming a stress free person.
By doing this, a new file is opened in our memory banks and the new file needs a blueprint.
Using the information from this book, we will build a new blueprint. We use as many senses as possible to do this. Once a new blueprint is built, the old blueprint about stress will be gone. Have a little patience with yourself and give it some time to replace the old one. Also, have patience until the *workers,* your body's cells, get used to the new command and start fulfilling the new assignments. Be persistent in continuously feeding your mind with the right kind of *food* and pretty soon a stress free person will become a reality.
Both methods; the reasoning and the substitution, can be used freely everyday for dealing with things or situations that might cause stress. Both of them are working and they are easy to apply. It is up to us to do this if we really are looking for a permanent solution to our problems. By doing this, we eliminate many potential stressors that might otherwise resulted in stress.
Now, let's go further and discus about six steps we can take when we are dealing with some painful situations.

When bad things happened to peaceful people.
Six steps in dealing with difficult situations.

- But, it hurts so badly... why, tell me why? -

By now, we have a much better understanding of how our mind works and how we can become our own ally in designing / creating our own environment.
Let's discuss how to deal with extraordinary negative situations or events that we might go through due to unforeseen circumstances.

Chapter 11.   Healing the past.

The recent events the American people went through in September 2001, left many people with a lot of unanswered questions. Why did this happen? How come events like these could take place here? How could people be so cruel? Why did it happen to us?

Well, let's leave these questions to experts and focus our attention on another questions that is very important also: How do we cope with this? What we can do to put this behind and start healing from wounds created by tragedies like these and what role we play in our own healing?

Before we do this, it might be very helpful to understand why we are emotionally affected when these things happen.

We have learned earlier, that our propulsion mechanism has the role to identify, explore, absorb, understand, enjoy, and finally own the *environment* we live in. Our dear ones, friends and relatives also become part of this *environment* that we already own. Once we have a certain *ownership* over them, they go under the protection and jurisdiction of our self-defense mechanism. That's why we care and do our best to protect them from anything that might cause any harm. Having *ownership* over them, they become our own *possessions*. When something bad happens to them; we are affected also. When they suffer, we suffer. When some of them die a part of us dies also. That's why it hurts so badly and feels like our pain is unbearable.

All the bits of information, with all the positive emotions attached to them, are deposited in our memory banks into a specific file. As we have learned earlier, this file has also a blueprint that our subconscious mind uses to direct our behavior towards them. When something bad or terrible happen to any of our dear ones, the conscious mind understands what happened. But for our behavior to change, it takes a while until the subconscious mind overrides the existing blueprint with the new one created by the new situation. It takes some time and a conscious effort to realize the reality, accept it and look for the proper reaction to the new situation. Until this happens, even though we consciously see what happened, our subconscious mind still directs our behavior by using the existing blueprint. That's why many of us are in shock or in denial having a hard time to cope with the new situation. Unless the existing blueprint is replaced with a new one, our subconscious mind has the tendency to reject the new information; directing the behavior through the existing blueprint. The more the new situations are accepted consciously, the more it hurts because of the conflict between the existing blueprint and the new one that starts to take form through the conscious acceptance of the new reality. Little by little, it takes shape and tries to replace the other.

So, it's important to understand these things and consciously take the necessary decisions to get the best out of any difficult situation.

Now let's examine the six steps we need to go through.

First, we need to acknowledge that all of us are affected by these kinds of events; some more directly than others. It's a terrible thing to hear when they happen but it's even worst to be personally affected by these tragic events.

The reality is that living in the 21st Century, we can see and benefit from the greatest scientific discoveries. But also we know that there are people that use these advanced technologies to achieve their dark and diabolic goals. The human mind, when used properly, can bring the human efforts to marvelous achievements. When used to do evil, it's able to conceive the worst imaginable destruction to its own kind.

This is the reality of the world we live in. This makes one aware of the responsibility each of us has to do in the development and advancement toward the good and well being for all. Let's tell it like it is and not deny the reality; no matter how painful it might be.

- Yes, sometimes bad things happen to peaceful people. -

Second, we need to recognize that we play a major role in our own recovery.

We are the ones that feel the emotions produced by our absorbing the information concerning these events or situations. We are the ones that play a major role in our recovery; by the way we look at them and the meanings we give them. Of course, in the short run we might have been shocked and under a great deal of pain. That is understandable and kind of a normal reaction. But, we need to understand that to recover and benefit in the long run, we are responsible to take the necessary steps. We might need some help from others in coping, but the major responsibility still falls on our shoulders. By getting involved in our recovery and also by trying to help others affected by these events and situations, we are making our recovery easier and shorter.

- So, start helping yourself before counting on others to help you. -

Third, even though the events were unbelievable and affected many of us very much, this is only an episode of our lives. This is not our entire life and any event no matter how powerful effect might have over us, is just a part of a bigger picture. A wedding, for example, is considered by many to be the most important events in one's life. A lot of time energy and money is invested in it and sooner or later, it becomes an episode of our life. The same thing happens with a major negative experience. Sooner or later they too become just an episode in our life. But, we as a whole are more that just an episode of our lives.

- Remember, you are more than just what happens to you. -

Fourth, it's only human to grief. We all have this inner need to express our sorrow and emotions when dealing with these kinds of situations. It's ok to cry, to express our indignation and pain. It's also ok to write a letter and express in it our feelings. Of course we don't mail it. The reason being is to let out this inner energy that is produced as a result of being involved in these situations or events.
Now, you may say that it's easy for me to talk about these things when I wasn't directly affected by these kinds of experiences. Actually I was, during my life, I been through many painful experiences.
When I was ten years old, my father died from burns in a terrible accident. When I went with the family to his funeral, I could not recognize his face. He was terribly burned from the accident. I looked at his face and with my broken heart I asked myself:
Why? Why did this happen to us?
I didn't receive any satisfactory answer for my inner question, but I learned to accept it; maybe one day I might find out why. It might not be today but that day will surely come.
When I was twenty-one, back in Europe, I use to work as a professional driver for the City. From time to time, I drove the mortuary minivan; sometimes locally or long distance. One day my boss sent me to a hospital to pick up a man (a husband and a father) that just died in a work accident. I was to deliver him to his family in a village about 150 miles away. I left from my City during the day and I got there in the evening. The house was full of relatives and other neighbors crying and mourning the lost of this man. Once they brought him inside the house, one of his children, his seven-years old daughter, started crying with a loud childish voice begging him to come back to life.
"Daddy! my daddy, my daddy!!, I want you back, I want you back, don't go daddy!, don't go, don't go…"
"What can I do without you my daddy, what can I do…? Please daddy, please come back!"
"Why are you leaving me daddy? What did I do to you, please come back, please daddy!!"
My words cannot express that scene, they seem too poor and ineffective; it was like a very painful drama that words couldn't describe. I was twenty-one, recently discharged from the army, where I was trained to be brave and strong. Not being able stand to see this scene any longer, I went outside because I didn't want these people see my eyes full of tears. Never in my life did I witness such a manifestation of sorrow and pain from a child. It felt like I should be leaving this world and go away someplace where there is no pain and sorrow. I relived in my mind the picture of me as a ten years old child standing helpless in front of my father's coffin, not knowing what to do except get away from this world full of sorrow and pain.

The image of that helpless child begging for her father not to leave her left a deep and lasting impression in my mind.
Did we come on this earth only to suffer or for a better reason?

- Yes, tears of sorrow are medication for healing. -

Fifth, no matter how difficult an event might be, there comes a time to let them go. We do this not because we loose interest in the loss of our dear ones, but we understand that we are under obligation to go ahead with our life. Continuing to care for those that still are with us and need our help is our responsibility. Another reason we do this, is in the memory of those we lost. We come to the realization that if they could send us a message on what to do with our lives, they would want us to continue on; getting the best out of it.
I remember when I was a kid; I learned a short poem that might fit our situation.
"Do not despair when fate has put you down,
And do not cry, because of its destine,
Cause' after tribulations, the life looks even better,
As after rain, the sky is much serene"
Yes we all suffer, we loose some of dear ones and at present we might not understand why. There is a reason for it and sooner or later we might find that truth. Until then, we learn to accept the reality and go ahead with our lives. This is for our sake, the sake of the ones that we still have with us and also in the memory of those we lost.

- Forget your tribulations, but never forget what they teach you. -

Sixth, what can we learn from these experiences and what can be done to stop them from happening again? Since we cannot turn back the time and prevent these things from happening; at least we can learn a lesson from them. Even though they have been very painful to most of us; something good might come out of them.
Many of us who lost some of our dear ones, might wish we had a better relationship with them, to spend more time and show them more love / attention. Now it is too late, they are gone, but we can learn to do more for the others that are still here. We still have many other friends and relatives left
Maybe, we can learn to appreciate our relationships with our friends, relatives; understand them better and get closer to them.
Not that the ones we lost are less important but we need to pick up the pieces and continue our life's journey to the best of our abilities.

- Out of ruins, let a better and stronger you come out. –

Even though some of our experiences are taking a heavy toll on us, we are just humans. It's human to grief, it's human to cry, but it's also human to go ahead with our lives no matter how difficult some of the experiences might have been.

Until now we have learned a few secrets of who we really are, what we're dealing with when it comes to stress and some solutions to this worldwide problem.
Now, we understand that anyone who knows the rules of the game can play the game the way they want to. When it comes to stress, we realized that this is also a *game* and by understanding and applying its rules, we

can play it the way we want to and win. Then we saw that through emotions, our body is the first to feel the results of the way our mind reacts to the *environment* that we are continuously interacting with.

We also understand that whatever we do, we do for a reason, based on our personal interpretation of our *environment*. Of course, now we know who are really the creators of our stressful environment. Not only this but now we have some simple and effective tools that will enable us to stop producing new stress, heal our past, so it won't have any stressful effect over us.

Let's go to the next secret, which is the best thing to do with what we have learned in order to truly benefit from our learning. Can we afford to let the knowledge we got from this book just be knowledge? Or, are we smart enough to transform it into wisdom by daily applying its principles in our lives? You may have heard the sayings:

"Use it, or loose it." Or "Repetition is the mother of skill."

Review Question: Which is the next door that needs to be closed on stress, and how do the reasoning and the substitution methods help us to implement this?

Answer:
- The next door we need to close on stress would be *healing of our past,* or eliminating the stress stored in the past in our memory banks.
- Using the reasoning method, we make peace with ourselves, our neighbors, our environment, and with our Maker.
- By using the substitution method, we trade the bad for the good. We do that by so-called switching position method, disassociation method, or the painted nail method.

Question: When bad things happen to peaceful people, what it might be useful to remember?

Answer:
- Even though at times the pain seems unbearable, the reality of the world we live in is that sometime bad things do happens to peaceful people.
- No matter how painful they may be, the sooner we get involved in our own recovery the faster it will happen.
- We understand that there is a difference between our life as a whole and an episode of it. We need to take care of more than just an episode of our life.
- Joy and pain are both part of being human. Manifesting both would be a normal thing and also a medication that helps the healing process.
- Sooner or later, the time will come to let go, and realize that this negative episode will become part of our past. We forget our tribulations, but remember the lessons that they taught us.
- As the rainbow, that gracious thing made up of tears and light, so out of ruins a better and stronger you could come out.

"The past has been a great player in our present stressful life. By healing it, we become free of its negative influence, and to live the present free of stress."

Secret # 12.

"Wisdom is the practical application of knowledge people continuously acquire."

Chapter 12. Make Up Your Mind.

- Some people "love" misery of stress so much they spend all their life in it, how about you?-

Until now, we have learned that first we need to raise the level of awareness to a level where we are starting to appreciate the value of truthful information pertaining to the process of stress. Once the level of awareness increases, the desire to eliminate stress starts to develop.

The more we desire, the more we will look for information that will help increase the awareness. When the desire is powerful enough, we will make a decision to do something about the stress. Because the level of awareness keeps rising, we learned how to properly motivate ourselves in following the right steps in the process of forming a new habit.

Having enough motivation, we are able to keep ourselves on track or to self- discipline ourselves in such away that we could easily master the ability to recognize in advance potential stressors and take the necessary steps to eliminate them, before we loose control and concentration. In other words we have replaced the old blueprint from the subconscious mind that says we have to live with stress, with a new and better one.

The new one says that by applying the right knowledge, we are able to eliminate stress, not just manage it.

We learned that our mind continuously absorbs information through our senses, and to each event based on the meaning given it becomes a positive or negative situation.

By giving positive meaning, we are linking this information to the propulsion mechanism, which in turn triggers a positive emotion in our body. But if we give a negative meaning to it, based on the same laws that do not change, we're linking the information to self-defense mechanism. As a result the mechanism in our body triggers a negative emotion, bringing to our conscious awareness that there is danger near by.

Understanding this vital principle, we realize basically there aren't any stressors out there.

The stressful effect that we usually feel is the negative emotions previously attached to these situations; by linking them to the self-defense mechanism.

We cannot change the past, but we can remove negative feelings that we have previously attached to them. So, the next time in the future when we start thinking about the past, reliving these negative feelings again isn't necessary. Once done, these particular situations present no more potential stressful effects. To eliminate the negative feelings from stressful situations, we need to master a habit of disassociation by using the reasoning or substitution method.

Knowing once we are into a stressful situation we loose control and concentration, we need to apply this new habit of reasoning, which will be triggered by our brain before we get in the situation.

Since we are warned in advance by this new habit an incoming *stressful situation* might occur, we consciously take the right steps in eliminating its stressful effects. Remember:
"Everybody is a slave to things they cannot control."
But nobody is slave to things that they're able to master well. And the good news is:
"By knowing the truth, the truth will set you free."
Knowing this principal, we have the choice to free ourselves from the negative effects that stress has over us, by the simple fact that we learned to master this new habit of dealing with potential stressful situations in advance. We all know and are aware of the fact that the best way to deal with a stressful situation is not to get into it. That's why we need to form this new habit. Having this habit formed and firmly in place, it'll be triggered by our brain any time we get close to a potential *stressful situation.*

Understanding the importance of reasoning and substitution methods, we will make sure to disassociate the negative feelings previously attached. By doing that, the next time when we are facing the same kind of situations we will remember the meaning of it, but there will no longer be any stressful effects. It will be just an unpleasant past experience that doesn't present any danger in causing stress.
So, basically stress is not the information itself, but is caused by the meaning we give to it. If we think that it is a stressor it'll becomes a stressor. But if we change the meaning from stressor to just information that requires special attention, then we just treat it like any other sensitive thing. By doing this, we don't have any negative feelings attached to it. So, we basically we have eliminated the potential stressors.
The problem comes from the fact that people were never taught about the way their mind works and unaware of, learned the habit of giving negative meanings to many situations. Without being aware of this principal, they are the creators of their own stressful environments.
The only solution is to learn to replace these *bad habits* of misdiagnosing information coming from the outside environment, with the right habit of seeing things from a positive point of view, and give the right meaning to it. Proceeding this way we are not linking them to the self-defense mechanism, so it can have a stressful effect over us. Instead we are attaching a positive feeling to it, by linking them to the propulsion mechanism. A result we can have a clear mind to reason the situation and come up with the right solution.

Remember, if you are looking for negativity, it's guaranteed you'll find negativity, no matter how perfect somebody or the situation might be. But, if you are looking for positive, you'll be surprised in realizing there is a positive side to it too. This is *your* responsibility to achieve. Start to appreciate the value of positive information, and by gaining understanding, you'll take the necessary steps in eliminating stress forever. Remember that aware or not, we are designed to absorb information continually as long as we are alive. So, it's important to start being selective with information allow to enter our minds. There is a large variety of negative information out there, that we just don't need them, and more than that, this will affect us negatively in the future. As we saw earlier, anything that we have learned today, will become food for thought for tomorrow. In other words, memory that is going to affect the way we think tomorrow.
So, remember: Stop saving the wrong things, and start accumulating the things that really matter and will help you in the future.

Now, we all know that life on earth develops in three dimensions. We have three elements called: Time, Space, and Matter. Humans are superior to any other creature, are aware of their own existence and can perceive these three elements as a part of their life. Knowing that our life is limited to time, space, and matter, we might keep in consideration that we're responsible for the way we deal with these three elements. Understanding their purpose and importance in our life, we could purposely learn how to manage them for our own benefit. On the other hand, unaware of their importance in our life, we could mismanage them, and as result our life could become an unpleasant experience.

Remember that our life is basically the conscious process of administration of these three elements. And, the more we are aware of this, the healthier our lives can become.
Therefore, it's important to recognize that it is our responsibility to learn to properly manage our life. The more active we are in managing it, the more we'll live it according to our wishes. The less active we are, the more we live it according to other people's wishes. Take control of it, or let others to do it for you. .

Chapter 12. Make-up your mind.

Now, we'll focus on the element that is called: Time. We all realize that time is a relative term, but by applying our personal situation, time is something that is perceived in three steps. One is the past, which we already have experienced. Second is the present, which is the one we consciously perceive now. And of course the future, which is the one that'll come tomorrow.

We mentioned previously, as conscious human beings, we continuously absorb information from the environment and also give them a meaning by associating states of mind, or feelings to them. Once this process is finished, it becomes a memory that'll be available for a future point of reference. In other words, our brain always compares new information it receives in the present with the ones already existing. Once a match is found, if we perceive that it'll be in our best interest, the information is recalled.

If in the past, that particular memory had negative meaning attached to it, unaware of, we'll feel that feeling again. Understanding this, we have a choice to be selective about the kind of meanings we give to the information surrounding us. Contending with past information we don't have any power to change past events, but we do have a choice to change the meaning we gave them. Without being aware of, we do this many times in our life. For example:

Let's see how we make friends. Suppose you have a friend for three years. Now, he / she is your best friend. But were they your best friend three and a half years ago? No. Just an acquaintance. How about four years ago? Maybe they were strangers. After you met him / her, they became an acquaintance and progress to becoming a best friend. Now, did you change the past, in order to do this?

No, but you changed the meaning you gave to him / her, from a stranger to a friend and eventually, best friend. Knowing this principle of removing the meaning of particular information with a different one, we can apply it consciously to any situation needed. In our case, we use this principle to eliminate stress.

So what we do is, we learn how to remove the cause of stress that is, the negative part of memory, and replace it with something different that'll not result in stress.

We have learned earlier the necessary steps needed to consciously change an old habit that was resulting in stress and replacing it with a new one that will result in a stress free life. Now, let's recall how old habits were formed, and what determines their reaction as impulses that are triggered instantaneously by our brain in certain situations. A good way to learn and understand how something functions is to first understand the purpose of its designer. Then, the better we understand its purpose, the easier it'll be to understand why it functions the way it does.

Let's take an example:

A car is a complex piece of machinery, with many systems and components, which are designed to work together. As result the car is in good condition to be used for the purpose that it was designed.

Now, the more you know about cars, the more you're aware that its components need to be in the proper place and in working condition. If we find out something is wrong with it, we might consider taking it to the mechanic.

The less you know about it, the easier you could be misled about its condition In a case like this, you have two choices: One, you could depend on other opinions about the condition of your car. Or, you could start learning about how the car functions, and the necessary things needed to give a right diagnostic; eventually repair it. Most of us prefer to leave this job to the mechanic, and just write the check for the amount requested. But, when it comes to our future, we might consider learning some things that will enable us to understand and control our life the way we want. We shouldn't leave it in the hands of others to decide what is best for us, and how to live our life. We are more important than a car. We might be able to replace a car at any time, by buying another one, but as regards to our life and future at least now, we know about this one.

So, it might be wise to look for necessary information that'll help you design your future according to your wishes, and not letting others to do it for you. If it's precious enough for you, then learn how to master it properly. The best time to start is right now.

"Repetition is the mother of skill"

Let's Remember.

- The final test; applying what we have learned. -

So far we have learned that as long as we are alive, we constantly receive information from the outside environment. The information is modeling our thinking abilities, based on the meaning that was given. Not paying attention to the meaning we given them, they might become habits resulting in potential stressors. This is what we have done in the past. Like a garden without gardener, we let our mind be filled with any information, not being aware of negative results that could come out of it. Nobody taught us to be selective, and control information that we get from the outside. .
But, now once we have learned that we are responsible for doing this, we can consciously select the *quality* of information that we choose to accept. Like a good gardener, we do a thorough clean up of our mind from anything that might cause us stress.

In regards to new information, we have learned to see them through a positive light, and by doing that we stopped associating negative feelings towards them.

Proceeding this way, we train our mental abilities to see what is good about everything in life, and give them positive meanings.

Also we learned that habits are learned behaviors, and we can change the ones that might be potential stressors. We do this by changing old blueprints with new and better ones. We can learn to be patient, and act with patience, as easy as we get upset when things go wrong. We always have a choice.

We learned that stress is not a cause, but a symptom of a cause and we need to go to the roots of the cause. To see where stress is coming from, eliminate the roots, and then stress automatically will disappear. It's like a tree with many branches. We could day and night keep cutting branches here and there, but they'll grow back again. We need to get to its roots and destroy them and then all the branches will die off.

Also, we have learned in our brain every second neuron-associations between audio and visual information are created that we constantly receive from the outside environment. To each of these, we also give a meaning, which could be positive, and will be linked to the propulsion mechanism. As a result, there are positive feelings attached to them. On the other hand, we can give them a negative meaning but they are getting linked to the self-defense mechanism and a negative feeling will be attached to them.

We saw that stress is not the information itself, but the previous negative meaning that we have attached to it from the past. When we recall it, we start to feel the same negative feeling that we have experienced in the past. We know and recognize now that stress does not just occur in any kind of situation. It occurs only when there is a negative meaning given to the information.

By understanding that we are a design for a purpose with the capacity to absorb information all the time, we realize that any change that we might face rises the level of awareness of our nervous system for our

enjoyment or protection and should not be mistaken with stress. If we attach negative feeling to these levels of awareness then they might become potential stressors, but otherwise they just vary in their intensity without stressing effect. This is an important thing that we need to remember. Because unaware of, we are blaming the creation of stress on the process of change. By doing this, we get stuck with unlimited numbers of potential stressors, that we will never be able to control or manage properly. Why?
Because having infinite possibilities of changes, this will result in infinite possibilities of stressors.

To prove that the stress is not the information itself, but the negative feeling attached to it, I will like to ask you a question: We know that in any decision that our mind makes always will be toward pleasure and away from pain. All the scientific communities agree with this statement. If this is the case, why in the world does our brain leave a person in a state of stress for so long? There are people who are living in advance stages of stress. Why does their brain make the decision to keep them in this state, when we all know that it produces a lot of pain? How come the brain, of so many millions today, are not aware that stress is wrong for them? I would like a satisfactory answer to this question. Well, there is one, and it has to come from somebody who really understands what stress is. Let's take another example:

Skydiving is for some people an exciting adventure and they of us will go to a great extent to enjoy this kind of fun. Well let's say that two friends are in an airplane for an exercise. Both of them are excited, and are anxious waiting for the trill. Right before they jump, one of them tell the other:

"Well my friend, you know when we left the ground I forgot to take both parachutes, so I am going down, and it's up to you if you want to jump without it"

What do you think is going to be the other's reaction?

Prepared for the excitement, he never thought that by jumping he would lose his life. Since there is no more parachute, right the way his whole attitude towards jumping has instantly changed. Why? Because in his mind he knows that jumping with the parachute is a thrilling experience, but jumping without it is associated with death. Instantly, he will change his mind about jumping.
From a high level of awareness that is produced by jumping with the parachute, right the way by being attached to it the fear of death, the same situation becomes a potential stressor.
To better illustrate this, let's suppose that both of them have jumped from the airplane. And of course that going down, both of them will be experiencing a high level of excitement. Now let's say that half way down, one tell the other that he forgot to put the others parachute in his backpack.
What's going to happen immediately with the one who just found out that he has no parachute?
For sure, it will be a terrifying moment, because as soon as he realizes that there is no more parachute, instantly an attachment to this exciting feeling is a very negative one; a fear of death.

Even though this is just an example, we can imagine what could possibly happen, and how we could instantly attach a negative meaning to information that basically has no stressful effect. What makes it stressful is the negative feeling that we attach to it. This is what basically is stressing us, not the situation itself. So, the situation is still the same, two people jumping from the airplane to have some fun.
But in their memory, the information to jump with the parachute is understood as fun, but to jump without it is death. In other words, jumping with the parachute is linked to the propulsion mechanism that triggers excitement and joy, but jumping without it, is linked to the defense mechanism, which of course triggers a negative feeling. When the level of awareness increases, and that person realizes that there is no parachute, fear of death comes in the mind immediately.
Let's say that after one minute of terrifying experience, his friend tells him:
"Just kidding, your parachute is fine, I just wanted to scare you a little bit "
What do you think is going to happen then?
The friend's state of mind will change back. If you ask him later about this experience, he will tell you that the feelings were very real, not just a joke.
Even though he didn't have to go down to his death without parachute, negative feelings were felt. Anyone would have had the same feelings if they didn't have a parachute and still jump from the airplane.

We can clearly see from this experience, that the situation itself does not stresses us, it might raise the level of awareness, but the meaning given to it determines the feeling that are felt. Remember:
"It's not what happens to you, but what you do with what happens to you"

If we go back to the history of the Roman Empire, we find out that shortly after the death of Christ in the first century, Christians were badly persecuted by authorities. They went so far to sent many to die in Romans arenas; eaten by wild beasts.
The history accounts shows; these people went to their death without fear, not fighting for their survival. Now, before they became Christians, like any other people they were afraid of death, and would do anything to save their lives. But once they embraced the Christian faith, what they basically did is changed their belief, and in their minds have removed the fear of death. When they were thrown to wild beasts, even though it meant death for them, it was not a fearful experience. In other words, they have changed their old blueprint about death with a new one. They still felt the pains of death, but totally different than others who felt the pains of death combine with the fear of death. We can see, that even though the situations might be the same but the way we look at them makes a lot of difference. A feeling of calmness and control of a situation contrasted with a feeling of despair and anguish because of inability to control the event. It all depends on how we view it.

Going back to our question: "Why does our brain chooses to put and keep us into a stressful situation, even though it's aware of what it is doing?"
This is a very valid question, and by understanding what stress really is we could answer it easily. As we learned earlier, our subconscious mind attaches feelings to the information that we receive from the environment based on our conscious decision. In other words, every second we consciously give a negative or a positive meaning to the information that we receive, and by doing that unconsciously we are attaching a positive or negative feeling to it. Once a neuron-association is made, it goes in our memory banks and stays there to be used as reference in the thinking process, or to be retrieved in the future.
When retrieved, the memories are brought from the unconscious level to the conscious level and we remember what happened. Not only do we remember it, but we also feel that same feeling that were previously attached. When that situation has attached to a negative feeling, we start to feel it and eventually we get stressed. Since we are unaware of it, we blame the present environment or situation, thinking that they are the stressors. Unless we remove this negative feeling previously attached to this information, we keep feeling the same negative state, any time we remember that particular situation.
The subconscious mind receives the command to *remember* the memory, not to remove the negative feeling attached to it, and that's why we'll keep feeling it. Worst of all, we might give more negative meaning to the same negative memory, so the next time in the future when we *remember* it again stress is felt even more.
What we need to do is remove or erase negative feeling from it, and attached a different feeling that does not have a stressful effect. That's the right way to deal with and eliminate stress.
Only by understanding this fundamental truth about ourselves, can we properly deal with any situation that we might encounter, no matter how stressful it might be for others. This is the right way to deal with it. So what's the answer?
The answer is when we recall a memory from the past we are giving to our subconscious mind a command to retrieve the memory, not to remove the negativity. Unless we consciously remove that negative state from memory, our subconscious mind will keep retrieving it and putting it back the way it was, until we decide to give a different meaning to it. If we decide to do this, our subconscious mind will do this right away, and attach any meaning wanted to it.
Let's take an example to better illustrate:
Suppose you have a computer, and you let somebody to work with it. They add some of their own files to the computer; information that you do not like at all.
Now, what will your computer will do, when you type the name of the files that belongs to your friend? Even though this is your computer, it'll open the files you requested, and give

you the information. The computer itself will never do any changes to the files, unless you do. It will only open for viewing these files.

The same thing happens with our mind, unless we do the removing of the negative feelings, the brain will only retrieve information, and we'll feel the feelings previously attached to them.

The subconscious mind works in many ways much like a computer does. It receives commands, and act based on the commands. So, unless it receives the command to remove the negative feeling, it will not do this even though these negative feeling have a stressful effect over us. It was design to respond to our conscious commands. We need to learn to use it properly, and of course that it will act properly. We need to stop blaming the environment for our stress, because it is not, and we need to learn how to remove negative part of associations from memory, and stress will disappear.

Scientists have discovered that individuals, who learned to solve problems fast from childhood, are more likely to be stress-free, than the others who always have problems.

Why is that? By learning to solve them fast, they don't have any. In other words they handle each very fast, they don't wait and wait thinking maybe the problems will go away. But as grown ups, we many times keep telling ourselves: "I have so many problems, and I don't know what to do about them." In other words, I do *own* many problems; they are mine.

Then the brain makes sure that we possess unsolved problems. A simple way to avoid this is to make a habit of changing the word problems, with the word challenges. If you call them *challenges* instead of *problems*, they are much easier to solve, because most everybody is open to a challenge, but none of us likes to have problems. As we have mentioned earlier, we continually attach meanings to words and situations. Think a little what kind of feelings have we all attached by the word *problems* in the past? Well, we should recognize that we have attached negative feelings. When we have a problem, what kind of feelings will we experience? Well, what has been attached to it; is a negative.

How about the word *challenge*? Most probably none of us have attached to it a negative meaning, but instead a feeling of power and courage. Therefore when we have a problem we feel hopeless, but when we have a challenge, we feel energized, and ready to deal with it.

Remember: It's your choice to *have a problem* which means to own a problem, or you could chose *to have a challenge*, so that you don't have or own any problems. You just have a challenge to face, that of course it's not a big deal. You could solve it much easier than any problem. You might want to remember that to *have a problem* means having stress, but on the other hand you could have *a challenge* which could gives you the source of motivation.

By being aware of this simple truth, and using it properly, we eliminate many potential stressors. We need to learn this new habit of looking at things and situations different than before. Most people don't do this, and they are the ones that are having a hard time dealing with stress. It is just a matter of recognizing the importance of this information, and to learn and repeat them, until they become new habits. Once they are new habits, we'll use them freely and automatically, like any other habit that we have. In other words, we have built a new and better blueprint for our subconscious mind to work with in this subject. Remember the story with the servant and the rich man? The food is not in the short supply, just the managing of it. We know most of these things; we need just to arrange them in the proper order. And once we do that, the whole scenery will change. The impossible stressful situations will then become possible.

Another set back in dealing with stress, is the fact that today most if not all the researchers in this area are following the idea, that stress is caused by change, and none of them tried to challenge it, even though as many have said:

" It's not possible to get sweet and salty water, at the same time, from the same well"

This is what the researchers in the area of stress are doing.

They believe that when the body reacts to any demand, it produces stress. Some of these changes are positive, and some are negative. If we take a closer look at this idea, we might recognize that this is just impossible, because humans react different to stress. Some of us are stress by some things, but others are not. The truth is, that when our body reacts to any demand upon it, it does not produce stress, but humans are equipped with consciousness and we can understand the change we are going through. *Our level of awareness* changes when we meet any demand. The higher the level of awareness is, the higher the level of emotion that is attached. These chances of awareness could be understood as pleasure producing demands that will be linked to the propulsion mechanism. Or, they could also be understood as pain producing demands that will be linked to the self-defense mechanism.

When they are linked to the propulsion mechanism they result in positive states of mind and we become positively excited, or happy. But, when they are linked to the self-defense mechanism, they result in negative states of mind and we become unhappy or even stressed.

That's why it's very important to learn to be positive thinkers because by doing that, we are attaching positive feelings to all our demands, and as result there isn't any *stress* attached.

Now, some might ask, how come I have the courage to challenge all the professionals and researchers in stress management, who have been studying this subject many years?
Well, first of all we might be aware of the fact that:
"Necessity is the mother of inventions. "
I started studying the subject of stress for my own benefit, due to my difficult situations that I had gone through in my life. Being the kind of person that: Does not start to fix something, unless he finds the root of the problem, I started to get educated in this area.
Going through many difficult situations in life, I had the opportunity to experience stress to a high degree.
I knew what was missing, I just had to find the source of it, and know what to do with it. Soon I realized, that this area in life is new for me, so, I decided that if I had to start learning at this stage in life, I'll better learn from the best experts, because I might not have the time and patience to go through a trail and error process that could take too much time. So, I decided to learn from top researchers in this area.
Soon, I realized that most specialists in this area are following the path that pioneer of stress research, Dr. HANSE SELYE, had drawn many years ago.

Knowing from early childhood, I always had a choice in what I wanted to do, and that there were two kinds of consequences for my actions, soon I came to realization that there is something missing in this theory that stress is: "Our body response to any demand upon it."
I feel stressed, not because of the environment, but because of what I believe what the environment is. So, I started to learn how our mind works, and how the thinking process takes place. Understanding how the neuron-associations take place in our brain, and how each of them we attach a feeling, by the meaning given to them, I realized that unconsciously or not we are the ones that have control over the meaning we give to the environment. This results in attachment of either negative, or positive feelings to it.
Also, by learning that 90 % of our response to the environment is habitual, I realized that because we do have many *bad habits,* and one of them is to give a negative meaning to the environment. In other words we tend to be negativists, to see darkness, instead of light in the environment. I saw the necessity to learn how to change these negative habits into positive ones and by doing that I changed the meaning that I gave to the environment. Having a positive attitude or perceiving the environment through a positive view, the sources of stress have disappeared.

Now, there were other sources of stress that comes from inside of me, and I used to blame them on the environment. Once I understood these things, I started to be confronted with a dilemma.
Knowing that in any decision that our mind makes, it always should result in pleasure and away from pain. Then I started to ask myself this question: Why in the world would my brain let me stay in a stressful situation, and why doesn't it warn me in advance, of a danger? Everybody knows that stress is a negative feeling, and nobody likes it. I realized something is missing here.
By careful examination, I came to the conclusion, these are not part of the present, but part of past memories that I unconsciously retrieve from time to time, and relived the same feelings that I previously attached to them. So, the feelings of stress that I might feel in certain situations have nothing to do with the present.

They are the negative feelings that were previously attached to these situations. Now, when my brain *retrieves* these memories, I feel the same feelings that I have felt in the past when that memory was formed. And, because I have attached these feelings in the past, I have the choice to remove or erase these negative feelings from these memories, and attach a positive, or just no feelings at all. Then the next time, when I retrieve these memories, there won't be stressful effects to feel, but whatever I have attached them, positive or no feelings at all. I understood that the present is OK, as long as I see it OK. But, if I decide to see it different, it becomes different. In other words, whatever I choose to believe to be the truth, will become truth for me, even though everybody else might see it differently.

See, I had the past, which was different than the present. I do have a choice to believe the past, and feel the negativity that was previously attached to it. Or, I do have a choice to believe the present, and feel the positive feelings that I am attaching to it. But also, I have the choice to make sure what I decided to believe it's true or not, and if not, I have the choice to change my beliefs. This is my own responsibility.

From my childhood, I have learned many things the wrong way, and the information still makes the data base for my present thinking ability. Unless I recognize this, and remove these out of my mind, I will act the same old wrong way, and of course, I have nobody else to blame, but myself. In other words, I have a choice to follow my old blueprints, or to replace them with new and better ones.

Like it or not, all the time I am learning and things I learn are added to the data base for my thinking ability, and unless I become selective in the quality of information I let to enter my mind, I will fulfill the old saying: "By keep doing what you were doing, you will be getting what you're getting." So, I need to choose the information I let enter my mind. By being selective, I have the opportunity to master new habits. My brain will trigger these anytime they are needed for my own protection, before I have to deal with a difficult situation or challenge. Thus, I'll have a clear mind when I make a decision. I also realized that, to give a correct meaning to new information, I needed to make sure that the past does not interfere with the present. I consciously decide the meaning of the new information. The past affects the present, and eventually the future, and the only way to solve this, is to make sure that *the past stays the past* never coming back. I could learn from it and I still do, but as a reminder, not as a controlling factor over the present. To accomplish this, I realized the necessity of removing negative feelings previously attached to some events from the past that could become potential stressors in the future. In other words, *forgive* or *heal the past,* and go on with my life in the way I consciously decide to, not overshadow by the negative events of the past.

Understanding these things and their importance, I realized that it's my duty to do something about my life, which I did, and since it does not matter what kind the situation I might have to go through, there is no more stress for me, and believe it or not, I am still amazed how simple this is, and why hasn't this been discovered? Of course, being aware of how useful this kind of information is, I decided to put them into a book, and make them available to anybody who is interested in doing something about the killing effect of stress.

There is a big difference between knowledge and wisdom.

Having knowledge means that we took the time to expose our mind to specific information. Having wisdom is deeper than that. When we do apply the knowledge we posses, then our knowledge becomes wisdom. So, we need to be more than knowledgeable people, we need to be wise and apply what has been learned.

You might have heard about *Silicon Valley*. It is known as the area that in recent years has created more millionaires than any other place in the world. But did you know how this was possible? These people acquired a lot of knowledge about the computer. But beside that, they realized that the only way to really benefit from their knowledge was to find a way to apply this knowledge. That's why they're in this position now. They did something with their knowledge. And the reality is that by applying the knowledge they possessed, it paid off big. So, the same thing will happen with the information from this book. It will not make you a millionaire, but will make you a stress-free and happy person, which sometimes is better than being a millionaire.

At the beginning of this book we talked about a powerful paradigm shift from one that keeps us slaves to the cruel enemy; stress, to a new and better one. I think that by paying serious attention and continuously applying the information we already learned from this book, that powerful paradigm shifting could take place thus enabling us to become stress-free persons. Yes, a dream of living a stress free life is possible. As you can see, it's much closer that it was before you started reading this book.

Because of the simplicity of the information, the material in the book is presented in such a way anybody could understand, not only for professionals in this area. Once anybody reads and understands this material, they'll soon become well aquatinted with it. Most things are known, but we were just not aware of them, so we could use them the right way.

Take a closer look at them, give them the importance you should, and pretty soon you'll discover that negative effects of stress could really be eliminated, and the way to do it, is pretty much simple and easy. You spend much time and energy on so many other things that you need to do. Now do something for yourself, take time and see if this is true or not, try to convince yourself; you do not have to believe me. Apply the simple information, and see how many changes towards the better they'll produce in your life.

Now, we are getting to the end of our wonderful journey and we went through the twelve secrets of eliminating stress forever. We can happily say that we traveled the rough road from slavery to freedom. We have seen that the dream of living a stress free life is no more an impossible dream, but a much closer reality that previously perceived. It's up to us to do our share in bringing it into reality. The tools we need are here, it's our turn now not to let them *rust*, but to use them for improving our lives and those around us.
We realize now that anyone who knows the rules of a game can play the game the way they want to. Eliminating stress is like dealing with a new game. Understanding and applying its rules, we too can play it the way we want to and win. Our emotions are the first results our body's feels when our mind interacts with the environment. Whatever we do, we do it for a reason, based on our personal interpretation of our *environment*. Knowing that we can stop being the creators of our stressful environments. We start using the simple and effective *new tools* that enable us to stop producing new stress. Beside this, we also know now how to *heal our past* so it won't have any stressful effect over us. Even more than that, now we have enough practical knowledge to apply, so we can create a better present and future.

In chapter 1 of this book we mentioned the scientific method. Now, that we're arriving at the end of our journey, let's review to see if what we planned has been accomplished by us.

1. We made the observations.

Having a better understanding of stress, we can now safely say that we are qualified enough to carefully observe what stress really is. We realized that it isn't our response to just any stimuli, but only to the ones that we perceive as negative, or the ones we may be unable to cope with. Also we have seen that sometimes stress occurs even though there are no stressful situations. We know that some people go through cycles of stress that affects their life pretty often without any specific physical cause.

2. We asked many related questions.

We asked a series of questions referring to stress. We have seen the popular idea that stress is caused by the fact that in our journey through life we go from one stressful situation into another. But now we know better and understand that there are basically two sources of stress:
1. New stress that is the result of our perceiving and as result giving a negative meaning to a particular stimulus.
2. Reliving old stress by recycling memories from the past that previously had negative emotions attached to them.

The first source of stress, the *new stress* was the result of giving a negative meaning to new information that we came in contact with. Doing that we were making negative neuron-associations and stored them in our memory banks. Most of these are the result of our cultural and environmental conditioning. In other words, we did what we saw others doing without conscious thought whether it was right or wrong. If we keep doing what we were doing, we'll keep getting what we were getting. But by changing the old blueprints with new and better ones, we start to behave different. This behavior enables us to get much better results. By embracing the new paradigm of stress, we are able to plan and design our future, a life where stress is just an option and not a way of life. Of course this will not come over night, but by daily applying what we have learned, with patience, discipline, and perseverance, we too can live a stress free life.

3. We formed two hypotheses.

Based on our observations we made two hypotheses, hypothesis A and hypothesis B.
In Hypothesis A, knowing that we humans are surrounded by a wonderful and delightful environment, we conclude that we were designed as wonderful human beings with the inborn right to live a happy and stress free life.
In Hypothesis B, we conclude what the roots of stress are, and the real sources for it:
 1. By perceiving any stimuli as negative, we either consciously or unconsciously give a negative meaning to them. The subconscious part of our brain takes the stimuli as negative and therefore is harmful to our well-being and triggers the protecting self-defense mechanism. Understood as negative, it is processed and transformed into an electro-chemical reaction (negative emotion) that is sent through the nervous system throughout our body.
 2. When we are not aware of it, we relieve a memory that has a negative feeling attached to it in the past.

4. We tested the hypotheses.

Hypothesis A. Starting with chapter 3. "Human body" through chapter 8, we discussed in details who really are we. Based on all the information that we presented, we can safely say that we indeed are wonderful human beings deserving to live a happy and stress free life.
Hypothesis B. The information contained in Chapter 9, "Who really are the stressors" helped us to understand who we're dealing with when it comes to stress.

5. We analyzed the results.

Realizing that we all are humans equipped with free will, we have an option to decide whether to follow the old blueprints and behave the old way and of course get the same old results. Or on the other hand, we can apply what we just learned and replace these old blueprints with new and better ones by taking a conscious decision to do that. This is just a matter of behavioral change. By changing our blueprints that trigger our behavior, we automatically change the behavior. Remember: GIGO (garbage in garbage out,)

6. We drew a conclusion.

By embracing the new paradigm of stress, we empower ourselves to take control of our life by becoming the ones that decide the way we feel about any situation or event. Proceeding this way, we too can live a happy and stress free life.

7. We communicated the results.

Coming to the end of our journey through this wonderful book, you found out that you too can, and deserve to live a happy and stress free life.

Finally, we got to the end of our journey. If we recall in part one of this book: "Who really are we?" we acquired enough information to believe that no matter what kind of *label* we or others may put on us, each of us is a wonderful human being. Doesn't matter who we are or where we come from, we all deserve to live a stress free life. Then in part two: "What are we dealing with?" we came to the realization of what stress really is, where it comes from, and the role we have been playing in the creation of our stressful environment. Now, at the end of part three: "When the impossible becomes possible" we are equipped with enough tools to bring our dream of living a stress free life into a daily reality.
There are some things that have been repeated many times in this book. That was done for a reason. We know that to effectively practice something we need to understand it first. Through repetition that is the mother of skill, we get this understanding.

There is a bright light at the end of the tunnel, and it is here for you to grab it. Look at it, embrace it, and master it. It's true, it's simple, it's achievable, and it's up to you. I think you have struggled enough with worries and stress, without knowing that there is an easy way out. Now, this is made available to you just for the taking.
Do it for yourself, and for your family, just do it. And may all your good dreams come true.

"…………Then, wiping the dust from the old violin, and tightening the loose strings,
He played a melody pure and sweet as caroling angel sings.
The people cheered, but some of them cried,
"We do not quite understand what changed its worth." Swift came the reply:
"The Touch of the Master's Hand"…………"

Please don't get me wrong; I don't pretend to be the Master, I am just a simple messenger.

"An old chapter of your life has just been closed. A new one is opening in the front of your eyes. You are a wonderful human being and deserve to live a stress free life. Don't let anybody deny your inborn right. Your life is the most wonderful journey you'll ever take. Enjoy the ride."

Review Questions:

Question 1: Why it is useful to take a serious look at this matter of stress, and who plays a major role in it?

Answer:
- Dealing with stress is a personal matter. Since we are the ones that play the major role of the stress problems, we should also play the major role of the solution. There is no substitute for this, either we do it, or it remains undone.

"If it is to be, it's up to me"

Question 2: In the light of the example used in the beginning about the car whose *health* starts to deteriorate, what it might be useful to consider?

Answer:
- A *paradigm shift* from its management to the real source of the problems; our driving habits.

"By changing our paradigm of stress from stress management to eliminating stress, we learn to use our body according the laws and principle they were designed to and then the impossible becomes possible."

Question 3: In order to play the game of life in such a way that we win it, what is required from us?

Answer:
- Like any other games it also has its own rules that we need to understand and obey in order to win this game of life.

"Acquiring knowledge will make us knowledgeable people. Acquiring accurate knowledge and continuously applying it will help us to win the game of life."

Question 4: Why it is that no one has yet won the *game* of stress?

Answer:
- It's close to impossible to play and win a game if their rules are not understood and applied properly.

"Acquiring knowledge about the old paradigm of stress will make us managers over something that nobody likes; stress. Acquiring accurate knowledge about the new paradigm and continuously applying it will help us to win the game of stress."

Question 5: What will be a great help in winning the *game* of stress?

Answer:
- Understanding it we start benefiting from our amazing abilities that we all posses. This will help us win this so called *unwinable* game.

"We are not just human beings. We are wonderful human beings designed with amazing abilities."

Question 6: What does our body needs in order to be able to function properly?

Answer:
- We need clean air, healthy foods and proper information in order to personally grow and properly deal with the environment.

"The quality of these three ingredients (clean air, healthy food and proper information) generates the strength of our spirit, the fire within that keeps all of us alive."

Question 7: What does our mind uses to implement our behavior?

Answer:
- Like any other sophisticated accomplishments, our mind uses a blueprint to dictate our behavior.

"Through Reasoning, we choose what we accept. Through Imagination, we combine the information accepted. Emotions, are the results we feel after our mind has combined what we have chosen to accept."

Question 8: What are the first three components of creating and changing our behavior?

Answer:
- Awareness; the first step in perceiving what happens around us.
- Desire, once the level of awareness increases to a specific level, it triggers an inner craving or desire toward that specific information or away from it.
- Decision, when the awareness gets to higher level, the desire becomes strong enough to condition us to make a decision.

"We all were born as wonderful human beings. What we are today is what we made ourselves through our behavior."

Question 9: What is the fourth component of creating and changing our behavior and the driving forces behind it?

Answer:
- The fourth component is motivation that usually is driven by fear or pleasure.

Question 10: What is the fifth component of creating and changing our behavior and what's behind it?

Answer:
- The fifth component is discipline. The factors that dictate it are: Self control, responsibility, courage, consistency and persistency.

"Through these five steps, awareness, desires, decision, motivation and discipline, we can keep ourselves slaves to the merciless environment, or we can free ourselves from the bondages of stress."

Question 11: What is the propulsion mechanism, and what kind of needs does it trigger?

Answer:
- The propulsion mechanism is the figurative engine that continuously generates inner drives to identify, explore, absorb, understand, enjoy and own the *environment* we are surrounded with.
It works at the conscious and subconscious level, and it generates our personal and universal needs.

Chapter 12. Make-up your mind.

"We can use our propulsion mechanism as the best tool in our journey to freedom from stress. It will generate all the motivation that is needed to finish the race and win it."

Question 12: How do you describe the self defense mechanism and what are the factors that activate it?

Answer:
- If the propulsion mechanism would be the *engine* that generates our inner driving force, the self-defense mechanism would be the *breaking system* design to protect us from anything that might cause us harm.
- This system works at conscious and subconscious levels and is activated by information coming from inside of us and from the outside environment.

"Getting a better understanding of our protective guardian, it will stop being a source of stress and become a helper on our journey to a stress free life."

Question 13: What are the six major groups of the so-called stressors, and what can we do about them?

Answer:
- Our vocabulary plays a major role in the quality of *food* our mind digests. The quality of our speech reduces and increases the emotional quality of our life.
- The uselessness of knocking on locked doors. Before you start to work hard, you should make sure it's in the right direction.
- Some things no matter how much we want still are impossible to solve.
- Dreams are the first steps in accomplishing any great thing. The best dreams to dream are the achievable dreams.
- Our inner needs and fears. Are they our friends or foes? The inner drivers of our behavior let us have them as our best friends.
- Our past is no more a major negative factor in our stressful life, but is just a reference guide.

"If these six major group of stressors would be a monster with six heads, what would happen if one by one we are to cut down all of its heads? The monster will have no more power over us."

Question 14: In order to solve the mystery of stress, what is the first door we need to shut and how do we implement that?

Answer: The first door is to stop producing new stress. We implement this as follows:
- The best way to win a war is not to start one, so we avoid stress before it happens.
- Every great thing accomplished was started with a dream in somebody's mind. By creating positive new events and situations, we start dreaming achievable dreams long enough until they become a realty.
- Becoming aware of the uselessness of saving fake money, we stop depositing negative information in our mind.
- Regardless of how we used our body in the past, now we get a new ally, our own body.
- Realizing that by opening old coffins we do ourselves a disfavor, we avoid unnecessarily thinking about our past.
- Finally, when life gives us more lemons than we actually need, with the help of humor power we add sweetness to them and go in the lemonade business.

Chapter 12.   Make-up your mind.

"If these six areas would form a six layers body armor, wouldn't it be wise for us to wear our armor all the time?"

Question 15: Which is the next door that needs to be closed on stress, and how do the reasoning and the substitution methods help us to implement this?

Answer:
- The next door we need to close on stress would be *healing our past,* or eliminating the stress stored in the past in our memory banks.
- Using the reasoning method, we make peace with ourselves, our neighbors, our environment, and with our Maker.
- By using the substitution method, we trade the bad for the good. We do that by so-called switching position method, disassociation method, or the painted nail method.

Question: When bad things happen to peaceful people, what it might be useful to remember?

Answer:
- Even though at times the pain seems unbearable, the reality of the world we live in is that sometime bad things do happens to peaceful people.
- No matter how painful they may be, the sooner we get involved in our own recovery the faster it will happen.
- We understand that there is a difference between our life as a whole and an episode of it. We need to take care of more than just an episode of our life.
- Joy and pain are both part of being human. Manifesting both would be a normal thing and also a medication that helps the healing process.
- Sooner or later, the time will come to let go, and realize that this negative episode will become part of our past. We forget our tribulations, but remember the lessons that they taught us.
- As the rainbow, that gracious thing made up of tears and light, so out of ruins a better and stronger you could come out.

"The past has been a great player in our present stressful life. By healing it, we become free of its negative influence, and to live the present free of stress."

Question 16. Why the need for a new paradigm has arrived?

Answer:
- As science continuously progresses, so does our understanding of the human behavior. The new understanding of how we ourselves define the quality of the environment that we live in, through our attitude towards it generates the necessity of a new paradigm.

"This new paradigm is no longer based on what the environment is doing to us, but it's based on what we do with what happens to us."

Question 17. Why is the new paradigm far superior to the old one?

Answer:
- We are no longer at the discretion of a cruel and merciless environment. It empowers us to take

charge of our life, giving us the necessary tools to succeed in freeing us from the bondages of stress.

"Like an accurate map that gives us clear and easy to follow instructions on how to get where we want to go compared to a barely visible outdated hand written sketch, so the new paradigm is superior to the old one."

Question 18. How does the new paradigm help us to live a stress free life?

Answer:
- It helps us to understand that we are wonderful human beings, with the inborn right to live a stress free life.
- It clarifies the real causes of stress.
- Once we understand that we deserve to live a stress free life, and have the accurate knowledge of how we play a major role in the quality of the environment we live in, it help us to combine this knowledge in such a way that we become the designers of our new life, where we decide the way we interpret its polarity.

"Indeed we all are wonderful human beings, equipped with amazing abilities, and deserving to get a chance of living a stress free life."

www.ingramcontent.com/pod-product-compliance
Lightning Source LLC
Chambersburg PA
CBHW081219170426
43198CB00017B/2660

9 780971 950009